Hermann Oldenberg, F. Max Müller

The Grihya-Sutras

Rules of Vedic Domestic Ceremonies - Vol. 1

Hermann Oldenberg, F. Max Müller

The Grihya-Sutras
Rules of Vedic Domestic Ceremonies - Vol. 1

ISBN/EAN: 9783337158750

Printed in Europe, USA, Canada, Australia, Japan

Cover: Foto ©Thomas Meinert / pixelio.de

More available books at **www.hansebooks.com**

THE

SACRED BOOKS OF THE EAST

TRANSLATED

BY VARIOUS ORIENTAL SCHOLARS

AND EDITED BY

F. MAX MÜLLER

VOL. XXIX

Oxford

AT THE CLARENDON PRESS

1886

RULES OF VEDIC DOMESTIC CEREMONIES

TRANSLATED BY

HERMANN OLDENBERG

PART I

SÂNKHÂYANA-GR*I*HYA-SÛTRA
ÂSVALÂYANA-GR*I*HYA-SÛTRA
PÂRASKARA-GR*I*HYA-SÛTRA
KHÂDIRA-GR*I*HYA-SÛTRA

Oxford

AT THE CLARENDON PRESS

1886

CONTENTS.

⁎ The Second Volume will contain a GENERAL INTRODUCTION to the G*r*ihya-Sûtras.

SÂNKHÂYANA-GRIHYA-SÛTRA.

SÂṄKHÂYANA-GRIHYA-SÛTRA.

THE Grihya-sûtra ascribed to Sâṅkhâyana, which has been edited and translated into German by myself in the XVth volume of the Indische Studien, is based on the first of the four Vedas, the Rig-veda in the Bâshkala recension[1], and among the Brâhmaṇa texts, on the Kaushîtaka. Its reputed author, whom we ordinarily find called by his family name, Sâṅkhâyana, had the proper name Suyagña. This we may infer from the lists of Vedic teachers given in different Grihya texts where they describe the Tarpaṇa ceremony. Though in these lists the order of names varies very much, yet the two names Suyagña and Sâṅkhâyana are constantly placed side by side, so that this fact alone would render it probable that they belonged to the same person. Thus we read in the Sâṅkhâyana-Grihya IV, 10 = VI, 1 :

Kaholam Kaushîtakim, Mahâkaushîtakim, Suyagñam Sâṅkhâyanam, Âsvalâyanam, Aitareyam, Mahaitareyam.

Here we have grouped together the two Brâhmaṇa authors (with the fictitious doubles, the great Kaushîtaki, the great Aitareya) and the two corresponding Sûtra authors belonging to the two chief branches of the Rig-veda literature; first comes one Brâhmaṇa author (for Kahola Kaushîtaki is one person) with the Sûtra author connected with him, then the second Sûtra author and the corresponding Brâhmaṇa teacher.

In the Sâmbavya-Grihya (Indische Studien, XV, 154) the corresponding passage runs thus:

Gârgya- Gautama- Sâkalya- Bâbhravya- Mâṇdattavya

---

[1] See IV, 5, 9.

[sic]- Mâṇḍûkeyâ*h* Suya*gña*- Sâ*m*khyâyana- *G*âtukar-*ny*eyâ*h* [sic] Pai*m*ga [sic]- *S*âmbavy'-Aitareyâ*h*.

The same *G*rihya still more explicitly bears witness to the name of Suya*gña Sâṅkhâyana*, by adding at the end of the list from which these names are quoted the following words: Suya*gña Sâkhâyanas* [sic] t*ri*[pya]tu, i. e. 'May Suya*gña Sâṅkhâyana* satiate himself (with the water offering).'

In the Âs*valâyana-Grihya* III, 4, we read:

Kahola*m* Kaushîtaka*m* Mahâkaushîtaka*m* Paiṅgya*m* Mahâpaiṅgya*m* Suya*gña*m *S*âṅkhâyanam Aitareyam Mahaitareyam.

We may also quote here a Kârikâ given by Nârâya*n*a [1] in his great commentary on the *S*âṅkhâyana-Gr*i*hya (I, 1, 10):

Atrâra*n*ipradâna*m* yad adhvaryu*h* kurute kva*k*it [2] mata*m* tan na Suya*gñ*asya, mathita*m* so 'tra ne*kkh*ati.

It would perhaps be hazardous to claim for the author of this Kârikâ the authority of an independent witness, for very likely he may have derived his knowledge from the lists of teachers which we have quoted before. But at all events the concordance of the three *G*r*i*hya texts furnishes a proof which, I think, cannot be set aside by another testimony which we must mention now. At the end of the Kaushîtaki-Âra*n*yaka (Adhyâya 15) we find a Va*m*sa or list of the teachers by whom the knowledge contained in that Âra*n*yaka is supposed to have been handed down. The opening words of this list run thus:

'Om! Now follows the Va*m*sa. Adoration to the Brahman! Adoration to the teachers! We have learnt (this text) from Gu*n*âkhya *S*âṅkhâyana, Gu*n*âkhya *S*âṅkhâyana from Kahola Kaushîtaki, Kahola Kaushîtaki from Uddâlaka Âru*n*i, &c.'

It is a very natural supposition that the author of this list intended to begin with the name of the Doctor eponymus, if we may say so, of the Sûtras of his school, and then to proceed to name the Doctor eponymus of the Brâhma*n*as, and after him the more ancient teachers and

---

[1] Manuscr. Chambers 712 (Berlin Royal Library), fol. 12 b.
[2] Comp. Pâraskara-G*ri*hya I, 2, 5: ara*n*ipradânam cke.

sages. But whether the author of this passage really supposed this Gu*n*ākhya *S*āṅkhāyana to be the author of the
*S*āṅkhāyana-sûtras, or not, we shall be justified in following
rather the unanimous statements of the texts previously
quoted, and in accepting in accordance with them, as the
full name of our Sûtrakâra, the name Suya*g*ña *S*āṅkhāyana.

The Gr*i*hya-sûtra which has been here translated presupposes, as all Gr*i*hya-sûtras do, the existence of the
*S*rauta-sûtra, with which it is intimately connected and
which is referred to in the Gr*i*hya in several instances[1].

Here the question arises whether the Gr*i*hya-sûtra was
composed by the same author to whom the authorship of
the *S*rauta-sûtra belongs, so that the two texts form together, and would, in the conception of their author, be
intended to form, one great body of Sûtras, or, on the other
hand, whether the Gr*i*hya-sûtra is a later addition to the
*S*rauta-sûtra. On this question I have ventured, in the
preface to my German edition of *S*āṅkhāyana[2], to offer a few
remarks which, however, I feel bound to say do not seem to
myself quite decisive. I there pointed out that the Gr*i*hya-
sûtra contains a few aphorisms which we should rather expect
would have found their place in the *S*rauta-sûtra, if the two
texts were composed by the same author and on a common
plan[3]. But, apart from the possibility that in a work of such
considerable extent as that collection of Sûtras would be,
such trifling incongruences or irregularities might very
easily escape the attention even of a very careful author,
there is still another objection that may be urged against
the inference drawn by me from such passages. It can be
shown[4] that the Gr*i*hya texts which we possess are based
to some extent on one common original, from which they
have taken verbatim, or nearly verbatim, a certain number
of aphorisms. Thus if we were to suppose that *S*āṅkhāyana,

---

[1] See, for instance, Gr*i*hya I, 16, 1 (*S*rauta IV, 16, 2).
[2] Indische Studien, vol. xv, pp. 11, 12.
[3] The Sûtras with reference to which I made that observation are I, 8, 14;
14, 13–15; II, 15, 10. Comp. *S*rauta-sûtra II, 7, 12; IV, 21.
[4] I intend to give some proofs of this in the General Introduction to the
Gr*i*hya-sûtras which will be given in the second volume of these translations.

or whosoever the author of this Grihya-sûtra may have
been, found the aphorisms on which I once based my argument, in that original text, this would explain the occurrence of those passages in a portion of the great body of
Sûtras different from that in which we should expect to
meet them. Now several of the passages in question recur
identically in other Grihya texts, so that we may infer
indeed that they are taken from that lost original, and we
have no means to judge whether the other similar passages
are not taken from it also. I believe, therefore, that the
opinion which I once pronounced regarding the relation in
which the two Sûtra texts stand to each other, cannot be
vindicated, and that it is better to leave that question un-
answered until perhaps further discoveries throw a new light
on it.

For the reconstruction of the correct text of the Sâṅkhâyana-Grihya, and occasionally also for its interpretation, it
is of considerable importance that we possess, besides the
Devanâgarî MSS. of the text and of the commentaries, a
South Indian MS. written in the Grantha character (MS.
Whish 78 in the library of the Royal Asiatic Society,
London) which contains a Grihya based on that of Sâṅkhâyana and following it, during the greater part of the work,
nearly word for word[1]. It is designated in the MS., at the
end of the single Adhyâyas, as 'Kaushîtaka-Grihya.' It
therefore professes to follow the teaching of the same Brâhmana which is adhered to also by the Sûtra school of
Sâṅkhâyana. A metrical commentary, which in the MS.
follows after the text, names in its opening Sloka a teacher
Sâmbavya as the author of this Sûtra. The Sloka runs thus:

Natvâ Kaushîtakâkâryam Sâmbavyam sûtrakrittamam
grihyam tadîyam samkshipya vyâkhyâsye bahuvismritam.

('Having bowed to the most excellent author of Sûtras,
to Sâmbavya, the Âkârya belonging to the Kaushîtaka
school, I shall compose a short commentary on his Grihya,
which has been forgotten by many.')

The name of this Sâmbavya does not occur among the

---

[1] Comp. the statements given with regard to that text in my German edition
of Sâṅkhâyana, Indische Studien, XV, 4 seq.

teachers enumerated in the description of the Tarpa*n*a
ceremony, neither in *S*ânkhâyana IV, 10, nor in Â*s*valâyana III, 4; but in the list of the *S*âmbavya-G*ri*hya itself
it is found (see above, p. 4); and besides it seems to me
also to be mentioned in Â*s*valâyana-G*ri*hya IV, 8, 24, in
which passage it will scarcely be considered too bold to
conjecture *S*âmbavya instead of *S*â*m*vatya.

Though the MS. of the *S*âmbavya-G*ri*hya is very con-
fused, and full of blunders of all sorts, yet it deserves to be
attentively studied by all scholars who are accustomed to
look, if not in theory yet in practice, on the agreement of
a few Vedic text MSS., or of a few Indian commentaries,
as if it had a claim to an unassailable authority to which
European Orientalists would have no right to deny their
faith. In the *S*ânkhâyana-G*ri*hya a number of passages
are found in which corrupt readings or perverse explanations are supported by all the *S*ânkhâyana MSS. and
by all the *S*ânkhâyana commentaries, and if, by a rare
and fortunate chance, the *S*âmbavya Grantha MS., which
is unaffected by the blunders of the Devanâgarî MSS.,
had not been discovered in the south of the peninsula,
these readings and explanations would seem to rest on the
unanimous agreement of tradition. Perhaps it seems un-
necessary to dwell on this point, for very few Orientalists,
if any, would be prepared to assert that Indian tradition is
infallible. But when looking over many of the editions
and translations of the Vedic texts, even such as have been
published in the last years, one finds plentiful occasion to
observe that in hundreds of passages tradition has been
practically treated, by scholars of very high merit, as if it
had an authority not very far removed from infallibility.
A case like that of which we have to speak here, in which
a whole set of MSS., and occasionally also of commentaries,
can be tested by a MS. of a nearly related text, written in
a different character and in a distant part of India, will
strengthen our belief that we are right in judging for ourselves, even if that judgment should oppose itself to such
authorities as Nârâya*n*a or Râma*k*andra or *G*ayarâma.

Perhaps it will not be out of place to add here, as an

illustration of these remarks, a few observations on one of
the passages in which the rejection of the traditional Sânkhâyana reading, together with the traditional Sânkhâyana
explanation, is confirmed by the Sâmbavya MS., though
no doubt, even without the aid of that MS., we ought to
have formed the right conclusions for ourselves.   At Sânkhâyana II, 4, 1. 2 the traditional reading is:

Mama vrate h*r*idaya*m* te dadhâmi mama *k*ittam anu
*k*itta*m* te astu | mama vâ*k*am ekamanâ *g*ushasva B*r*ihas-
patish *t*vâ niyunaktu mahyam iti | kâmasya brahma-
*k*aryasyâsâv iti.

Sânkhâyana is treating here of the Upanayana, or the
initiation of the student who is received by a teacher and
intends to study the Veda with him.   The teacher on that
occasion is to pronounce the Mantra which we have just
transcribed, and which translated into English would run
thus:

'Under my will I take thy heart; after my mind shall thy
mind follow; in my word thou shalt rejoice with all thy
heart; may B*r*ihaspati join thee to me.'   'Of the Brahma-
*k*arya of Kâma (or lust), N. N.!'

The MSS. give the end of the passage as we have printed
it above, kâmasya brahma*k*aryasyâsâv iti.   This
Nârâya*n*a explains in the following way.   Brahma*k*arya
here means the observances which the student has to keep
through certain periods of time before the different texts
which he has to learn can be taught him.   First comes
the Sâvitrî verse, for which he prepares himself by observing the sâvitra vrata; this lasts either one year, or three
days, or the Sâvitrî can also be taught him immediately
(see chap. 5, 1–3).   Then follows the *s*ukriya vrata, of
three days, or twelve days, or one year, or any other period
of time according to the teacher's pleasure (chap. 11, 10);
by this vrata the student is enabled to study the main
portion of the Veda.   Finally come the *s*âkvara, vrâtika,
aupanishada observances, each of which has to last one
year, and which refer to the different parts of the Âra*n*yaka
(see chap. 11, 11 seq., and the sixth book).   Now the formula
of which we treat here refers principally to the sâvitra

vrata. The teacher announces to the student how long he has to keep that vrata. He says (Sûtra 1), 'May Brihaspati join thee to me (Sûtra 2) for a brahma*k*arya (i. e. a vrata) of such and such (kâmasya) a time (one year, three days, &c.), N. N. 1' Kâma (the pleasure) would thus stand here as an expletive which was to be replaced in each single case by the indication of the real space of time that depended on the teacher's pleasure ('... niyunaktu mahya*m* sâ*m*vatsarikasya trairâtrikasya vânvakshikasya vâ sâvitrasya brahma*k*aryasyâmukâmuka*s*armann iti vâkyasa*m*yogo g*ñe*ya*h*'). The same should take place at the corresponding forms of Upanayana which had to precede the entrance of the student upon the *s*ukriya, *s*âkvara, &c. observances. This is the explanation of Nârâya*n*a, with which Râma*k*andra and all the other commentaries agree. It will scarcely be necessary to observe that the singular use of k â m a, on which this traditional explanation rests, is neither in accordance with the meaning of the word, nor supported by any parallel texts. So, even before I had the opportunity of collating the *S*âmbavya MS., I had no doubt that the system of the Vratas has nothing at all to do with our Sûtra, and that its text should be made intelligible by a slight alteration touching only the quantity of the a in two syllables, by writing, K â m a s y a b r a h m a *k* â r y a s y a s â v i t i (thou art the Brahma*k*ârin of Kâma, N. N.!), as we read in Âsvalâyana I, 20, 8, k a s y a b r a h m a *k* â r y a s i, p r â *n* a s y a b r a h m a *k* â r y a s i. Afterwards I found that the Grantha MS. of *S*âmbavya gives the very reading which I had conjectured.

Passages like this are not very rare in the G*r*ihya-sûtras. In the other Sûtras we are not in the same favourable position of possessing a MS. which enables us, as the Grantha MS. of *S*âmbavya does, to test their text.

We cannot conclude these introductory remarks without speaking of the later additions tacked on at the end of the original body of the *S*âṅkhâyana-G*r*ihya-sûtras[1]. There are unmistakable indications that the fifth and sixth books are later additions. The fifth book is

---

[1] Comp. the remarks in my German edition of *S*âṅkhâyana, Ind. Studien, XV, 7.

designated as a pari*s*ish*t*a in a Kârikâ quoted by
Nârâya*n*a:

> pari*s*ish*t*âd âvasathyc pârva*n*âtikrame *k*aru*h*
> Vai*s*vânarâyâgnayc *k*âgnayc[1] tantumate tathâ.

('According to the Pari*s*ish*t*a, if one of the half-monthly
sacrifices has been omitted, a mess of rice should be offered
on the sacred domestic fire to Agni Vai*s*vânara and to
Agni Tantumat.')

The passages of the 'Pari*s*ish*t*a' here referred to are the
two first aphorisms of V, 4:

'Now if a half-monthly sacrifice has not been performed,
one or the other of them, then a mess of rice (is to be
offered)—

'With (the words), "To Agni Vai*s*vânara svâhâ! To
Agni Tantumat svâhâ!"'

There are, besides, several passages in which Nârâya*n*a
himself mentions the fifth book under the designation of
Pari*s*eshâdhyâya[2]. And even if we had not the authority of
the Kârikâ and of Nârâya*n*a, the contents alone of the fifth
book would raise our suspicion against its genuineness.
The matter ordinarily treated of in the G*ri*hya texts is
brought to an end in Adhyâyas I–IV; in the fifth book
we find diverse supplementary additions on points discussed before; rules, which no doubt would have been given
at their proper place, had the fifth book been composed at
the same time, and by the same author, as the preceding
books[3]. Besides, we find different prâya*sk*itta oblations
treated of, and a description of two ceremonies which are
mentioned, as far as I know, in no other G*ri*hya-sûtra,
but belong to the rites frequently described in such works
as Purâ*n*as, Parisish*t*as, and later Dharma texts: the consecration of ponds or wells (chap. 2), and the consecration
of gardens (chap. 3).

There can thus be little doubt as to the secondary
character of the fifth book. And this alone suffices to

---

[1] vâgnaye the MS.

[2] Nârâya*n*a on I, 9, 3; 10, 2.

[3] The Paddhati inserts the paraphrase of several of these rules into the
explanation of the first Adhyâya.

furnish an important argument in favour of the same view with regard to the sixth book also. This view is furthermore supported by the opening invocation in that book, addressed to Brahman and to a number of mythological beings and Vedic sages and teachers. It is evident that by such an invocation this book is characterised as a separate treatise, presupposing of course the main body of the *Sânkhâyana*-sûtras, but not forming part of it in the same sense in which, for instance, the second or the third Adhyâya does. The object of that treatise is the exposition of the ritual connected with the study of the Rahasya texts. The sixth book, composed no doubt by a later adherent of the *Sânkhâyana* school, returns, in fact, to, and enlarges on, matters that have already found their proper place in the original G*ri*hya-sûtra at II, 12, and partly also at IV, 7.

SÂNKHÂYANA-GR/HYA-SÛTRA.

ADHYÂYA I, KHANDA 1.

1. Now henceforth we shall declare the Pâka-yagñas.

2. When (a pupil) is going to return (from his teacher), let him keep that fire (as his domestic fire) on which he has put the last piece of wood (as required by the regulations for a student),

3. Or (he should keep) his nuptial fire.

1, 1. The ceremonies to be treated of are defined here as the Pâkayagñas (i. e. oblations of cooked offerings) just as in the opening sentence of the Pâraskara-Gr/hya they are called gr/hya-sthâlîpâkâs. This is indeed the most characteristic form of offerings belonging to the domain of the Gr/hya ritual, though it would not be correct to state that the Gr/hya-sûtras treat exclusively of sacrificial ceremonies of this kind.

2. As to the duty of the Vedic student of putting every day a piece of wood on the sacred fire of his teacher, see below, II, 6. 8, and compare the Gr/hya-samgraha-parisishta II, 58. According to a Kârikâ given by Nârâyana, and the Karmapradîpa (I, 6, 13), the prescription of this Sûtra regarding the time for the kindling of the sacred fire refers exclusively to the case of vâgdâna (betrothal). Comp. also Dr. Bloomfield's note on the Gr/hya-samgraha-parisishta I, 76 (Zeitschrift der Deutschen Morgenländischen Gesellschaft, XXXV, 560). In the Kârikâ it is stated that if the betrothed girl dies after the fire has been kindled, but before the marriage, the sacrificer is not to forsake his fire, but to marry another girl; if he cannot find a bride, he should make the fire enter into himself according to the rules given by Sânkhâyana-Gr/hya V, 1, and himself become uttarâsramin, i. e. enter one of the two final Âsramas.

4. Some declare (that the domestic fire should be kindled) at the time of the division of the inheritance.

5. Or that after the death of the householder the eldest one himself (should kindle it).

6. (It should be kindled) on the day of the new moon of the month of Vaisâkha or on another (new moon day).

7. Some say (that the fire should be kindled) according to the (sacrificer's) wishes under the (corresponding) constellation.

8. He should light his fire at one of the following places, viz. in the house of a Vaisya who is rich in

---

5. Nârâyana: 'If the fire has not been kindled at the time stated above, then, after the householder ... i.e. the father, even if he should not have performed the âdhâna, or the elder brother has died, the eldest son (or the son who after his elder brother's death has become the eldest), after he has performed the Sapindîkarana (for the dead father or brother; see below, IV, 3, and the ninth chapter of the Parisishta [book V]), even if he has not divided the inheritance with his younger brothers (so that the time stated in the fourth Sûtra would not have arrived), should kindle the fire himself, i.e. without an officiating priest (ritvig). . . . Or the Sûtra should be divided into two; prete vâ grihapatau (or after the death of the householder), and svayam gyâyân (the eminent one himself), i.e. of Brâhmanas, Kshatriyas, and Vaisyas a gyâyân, which means a most eminent person, a Brâhmana, performs the Pâkayagñas himself; for the two other castes the Pâkayagñas have to be performed through an officiating priest : this is the meaning of this svayam (himself).' I have given this note of Nârâyana as a specimen of the entirely arbitrary and obviously misleading explanations which are unfortunately so frequently found in this author, as indeed in most of the other Sûtra commentators. As to the true meaning of this svayam I still adhere to the explanation which I proposed in my German edition of the text (p. 118), that in case no division of the inheritance takes place, the sacred fire should be kindled on behalf of all the joint-proprietors, but that only the eldest brother should act personally (svayam).

8. Or, 'at (the fire of) a person rich in cattle, in the house of a Vaisya,' &c.? The commentators (see p. 118 of the German

cattle, at a frying-pan, or (at the fire of) one who offers many sacrifices.

9. Some say that (the fire should be fetched from one of the above-mentioned places) in the evening and in the morning.

10. The inauguration (of the fire) by an evening offering should be learnt from the Adhvaryus, according to (my) teacher.

11. In the morning he shall offer a full oblation with a verse sacred to Vishnu, or silently.

12. The time for setting it (i.e. the domestic fire) in a blaze and for sacrificing on it has been explained by (the rules given with regard to) the Agnihotra.

---

edition) differ as to whether in purupasu-viskula one or two alternatives are contained, and it is interesting to see that the Sûtra authors themselves differed in this respect; Pâraskara (I, 2, 3), when declaring from what place the fire should be fetched, speaks of the house of a Vaisya rich in cattle; Âsvalâyana, on the contrary, who in the Grihya-sûtra does not expressly treat of the kindling of the domestic fire, in the corresponding passage of the Srauta-sûtra (II, 2, 1), gives the rule that the dakshinâgni is to be fetched 'from the house of a Vaisya or from a rich person.'

9–11. I now differ from the opinion which I pronounced in my German edition with regard to the relation in which these three Sûtras stand to each other. I think they ought to be understood thus: 9. Some teachers say that the fetching of the fire from its yoni, as taught in Sûtra 8, ought to be done twice; in the evening, so that the fire, after the necessary rites have been performed, goes out, and then again in the morning. 10. But my (the author's) teacher (comp. as to âkâryâh, Kâtyâyana's Srauta-sûtra I, 3, 7; Professor Garbe's note on Vaitâna-sûtra 1, 3) is of opinion that the fire should be fetched only once, and that with this fire the ceremonies which are taught by the Adhvaryus are to be performed in the evening (see, for instance, Kâty. IV, 7. 8, which passage is paraphrased here by Nârâyana). 11. In the morning (according to the same teacher, not, as I once understood this passage, according to the eke referred to in Sûtra 9), a full oblation is to be offered, &c.

12. Srauta-sûtra II, 6, 2 seq.

13. And 'invested with the sacrificial cord,' &c., all these rules, as far as they are applicable, should be applied (here also) in consequence of the unity of the ritual.

14. With regard to this they quote also (the following *Sloka*):

15. 'The kinds of Pâkayagñas, the kinds of Haviryagñas, and again the kinds of Soma sacrifices,

'Twenty-one by number, these are proclaimed to be the kinds of sacrifice.'

KHANDA 2.

1. At the end of the sacrificial acts (follows) the distribution of food to Brâhma*n*as.

2. Voice, (pleasantness of) form, age, learning, moral character, (right) conduct are the qualities (required in the Brâhma*n*as who are to be invited thereto).

---

13. *Srauta-sûtra* I, 1, 6. 7: *yagñopavîtî* devakarmâ*n*i karoti, prâ*k*inâvîtî pitryâ*n*i, &c. The unity of the ritual of course means the unity of the two great domains of the *Srauta* and G*ri*hya ritual.

15. With regard to the twenty-one kinds of sacrifice compare, for instance, Gautama VIII, 18–20; Max Müller, Z. D. M. G. IX, p. lxxiii; Weber, Indische Studien, X, 326. The seven kinds of Pâkayagñas are the Ash*t*akâ sacrifices (see below, III, 12 seq.), the sacrifices offered at each Parvan (I, 3), the *Srâddha* (or funeral) sacrifices (IV, 1 seq.), the sacrifice of the *Srâva*nî full moon (IV, 15), of the Âgrahâya*n*î (IV, 17 seq.), of the *K*aitrî (IV, 19), and of the Â*s*vayugî (IV, 16). The seven Havis sacrifices (belonging, as is the case also with the third division of sacrifices, to the *Srauta* ritual) are the Agnyâdheya, the Agnihotra, the sacrifices of the full and new moon, the Âgraya*n*a, the three *K*âturmâsya sacrifices, the Nirû*dh*apa*s*ubandha, and the Sautrâma*n*î. The seven kinds of Soma sacrifices (of which the more ancient texts mention only three or four sa*m*sthâs, see Weber, Indische Studien, IX, 120) are the Agnish*t*oma, the Atyagnish*t*oma, the Ukthya, the Sho*d*a*s*in, the Atirâtra, the Aptoryâma.

3. Learning, however, outweighs every (other qualification).

4. A learned one should not be passed over.

5. 'The threefold (knowledge, viz. that) which refers to the deities, that which refers to the Âtman, and that which refers to sacrifice,

'(Handed down) in the Mantras and in the Brâhmaṇa : this is called learning.

6. 'A performer of the sacred rights, a man who has studied (the Veda), who is old in learning and devoted to austerities :

'He who gives food (even) once to such (a Brâhmaṇa), hunger will not befall that man any more.

7. 'Whatsoever deity he may wish to satiate at any sacrifice,

'Destining it to that (deity) in his mind, he shall give (the food) to a person like that.

8. 'An oblation deposited in a person like that will never miss its way to the deity;

'Treasure of men, vessel of gods (in which they receive what is given to them) he is called.'

KHAṆDA 3.

1. Now (follow) the ceremonies of the days of the new and full moon.

He fasts.

2. In the morning, when the sun shines on the

3, 1. Most probably this rule should be divided into two Sûtras, so that atha darsapûrṇamâsau would stand as the heading of the chapter; comp. below, chap. 18, 1, atha katurthîkarma; chap. 24, 1, atha gâtakarma, &c.

2. 'If this is expressly stated, the oblation is to be made in night-time; for instance, at the Vâstoshpatiya ceremony it is stated, "The tenth oblation of the Sthâlipâka, to Agni Svishṭakrit at night" (see below, III, 4, 8).' Nârâyaṇa.

top of the great trees, that is the most auspicious time for all kinds of sacrifices, unless there be a special rule.

3. With a genial mind, clean, on a pure, protected spot, having cooked a full, thin mess of rice, he offers that cooked oblation to the deities of the festivals of the new and full moon, distributing it in the due way.

4. In the oblations of cooked food the acts of taking (the intended oblation), of putting it down (near the fire), and of sprinkling it (with water) are performed with regard to the deities of the (respective) Mantras.

3. On vighana, which I have translated thin, see the note in the German edition, pp. 119 seq.

The deities of the festivals of the new and full moon (i. e. of the rites which in the Srauta ritual correspond to that taught here) are, at the full moon, Agni and Agnîshomau, at the new moon, Agni, Vishnu, and Indrâgnî, who are preceded in both cases by Agni and Soma as the deities of the two âgyabhâgas (see below, ch. 9, 7), and followed by Agni Svish/akrit. For more detailed statements see Hillebrandt, Das altindische Neu- und Vollmondsopfer (Jena, 1879), pp. 102 seq.

4. For instance, the taking of the portion of food destined to Agni should be performed with the Mantra: Agnaye tvâ gush-tam grihnâmi, &c. A number of ceremonies common to the Sthâlipâka ritual and to the ordinary ritual of Âgya oblations, such as the strewing of Kusa grass round the fire, the ceremonies regarding the Pavitras (strainers), &c., have to be supplied here from the Âgya ritual given below (ch. 7 seq.); this may be looked upon as an argument in favour of our conjecture which will be stated in the preface (vol. ii of the Grihya-sûtras), that our text, as probably is the case also with the Pâraskara-sûtra, is based on an original, the opening sentences of which are preserved to us in Sânkh. I, 5, 1-5 = Pâraskara I, 4, 1-5, so that the first chapters of Sânkhâ-yana, and among them the exposition of the festivals of the full and new moon, would have been prefixed to the original commencement of the text.

5. And the rules about the portions to be cut off (from the sacrificial food, are valid).

6. But before the sacrifices of the new and full moon one should make offerings to the deities of the Anvârambhanîya ceremony.

7. The time for the new moon sacrifice is not elapsed until the full moon, nor that for the full moon sacrifice until the new moon.

8. And some say that the morning oblation may be made at the time of the evening oblation, in the case of danger.

9. But the time is fixed, as at the Agnihotra an expiation has been prescribed for him who has neglected the time.

10. At the two daily oblations one should use as sacrificial food either rice or barley or grains.

11. In case these are not at hand, other (sorts of sacrificial food are) not prohibited.

12. Some say that if he uses grains, he should wash them.

13. With the other (kinds of food) no such preparation takes place.

---

5. On the avadânadharmâs comp. Weber, Indische Studien, X, 95; Hillebrandt, Neu- und Vollmondsopfer, pp. 122 seqq.

6. The Anvârambhanîyâ-ishti is the sacrifice taught in the Srauta texts which is to be performed before the sacrificer for the first time offers the Darsapûrnamâsa sacrifice. See Weber, Indische Studien, X, 330; Hillebrandt, loc. cit., p. 185. The deities of this ceremony are Agnîvishnû, Sarasvatî, and Sarasvat.

7. Comp. the expiatory sacrifice prescribed in the Parisishta book, V, 4.

8. The text here passes over from the two monthly sacrifices to the two daily ones, which correspond to the Agnihotra of the Srauta ritual.

14. In the evening (he makes the oblation) to Agni, in the morning to Sûrya,

15. And after both silently to Pragâpati.

16. Some (say that) before the first oblation a piece of wood (is to be put on the fire).

17. The sprinkling with water as indicated (in the Srauta-sûtra).

KHANDA 4.

1. When he has risen in the morning and has sipped water, let him daily repeat his recital.

2. (This consists of, or is accompanied by, the following texts :) the two verses, ' To-day, god Savitar ' (Rig-veda V, 82, 4–5); the hymn, ' Go away, Manasaspati ' (X, 164); the hymn, ' Right and truth ' (X, 190); the verses, ' Look down, ye Âdityas,' to the end of the hymn (VIII, 47, 11–18);

14, 15. These are the same deities who are worshipped also at the Agnihotra.

17. Srauta-sûtra II, 6, 9–11. Comp. p. 120 of the German edition.

4, 1. The Paddhati of Râmakandra understands svâdhyâyam adhîyîta as a prescription to perform the daily Brahmayagña (comp., for instance, Âsvalâyana-Grihya III, 2 ; Âpastamba I, 11, 22 seq.), which consists in the recitation of portions of the Veda ; the hymns and verses stated in Sûtra 2 are, according to the same authority, to be repeated immediately after the recitation of the svâdhyâya ('svâdhyâyânantaram'). Nârâyana, on the contrary, considers that the svâdhyâya prescribed in Sûtra 1 consists of those very hymns and verses which are indicated in the second Sûtra. As to the Brahmayagña, he says that the ka at the end of the second Sûtra may be referred to it ('the word ka means that texts procuring a long life, such as Rig-veda I, 89, should be murmured, or an injunction of the Brahmayagña is intended'). At all events it is very difficult to believe that the recitation of the texts stated in this chapter should be quite independent from the daily Brahmayagña. About the performance of the Brahmayagña in our days comp. the note of Professor Bühler, Sacred Books of the East, vol. ii, p. 43.

the verse, 'O Indra, the best treasures' (II, 21, 6);
the verse, 'The swan dwelling in purity' (IV, 40, 5);
the verse, 'Adoration to the great ones' (I, 27, 13);
the verse, 'What we fear, Indra' (VIII, 50, 13); the
verse, 'And of the sleep' (I, 120, 12); the verse, 'He
who says to me, O king' (II, 28, 10); the hymn,
'Let glory be mine, Agni' (X, 128); and the five
verses, 'Bliss may create for us' (V, 51, 11 seq.).

KHANDA 5.

1. There are four kinds of Pâkayagñas, viz. the
HUTA, the AHUTA, the PRAHUTA, and the PRÂSITA.

2. On the following five occasions, viz. the wedding, the tonsure (of the child's head), the initiation
(of the Brahmakârin), the cutting of the beard, and
the parting of the hair, (on these occasions) in the
outer hall—

3. To a place that has been smeared (with cowdung), which is elevated, and which has been
sprinkled (with water), he carries forward the fire,

4. Having kindled it by rubbing, according to
some teachers, at his marriage.

5. During the northern course of the sun, in the

5, 1. This Sûtra and the following ones down to the fifth are
identical with Pâraskara I, 4, 1–5; it seems to me that we have
here before us the opening Sûtras of a lost text from which this
passage has been copied both by Sâṅkhâyana and Pâraskara.
Comp. the preface of the second volume of the Grihya-sûtras.
With regard to the fourfold division of Pâkayagñas stated here
comp. below, chap. 10, 7.

2. Comp. the Kârikâ quoted by Nârâyana, 'vivâhâdishu bâhyo
'gnir mandape ka tad ishyata iti.'

3. On the Agni-pranayana comp. the details given in the Grihya-
samgraha-parisishta (Zeitschrift der Deutschen Morgenländischen
Gesellschaft, vol. xxxv), I, 64–69.

time of the increasing moon, on an auspicious day he shall seize the hand of a girl,

6. Who should possess (the auspicious) characteristics (required),

7. Whose limbs should be proportionate,

8. Whose hair should be smooth,

9. Who should also have at her neck two curls turned to the right.

10. (Of such a girl) he shall know that she will give birth to six men.

KHANDA 6.

1. If he will acquire a wife, let him recite over the wooers (whom he sends to the girl's father) when they go away, the verse, 'Thornless' (Rigveda X, 85, 23).

2. When they arrive, they take flowers, fruits, barley, and a pot of water.

3. They say thrice, 'Here I am, sir!'

4. When these words have been uttered, they ask the girl in marriage, reciting the clan names, the dwellers turning their faces to the east, the visitors to the west.

5. When the matter pleases both sides, let them touch a full vessel into which have been put flowers,

---

9. On âvartau comp. the note in the German edition, p. 121.

6, 1. 'The wooers, i.e. his own father, &c.' Nârâyana.

3. 'When the father of the suitor and the others, together with their Âkârya, have arrived at the house of him who is to give away the girl, they station themselves in the hall, and the father of the suitor says thrice, "Here am I, N. N. (amukasarman), Sir!"—in these words he announces himself three times . . . . For at the house of the person who gives the girl away, there arrive also, in order to see the festivities, many other people. In order to distinguish himself from these, he pronounces his name.' Nârâyana.

fried grain, fruits, barley, and gold, and let them
recite (the formula), 'Undisturbed art thou, the
undisturbable vigour of the gods, not cursed, protecting against a curse, unexposed to a curse.
Might I straightway attain to truth. Put me into
prosperity.'

6. With the verse, 'Offspring may produce us'
(Rig-veda X, 85, 43), the Â*k*ârya of the girl's
(family), standing up, places (the vessel) on her
head (saying), 'Offspring I put into thee, cattle
I put into thee, splendour and holy lustre I put
into thee.'

KHA*ND*A 7.

1. When assent has been declared (by the girl's
father, the bridegroom) sacrifices.

2. He besmears a quadrangular space with cowdung.

3. (Let him consider in the ceremonies to be
performed,) of the two eastern intermediate directions, the southern one as that to which (the rites)
should be directed, if the rites belong to the Manes,

6. The position of the words as well as the sense favours combining the genitive kanyâyâ*h* with â*k*ârya*h*, not with mûrdhani, though Râma*k*andra says that the varapaksha*k*ârya is to
be understood.

7, 1 seq. Here follows a description of the sacrifice which is to
be performed when the girl's father has declared his assent
(prati*s*rute) to give her away in marriage: this is the general
model for all G*ri*hya sacrifices.—'Varo *g*uhoti,' Nârâya*n*a.

3. 'He here states an exception to the rule, "The ceremonies
sacred to the Manes are directed towards the south" (*S*rauta-sûtra
I, 1, 14) . . . . He should consider the south-eastern direction,
sacred to Agni, as that to which the ceremonies are to be directed
(prâ*k*îm pûrvâ*m* kalpayet) which are sacred to the Manes, such as

4. The northern one, if the rites belong to the gods,

5. Or rather the east (itself) according to some (teachers).

6. He draws in the middle (of the sacrificial ground) a line from south to north,

7. Upwards from this, turned upwards, to the south one line, in the middle one, to the north one.

8. These he sprinkles (with water),

9. Carries forward the fire with the verse, 'I carry forward Agni with genial mind; may he be the assembler of goods. Do no harm to us, to the old nor to the young; be a saviour to us, to men and animals,'

10. Or (he carries it forward) silently,

11. Then he wipes with his wet hand three times around the fire, turning his right side to it. This they call SAMÛHANA (sweeping together).

---

prescribed in the Sûtra, "Let him make oblations every month to the Fathers" (IV, 1, 1) . . . . He states an exception to the rule, "The ceremonies sacred to the gods are directed towards the east" (*S*raut. I, 1, 13) . . . . The northern of the two eastern intermediate directions, sacred to Îsâna, should be considered as that to which the ceremonies sacred to the gods, such as oblations, &c., are to be directed.'—Comp. Âsvalâyana-*S*raut. I, 12, 4.

6–7. See the quotations from Râma*k*andra's and Nârâya*n*a's commentaries, p. 123 of the German edition. An illustration of the form of the sthan*d*ila with the lines drawn thereon is given by Dr. Bloomfield in his note on the G*ri*hya-sa*m*graha-pari*s*ish*t*a I, 52 seq.; instead of the three lines, however, which are here prescribed in Sûtra 7, there are four indicated in accordance with the doctrine of that Pari*s*ish*t*a and of Gobhila himself, which are stated to be sacred to P*ri*thivî, Pra*g*âpati, Indra, and Soma, while the line turned from south to north is sacred to Agni.

9. On the Agnipra*n*ayana (carrying forward of the fire) see the G*ri*hya-sa*m*graha-pari*s*ish*t*a I, 64–69.

12. Once, turning his left side to it, in the rites belonging to the Manes.

KHANDA 8.

1. Now (follows) the strewing (of grass) around (the fire).

2. He strews eastward-pointed Kusa grass around it, in three layers or in five layers,

3. Beginning on the east side, then to the west, then to the west.

4. He covers the roots (of the grass-blades) with the points.

5. And all kinds of rites are to be performed beginning south, ending north.

6. He places the Brahman south with the words, BHÛR BHUVAH SVAH,

7. Adorns him with flowers,

8. Carries forward on the north side the Pranîtâ waters with the words, 'Who carries ye forward?'—

9. Takes up with the left hand the Kusa blades, and arranges them (on the ground) with the right hand,

---

8, 1. Comp. the passages quoted in Professor Eggeling's note on Satapatha Br. I, 1, 1, 22.

6. Ordinarily there was no real Brahman present, and his place was filled by a bundle of Kusa grass that represented him. Nârâyana states that this bundle should consist of fifty blades of Kusa grass. Comp. also the Grihya-samgraha-parisishta I, 89-90.

8. Comp. the passages quoted by Dr. Bloomfield, Zeitschrift der Deutschen Morgenländ. Gesellschaft, vol. xxxv, p. 565, note 2.

9. This Sûtra shows that the paristarana, though already treated of in Sûtras 1-4, is not to be performed till after the 'carrying forward' of the Pranîtâ water. Comp. Nârâyana's note on Sûtra 1 (p. 123 of the German edition). That this is indeed the order of the different acts is confirmed by Pâraskara I, 1, 2.

10. Bending his right knee,

11. The left when worshipping the Manes.

12. The strewing around (of the grass) is not necessary in the Âgya offerings,

13. Nor in the standing offerings, according to Mândûkeya.

14. He now measures off with the span (of his hand) two Kusa blades, which are not unequal, with unbroken points, bearing no young shoots in them, and severs them (from their roots) with a Kusa blade, saying, ' Purifiers are ye.'

15. There are two or three (of these Kusa strainers).

16. He holds them with their points to the east and sprinkles them (with water, saying), ' Belonging to Vishnu.'

17. With the two Kusa blades he sprinkles (water) around the fire three times, keeping his right side turned towards it,

18. Takes up the Âgya pot with the words, 'Milk of the cows art thou ;'

19. Puts it on the fire with the words, ' For sap thee ;'

20. Takes it from the fire towards the north with the words, ' For juice thee ;'

21. And holding the two (Kusa) strainers with their points to the north, seizing them on both sides

---

13. ' In the standing offerings, such as the Vaisvadeva sacrifice in the morning and in the evening.' Nârâyana.

14–16. Vâgasaneyi Samhitâ I, 12 a.

18. Vâg. Samh. IV, 3 a.

19. Vâg. Samh. I, 22 d.

20. Vâg. Samh. I, 30 c.

21. Vâg. Samh. I, 12 b.—The division of Sûtras 21 and 22 should be after iti, not, as the Indian tradition has it, after rasmibhih.

with his two thumbs and fourth fingers, he bends
them down, the points upwards, and dips them into
the Âgya with the words,

'By the impulse of Savitar I purify thee with
this uninjured purifier, with the rays of the good
sun.'

22. (This) preparation of the Âgya (takes place)
each time.

23. Let him not offer (Âgya) which has not been
(thus) prepared.

24. Also the waters in the Sruva spoon (he purifies) with the words, '(By the impulse) of Savitar
(I purify) you.'

25. This (is called) the PRANÎTÂ and the PROK-
SHANÎ water.

KHANDA 9.

1. The Sruva spoon (serves as) a vessel.

2. According to the purpose the properties (of
the different things to be used at each oblation)
should be chosen.

3. Taking up Kusa blades with the left, and the

24, 25. Râmakandra: 'He pours water into the Sruva and
purifies this also, as he had done with the Âgya (Sûtra 21) . . . .
He then pours a little portion of that water on to the Pranîtâ water
(see above, Sûtra 8), and with the rest, which is called the Prok-
shanî water, he sprinkles the sacrificial food, the fuel, and the
Barhis.'

9, 1. 'When no special rule is stated, the Sruva is to be under-
stood as the vessel (for the offering). Thereby the rule, "The
Guhû is the vessel" (Srauta-sûtra III, 19, 5) is abolished (for the
Grihya rites).' Nârâyana.

3. The manner of holding the Sruva in which the Âgya is, is
described by Kâtyâyana, Sraut. I, 10, 6 seq., Stenzler's note on
Pâraskara I, 1, 4.

Sruva at its bottom with the right hand, with the words, 'The hand of Vishnu art thou '—

4. He offers with the Sruva the Âgya oblations.

5. Beginning from the north-west side of the fire he offers (the Âgya) unintermittingly on the south side (of the fire) with (the verse), 'Thou Agni art full of foresight' (Rig-veda I, 31, 10).

6. Beginning from the south-west side of the fire he unintermittingly offers on the north side with (the verse), 'To whom these snowy mountains' (Rig-veda X, 121, 4).

7. To Agni belongs the northern Âgya portion, to Soma the southern.

8. In the middle (are made) the other oblations,

9. (With the words,) 'Agni is the begetter; may he give to me N. N. as my wife; svâhâ!

'Soma is rich in wives; may he make me rich in wives by N. N.; svâhâ!

'Pûshan is rich in kindred; may he make me rich in kindred by the father, the mother, the brothers of N. N.; svâhâ!'

10. At the Âgya oblations the offering of the two Âgya portions and of the Svishtakrit oblation is not standing,

---

4. As to the characteristics of Âgya (sacrificial butter), which is the substance offered at most of the Grihya sacrifices, comp. the statements of the Grihya-samgraha-parisishta I, 105 seq.

5. Avikkhinnam (unintermittingly) is explained in Nâr.'s commentary by ekadhârayâ.

8 seq. Here are indicated the chief oblations of this sacrifice (anyâ âhutayah pradhânabhûtâh, Nâr.), or the âvâpa (the insertion, Sûtra 12) which comes between the standing introductory and concluding oblations.

10. On Svishtakrit, comp. Weber, Indische Studien, IX, 217.

11. Nor in the standing oblations, according to Mâ*nd*ûkeya.

12. The place for the insertion is the interval between the Mahâvyâh*ri*tis, the general expiation, and the oblation to Pra*g*âpati.

---

11. See chap. 8, 13.

12. This Sûtra prescribes where the âvâpa, i.e. the special characteristical offerings of each sacrifice, is to be inserted between the regular offerings that belong to the standing model. The same subject is treated of in the *S*rauta-sûtra in the two rules, I, 16, 3 and 4: 'Whatsoever is offered between the two *Â*gya portions and the Svish*t*akr*i*t, that is called âvâpa; this is the chief part (pradhâna) (of the sacrifice); the other (oblations) are subordinate thereto (tadangâni).' The position of the âvâpa among the other oblations is indicated by Pâraskara in the following rule (I, 5, 6): 'Between the general expiation and the oblation to Pra*g*âpati, this is the place for the âvâpa.' (The word vivâhe at the end of this Sûtra seems to me to belong not to this rule, but to Sûtra 7.) Our Sûtra is identical with that of Pâraskara word for word; only instead of sarvaprâya*s*kitta, as Pâraskara has, we read here, mahâvyâh*ri*tisarvaprâya*s*kitta. This means, I believe, that the âvâpa, preceded and followed by the Mahâvyâh*ri*ti oblations (comp. below, I, 12, 13), should be placed between the Sarvaprâya*s*kitta and the Prâ*g*âpatya oblation. The oblations made with the Mahâvyâh*ri*tayas are four in number; the corresponding formulas are: bhû*h* svâhâ, bhuva*h* svâhâ, svâ*h* svâhâ, bhûr bhuva*h* sva*h* svâhâ (comp. below, chap. 12, 12). The Sarvaprâya*s*kitta (general expiation) consists of two oblations, one with the three Mahâvyâh*ri*tayas, the other with the verse ayâs *k*âgne, quoted in the *S*rauta-sûtra III, 19, 3, and in Â*s*valâyana's *S*rauta-sûtra I, 11, 13. (On the Sarvaprâya*s*kitta in the *S*rauta ritual, compare Hillebrandt, Neu- und Vollmonds-opfer, p. 166.) The Prâ*g*âpatya oblation is performed with the formula Pra*g*âpataye svâhâ. The discussions of Nârâya*n*a on this Sûtra (see p. 125 of the German edition) evidently fail to bring out the true meaning of the text; according to this commentator the oblations follow each other in this order: the two Â*g*yabhâgas, the principal oblations (pradhânâhutaya*h*), the Svish*t*akr*i*t, the four Mahâvyâh*ri*ti oblations, the two Sarvaprâya*s*kitta oblations, the Prâ*g*âpatya oblation. Finally we may mention the corrupt form in which the corresponding passage of the *S*âmbavya-sûtra is pre-

13. If the oblation consists in Âgya, let him seize the Kusa blades in his left hand with his right hand at their points and with the left at their roots, and let him wet their points (with Âgya) in the Sruva, the middle and the roots in the Âgya pot;

14. In the oblations of cooked food, however, the points in the Sruk, the middle in the Sruva, the roots in the Âgya pot.

15. When he then has thrown them (into the fire) with the words, 'Agni's garment art thou,'

16. And has put on (the fire) three pieces of wood,

17. (Water) is sprinkled round (the fire) as stated above.

18. Oblations for which only the deities are indicated, but no texts prescribed, are to be made merely with the word Svâhâ, 'To such and such a deity svâhâ! To such and such a deity svâhâ!'

19. The ritual (here) declared of the sacrifice (to

---

served in the MS. There the two Sûtras 10 and 11 are placed before the Mantra in Sûtra 9. This Mantra then is given down to svâheti, then follows âgyena, which seems to me to form part of the same Sûtra, and to refer to the oblations to which the Mantra belongs. Then the MS. goes on: mahâvyâhritishu sarvaprâyaskittâram (sic) etad âvâpasthânam âgyahavishi vyâhritishu sarvaprâyaskittâram (the syllables prâyaskittâram seem to be expunged) svishtakrito sthâlipâke. In the commentary I find the following Slokas, which I give exactly as they are read in the MS.: tisrinâm vyâhritînâm ka prâyaskittâhutîr api yad antaram tad âpâpasthânam sarpihpradhânake. sthâlipâke vyâhritînâm yat tat svishtakritottaram âhutînâm pradhânânâm nânâdaivatakhandasâm yas tu kâlas tad âvâpasthânam itâkyate budhaih tatas tat tam ma ârabhya prâyaskittâhutih kramât.

17. See above, chap. 8, 17.

19. This Sûtra, though reckoned in the Indian tradition to

be performed) when (the father's) assent (to give away his daughter) has been declared—

KHANDA 10.

1. Forms the standard for all sacrifices that procure happiness,
2. And for all Âgya offerings,
3. For the sacrifice of animals which are tied to a branch,
4. And for the offerings of boiled (rice) grains and of cooked food.
5. These are performed, all the offerings of cooked food, without PRAYÂGA and ANUYÂGA oblations, without (the invocation of) the ILÂ, without NIGADA recitation, and without SÂMIDHENÎ verses.
6. There are also the following *S*lokas :

---

chap. 9, seems to me clearly to belong to the next chapter, and to contain the subject, to which the predicate is given in 10, 1. For prati*s*rute, see chap. 7, 1.

10, 1. 'As in the *S*rauta ritual the sacrifice of the full and new moon forms the standard for the ish*t*is, the pa*s*ubandha, &c., thus the prati*s*rut-kalpa is the standard for the vikr*i*tis of the Smârta ritual, such as the *g*âtakarman (chap. 24), &c.' Nârâya*n*a.

3. 'It is the standard of the sacrifices prescribed in the rules, "The animal (offered) to the teacher is sacred to Agni; to an officiating priest, to Br*i*haspati, &c."' Nârâya*n*a. This refers to the sacrifice of animals which forms part of the Arghya ceremony; see II, 15, 4 seq.

4. *K*arû*n*â*m* pâkaya*g*ñânâ*m* *k*a. Nârâya*n*a.

5. On the five Prayâgas and the three Anuyâgas (introductory oblations and oblations following on the principal offerings) prescribed in the *S*rauta ritual, comp. Hillebrandt's Neu- und Vollmondsopfer, pp. 94 seq., 134 seq. On the Ilâ, see ibid., 122 seq. ; on nigada, Weber's Ind. Studien, IX, 217, &c. ; on the Sâmidhenî verses, Hillebrandt, loc. cit., pp. 74 seq. On this Sûtra compare also the passage in Kâtyâyana's *S*rauta-sûtra, VI, 10, 22 seq.

7. '(An oblation is called) HUTA, (if made) by the performing of the Agnihotra; AHUTA (i.e. unsacrificed, if) by the Bali offering; PRAHUTA (i.e. sacrificed up, if) by a sacrifice to the Manes; PRÂSITA (i.e. tasted, if) deposited as an offering in a Brâhmana.

8. 'Without raising his knees, with spread knees let him always offer his oblation; for the gods never accept an offering (that has been made holding the hand) not between (the knees).

9. 'But when he has repeated a text sacred to Rudra, to the Rakshas, to the Manes, to the Asuras, or that contains an imprecation, let him touch water, and so also when he has touched his own body.'

KHANDA 11.

1. Now when the bride is to be carried away (to the bridegroom's house) that night, or on the next, or on the third night,

2. On that night, when (the darkness of) night is gone, they wash the girl up to her head with (water that has been made fragrant by) all sorts of herbs and the choicest fruits together with scents; ·

---

7. Comp. chap. 5, 1.

8. Comp. the Grihya-samgraha-parisishta I, 46, and the note, Zeitschrift der Deutschen Morgenl. Gesellschaft, XXXV, 556. Nârâyana: dakshinam bâhum gânvor antare kritvety arthah, sarvadâ sarvasminn api karmani havir homadravyam guhuyât.

9. This verse is found also in the Karmapradîpa III, 8, 4.

11, 1. The ceremony described in this chapter is called Indrânî-karman. The goddess Indrânî is mentioned in Sûtra 4 among the deities to whom Âgya oblations are made.

2. Nisâkâle, nisâ madhyastham praharadvayam, tasmin kâle atîte. Nârâyana.

On the anvârambha, comp. Weber's Indische Studien, IX, 224.

3. They put on her a newly-dyed garment or (a new one) which has not yet been washed;

4. Then (the Âkârya of the bride's family) makes the girl sit down behind the fire, and while she takes hold of him he sacrifices with the Mahâvyâhritis, and then he makes Âgya oblations to Agni, to Soma, to Pragâpati, to Mitra, to Varuna, to Indra, to Indrânî, to the Gandharva, to Bhaga, to Pûshan, to Tvashtar, to Brihaspati, to the king Pratyânîka.

5. After they have regaled four or eight women, who are not widows, with lumps of vegetables, Surâ, and food, these should perform a dance four times.

6. The same deities (they worship also) on behalf of the man,

7. And Vaisravana and Îsâna.

8. Then follows the distribution of food to Brâhmanas.

KHANDA 12.

1. The bridegroom, who has bathed and for whom auspicious ceremonies have been performed, is escorted by happy young women, who are not widows, to the girl's house.

2. To these he shall not behave unobsequiously, except where forbidden food or a transgression is concerned.

3. Having obtained their permission, he then gives her the garment with (the verse), 'The Raibhi was' (Rig-veda X, 85, 6).

---

4. The 'king Pratyânîka' has given origin to a very curious misunderstanding in the Sâmbavya-Grihya and its commentary; see p. 127 of the German edition.

4. With (the verse), 'Mind was the cushion' (ibid. 7) he takes up the salve-box.

5. The verse for the anointing is, 'May the Visve devâs anoint (or, unite),' (ibid. 47.)

6. 'As this (has protected) Saki the beloved one, and Aditi the mother of noble sons, and Apâlâ who was free from widowhood, may it thus here protect thee, N. N.!'—with these words (the bridegroom) gives her into her right hand the quill of a porcupine (and) a string of three twisted threads,

7. With the verse, 'Shape by shape' (Rig-veda VI, 47, 18) a mirror into the left.

8. Her relations tie (to her body) a red and black, woollen or linen cord with three (amulet) gems, with the verse, 'Dark-blue and red' (Rig-veda X, 85, 28).

9. With the verse, 'Full of honey the herbs' (Rig-veda IV, 57, 3), (the bridegroom) ties (to her body) Madhûka flowers.

12, 5. On the ceremony of 'salving together' (samangana), comp. Pâraskara I, 4, 14; Gobhila II, 2, &c. Professor Stenzler is certainly wrong in translating Pâraskara's samangayati by 'heisst sie beide zusammentreten' (according to Gayarâma's expli- cation, sammukhîkaroti). It is clear from Sânkhâyana, that a real anointing of bridegroom and bride took place. This was per- formed, according to Gobhila, by the 'audaka' (this seems to be the same person that is mentioned in Pâraskara I, 8, 3), of whom it is said, pânigrâham (i. e. the bridegroom) mûrdhadese 'vasinkati, tathetarâm. Nârâyana, on the contrary, in his note on our pas- sage, says that it is the bridegroom who anoints the eyes of the girl with the verse quoted. But the word sam-angana, and the obvious meaning of the whole rite, make it rather probable that both were anointed, and that this was done by a third person.

6. Comp. below, chap. 22, 8, where the use of a porcupine's quill is prescribed at the sîmantonnayana ceremony; and see chap. 22, 10.

10. At the wedding one cow, when the Argha ceremony has been performed; in the house one cow: these are the two Madhuparka cows.

11. (The bridegroom) makes the girl sit down behind the fire, and while she takes hold of him he makes three oblations with the Mahâvyâhr*i*tis.

---

10. As to the meaning of arhayitvâ I differ from the opinion of Nârâya*n*a (see his note on p. 127 of the German edition), who takes gâm as the object of this verb (gâm arhayitvâ pû*g*ayitvâ mâtâ rudrâ*n*âm ity r*i*k*am* *g*apitvâ [comp. Pâraskara I, 3, 27]). The real meaning of arhayati is, to perform the Argha ceremony for a guest. Evidently in this Sûtra two different occasions are stated on which the Argha reception, eventually with the killing of a cow, should be performed; firstly, the bridegroom should be so received in the house of the bride's father; secondly, when the newly-married people have arrived at their own house, an Argha reception should there be offered to them, perhaps, as the commentaries state, by the Â*k*ârya.

11. According to Nârâya*n*a it is the Â*k*ârya who performs the rite prescribed in this Sûtra; Râma*k*andra, on the contrary, refers it to the bridegroom, which seems to me right. Comp. Gobhila II, 1.

In *S*âṅkhâyana's description of the wedding ceremonies the point at which the bride passes over from the paternal power into that of her new husband is not expressly indicated. Pâraskara (I, 4, 15) clearly indicates it (pitrâ prattâm âdâya), and in the Pari*s*ish*t*a of the Â*s*valâyana-Gr*i*hya this act of handing over the girl is treated of in detail (I, 22). On this depends the description in the Prayogaratna, fol. 69; comp. also Colebrooke's Miscell. Essays, I, 210. The Paddhati of Râma*k*andra does not fail to mention the kanyâpradâna, but I do not think that the succession of the different rites is stated there correctly. According to the Paddhati the bridegroom goes to the house of the girl's father, and there, after the madhuparka has been offered, the bride is given over to him; he then (labdhavadhûka*h*) goes (chap. 12, 1), accompanied by young women, to the kautukâgâra, where the ceremonies described in chap. 12, 3 seq. take place. Pâraskara, on the contrary, describes the handing over of the garments, the anointing, &c., as preceding the giving over of the girl, and indeed it is scarcely possible to see in the acts of dressing, adorning the girl, &c., in which both the bridegroom and her relations

12. A fourth (oblation) with (the three Mahâvyâhritis) together is to be understood from this rule.

13. In this way, where no express rule is stated, in all sacrifices that procure happiness, one is to sacrifice before and afterwards with these same (Mahâvyâhritis).

KHANDA 13.

1. 'Be queen with thy father-in-law,' with this verse (Rig-veda X, 85, 46) her father or brother sacrifices with a sword's point on her head, or with the Sruva, standing while she is sitting, with his face turned to the west, while her face is turned to the east.

2. 'I seize thy hand for the sake of happiness' (Rig-veda X, 85, 36), with these words (the bridegroom) seizes with his right hand her right hand with the thumb, both hands being turned with the palms upwards, he standing while she is sitting, with his face turned to the west, while her face is turned to the east.

3. And when he has murmured the following five verses,

4. (He continues thus,) 'This am I, that art thou;

take part, anything but preparatory performances that precede the decisive moment. The sacrifice, on the contrary, which the bridegroom performs, according to chap. 12, 11, in common with his bride, seems to presuppose that he has already received her from her father; and the ceremonies described in chap. 13, the pânigrahana, the pronouncing of the Mantra, chap. 13, 4, which reminds one of the Roman formula ubi tu Gaius, the seven steps—all that should be understood not as intended to establish the power of the husband over his wife, but as presupposing that power and showing an exercise of it.

13, 4. Nârâyana states that here four Brâhmanas should repeat that art thou, this am I ; the heaven I, the earth thou; the *Rik* art thou, the Sâman I.   So be thou devoted to me.

'Well! Let us here marry.   Let us beget off-spring.   Let us acquire many sons who may reach old age.'

5. (The Â*k*ârya) fills, with the words bhûr bhuva*h* sva*h*, a new water-pot,

6. Throws into it (branches) with milky sap and leaves, of a tree the name of which is masculine, together with Ku*s*a grass,

7. And gold, according to some (teachers),

8. And hands it over to a student who observes silence.

9. They should walk round this Stheyâ water, (placed) to the north-east, so that they turn their right sides towards it.

---

the Sûryâ hymn (Rig-veda X, 85) to the bride.   That, according to *S*ânkhâyana, that hymn is recited at the wedding, is clear from chap. 14, 12.

6. Sakshîrânt sapalâsânt saku*s*ân.   Nârâya*n*a's commentary divides sa ku*s*ân, and refers sa to the â*k*ârya.   But this sa would be superfluous, and the substantive to which sakshirân and sapalâ*s*ân are to be referred, is, as both the nature of the case and the corresponding passages show, *s*âkhân and not ku*s*ân.   Comp. the *S*rauta-sûtra IV, 17, 5 : palâsa*s*âkhâ*m* sapa-lâsâ*m* nikhâya, and a passage concerning the very rite here described, Âsvalâyana-pari*s*ish*t*a I, 24: audumbaryârddhayâ (read, ârdrayâ?) *s*âkhayâ sapalâ*s*ayâ sahira*n*yapavitrayâ sadûrvâpavitrayâ.   The MS. of the *S*âmbavya-sûtra has sa-kshîrân palâ*s*ân saku*s*ân.

9. 'The Stheyâ water has to be so placed that when the bride and the bridegroom walk (their seven steps, see chap. 14, 5 seq.), their right sides are turned towards it.'   Nârâya*n*a.   Comp., re-garding the Stheyâ water and its bearer, the G*ri*hya-sa*m*graha-pari*s*ish*t*a II, 26. 30. 35.

10. And after (the Âkârya) has placed a stone towards the northern direction,

11. (The bridegroom) makes her rise with the words, 'Come, thou joyful one,'

12. And makes her tread with the tip of her right foot on the stone, with the words, 'Come, tread on the stone; like a stone be firm. Tread the foes down; overcome the enemies.'

13. He then leads her round the fire so that their right sides are turned to it,

14. And gives her a second garment with the same text (chap. 12, § 3).

15. Her father or brother pours out of a basket fried grain mixed with Samî leaves into her joined hands.

16. The spreading under, the sprinkling over, and the second sprinkling over (are done) with Âgya.

17. She sacrifices those (fried grains).

KHANDA 14.

1. 'This woman, strewing grains, prays thus, "May I bring bliss to my relations; may my husband live long. Svâhâ!"'—while the husband murmurs (this) text, she sacrifices standing.

2. (All the ceremonies,) beginning from the tread-

---

17. I believe that the words forming this Sûtra, tâ ñ guhoti, are taken from the same lost old Grihya text which Sânkhâyana has followed word for word also in I, 5, 1–5 and elsewhere. This is made probable by the comparison of Pâraskara I, 6, 2. The author of our text, while literally adopting the words of his original, has not quite succeeded in welding them together with his own statements; thus the sacrifice of grains is treated of in this Sûtra and in the first Sûtra of the next chapter, as if there were two different acts, while indeed it is one and the same.

14, 2. The treading on the stone is prescribed in chap. 13, 12.

ing upon the stone, (are repeated) in the same way for a second time,

3. And in the same way a third time.

4. Silently, if they like, a fourth time.

5. (The Âkârya?) makes (them) step forward in a north-eastern direction seven steps (with the words),

6. 'For sap with one step, for juice with two steps, for the prospering of wealth with three steps, for comfort with four steps, for cattle with five steps, for the seasons with six steps. Friend be with seven steps.'

7. (The Âkârya?) 'appeases' those (foot-steps) with water.

8. With the three Âpohishthiyâ verses (Rig-veda X, 9, 1–3) he wipes (them) with the Stheyâ water,

9. And sprinkles it on their heads.

10. (The bridegroom then) says, 'I give you a cow.'

11. Let him give something to the Brâhmanas each time at the Sthâlîpâkas and other rites;

12. To him who knows the Sûryâ hymn the bride's shift.

5, 7. According to Nârâyana it is the teacher who makes them walk the seven steps; the Paddhati says that the bridegroom or the Âkârya causes her to do so. Comp. Pâraskara I, 8, 1; Âsvalâyana I, 7, 19, &c.

8. Comp. chap. 13, 9.

9. Probably we should read mûrdhanî (acc. dual.), not mûrdhani. Âsvalâyana has sirasî. Of course the heads of both the bridegroom and the bride were sprinkled with water; comp. Âsvalâyana I, 7, 20, &c.

12. The Sûryâ hymn is Rig-veda X, 85. Comp. the note above on chap. 13, 4.

13. A cow is the optional gift to be given by
a Brâhma*n*a,

14. A village by a Râganya,

15. A horse by a Vai*s*ya.

16. A hundred (cows) with a chariot (he gives to
a father) who has only daughters.

17. To those versed in the sacrificial rites he
gives a horse.

KHANDA 15.

1. The three verses, ' I loosen thee' (Rig-veda X,
85, 24), when she departs from the house.

2. 'The living one they bewail' (Rig-veda X,
40, 10), if she begins to cry.

3. The wife then smears the axle of the chariot
with clarified butter with this (verse), 'They feasted,
they got drunk' (Rig-veda I, 82, 2),

13-15. These Sûtras, treating of the fee for the sacrifice, are
identical with Pâraskara I, 8, 15-18. Apparently they are taken
from the same lost original from which several identical passages
in the Sûtras of Pâraskara and *S*ânkhâyana seem to be derived
(see the notes on chap. 5, 1 ; 13, 7). They stand rather out of
place here, for they return to the same subject which had already
been treated of in Sûtra 10, though in that Sûtra, as very frequently
is the case in our text and in similar ones, only the case of the
bridegroom being a Brâhma*n*a has been taken notice of.

16. Comp. the passages quoted by Professor Stenzler on Pâraskara I, 8, 18. Nârâya*n*a has the following note : ' To a duhit*r*i-
mat, i. e. to the father of a girl who has no brother, he shall give
a hundred cows and besides a chariot, in order to destroy the guilt
brought about by marrying a girl who has no brother.' Possibly
we should here emancipate ourselves from the authority of the
commentators, and explain duhit*r*imat 'he who gives his
daughter in marriage,' the bride's father. Comp. Âpastamba II,
11, 18 ; II, 13, 12 ; Weber, Indische Studien, V, 343, note 2.

15, 3. Probably the use of this verse on this occasion rests on the
assonance of its opening word aksha*n* and aksha (rathâksha).

4. And with the two (verses), 'Pure are thy
wheels,' 'Thy two wheels' (Rig-veda X, 85, 12. 16),
of the two wheels the first with the first (verse)
and the second with the second (verse),

5. And the two bulls.

6. After (the wife?) has put, with this (verse),
'In the box of the wheel' (Rig-veda VIII, 80, 7),
a branch of a fruit-bearing tree into each of the
holes destined for the pins,

7. Or, if (such branches) are (already) fixed, has
recited (that verse) over them,

8. They then harness the two bulls with the two
(verses), 'Harnessed be thy right one' (Rig-veda I,
82, 5–6), (the bridegroom) reciting the half-verse,
'White the two bulls' (Rig-veda X, 85, 10), over
them when they have been harnessed.

9. Now should any part of the chariot break or
burst, let him take the girl to the house of one who
keeps the sacred fires,

10. And repair (the damage) with the verse,
'Cover thyself with the Khadiras' (Rig-veda III,
53, 19).

11. A knot with the verse, 'Him like a horse'
(Rig-veda X, 143, 2).

12. He then murmurs the five verses, 'May prosperity give us' (Rig-veda V, 51, 11–15).

13. 'Adorned with Kimsuka flowers' (Rig-veda X,
85, 20), when she mounts the chariot;

14. 'May no waylayers meet us' (ibid. 32), at
a cross-way;

15. 'Which the woman's' (ibid. 31), near a cemetery;

16. The half-verse, 'O tree with thy hundred

---

6. See Nârâyana's note on samyâgarta, p. 129 of the German
edition.

branches' (Rig-veda III, 8, 11), he mutters near a
big tree;

17. 'The good protectress' (Rig-veda X, 63, 10),
when she ascends a ship;

18. 'Carrying stones' (Rig-veda X, 53, 8), when
she crosses a river;

19. Optionally (he) also (murmurs the same verse,
if that is done) with the harnessed chariot;

20. 'Up may your wave' (Rig-veda III, 33, 13), at
deep places (in the river);

21. And (at such places) let her not look out.

22. The seven verses, 'Here may delight' (Rig-
veda X, 85, 27 seq.), when she has reached the house,
omitting the verses already employed.

KHANDA 16.

1. 'A bull's hide'—this has been declared.

2. On that hide the husband makes her sit down
and sacrifices, while she takes hold of him, four oblations (with the following formulas),

3. 'With god Agni, with the earth-world of the
worlds, and the Rig-veda of the Vedas: therewith
I appease thee, N. N., svâhâ!

'With god Vâyu, with the air-world of the worlds,

16, 1. In chap. 13, 22 it is said that the bride arrives at the
house; in 16, 12, that she enters the house. Probably we are to
understand, therefore, that the sacrifice prescribed in this chapter,
Sûtras 2 seq., is performed before the house, like the Vâstosh-
patîya karman (below, III, 4). The words, 'has been declared,'
refer to the Srauta-sûtra (IV, 16, 2), 'Having spread a red bull's
skin, with the neck to the north or to the east, with the hair outside, behind the fire, they sit down,' &c.

2. On anvârambha comp. the quotation in the note on
chap. 11, 2.

with the Yagur-veda of the Vedas : therewith I appease thee, N. N., svâhâ!

'With god Sûrya, with the heaven-world of the worlds, with the Sâma-veda of the Vedas : therewith I appease thee, N. N., svâhâ!

'With god Kandra, with the world of the quarters (of the horizon) of the worlds, with the Brahma-veda of the Vedas : therewith I appease thee, N. N., svâhâ!'

4. Or, 'Bhûh! What harm dwells in thee, bringing death to thy husband, death to thy husband's brother, that I make death-bringing to thy paramour, N. N., svâhâ!'—thus the first (of the before-mentioned formulas) may be joined with the first Mahâvyâhr/ti, the second with the second, the third with the third, the fourth with (the three Mahâvyâhr/tis) together.

5. With (the verse), 'With no evil eye' (Rig-veda X, 85, 44), let him besmear (her) eyes with Âgya salve.

6. (The bridegroom,) having touched the ends of her hair with the three (verses), 'How may us the resplendent one . . .' (Rig-veda IV, 31, 1–3),

7. And having quickly recited the four verses, 'And those divine medicines' (Rig-veda VIII, 18, 8), at the end (of that text) with the word svâhâ (pours out) the remainder on (her) head.

8. Here some place a boy of good birth on both sides, in her lap, with this (verse), 'Into thy womb' (see below, chap. 19, 6),

---

8. It should be noted that the verse â te yonim is quoted here only with the Pratîka, while its full text is given below, chap. 19, 6. Can the Sûtras describing this ceremony with the kumâra ubhayatah-sugâta be a later addition?

9. Or also silently.

10. Into this (boy's) joined hands (the bridegroom) gives fruits and causes (the Brâhmaṇas) to wish an auspicious day.

11. Thus she becomes the mother of male children.

12. With the rest of the hymn, 'Stay ye here both' (Rig-veda X, 85, 42 seq.), they make them enter the house.

KHANDA 17.

1. With the verse, 'I praised Dadhikrâvan' (Rig-veda IV, 39, 6), let them drink together curds.

2. Let them sit silent, when the sun has set, until the polar-star appears.

3. He shows her the polar-star with the words, 'Firm be thou, thriving with me!'

4. Let her say, 'I see the polar-star; may I obtain offspring.'

5. Through a period of three nights let them refrain from conjugal intercourse.

6. Let them sleep on the ground.

7. Let them eat together boiled rice with curds, with the three verses, 'Drink and satiate yourselves' (Rig-veda VIII, 35, 10).

8. Let them serve the nuptial fire in the evening and in the morning with the words, 'To Agni svâhâ! To Agni Svishṭakṛit svâhâ!'

9. 'Let the two men Mitra and Varuṇa, let the two men, the Asvins both, let the man Indra and also Agni make a man grow in me. Svâhâ!'—with

---

17, 2, 3. I have changed in the translation the division of these Sûtras; the native authorities divide after dhruvadarsanât, while I propose to divide after astamite.

(these words she offers) the first oblation if she is
desirous of pregnancy.

10. For ten days they are not to set out (from
home).

KHANDA 18.

1. Now the rites of the fourth day.

2. When the three nights have elapsed, he makes
offerings of cooked food (with the texts),

3. 'Agni! Thou art expiation; thou art the expiation of the gods. What substance dwells in her
that brings death to her husband, that drive away
from her.

'Vâyu! Thou art expiation; thou art the expiation
of the gods. What substance dwells in her that
brings sonlessness, that drive away from her.

'Sûrya! Thou art expiation; thou art the expiation of the gods. What substance dwells in her
that brings destruction to the cattle, that drive away
from her.

'To god Aryaman the girls have made sacrifice,
to Agni; may he, god Aryaman, loosen her from
this, and not from that place.

'To god Varuna the girls have made sacrifice, to
Agni; may he, god Varuna, &c.

'To god Pûshan the girls have made sacrifice, to
Agni; may he, god Pûshan, &c.'

4. The seventh oblation with the verse, ' Praĝâ-
pati' (Rig-veda X, 121, 10).

5. The eighth to (Agni) Svishtakrit.

18, 3. As to preto muñkâtu mâmutah compare Pâraskara I,
6, 2: preto muñkatu mâ patch. This passage shows what
itah and amutah refer to. Comp. Professor Weber's note 3 at
Indische Studien, V, 347.

1. Let him pound the root of the Adhyâ*nd*â plant and sprinkle it at the time of her monthly period with the two (verses), 'Speed away from here; a husband has she' (Rig-veda X, 85, 21. 22), with svâhâ at the end of each, into her right nostril.

2. 'The mouth of the Gandharva Visvâvasu art thou'—with these words let him touch her, when he is about to cohabit with her.

3. When he has finished, let him murmur,

4. 'Into thy breath I put the sperm, N. N.!'

5. Or, 'As the earth is pregnant with Agni, as the heaven is with Indra pregnant, as Vâyu dwells in the womb of the regions (of the earth), thus I place an embryo into thy womb, N. N.!'

6. Or, 'May a male embryo enter thy womb, as an arrow the quiver; may a man be born here, a son after ten months.

'Give birth to a male child; may after him (another) male be born; their mother shalt thou be, of the born, and (to others) mayst thou give birth.

'In the male verily, in the man dwells the sperm; he shall pour it forth into the woman : thus has said Dhâtar, thus Pragâpati has said.

'Pragâpati has created him, Savitar has shaped him. Imparting birth of females to other (women) may he put here a man.

'From the auspicious sperms which the men pro-

19, 6. The first verse is that quoted already at chap. 16, 8. The text of the verses quoted in this Sûtra is very corrupt; see the notes on p. 36 of the German edition.

duce for us, produce thou a son; be a well-breeding cow.

'Roar, be strong, put into her an embryo, achieve it; a male, thou male, put into her; to generation we call thee.

'Open thy womb; take in the man's sperm; may a male child be begotten in the womb. Him thou shalt bear; (having dwelt) ten months in the womb may he be born, the most excellent of his kin.'

KHANDA 20.

1. In the third month the Puṃsavana (i.e. the ceremony to secure the birth of a male child),

2. Under (the Nakshatra) Pushya or Sravaṇa.

3. Having pounded a Soma stalk, or a Kusa needle, or the last shoot of a Nyagrodha trunk, or the part of a sacrificial post which is exposed to the fire,

4. Or (having taken) after the completion of a sacrifice the remnants from the Guhû ladle,

5. Let him sprinkle it into her right nostril with the four verses, 'By Agni may good' (Rig-veda I, 1, 3), 'That sperm to us' (III, 4, 9), 'May he succeed who lights fire' (V, 37, 2), 'Of tawny shape' (II, 3, 9), with Svâhâ at the end (of each verse).

20, 3. On suṅgâ compare the note of Nârâyaṇa and the verse quoted from the Karmapradîpa, p. 131 of the German edition.

On kusakaṇṭaka Nârâyaṇa says, kusakaṇṭakam kuso darbhas tasya kaṇṭakaḥ sûkî (sûka, MS. Berol. Orient. fol. 602) tâm vâ peshayitvâ. I do not understand why the commentators of Pâraskara, whom Professor Stenzler has followed in his translation of Pâr. I, 14, 4, make kaṇṭaka equal to mûla.

5. Nasto dakshiṇataḥ stands here as in chap. 19, 1. Âsvalâyana I, 13, 6 has dakshiṇasyâm nâsikâyâm, and so has also

KHANDA 21.

1. In the fourth month the Garbharaksha*na* (i.e. the ceremony for the protection of the embryo),

2. Sacrificing six oblations from a mess of cooked food with (the six verses of the hymn), ' Agni, joined with the prayer' (Rig-veda X, 162),

3. With (the verses), ' From thy eyes, thy nose' (Rig-veda X, 163), verse by verse besmearing her limbs with Âg*y*a salve.

KHANDA 22.

1. In the seventh month, at her first pregnancy, the Sîmantonnayana (or parting of the hair).

2. He causes her, after she has bathed and put on a (new) garment which has not yet been washed, to sit down behind the fire.

3. He sacrifices, while she takes hold of him, with the Mahâvyâh*r*itis.

4. He cooks a mess of food,

5. According to some (teachers) boiled rice with Mudga beans.

6. The implements used and the Nakshatra should be of male gender.

7. (He then sacrifices with the following texts,) ' May Dhâtar give to his worshipper further life and safety; may we obtain the favour of the god whose laws are truthful.

' Dhâtar disposes of offspring and wealth; Dhâtar has created this whole world; Dhâtar will give a

---

Pâraskara I, 13. Comp. the natthukamma treated of in the Pâli Buddhist texts (Mahâvagga VI, 13) and in the medical literature.

son to the sacrificer: to him you shall sacrifice, an offering rich in ghee.'

(Besides) with the three verses, 'Negamesha, fly away' (Rig-veda Khailika sûkta, after X, 184, vol. vi, p. 31), and in the sixth place the verse, ' Pragâpati' (Rig-veda X, 121, 10).

8. (The husband then) parts her hair, upwards, beginning from the middle, with a porcupine's quill that has three white spots, or with a Darbha needle together with unripe Udumbara fruits, with the words, 'Bhûr bhuva*h* sva*h*.'

9. He lays down (the thing he has used) in her lap,

10. Ties (the fruits) to a string of three twisted threads and fastens them to her neck with the words, ' Rich in sap is this tree ; like the sappy one be thou fruitful.'

11. (The husband) then says to lute-players, 'Sing ye the king—

12. ' Or if anybody else is still more valiant.'

13. Having poured fried grain into a water-pot, let him cause her to drink it with the six verses,

---

22, 8. Comp. above, chap. 12, 6.

10. Nârâya*n*a : tis*ri*bhis tantubhir v*ri*tte sûtre udumbaraphalâni . . . gale . . . badhnâti. I have translated accordingly. Pâraskara I, 15, 6 uses the same expression tri v*ri*t. Professor Stenzler there translates it, on the authority of *Ga*yarâma, 'dreifache Haarflechte,' and says in his note on that passage that, according to *S*âṅkhâyana, he would have to tie the things with a threefold string to the neck of the woman, as if *S*âṅkhâyana's statement were different from that of Pâraskara. But both authors have the same word, and only the commentators differ in their explanations thereof.

11. Âsvalâyana more explicitly says (I, 14, 6), Soma*m* râgâna*m* sa*m*gây et â m iti.

13. In my German translation there is a mistake which should be corrected. I have there referred shal*ri*ka to the verses Râkâm

'May Vish*n*u take care of thy womb,' 'I call Râkâ'
(Rig-veda X, 184, 1 ; II, 32, 4-8).

14. Let him then touch her (with the words),

15. 'The winged one art thou, the Garutmat;
the Triv*ri*t (stoma) is thy head, the Gâyatra thy
eye, the metres thy limbs, the Ya*g*us thy name, the
Sâman thy body.'

16. Let him cause her to sing merrily,

17. Wearing, if she likes, many gold ornaments.

18. A bull is the fee for the sacrifice.

KHANDA 23.

1. Let him pound the roots of the plants kâkâtanî,
ma*k*aka*k*âtanî, kosâtakî, of the egg-plant, and of the
indigo plant, and besmear (therewith) the place in
which she is going to be confined, in order to drive
away the Rakshas.

KHANDA 24.

1. Now the *G*âtakarman (i. e. ceremony for the
new-born child).

---

aham, which are actually. only five in number. The six verses
are Vish*n*ur yonim, &c., and the five verses mentioned.

15. Vâ*g*asaneyi Sa*m*hitâ XII, 4.

16, 17. Nârâya*n*a: modamânîm harshayuktâm tâm mân-
galikair gîtair gâyayet . . . mahâhemavatim bahvâbha-
ra*n*ayuktâm vâ gâyayet.

24, 1. Comp. Dr. Speijer's essay on the *G*âtakarman (Leiden,
1872). Nârâya*n*a observes that, as it is prescribed below (chap.
25, 4) that a mess of food is to be cooked in the sûtikâgni, here
the sûtikâgni is established, and sacrifice is performed therein.
The Sûtra 1, 25, 4, from which it is to be inferred that the sûtikâgni should be kept, is considered, accordingly, as a *G*ñâpaka
(see Professor Bühler's notes on Âpastamba I, 11, 7; Gautama

2. Let (the father) breathe three times on the new-born child and then draw in his breath with the words, 'Draw in your breath with the *Rik*, breathe within with the Ya*g*us, breathe forth with the Sâman.'

3. Let him mix together butter and honey, milk curds and water, or grind together rice and barley, and give it to eat (to the child) thrice from gold (i.e. from a golden vessel or with a golden spoon),

4. With (the verse), 'I administer to thee honey food for the festival, the wisdom ("veda") raised by Savitar the bountiful; long-living, protected by the gods, live a hundred autumns in this world, N. N.!'— (with these words) he gives him a name beginning with a sonant, with a semivowel in it, consisting of two syllables, or of four syllables, or also of six syllables; he should take a k*ri*t (suffix), not a taddhita.

5. That (name only) his father and his mother should know.

6. On the tenth day a name for common use, which is pleasing to the Brâhma*n*as.

7. Let him pulverise black and white and red hairs of a black ox, intermix (that powder) with those four substances (see Sûtra 3), and give it to eat (to the child) four times: such (is the opinion of) Mâ*nd*ûkeya.

I, 31; Nârâya*n*a's note on chap. 25, 4, p. 133 of the German edition).

2. Abhyavânya should be corrected into abhyapânya, as in IV, 18, 1 nearly all the MSS. read nivâta instead of nipâta. The *S*âmbavya MS. reads in the text, trir abhyânyânuprâ*n*ya; in the commentary trir a*n*yapâ*n*yânuprâ*n*yâ. Comp., on the terminology of the different vital airs, Speijer, *G*âtakarma, p. 64 seq.; Eggeling, S. B. E., vol. xii, p. 20.

8. If he likes (let him do so) with the words, 'Bhû*h*! The Rig-veda I lay into thee, N. N., svâhâ! 'Bhuva*h*! The Yagur-veda I lay into thee, N. N., svâhâ! 'Sva*h*! The Sâma-veda I lay into thee, N. N., svâhâ! 'Bhûr bhuva*h* sva*h*! Vâkovâkya (colloquies), Itihâsa, and Purâ*n*a—Om! All the Vedas I lay into thee, N. N., svâhâ!'

9. The production of intelligence (is performed) by thrice saying in his right ear, 'Speech!'

10. And let him recite over (the child the following text), 'Speech, the goddess, united with mind, together with breath, the child, uttered by Indra— may she rejoice in thee, the goddess, for the sake of joy, the great one, the sweet sounding, the music, full of music, the flowing, self-produced.'

11. Let him tie a piece of gold to a hempen string,

12. And bind it to (the child's) right hand until (the mother) gets up (from childbed).

13. After the tenth day let him give it to the Brâhma*n*as,

14. Or keep it himself.

KHANDA 25.

1. After ten days the getting up (of the mother from childbed).

---

8. Veti vikalpârthe. bhûr *ri*gvedam ityâdi*k*aturbhir mantrair asâv ity atra pûrveva (read pûrvavat?) kumâranâmagraha*n*apûrvakam kumâra*m* prâsayet. Nârâya*n*a.

12. Bâlasya dakshi*n*e haste. Nârâya*n*a.

25, 1. After ten days the impurity (a*sauk*a) that falls on the mother at her confinement, ceases; see Gautama XIV, 16; Manu V, 62; Vasish*th*a IV, 21.

2. Father and mother with washed heads, wearing (new) clothes which have not yet been washed;

3. And so also the child.

4. Let (the father) cook a mess of food in that same fire that has been kept from her confinement,

5. And let him make oblations to the Tithi of (the child's) birth and to three constellations with their (presiding) deities.

6. Let him place in the middle the oblation to that constellation under which (the child) is born; the deity, however, is constantly to precede (the corresponding Nakshatra).

7. (He then makes two other oblations with the verses,) '(May) this Agni, the excellent one, (give) thee to-day life for (our) prayers; give us life that we may live long,'—(and,) 'Life-giving, Agni, be strong by Havis; may thy face and thy seat be full of ghee; drinking ghee, the sweet honey of the cow, protect, as a father (protects) his son, here N. N.' The tenth oblation of the mess of cooked food with the verse, 'Thou, Soma, givest bliss to the old one' (Rig-veda I, 91, 7).

8. Having pronounced aloud (the child's) name,

9. And caused the Brâhma*n*as to say auspicious words,

10. And having sacrificed in the same way every month to the Tithi of (the child's) birth,

11. He sacrifices, when one year has expired, on the (ordinary) domestic fire.

---

4. Comp. the note on chap. 24, 1.

7. The first Mantra is corrupt; in the Âsvalâyana-*S*rauta-sûtra (II, 10, 4) its text runs thus, âyush *t*e vi*s*vato dadhad ayam agnir vare*n*ya*h*, &c. Comp. Atharva-veda VII, 53, 6.

11. 'The words "every month" (Sûtra 10) retain their value

1. To Agni, to the Krittikâs.
2. To Pragâpati, to Rohinî.
3. To Soma, to Mrigasiras.
4. To Rudra, to the Ârdrâs.
5. To Aditi, to the two Punarvasus.
6. To Brihaspati, to Pushya.
7. To the Serpents, to the Asleshâs.
8. To the Manes, to the Maghâs.
9. To Bhaga, to the two Phalgunîs.
10. To Aryaman, to the two Phalgunîs.
11. To Savitar, to Hasta.
12. To Tvashtar, to Kitrâ.
13. To Vâyu, to Svâti.
14. To Indra and Agni, to the two Visâkhâs.
15. To Mitra, to Anurâdhâ.
16. To Indra, to Gyeshtha.
17. To Nirriti, to Mûla.
18. To the Waters, to the Ashâdhâs.
19. To the Visve devâs, to the Ashâdhâs.
20. To Brahman, to Abhigit.

(here also). Thus the sûtikâgni is to be kept through one year. After the lapse of that year one should sacrifice every month on the domestic fire as long as his life lasts. As it is said " in the domestic fire," the sûtikâgni is not to be kept any longer.' Nârâyana.

26, 1. This chapter is not found in the Sâmbavya-Grihya, and Nârâyana expressly designates it as kshepaka khanda. It is a sort of appendix to the Sûtras 25, 5. 6; a sacrifice having there been prescribed to three Nakshatras with their presiding deities, an enumeration of the Nakshatras and deities is here given. Compare, on similar lists, Weber's second article on the Nakshatras (Abhandlungen der Berliner Akademie der Wissenschaften, 1861), pp. 289 seq., 315, 367 seq.

21. To Vish*n*u, to *S*rava*n*a.
22. To the Vasus, to the Dhanish*th*âs.
23. To Varu*n*a, to *S*atabhisha*g*.
24. To A*g*a ekapad, to the Prosh*th*apadâs.
25. To Ahi budhnya, to the Prosh*th*apadâs.
26. To Pûshan, to Revatî.
27. To the two A*s*vins, to the two A*s*vinîs.
28. To Yama, to the Bhara*n*îs.

K*H*A*ND*A 27.

1. In the sixth month the Annaprâ*s*ana (i.e. the first feeding with solid food).
2. Goat's flesh, if he is desirous of nourishment,
3. Flesh of partridge, if desirous of holy lustre,
4. Fish, if desirous of swiftness,
5. Boiled rice with ghee, if desirous of splendour—
6. (Such) food, prepared with milk curds, honey, and ghee, he should give (to the child) to eat.
7. After he has made oblations with (the verses), 'Lord of food, give us food, painless and strong; bring forward the giver; bestow power on us, on men and animals;' 'Whatsoever' (Rig-veda IV, 12, 4); 'Even of great' (ibid. 5), 'Him, Agni, (lead) to long life and splendour; sharp strength (mayst thou), Varu*n*a, king Soma, protection may Aditi, like a

---

27, 2–6. These rules stand here, in the beginning of the chapter, as introductory remarks; the act of feeding itself (Sûtra 10) does not follow till after the sacrifice and the other performances prescribed in Sûtras 7–9.

3. This rule evidently rests on the allusion of taittira (partridge flesh) to the Taittirîya school.

7. Both metre and construction show that the Pâda imam Agna âyushe var*k*ase is incomplete; the *S*âmbavya-Gr/hya and Taitt. Sa*m*hitâ II, 3, 10, 3 add kr/dhi after var*k*ase.

mother, afford to him, and all the gods that he may reach old age'—

8. And has recited over (the child) the verse, ' Powers of life, Agni' (Rig-veda IX, 66, 19),

9. And has set him down on northward pointed Kusa grass with (the verse), ' Be soft, O earth' (Rig-veda I, 22, 15)—

10. The act of feeding is performed with the Mahâvyâh*ri*tis.

11. Let the mother eat the remnant.

KHANDA 28.

1. After one year the *Kûd*âkarman (i.e. the tonsure of the child's head);

2. Or in the third year;

3. In the fifth for a Kshatriya;

4. In the seventh for a Vaisya.

5. Having placed the fire (in the outer hall; see chap. 5, 2)—

6. And having filled vessels with rice and barley, sesamum seeds and beans,

7. And having put down northwards bull-dung and a layer of Kusa grass for receiving the hair, a mirror, fresh butter, and a razor of copper,

8. He pours cold water into warm with (the verse), ' Mix yourselves, ye holy ones, with your waves, ye honied ones, mixing milk with honey, ye lovely ones, for the obtaining of wealth.'

9. ' May the waters moisten thee for life, for old age and splendour. The threefold age of *G*amadagni, Kasyapa's threefold age, the threefold age of

---

28, 1. *Kû*/âkarman literally means, the preparing of the lock or the locks (left when the rest of the hair is shaven).

Agastya, the threefold age that belongs to the gods, that threefold age I produce for thee! N. N.!'—with these words he sprinkles the right part of his hair three times with lukewarm water.

10. Having loosened the tangled locks, according to some (teachers), with a porcupine's quill,

11. And having anointed (his hair) with fresh butter,

12. He puts a young Kusa shoot among (the hairs) with the words, 'Herb, protect him!'

13. Having touched the hair and the Kusa shoot with the mirror,

14. He takes up the copper razor with the words, 'Sharpness art thou; the axe is thy father. Do no harm to him!'

15. With (the words), 'The razor with which in the beginning Savitar, the knowing one, has shaven the beard of king Varuna, and with which Dhâtar Brihaspati has shaven Indra's head, with that, ye Brâhmanas, shave this (head) to-day; blessed with long life, with old age be this man N. N.!' he cuts the tips of the hairs and the Kusa shoot.

16. In the same way a second time; in the same way a third time.

17. In the same way twice on the left side.

18. Under the armpits a sixth and a seventh time at the Godânakarman (ceremony of shaving the beard).

19. The Godânakarman is identical with the Kûdâkarman.

---

15. The parallel texts show that instead of Brihaspatir we have to read Brihaspater, instead of adya, asya. So the correct translation would be, '. . . with what Dhâtar has shaven Brihaspati's and Indra's head, with that do ye Brâhmanas shave this head of this (child).'

20. (It is to be performed) in the sixteenth or in the eighteenth year.

21. At the third turn of shaving, however, he gives a cow and a garment that has not yet been washed.

22. Silently the rites (are performed) for girls.

23. To the north-east, in a place covered with herbs, or in the neighbourhood of water they bury the hairs in the earth.

24. To the barber the vessels of grain. To the barber the vessels of grain.

---

24. See Sûtra 6.

ADHYÂYA II, KHA*N*DA 1.

1. In the eighth year after the conception let him initiate a Brâhma*n*a,

2. With an antelope-skin,

1, 1. With regard to the standing terminology of the Upanayana, or the initiation of the student, we may observe that upa-nî does not mean, as, for instance, Professor Stenzler seems to understand it, 'to introduce a student to his teacher.' Thus Pâraskara's Sûtra II, 2, 1, ash*t*âvarsha*m* brâhma*n*am upanayet, &c., is translated by that distinguished scholar, 'Den achtjährigen Brâhma*n*a soll er (beim Lehrer) einführen,' &c. (comp. also Âsvalâyana-Gr*i*hya I, 19, 1). The texts clearly point to another translation of upa-nî, for they show that the person that introduces the student (upanayati or upanayate; the middle is used very frequently, for instance, *S*atapatha Brâhma*n*a XI, 5, 4, 1; *S*ânkh. II, 1, 25) is not the father or a relation of the youth who could be supposed to lead him to the teacher, but the teacher himself; he introduces (upanayati) him to the brahma*k*arya, or introduces him with himself, and the student enters upon (upaiti) the brahma*k*arya, or enters with (upaiti) the teacher; he who has thus entered upon studentship, is consequently designated as upeta (*S*ânkh. IV, 8, 1; Pâraskara III, 10, 10), and for the initiation, which is usually called upanayana, occasionally also the word upâyana is used (see the Mânava-Gr*i*hya I, 22, quoted by Professor Jolly in his article, Das Dharma-sûtra des Vish*n*u, p. 79). The following passages may be quoted here as supporting our opinion on this terminology. At *S*atapatha Brâhma*n*a XI, 5, 3, 13 Sau*k*eya says to Uddâlaka Âru*n*i, 'I will enter (as a student) with the reverend One' (upâyâni bhagavantam); and Âru*n*i replies, 'Come, enter (with me)!' (ehy upehi, 'and he initiated him' (ta*m* hopaninye). Ibid. XI, 5, 4, 16 it is stated that according to some a teacher who has initiated a Brâhma*n*a as a student (brâhma*n*am brahma*k*aryam upaniya) should abstain from sexual intercourse, for a student who enters upon studentship (yo brahma*k*aryam upaiti) becomes, as it were, a garbha, &c. Finally we may add that the Buddhist terminology regarding the entering into the order or upon a life of righteousness is clearly connected with that followed, for instance, in the dialogue between

3. Or in the tenth year after the conception.

4. In the eleventh year after the conception a Kshatriya with the skin of a spotted deer,

5. In the twelfth year after the conception a Vaisya with a cow-hide.

6. Until the sixteenth year the time has not passed for a Brâhmana,

7. Until the twenty-second for a Kshatriya,

8. Until the twenty-fourth for a Vaisya.

9. After that (time has passed), they become patitasâvitrika (men who have lost their right of learning the Sâvitri).

Saukeya and Âruni. As Saukeya there says, upâyâni bhaga-vantam, we frequently read in the Pâli books expressions like this, upemi Buddham saranam dhammañ kâpi anuttaram, &c. (Dhammap. Atthakathâ, p. 97, ed. Fausböll), and as Âruni replies, ehy upehi, Buddha says to those who wish to be ordained, ehi bhikkhu, svâkkhâto dhammo, kara brahmakariyam, &c. (Mahâvagga I, 6, 32, &c.; S. B. E., vol. xiii, p. 74, note).

The counting of the years not from the birth but from the conception occurs both in the Brahmanical and in the Buddhist ordinances, comp. H. O., Buddha, sein Leben, seine Lehre, seine Gemeinde, p. 354, note 1. Several Grihya texts (for instance, Âsv. I, 19, 1. 2) admit both ways of counting the years. The number of years given for the Upanayana of persons of the three castes (Brâhmanas 8–16, Kshatriyas 11–22, Vaisyas 12–24) is evidently derived from the number of syllables of the three metres which are so very frequently stated to correspond to the three castes, to the three gods or categories of gods (Agni, Indra, Visve devâs) &c., viz. the Gâyatrî, the Trishtubh, and the Gagatî. This is a very curious example, showing how in India phantastical speculations like those regarding the mystical qualities of the metres, were strong enough to influence the customs and institutions of real life.

9 seq. All these are standing expressions recurring nearly identically in most of the Grihya and Dharma-sûtras. In the rule contained in Sûtra 13 a number of the parallel texts have vivah-eyuh or vivâhayeyuh, others have vyavahareyuh. Comp. Vasishtha XI, 75; Indische Studien, vol. x, p. 21.

10. Let them not initiate such men,

11. Nor teach them,

12. Nor perform sacrifices for them,

13. Nor have intercourse with them.

14. Or (let them initiate students of) all (castes) wearing a (new) garment that has not yet been washed.

And wearing a girdle.

15. The girdle of a Brâhmana (shall be) made of Muñga grass,

16. That of a Kshatriya (shall be) a bowstring,

17. That of a Vaisya a woollen thread.

18. The staff of a Brâhmana (shall be) made of Palâsa or of Bilva wood,

19. That of a Kshatriya of Nyagrodha wood,

20. That of a Vaisya of Udumbara wood.

21. That of the Brâhmana shall reach the tip of the nose,

22. That of the Kshatriya the forehead,

23. That of the Vaisya the hair.

24. Or all (sorts of staffs are to be used) by (men of) all (castes).

25. Whatsoever (the student) wears at his initiation, is at the disposal of the teacher.

---

14. This Sûtra should rather be divided into two, as indicated in the translation. As to the mekhalâ(girdle)comp. below, chap. 2, 1.

21. There is no doubt that prânasammito (which Nârâyana explains thus, 'prâna is the wind [or breath]; [the staff should] reach to the place where the wind leaves the body, i. e. to the tip of the nose') should either be corrected into, or explained as, ghrânasammito; the Sâmbavya MS. has ghrânântiko brâhmanasya. Comp. Gautama I, 26, &c. The parallel texts agree in assigning the longer staff to the higher, not as Sânkhâyana does, to the lower caste.

26. Having had him shaved all round (his head) he should initiate him.

27. After (the student) has washed and adorned himself,

28. (And) after (the teacher) has sacrificed, both station themselves behind the fire, the teacher with his face turned to the east, the other with his face to the west.

29. Let him initiate him standing while (the other also) stands.

30. ['The firm, powerful eye of Mitra, glorious splendour, strong and prosperous, a chaste, flowing vesture, this skin I put on, a valiant (man).']

KHANDA 2.

1. 'Here has come to us, protecting (us) from evil words, purifying our kin as a purifier, clothing herself, by (the power of) inhalation and exhalation, with strength, this friendly goddess, this blessed girdle'—with these words, three times repeated, he ties the girdle from left to right thrice round.

---

26. After the introductory remarks given in the preceding Sûtras the ritual itself of the Upanayana is now described.

28. Nârâyana: hutvâ 'nâdesaparibhâshâtah (see above, I, 12, 13) purastâtsamgñakam hutvâ agnim sthâpitâgnim (see above, I, 5, 2) gaghanena . . . tishthatah.

30. This Sûtra is wanting in most of the MSS. (see the note, p. 48 of the German edition). It contains the Mantra with which the Agina (the hide mentioned in Sûtras 2, 4, 5 of this chapter) is put on. Nârâyana gives the Mantra which he says is taken from the Mâdhyandina-Grihya (in the Pâraskara-Grihya it is not found), after chap. 2, 3, and he states that the corresponding act to which it belongs has its place after the rites concerning the girdle (chap. 2, 1) and the sacrificial cord (2, 3).

2. (There should be) one knot, or also three, or also five.

3. He adjusts the sacrificial cord with (the words), ' The sacrificial cord art thou. With the cord of the sacrifice I invest thee.'

4. He fills the two hollows of (his own and the student's) joined hands (with water), and then says to him : ' What is thy name ? '

5. ' I am N. N., sir,' says the other.

6. ' Descending from the same *Ri*shis ? ' says the teacher.

7. ' Descending from the same *Ri*shis, sir,' says the other.

2, 2. Râma*k*andra : ' Let him make one, or three, or five knots, according to (the student's) Ârsheya,' i. e. accordingly as he belongs to a family that invokes, in the Pravara ceremony, one, or three, or five *Ri*shis as their ancestors. Comp. Weber, Indische Studien, vol. x, p. 79.

3. On the sacrificial cord (upavita) comp. the Gri*hya-sa*mgraha-pari*s*ish*t*a II, 48 seq.

4. Nârâya*n*a : Â*k*ârya âtmano mâ*n*avakasya *k*âṅgalî udakena pûrayitvâ, &c.

6, 7. A similar dialogue between the teacher and the student at the Upanayana is given in the Kau*s*ika-sûtra (ap. Weber, Indische Studien, X, 71). The student there says, ' Make me an Ârsheya (a descendant of the *Ri*shis) and one who has relations, and initiate me.' And the teacher replies, ' I make thee an Ârsheya and one who has relations, and I initiate thee.' As in this passage of the Kau*s*ika-sûtra the teacher is represented as having the power of making, by the Upanayana ceremony, an Ârsheya of the student, thus, according to the view expressed by Professor Weber (loc. cit., p. 72 seq.), *S*ânkhâyana would even give it into the teacher's power to make the student his samânârsheya, i. e. to extend his own Ârsheya on as many pupils as he likes. Professor Weber understands the sixth Sûtra so that the teacher would have to say, samânârsheyo bhavân brûhi (Nârâya*n*a : bhavân brû-hîti brahma*k*ârî bhavân brûhîty ata*h* [Sûtra 8] si*m*hâvalokananyâ-yenâtrânusha*g*yate. According to Râma*k*andra's Paddhati he is

8. 'Declare (that thou art) a student, sir.'

9. 'I am a student, sir,' says the other.

10. With the words, 'Bhûr bhuva*h* sva*h*' (the teacher) sprinkles thrice with his joined hands (water) on the joined hands (of the student),

11. And seizing (the student's) hands with (his own) hands, holding the right uppermost, he murmurs,

12. 'By the impulse of the god Savitar, with the arms of the two Asvins, with Pûshan's hands I initiate thee, N. N.'

13. Those who are desirous of a host (of adherents, he should initiate) with (the verse), 'Thee, (the lord) of hosts' (Rig-veda II, 23, 1).

14. Warriors with (the verse), 'Come here, do not come to harm' (Rig-veda VIII, 20, 1).

15. Sick persons with the Mahâvyâh*ri*tis.

---

only to say samânârsheya*h*). The student answers, samân-ârsheyo 'ham bho ; Professor Weber, who supplies the imperative asâni, translates this, ' May I have the same Ârsheya, sir l'

I think it more natural to simply translate the teacher's question, ' Art thou samânârsheya?' (or, supplying bhavân brûhi from Sûtra 8, 'Declare that thou art samânârsheya'), and the student's reply, 'I am samânârsheya, sir l' Thus we ought possibly to consider these formulas, which state a fictitious, ideal samânâr-sheyatva of the teacher and the students as a trace, and as far as I can see as the only trace, of an ancient rule requiring a real samânârsheyatva of teacher and student. As long as the ritual differences between the different Gotras, of which, as is well known, only a few traces have survived in the Vedic tradition, had retained their full importance, it can indeed scarcely have been considered as admissible that a young Brâhma*n*a should be confided to the guidance of a teacher who sacrificed and invoked the gods in another way than the customs of the pupil's own family required.

11. Nârâya*n*a : dakshi*n*ottarâbhyâm dakshi*n*a uttara upari yayos tau dakshi*n*ottarau, &c.

KHANDA 3.

1. 'Bhaga has seized thy hand, Savitar has seized thy hand, Pûshan has seized thy hand, Aryaman has seized thy hand. Mitra art thou by right, Agni is thy teacher, and I, N. N., both of us. Agni, I give this student in charge to thee. Indra, I give this student in charge to thee. Sun, I give this student in charge to thee. Visve devâs, I give this student in charge to you, for the sake of long life, of blessed offspring and strength, of increase of wealth, of mastership of all Vedas, of renown, of bliss.'

2. 'In Indra's course I move; in the sun's course I move after him'—with these words he turns round from left to right,

3. And grasping down with the span of his right hand over (the student's) right shoulder he touches the place of his heart with the words, 'May I be dear to thy inviolate heart.'

3, 1. Nârâya*n*a : 'Instead of asau (N. N.) he puts the name of the student in the vocative case.' I think rather that the teacher here pronounced his own name. Comp. asâv aha*m* bho, chap. 2, 5, &c., and the Mantra in Pâraskara II, 2, 20.

The text of the Mantra shows that the Â*k*ârya here seizes the hand of the Brahma*k*ârin; comp. Âsvalâyana I, 20, 4–6, where it is stated that he seizes the student's hand together with the thumb, quite in the way prescribed for the wedding at Sâṅkh. I, 13, 2. Comp. also Pâraskara II, 2, 17. Nârâya*n*a : mâ*n*avakasya gr*i*hita-sa*m*pu*t*a evâ*k*âryo Bhagas ta ima*m* mantra*m* *g*apan, &c.

2. Literally, 'he turns round, following his right arm.' Nârâya*n*a here has the following note, 'Â*k*âryo ba*l*or dakshi*n*am bâhu*m* *n*a*s*ta*m* aindrîm âvr*i*tam iti mantre*n*ânvâvartayet. ayam artha*h*, â*k*ârya ima*m* mantra*m* *g*aptvâ ta*m* ba*l*um *k*a vâ*k*ayitvâ pradakshi*n*â-varta*m* kârayet.' I believe that the commentator here, as he frequently does, instead of interpreting the text of Sâṅkhâyana, fathers

4. Having silently turned round from right to left,

5. And then laying his hand with the fingers upwards on his (i.e. the student's) heart, he murmurs:

KHANDA 4.

1. ' Under my will I take thy heart; my mind shall thy mind follow; in my word thou shalt rejoice with all thy heart; may B*ri*haspati join thee to me.'

2. ' Thou art the Brahma*k*ârin of Kâma, N. N.!'

3. With the same text (see chap. 3, 2) he turns round as before,

4. And touching with the span of his right hand (the student's) right shoulder, he murmurs:

---

on him statements belonging to other Sûtras, in this case probably to Â*s*valâyana I, 20, 9. As our text has not anvâvartya but anvâv*ri*tya, and in the Mantra not âvartasva but âvarte, we must conclude that he turned round himself, and, as far as the statements of the text go, did not cause the pupil to do so.

5. The gesture is the same as that prescribed in the Pâraskara-Gr*ih*ya I, 8, 8 to the bridegroom at the wedding; the Mantra there is identical with *S*âṅkh. II, 4, 1, the only difference consisting in the name of the god who is invoked to unite the two: at the wedding this is Pra*g*âpati, of course, because he is 'lord of offspring,' at the Upanayana, B*ri*haspati, the Brahman κατ' ἐξοχήν among the gods. It is very natural that at the Upanayana and at the Vivâha, which both are destined to establish an intimate union between two persons hitherto strangers to each other, a number of identical rites should occur, for instance, the seizing of the hand; see the note on Sûtra 1.

4, 1. Comp. Parask. I, 8, 8, and the note on chap. 3, 3. See also Atharva-veda VI, 94, 2.

2. As to Kâmasya brahma*k*âry asi, see my remarks in the Introduction, p. 9.

3. He turns round as described, chap. 3, 2. Nârâya*n*a here also explains paryâv*ri*tya paryâvartana*m* kârayitvâ. See our note above, loc. cit.

5. 'A student art thou. Put on fuel. Eat water. Do the service. Do not sleep in the day-time. Keep silence till the putting on of fuel.'

6. With (the words), 'Thine, Agni, is this piece of wood,' he puts the fuel on (the fire), or silently.

KHANDA 5.

1. After one year (the teacher) recites the Sâvitrî (to the student),

2. (Or) after three nights,

3. Or immediately.

4. Let him recite a Gâyatrî to a Brâhma*n*a,

5. A Trish*t*ubh to a Kshatriya,

6. A *G*agatî to a Vai*s*ya.

7. But let it be anyhow a verse sacred to Savitar.

8. They seat themselves to the north of the fire,

9. The teacher with his face turned eastward, the other westward.

5. According to Nârâya*n*a the student correspondingly answers. to the teacher's word, 'A student art thou,' 'I will' (asâni), to 'Put on fuel,' 'I will put it on,' &c. Eating water means sipping water after having eased oneself. On the putting on of fuel, comp. Sûtra 6 and chap. 10. The whole formula given in this Sûtra is already found in the *S*atapatha Brâhma*n*a XI, 5, 4, 5.

5, 1. The study of the Veda is opened by the Sâvitrî. Comp. *S*atapatha Brâhma*n*a, loc. cit., §§ 6 seq.

4–6. The Gâyatrî which the teacher shall recite to a Brâhma*n*a is the same verse of which it is said below, chap. 7, 11, that it belongs to Vi*s*vâmitra (Rig-veda III, 62, 10); the Trish*t*ubh which is taught to the Kshatriya is a verse ascribed to Hira*n*ya-stûpa, Rig-veda I, 35, 2; the *G*agatî which is to be repeated to a Vai*s*ya is Rig-veda IV, 40, 5, belonging to Vâmadeva, or Rig-veda I, 35, 9, belonging to Hira*n*yastûpa. See the note on chap. 7, 10.

9. The same position is prescribed, in the same words, for the study of the main part of the Veda, below, chap. 7, 3; during

10. After (the student) has said, ' Recite, sir!'—

11. The teacher, having pronounced the word OM, then causes the other one to say, 'Recite the Sâvitrî, sir!'

12. He then recites the Sâvitrî to him, the verse 'That glorious (splendour) of Savitar' (Rig-veda III, 62, 10); (firstly) pâda by pâda, (then) hemistich by hemistich, (and finally) without a stop.

KHANDA 6.

1. 'Waters are ye by name; happy ones are ye by name; sappy ones are ye by name; undecaying ones are ye by name; fearless ones are ye by name; immortal ones are ye by name. Of you, being such, may I partake; receive me into your favour'—with these words (the teacher) makes the student sip water three times,

2. And hands over to him the staff with the five

---

the study of the Âranyaka the position is slightly different (VI, 3, 2). According to Nârâyana this Sûtra would contain a nishedha of the Sûtras 828 and 829 of the Rig-veda-Prâtisâkhya (p. ccxcii of Professor Max Müller's edition).

10, 11. The Indian tradition divides these Sûtras after âkâryaḥ, so that the words adhîhi bho would have to be pronounced by the teacher. Thus also Nârâyana explains, âkârya adhîhi bho 3 iti mânavakam uktvâ, &c. In my opinion it is the student or the students who say adhîhi bho. Thus the Prâtisâkhya (Sûtra 831, ed. Max Müller) says, 'They invite him with the words adhîhi bho 3, all the students the teacher, having embraced his feet.' Comp. also below, IV, 8, 12, the greater part of which Sûtra is word for word identical with these rules; VI, 3, 6; Gautama I, 46; Gobhila II, 10, 38.

6, 1, 2. Râmakandra : '. . . with this Mantra which the teacher tells him, and which he (the student) pronounces, he sips water

verses, 'Blessing may give us' (Rig-veda V, 51, 11–15).

3. An optional gift is the fee for the sacrifice.

4. After (the teacher) has led him round the fire, turning his right side towards it, (the student) goes through the village to beg food.

5. (Let him beg,) however, of his mother first,

6. Or of a woman who will not refuse.

7. Having announced the alms to his teacher, he may eat (the food himself) with the master's permission.

8. The daily putting on of fuel, the going for alms, the sleeping on the ground, and obedience to the teacher: these are the standing duties of a student.

---

three times . . . He (the teacher) then gives him again the staff, which he had given him before silently.' I do not think that this double handing over of the staff agrees with the real meaning of the text; Gobhila also (II, 10) and Âsvalâyana (I, 22, 1) prescribe the daṇḍapradâna after the repetition of the Sâvitrî, without mentioning that the same had been already done before; Pâraskara II, 2, 11 speaks of the handing over of the staff before the recital of the Sâvitrî, and does not state that it should be repeated afterwards.

All these ceremonies, the teaching of the Sâvitrî as well as the daṇḍapradâna, were considered as forming part of the Upanayana, even though a longer or shorter space of time (chap. 5, 1–3) might elapse between the first arrival of the student at the teacher's house and the performing of these rites. This follows from chap. 11, Sûtras 2–4.

2. These five verses have already occurred above at I, 15, 12.

3. Comp. I, 14, 13–15.

4 seq. On the student's begging of alms compare the more detailed rules in Pâraskara II, 5; Âpastamba I, 3, &c.

7. Comp. the passages quoted by Professor Bühler on Âpastamba I, 3, 31 (S. B. E., vol. ii, p. 12).

1. Now (follows the exposition) of the study of the Veda.

2. Both sit down to the north of the fire,

3. The teacher with his face to the east, the other one to the west.

4. After (the student) has reverentially saluted the teacher's feet and has sprinkled his (own) hands (with water),

5. And has kneeled down with his right knee on young Kusa shoots at their roots,

6. And has grasped round (those Kusa shoots) in their middle with his hands, holding the right uppermost,

7. The teacher, having seized them at their tops

7, 1. Nârâyana: 'Now (atha), i.e. after the observance of the Sukriya vrata,' &c. On the Sukriya vrata which has to be undergone before the Anuvâkana treated of in this chapter can be performed, see the note on chap. 4, 1, and below, chap. 11, 9. One would have expected that in the arrangement of Sânkhâyana the rites belonging to the Sukriya vrata would precede the exposition of the Anuvâkana. Perhaps it was in consequence of the exact analogy of the Sukriya with the Sâkvara, Vrâtika, Aupanishada vratas, that the description of the former has been postponed till the latter had to be treated of.

Râmakandra's Paddhati has the following remark here, 'Now the way of studying the Veda, called Anuvâkana, is set forth. This can be done only after the Sukriya vrata has been enjoined on the student; before that nothing but the Sâvitrî can be taught to him.'

2 seq. Comp. above, chap. 2, 8 seq.

4. The way in which this reverential salutation should be performed is described below, IV, 12, 1 seq.

6. On dakshinottarâbhyâm, see chap. 2, 11 and Nârâyana's note there.

with his left hand, and with his right hand sprinkling
them with water, then makes the other say :

8. ' Recite the Sâvitrî, sir!' says the other.

9. ' I recite the Sâvitrî to thee!' says the teacher.

10. ' Recite the Gâyatrî, sir!' says the other.

' I recite the Gâyatrî to thee!' says the teacher.

11. ' Recite the verse of Vi*s*vâmitra, sir!' says the
other.

' I recite the verse of Vi*s*vâmitra to thee!' says
the teacher.

12. ' Recite the *R*ishis, sir!' says the other.

' I recite the *R*ishis to thee!' says the teacher.

13. ' Recite the deities, sir!' says the other.

' I recite the deities to thee!' says the teacher.

14. ' Recite the metres, sir!' says the other.

' I recite the metres to thee!' says the teacher.

15. ' Recite the *S*ruti, sir!' says the other.

' I recite the *S*ruti to thee!' says the teacher.

16. ' Recite the Sm*r*iti, sir!' says the other.

' I recite the Sm*r*iti to thee!' says the teacher.

17. ' Recite faith and insight, sir!' says the other.

' I recite faith and insight to thee!' says the
teacher.

---

8 seq. Comp. Weber's Indische Studien, vol. x, p. 131 seq.

10. Comp. the note on chap. 5, 4–6. Nârâya*n*a states, in
accordance with these Sûtras of the fifth chapter, that in case the
student belongs to the second or third caste, an Ûha (i. e. a corresponding alteration of the formulas; from the *S*rauta-sûtra, VI, 1, 3
the definition is quoted here *s*abdavikâram ûha*m* bruvate) takes
place. If he is a Kshatriya, he has to say, ' Recite the Trish*t*ubh,
sir!'—' Recite the verse of Hira*n*yastûpa (Rig-veda I, 35, 2), sir!'
A Vai*s*ya has to say, ' Recite the *G*agatî, sir!'—' Recite the verse
of Hira*n*yastûpa (or, of Vâmadeva, Rig-veda I, 35, 9 or IV, 40, 5),
sir!'

17. Comp. Indische Studien, X, 132, note 1.

18. In that way, according to what *Ri*shi each hymn belongs to and what its deity and its metre is, thus (with the corresponding indications of *Ri*shi, &c.) let him recite each hymn ;

19. Or also, if he does not know the *Ri*shis, deities, and metres, the teacher recites this verse, 'That glorious (splendour) of Savitar' (Rig-veda III, 62, 10), pâda by pâda, hemistich by hemistich, (and finally) without a stop, and says, when he has finished, 'This (verse belongs to Savitar; it is a Gâyatrî ; Vi*s*vâmitra is its *Ri*shi).'

18–20. I do not think that Professor Weber (Indische Studien, X, 132) has quite exactly rendered the meaning of these Sûtras when he says, 'The teacher then (i. e. after the formula of Sûtra 17 has been pronounced) teaches him first the *Ri*shi, the deity, and the metre of each Mantra. In case he does not know them himself for a Mantra, he recites the holy Sâvitrî (tat Savitur vare*n*yam). After this he teaches him in due order either (1) the single *Ri*shis, i.e. the hymns belonging to each *Ri*shi, or (2) the single Anuvâkas,' &c.— It does not seem quite probable to me that the student should have had to learn first the *Ri*shis, deities, and metres of the whole Veda, before the text of the hymns was taught him ; I rather believe that hymn by hymn the indication of the *Ri*shis, &c. preceded the anuvâ*k*ana of the text itself, and with this opinion the statement of Nârâya*n*a agrees, 'Evam pûrvoktena prakâre*n*a *ri*shidevatâ*kh*anda*h*pûrvaka*m* ta*m* ta*m* Agnim î*l*a ityâdika*m* mantra*m* mâ*n*avakâyâ*k*âryo *s*nubrûyât.'

19. According to Nârâya*n*a by esheti (literally, 'This [is the *Rik*]') it is meant that the teacher, after having recited the Sâvitrî in the three ways mentioned, should say to the student, 'This *Rik* is in the Gâyatrî metre. If recited pâda by pâda, it has three pâdas. Thus also this *Rik*, if recited hemistich by hemistich, has two Avasânas (pauses), the first at the end of the hemistich, the second at the end of the third *k*ara*n*a (or pâda). Thus also this *Rik* is recited without stopping ; at the end of the three *k*ara*n*as, or of the twenty-four syllables, the pause (avasâna) should be made. Thus I recite to thee the Sâvitrî ; I recite to thee the Gâyatrî ; I recite to thee the verse of Vi*s*vâmitra.' 'For,' adds Nârâya*n*a, 'if the Gâyatrî has been recited, the whole complex of the Veda being of that very

20. Let him thus recite (the hymns belonging to) each *Ri*shi, or (each) Anuvâka ;

21. Of the short hymns (in the tenth Ma*nd*ala) an Anuvâka,

22. Or as much as the master may think fit.

23. Or optionally he may recite the first and last hymn of (each) *Ri*shi,

24. Or of (each) Anuvâka,

25. (Or) one (verse) of the beginning of each hymn.

26. The teacher may optionally say at the beginning of the hymn, ' This is the commencement.'

27. This has been (further) explained in (the treatise about) the *Ri*shisvâdhyâya.

---

substance, a complete knowledge thereof has been produced.' The commentator then indicates a shorter form for the teacher's words which our Sûtra prescribes by esheti, 'This verse belongs to Savitar; it is a Gâyatrî; its *Ri*shi is Visvâmitra.'

21. The Kshudrasûktas are the hymns Rig-veda X, 129–191.

24 seq. This seems to be an abridged method by which students who had not the intention of becoming Vedic scholars, and probably chiefly students of the Kshatriya and Vaisya caste, could fulfil their duty of learning the Veda; a student who knew the first and last hymn of a *Ri*shi, or of an Anuvâka, was, as would seem from these Sûtras, by a sort of fiction considered as though he had known the whole portion belonging to that *Ri*shi, or the whole Anuvâka.

27. Nârâya*na* explains *Ri*shisvâdhyâya by mantrasa*m*hitâ. He says, 'The Anuvâ*ka*na which has been declared here, is to be understood also with regard to the svâdhyâya, i. e. to the Sa*m*hitâ of the Mantras.' I think there is a blunder in the MS., and instead of tad api svâdhyâye . . . g*ñ*eya*m* we ought to read tad *ri*shi-svâdhyâye . . . g*ñ*eya*m*. In this case we should have to translate the quoted passage, ' . . . is to be understood with regard to the *Ri*shisvâdhyâya, i. e. to, &c.'—I think, however, that the true meaning of the Sûtra is different from what Nârâya*na* believes it to be. The expression vyâkhyâtam apparently conveys a reference to another treatise in which the rules regarding the *Ri*shisvâdhyâya would seem to have been fully set forth. The Srauta-sûtra contains

28. When (the lesson) is finished, he takes the young Kusa shoots, makes of cow-dung a pit at their roots, and sprinkles water on the Kusa (shoots) for each hymn.

29. For the rest of the day standing and fasting.

KHANDA 8.

1. In the afternoon, having obtained by begging fried barley grains, he shall sacrifice them with his hand on the fire according to the rites of the Âgya oblations with the text, ' The lord of the seat, the

no passage which could be the one here referred to; we may suppose, therefore, that either a chapter of a Prâtisâkhya is quoted here, or a separate treatise on the special subject of the Rishisvâ-dhyâya. References to such treatises are found in the Sûtra texts in several instances, of which the most important is that in the Gobhila-Grihya I, 5, 13, 'On what day the moon becomes full, the knowledge thereof is contained in a special text; that one either should study or ascertain when the Parvan is from those who have studied it.'

28. Nârâyana: 'First stand the Mantras, then the Brâhmana, because it contains the viniyoga (the ritual use of the Mantras), then the Smriti texts such as Manu, &c. When he has repeated these texts to the student, after the end of the Anuvâkana, the teacher should take from the student the Kusa blades which had been taken up before for the sake of the Anuvâkana (see Sûtras 5 seq.),' &c.—The teacher is made the subject of this rule also by Râmakandra. On yathâsûktam Nârâyana observes that accord-ing to some teachers these water oblations were directed to the Rishis of the different hymns (rishîn uddisyeti kekit). This state-ment seems to be countenanced by IV, 6, 6. Comp. the note below on IV, 9, 1.

29. 'This rule concerns the Brahmakârin.' Nârâyana. See also Âsvalâyana I, 22, 11.

8, 1. This is the Anupravakaniyahoma treated of by Âsvalâyana at I, 22, 12 seq. There it is stated that this sacrifice should be per-formed as well after the recitation of the Sâvitrî as after the other

wonderful' (Rig-veda I, 18, 6 seq.), verse by verse, down to the end of the hymn,

2. Causing the teacher by (the gift of) food to pronounce auspicious wishes.

KHANDA 9.

1. In the forest, with a piece of wood in his hand, seated, he performs the Sandhyâ (or twilight devotion) constantly, observing silence, turning his face north-west, to the region between the chief (west) point and the intermediate (north-western) point (of the horizon), until the stars appear,

2. Murmuring, when (the twilight) has passed, the Mahâvyâhritis, the Sâvitrî, and the auspicious hymns.

3. In the same way in the morning, turning his face to the east, standing, until the disk of the sun appears.

10, 1. When (the sun) has risen, the study (of the Veda) goes on.

portions of the Veda, for instance, as the commentary there has it, after the Mahânâmnîs, the Mahâvrata, and the Upanishad have been recited. Nârâyana indicates the time of this sacrifice in the words, ' On that same fast-day (chap. 7, 29) in the afternoon.'

2. ' He shall, by pronouncing such words as svasti bhavanto bruvantu, dispose the teacher favourably so that he may say svasti!' Nârâyana.

9, 1. On the Sandhyâ ceremony comp. chiefly Baudhâyana II, 7. Samitpâni of course is not samyatapâni, as Nârâyana explains it. On anvash/amadesa comp. Professor Stenzler's note on Âsvalâyana III, 7, 4.

2. The Svastyayanas are texts such as Rig-veda I, 89 ; IV, 31.

10, 1. This Sûtra evidently should be placed at the end of the ninth chapter ; comp. IV, 6, 9. The fact that, as the commentary observes, the words nityam vâgyatah (chap. 9, Sûtra 1) are to be

KHANDA 10.

2. Every day in the evening and in the morning,

3. He establishes the fire (in its proper place), wipes (with his hand the ground) round (it), sprinkles (water) round (it), bends his right knee,

4. (And puts fuel on the fire with the texts,) 'To Agni I have brought a piece of wood, to the great Gâtavedas; may he, Gâtavedas, give faith and insight to me. Svâhâ!

'Firewood art thou; may we prosper. Fuel art thou; splendour art thou; put splendour into me. Svâhâ!

'Being inflamed make me prosperous in offspring and wealth. Svâhâ!

'Thine is this fuel, Agni; thereby thou shalt grow and gain vigour. And may we grow and gain vigour. Svâhâ!'

---

supplied here also points in the same direction. That this Sûtra has nothing to do with the Agniparikaryâ, of which the tenth chapter treats, becomes evident also from Râmakandra's Paddhati.

4. Nârâyana: samidham iti mantralingât samidhâm homah, mantraprithaktvât karmaprithaktvam iti nyâyât.

In the Atharva-veda XIX, 64, 1 the MSS. have Agne samidham âhârsham. Professors Roth and Whitney have conjectured in this passage agre instead of Agne. It is shown by our passage and the corresponding ones in the other Sûtras that the true reading is Agnaye. Instead of ahârsham we should read âhârsham, as all the parallel texts have. In the passage 'Firewood art thou; might we prosper,' there is a play upon words untranslatable in English, 'edho.sy edhishîmahi.' Perhaps instead of samiddho mâm samardhaya we should read samriddho mâm samardhaya. As the Mantra referred to the Samidh-offering, samriddha could very easily be supplanted by the participle of sam-idh. In the parallel texts indicated p. 139 of the German edition it should be, Vâg. Samh. II, 14 a.

5. Having then sprinkled (water) round (the fire),

6. He approaches the fire with the verse, 'May Agni (vouchsafe) to me faith and insight, not-forgetting (what I have learned) and memory; may this praiseful *G*âtavedas give blessing to us.'

[7. He makes with ashes the tripu*ndh*ra sign (the sign of three strokes) which is set forth in the (treatise on the) Saupar*n*avrata, which is revealed, which agrees with the tradition handed down by the ancients, with the five formulas ' The threefold age' (see above, I, 28, 9), one by one, on five (places), viz. the forehead, the heart, the right shoulder and the left, and then on the back.]

8. He who approaches the fire after having sacrificed thus, studies of these Vedas, one, two, three, or all.

KHA*ND*A 11.

1. Now (follows) the directing to the (special) observances.

2. The rules for it have been explained by the initiation.

3. He does not recite the Sâvitrî.

---

7. This Sûtra is wanting in one of the Haug MSS. and in the *S*âmbavya MS.; Râma*k*andra's Paddhati takes no notice of it. I take it for a later addition. It should be noticed that the words dakshi*n*askandhe . . . *k*a pa*nk*asu form a half *S*loka.

11, 1. On the four Vratas, of which the *S*ukriya precedes the study of the main part of the Veda, the *S*âkvara, Vrâtika, and Aupanishada that of the different sections of the Âra*n*yaka, see the note on chap. 7, 1 and the Introduction, p. 8. On the name of the *S*ukriya Râma*k*andra says, *s*ukriya*s*abdo vedavâ*k*î, tatsambandhâd vratam api *s*ukriyam.

2, 4. See the note on chap. 6, 1. 2.

4. Some say that the handing over of the staff forms the end (of this ceremony).

5. During the northern course of the sun, in the time of the increasing moon—

6. The teacher having abstained through one day and one night from sexual intercourse and from eating flesh—

7. With the exclusion of the fourteenth day and of the eighth (of the half-month),

8. And of the first and last, according to some (teachers),

9. Or on what day else the constellation seems lucky to him, on that day he shall direct (the student) to the duties of holiness according to the Sukriya rite.

10. Let him observe (those) duties through three days, or twelve days, or one year, or as long as the master may think fit.

11. The Sâkvara (observance), however, (is to be kept) one year.

12. (So also) the Vrâtika and Aupanishada (observances).

13. When the time has elapsed, when the duties

---

4. On the dandapradâna, see chap. 6, 2.

6. The pleonasm brahmakaryam upetya . . . brahmakârî should be removed by expunging brahmakârî, which is omitted in the Sâmbavya text. Comp. chap. 12, Sûtra 8; VI, 1, 2.

7. Comp. below, IV, 7, 7.

9. In the Sâmbavya text this Sûtra has a fuller form. It runs there thus, ' . . . he shall direct (the student) to the duties of holiness according to the Sukriya rite, the teacher saying, "Be a Sukriya-brahmakârin;" the other one replying, "I will be a Sukriya-brahmakârin." Thus also at the other observances he shall pronounce each time the name of the observance to which he directs him.'

10. Comp. above, II, 5, 1.

13. The Samyu Bârhaspatya, i.e. the verse beginning with the

have been observed, when the Veda has been studied
down to the _Samyu_-Bârhaspatya-(hymn), let (the
teacher then), should he intend to instruct (the
student) in the secret (part of the Veda), ascertain
the time (through which the student has to observe
the special rites) and the rules to be observed, from
the (special) directions (that are handed down on this
subject).

KHANDA 12.

1. After (the student) has eaten something in the
morning, in the afternoon, to the north-east—

---

words ta_k kham_ yor â v_ri_nîmahe, is the last verse of the Rig-
veda in the Bâshkala redaction. See below, the note on IV, 5, 9.

On kâlaniyama_m_, see Nârâya_n_a's note, pp. 140 seq. of the
German edition.

12, 1 seq. The Indian tradition (with the exception only, as far
as is known to me, of the _S_âmbavya commentary) refers the
ceremonies described in this chapter, like those treated of in chap.
11, as well to the _S_ukriya as to the _S_âkvara and the other Vratas.
This is not correct. The eleventh chapter gives the rites common
to the four Vratas; the _S_ukriya vrata is connected with no special
ceremonies beside those, so that the exposition of this Vrata is
brought to an end in that chapter. The last Sûtra of chap. 11
marks the transition to the special rites which are peculiar to the
three other Vratas, and are connected with the character of mystical
secrecy attributed to the Âra_n_yaka, and thus it is with the exclusion
of the _S_ukriya that the twelfth chapter refers only to those Vratas.
The difference which we have pointed out between the two chapters
finds its characteristic expression in Sûtras 9 and 11 of chap. 11,
compared with chap. 12, 13. 14; in the former Sûtras the statements there given are expressly extended to the _S_ukriya, the
_S_âkvara, the Vrâtika, and the Aupanishada, while in the latter
passage mention is made first of the Mahânâmnîs, i. e. the text
corresponding to the _S_âkvara vrata, and then the uttar_â_ni pra-
kara_n_âni (the following sections) are referred to, i. e. the Mahâvrata
and the Upanishad, so that the _S_ukriya vrata or the texts, the study
of which is entered upon by that Vrata, are left out here.
There is a good deal of confusion in the several commentaries

2. Having sacrificed, the teacher then asks him
with regard to those deities to whom he has been
given in charge (see above, chap. 3, 1), 'Hast thou
fulfilled the duties of holiness before Agni, Indra,
the Sun, and the Visve devâs?'

with regard to the succession of the different ceremonies taught in
this chapter. They all agree in stating that after the lapse of the
year through which the Vrata is kept, a ceremony is performed
called Uddîkshanikâ, i. e. the giving up of the Dîkshâ, or preparatory observance. This Uddikshanikâ consists chiefly in the
teacher's ascertaining whether the student has fulfilled the duties
involved by the Vrata (see Sûtras 2 and 3). Besides that, there is
no doubt that a repetition of the Upanayana (chap. 11, 2) also
formed part of the preparatory rites for the study of the Âranyaka.
As to the way in which these different ceremonies and the other
rites described in this chapter would have to be arranged according
to our text, it is perhaps best to follow the statements given in an
epitome from the bâlâvabodhanârtham Rishidaivatakhando-
paddhati (MS. Berol. Chambers, 199 a, fols. 13–16) ; the slight confusion therein is not difficult to get rid of. There we read, ' The
Sâkvara, however, is to be kept one year (chap. 11, 11). When
the Uddikshanikâ has been performed, and three nights (chap. 12,
6) or one day and one night (ibid. 7) have elapsed, the Upanayana
should be performed as above (chap. 11, 2), with this difference
that at the end of the formula mama vrate, &c. (chap. 4, 1) one
should say, " May Brihaspati join thee to me for the holy observance of the Sâkvara through one year, O Devadatta!" (On this
formula, resting on a misunderstanding of chap. 4, Sûtra 2, see the
Introduction, p. 8.) The rest is the same as at the Sukriya. Then,
when the year (chap. 11, 11) has elapsed, and the Uddikshanikâ has
been performed, and the three days or the night have passed (chap.
12, 6. 7), he should go out of the village ... and in the north-eastern
direction,' &c. (here follows the description of how the secret
doctrines should be taught to the student, according to Sânkh. VI).
The confusion showing itself in the double mention of the Uddikshanikâ, before and after the Upanayana, should no doubt be put
to the account of the excerptor or perhaps even of the MS. ; what
the meaning of the original Paddhati was is sufficiently shown in
the remarks on the following Vratas, for instance, on the Vrâtika
(fol. 16), ' Now follows the Vrâtika vrata. It lasts one year (chap.

3. If he answers, 'I have fulfilled them, sir!'—

4. The teacher three times envelops, from the left to the right, with a fresh garment the face (of the student) who is standing behind the fire, in front of the teacher, with his face to the east.

5. He turns the skirt (of that garment) upwards so that it cannot slip down,

6. (And says:) 'Leaving off for three days the putting on of fuel, the going for alms, the sleeping on the ground, and the obedience to the teacher, fast in the forest, in a god's house or in a place where Agnihotra is performed, keeping silence, with earnest care.'

11, 12). When the *Sâkvara* has reached its end [here we find added at the margin of the MS., "After the Uddîkshaṇikâ has been performed." These words ought not to be received into the text; in the corresponding passage on the Aupanishada vrata they are not found] he performs the whole ceremony, beginning from the smearing (of the Sthaṇḍila with cow-dung), the drawing of the lines, &c., as at the Upanayana . . . and then, when one year has elapsed, he performs the Uddîkshaṇikâ, and the rules [given in chap. 12, 9 seq.] are observed as above.' I think that here the meaning of the text is correctly represented; first comes the Upanayana, then follows the Vrata lasting one year, then the Uddîkshaṇikâ. After this ceremony the teacher gives to the student the directions mentioned in chap. 12, 16; then follow the three days, or the one night (chap. 12, 6. 7), and finally they both go out of the village to the north-east, and in the forest they recite the Rahasya.

On the whole ceremonies connected with the study of the Âraṇyaka the sixth book should be compared.

5. Nârâyaṇa: Vastrasya daśâḥ prântabhâga[m] uparishṭât kritvâ tathâ badhnîyâd yathâ na sambhraśyeta adhastân na patati tathâ vidheyam.

6. The things which the student here is ordered to leave off for three days are the same that are mentioned above, chap. 6, 8, as his standing duties. According to Nârâyaṇa this would be the Âdeśa mentioned in chap. 11, 13.

7. Here some (teachers) prescribe the same observances only for one night, during which he is to stand.

8. The teacher refrains from eating flesh and from sexual intercourse.

9. When those three days or that night has elapsed, going out from the village he shall avoid to look at the following (persons or things) that form impediments for the study (of the Veda):

10. Raw flesh, a *Kandâla*, a woman that has lately been confined, or that has her courses, blood, persons whose hands have been cut off, cemeteries, and all sorts of corpse-like (animals?) which enter (their dens?) with the mouth first (?), keeping them away from the place where he dwells.

---

8. Comp. chap. 11, 6.

10. With Sûtikâ is meant a woman during the first ten days after her confinement, for which period the *asauka* lasts.—Apahasta is rendered by Nârâyana by *khinnahasta*; the comment on the *Sâmbavya-Grihya* mentions âyudhânkitahastâms *ka*. The translation of the last words of this Sûtra (sarvâni *ka* savarûpâni yâny âsye na [or âsyena?] praviseyuh svasya vâsân nirasan) is absolutely uncertain. Nârâyana says that such animals as lions, serpents, &c. are designated in common use as savarûpâni. (This literally means, 'having the form of a corpse.' Immediately afterwards Nârâyana gives a nearly identical explanation of savarûpa as different from the one stated first. So perhaps we may conjecture that his first explanation rests on a reading sarparûpâni; comp. the reading sarvarûpa of Pâraskara.) Of these the animals entering their dwelling-places with the mouth first (âsyena) are to be understood here as forming, when looked at, an impediment for the study. Nârâyana then says that other authorities understand sava in the sense of a dead human body; then savarûpâni are beings having the form thereof (tadrûpâni), such as dogs, jackals, &c. The words yâny âsyena praviseyuh signify that the study is impeded also on the sight of lions, tigers, &c.; for these enter their dwelling-places with their faces first (? anumukhaih kritvâ). The words svasya vâsân nirasan mean,

11. Going out (from the village) in a north-eastern direction the teacher sits down on a clean spot, turning his face to the east.

12. When the sun has risen, he recites, in the way prescribed for the Veda-study, (the Âranyaka texts to the student) who is to keep silence and who wears a turban.

13. This rule is to be observed only for the Mahânâmnî verses.

14. At the sections however that follow (after the Mahânâmnîs) the other one hears while the teacher recites them for himself.

15. He gives (to the teacher) the turban, a vessel, a good cow.

16. (The teacher accepts the gifts) with the verses,

according to Nâr., 'when he—i. e. the teacher—goes out of his dwelling-place.' Râmakandra says that *savarûpa* either means lions, snakes, and other dangerous animals, or nails, horns, and other such things that fall off or are severed from the body. The text of the Sâmbavya MS. is sarvâni ka' syâmarûpâni yâvânyâ (?) praviseyuh, which the commentary explains, sarvâms ka bhakshyavargâms ka. I think there can be little doubt that the text of Sânkhâyana is correct (except that some doubt will remain as to âsyena or âsye na), the more so as the passage reoccurs, nearly identically, below at VI, 1, 4. 5. As to the translation we can only go so far as to venture the opinion that the Sânkhâyana text does not admit the interpretation given by Gayarâma, and accepted by Professor Stenzler (who compares Âpastamba I, 11, 27; Gautama XVI, 41) in Pâraskara II, 11, 3 for sarvarûpa, which consequently should, in our opinion, be rejected also in that passage of Pâraskara. For ascertaining the true meaning of *savarûpa* we shall have to wait until new parallel passages have been discovered.

12. The rules for the Anuvâkana have been given above in chap. 7.

13. The Mahânâmnî verses are given in the fourth Âranyaka of the Aitareyinas. See Sacred Books of the East, I, p. xliii.

'Thou him' (Rig-veda I, 18, 5), and, 'High in the sky' (Rig-veda X, 107, 2), or (he accepts them) all with the Pra*n*ava (i.e. the syllable O*m*).

17. Here some prepare a mess of rice for the Visve devâs at all sections (of the Âra*n*yaka);

18. For the gods to whom he has been given in charge, according to Mâ*nd*ûkeya.

KHANDA 13.

1. Now (follow) the rules regarding the staff.

2. Let him not leave a passage between himself and the staff.

3. Now should any one of these things, viz. staff, girdle, or sacrificial cord, break or rend, the same penance (takes place) therefore which (has been prescribed) at the wedding with regard to the chariot.

4. If the girdle cannot be repaired, he makes another and speaks over it (the following verses):

5. 'Thou who knowest the distinction of pure and impure, divine protectress Sarasvati, O girdle, prolong my vow unimpaired, unbroken.

'Thou, Agni, art the pure bearer of vows. Agni, carry hither the gods to our sacrifice and our oblation.

'Bearing the vows, the infallible protector of vows, be our messenger, undecaying and mighty. Giving treasures, merciful, Agni, protect us, that we may live, *G*âtavedas!'

6. And he ties the sacrificial cord to the staff.

7. Here it is said also:

---

18. Comp. the second Sûtra of this chapter.
13, 3. See above, I, 15, 9 seq.

8. 'Let him sacrifice the sacrificial cord and the staff, the girdle and also the skin in water after the completion of his vow with a Varuna-verse or with the essence (of the Vedas, i.e. the syllable Om).'

KHANDA 14.

1. Now (follows) the Vaisvadeva (sacrifice).
2. The rite of the sacrifice has been explained.
3. Let him pour oblations of prepared Vaisvadeva food in the evening and in the morning into the (sacred) domestic fire.
4. 'To Agni svâhâ! To Soma svâhâ! To Indra and Agni svâhâ! To Vishnu svâhâ! To Bharadvâga Dhanvantari svâhâ! To the Visve devâs svâhâ! To Pragâpati svâhâ! To Aditi svâhâ! To Anumati svâhâ! To Agni Svishtakrit

---

8. Nârâyana here quotes Rig-veda I, 24, 6, which is the first verse in the Rig-veda addressed to Varuna (i. e. to Varuna alone, not to Mitra and Varuna, &c.).

14, 1. The rules regarding the Vaisvadeva sacrifice stand here, as I have already pointed out in the German edition, p. 142, in a very strange position amid the matter that concerns the student, and before the description of the ceremony that concludes studentship (the Samâvartana; III, 1). On the first word of the chapter, atha, Nârâyana observes that thereby the householder is marked as the subject of the following rules. It seems rather forced to explain the position of this chapter, as Nârâyana does, by pointing out that in some cases, for instance when the teacher is away on a journey, a student also can eventually be called upon to perform the Vaisvadeva sacrifice (comp. below, chap. 17, 3).

2. This Sûtra shows, according to Nârâyana, that the Vaisvadeva offering does not follow the ordinary type of sacrifice (the Pratisrute homakalpa, as it is termed above, I, 9, 19), but the form described in the Agnikâryaprakarana, above, chap. 10, 3 seq.

svâhâ!'—having thus offered the oblations belonging
to those deities,

5. He then shall offer Balis (i.e. portions of food)
in the centre of the floor to the same deities; (then
another Bali with the words,) 'Adoration to Brahman
and to the Brâhma*n*as!' and (with the verse),
'Vâstoshpati, accept us' (Rig-veda VII, 54, 1) in the
centre of the floor to Vâstoshpati.

6. He then distributes Balis, from the left to the
right, through the different quarters (of the horizon,
to the presiding deities) in due order (with the
words),

7. 'Adoration to Indra and to those belonging to
Indra! Adoration to Yama and to those belonging
to Yama! Adoration to Varu*n*a and to those belonging to Varu*n*a! Adoration to Soma and to those
belonging to Soma! Adoration to B*ri*haspati and to
those belonging to B*ri*haspati!'

8. Then (turned) towards the disk of the sun,
'Adoration to Aditi and to the Âdityas! Adoration

---

5. 'He shall offer a Bali to those deities, i.e. to those ten deities
to whom he has sacrificed, to Agni, &c. (see Sûtra 4), addressing
them with the word, "Adoration (to such and such a deity")—
because in the other cases the word "adoration" (nama*h*) has been
prescribed for the Bali.' Nârâya*n*a.

6, 7. The distribution of Balis begins in the east, which is the
part of the horizon sacred to Indra; it then proceeds to the
south, the west, the north, which are sacred respectively to Yama,
Varu*n*a, and Soma. Finally the Bali belonging to B*ri*haspati
and the Bârhaspatyas is offered, according to Nârâya*n*a, to the
north-east.

8. The commentators (see p. 142 of the German edition) differ
as to whether âdityama*nd*ala means the disk of the sun towards
which this Bali should be offered, or a place or an apartment of
circular form (âdityama*nd*alarûpe ma*nd*alâgâre, as in my opinion
we ought to correct the reading in Nârâya*n*a's note).

to the Nakshatras, to seasons, to months, to half-
months, to days and nights, to years!'

9. 'To Pûshan, the path-maker; to Dhâtar, to
Vidhâtar, and to the Maruts' — (thus) on the
thresholds.

10. To Vishnu on the grindstone.

11. 'To the tree'—(thus) in the mortar.

12. 'To the herbs'—(thus) where the herbs are
kept.

13. 'To Parganya, to the waters'—(thus) near
the water-pot.

14. 'Adoration to Srî'—(thus) in the bed at the
head, 'to Bhadrakâlî' at the foot.

15. In the privy, 'Adoration to Sarvânnabhûti!'

16. Then (he throws a Bali) into the air, in the
evening with the words,' To the night-walkers,' in the
morning with the words, ' To the day-walkers,' and
with the verse,' Which gods' (Rig-veda I, 139, 11).

17. To the unknown deities to the north, and to
Dhanapati (i.e. the Lord of treasures).

18. With the sacrificial cord suspended over the
right shoulder he pours out the remnant to the south
with the verse, ' They whom the fire has burnt'
(Rig-veda X, 15, 14).

19. When he has made his offerings to gods,
fathers (i.e. Manes), and men, let him give food to a
Srotriya (i.e. to a learned Brâhmana).

20. Or let him give alms (of food) to a student.

21. Let him immediately afterwards offer food to
a female under his protection, to a pregnant woman,
to boys, and to old people.

---

21. Comp. Böhtlingk-Roth s. v. suvâsinî, and Professor Bühler's
note on Gautama V, 25.

22. Let him throw (some food) on the ground for the dogs, for the dog-butchers, and for the birds.

23. Let him eat nothing without having cut off (and offered as a Bali) a portion thereof.

24. (Let him) not (eat) alone,

25. Nor before (the others).

26. With regard thereto it has been said also in the *Rik*, ' In vain the fool gains food' (Rig-veda X. 117, 6).

KHANDA 15.

1. Should any one of the six persons (mentioned in the *S*rauta-sûtra and in the Sûtras 4–9) to whom the Arghya reception is due, visit (him), let him make (ready) a cow, a goat, or what (sort of food) he thinks most like (thereto).

2. Let the Argha not be without flesh.

3. On the occasion of a sacrifice and of a wedding let (the guest) say, ' Make it (ready).'

22, 23. Probably these Sûtras should be divided after iti.

23. 'Pûrva*m* means, he should not eat before his relations (bandhubhya*h* pûrva*m* prathamata*h*).' Nârâya*n*a.

15, 1. This Sûtra presupposes the *S*rauta-sûtra IV, 21, 1 : ' To six persons the Argha reception is due, viz. to the teacher, to an officiating priest, to the father-in-law, to a king, to a Snâtaka, to a friend.' Here the fourth person mentioned is the *s*va*s*ura, while in the G*r*ihya text the expression vaivâhya is used. It is difficult not to believe that both words are used in the same sense, and accordingly Nârâya*n*a says vivâhya*h* svasura*h*. Comp. Professor Stenzler's note on Pâraskara I, 3, 1 ; Âpastamba II, 8, 7 ; Gautama V, 27.

Sâmânyatama*m* sad*r*i*s*atama*m* mâshâdikam (mâkhâdikam the MS.) annam. Nârâya*n*a.

2, 3. These Sûtras are identical with Pâraskara I, 3, 29. 30. The following Sûtra of Pâraskara stands in the *S*ânkhâyana text as

4. The animal (offered) to the teacher is sacred to Agni;

5. If offered to an officiating priest, to Bri̇haspati;

6. If to the father-in-law, to Pragâpati;

7. If to a king, to Indra;

8. If to a friend, to Mitra;

9. If to a Snâtaka, to Indra and Agni;

10. Even if he performs more than one Soma sacrifice during a year, let only priests who have received (from him) the Arghya reception officiate for him, not such who have not received it.

11. Here it is said also:

Sûtra 10. Probably Pâraskara here represents the text which both Sûtrakâras follow, more exactly, and the enumeration given by Sâṅkhâyana in Sûtras 4–9 of the different categories of Arghyas with the corresponding deities, is an addition to that original stock of rules.

Apparently the two Sûtras 2 and 3 stand in contradiction to each other, as Sûtra 2 seems to prescribe that at the Argha meal in every case flesh should be given to the guest, and Sûtra 3 specifies only two occasions on which the killing of the Argha cow cannot be dispensed with. Perhaps the meaning is this, that it is not necessary, except in the cases of a sacrifice and of a wedding, to kill a cow expressly for that purpose, but that in any case, even if the cow offered to the guest be declined by him, the host should take care that some flesh be served at that meal. So says Nârâyana in his note on Âsvalâyana-Grihya I, 24, 33, 'Pasukaranapakshe tanmâmsena bhoganam, utsarganapakshe mâmsântarena.' Similarly the Buddhists distinguish between eating flesh and eating the flesh of an animal expressly killed in order to entertain that very guest.

6. The literal translation of vaivâhya would be 'a person related by marriage.' But comp. the note on Sûtra 1.

8. Priya of course does not mean gâmâtar, as is stated in a number of commentaries. Gobhila says, priyo-tithih.

11. Other persons, for instance a king, can claim the Argha reception not more than once a year. Comp. Âpastamba II, 8, 7; Gautama V, 28, 29, &c.

KHANDA 16.

1. 'At the Madhuparka and at the Soma sacrifice, at the sacred rites for fathers (Manes) and gods only animals may be killed, not elsewhere : thus has Manu said.

2. 'Both his teacher and his father, and also a friend who does not stay in his house as a guest : whatever these dispose, that let him do; such is the established custom.

3. 'Let him not consider as a guest a person living in the same village, or one that comes in returning from a journey; (but let him consider as a guest only) one who has arrived at his house where the wife or the fires (of the host) are.

4. '(The fire of) the Agnihotra, bulls, and a guest that has come in at the right time, children and persons of noble families : these burn up him who neglects them.

5. 'A bull, the Agnihotra, and a student, these three prosper only if they eat; there is no prosperity for them, if they do not eat.

6. 'Day by day the domestic deities approach the man who performs the domestic rites, in order to receive their share; (that) let him pour out to them.

KHANDA 17.

1. 'Even if a man constantly gather grass and perform the Agnihotra, a Brâhmana who stays (in his

---

16, 3. Comp. Gautama V, 40, &c.

4. On the right time for the arrival of a guest, see Gautama, loc. cit.

house) without receiving honour takes away all his good works.

2. 'One should give (even) if it were only a water-pot; one should sacrifice (even) if it were a piece of wood; (even) down to one hymn or to one Anuvâka the Brahmayag͂a is enjoined.

3. 'When on a journey let him not fast; (during that time) the wife keeps the vow. Let his son, his brother, or his wife, or his pupil offer the Bali oblation.

4. 'Those who perform this Vaisvadeva sacrifice in the evening and in the morning, they will prosper in wealth and (long) life, in fame and offspring.'

Khanda 18.

1. A student who is going to set out on a journey, speaks thus to his teacher:

2. 'Of inhalation and exhalation'—(this he says) in a low voice; 'Om, I will dwell'—this aloud.

3. (The teacher) in a low voice (replies), 'To inhalation and exhalation I, the wide-extended one, resort with thee. To the protecting god I give thee in charge. God Savitar; this student belongs to thee; I give him in charge to thee; protect him; do not forsake him.'

4. 'Om, hail!' the teacher aloud. 'Hail!' the teacher aloud.

Here ends the Second Adhyâya.

18, 2. Perhaps vatsyâmi (I will dwell) is a sort of euphemism for pravatsyâmi (I will go away).

1. A bath (shall be taken by the student) when he is going to return home (from his teacher).

2. 'A bull's hide'—this has been declared. On that hide he makes him sit down and have his hair and beard cut and the hair of the body and the nails.

3. Having had (the cut-off hair-ends, &c.) thrown away together with rice and barley, with sesamum-seed and mustard-seed, with Apâmârga and Sadâ-pushpî flowers,

4. Having sprinkled him (with water) with the Âpohish*thi*ya-hymn (Rig-veda X, 9),

5. Having adorned him,

6. Having dressed him with two garments with (the verse), 'The garments both of you' (Rig-veda I, 152, 1),

7. He then puts on him a golden ornament (with the words), 'Giving life and vigour' (Vâgasaneyi Sa*m*hitâ XXXIV, 50).

8. With (the verse), 'Mine, Agni, be vigour' (Rig-veda X, 128, 1), the veiling (of the head is done).

9. With (the verse), 'House by house the shining one' (Rig-veda I, 123, 4) (he takes) the parasol,

10. With (the verse), 'Rise up' (Rig-veda X, 18, 6), the shoes,

---

1, 2. Comp. above, I, 16, 1, and the note there.

4. Nârâya*n*a says here, ena*m* mânavakam abhishi*k*ya abhisheka*m* snâna*m* kârayitvâ. Comp. Pâraskara II, 6, 9 seq.

11. With (the verse), 'Long be thy hook' (Rig-veda VIII, 17, 10) he takes a bamboo staff.

12. Let him sit that day in solitude.

13. With (the verses), 'O tree! with strong limbs,' and, 'A ruler indeed' (Rig-veda VI, 47, 26; X, 152, 1) let him mount the chariot.

14. (Before returning home) let him first approach a place where they will perform Argha for him with a cow or a goat.

15. Or let him return (making his start) from cows or from a fruit-bearing tree.

16. With (the verses), 'Indra, give us best goods,' and, 'Be friendly, O earth' (Rig-veda II, 21, 6; I, 22, 15) he descends (from the chariot).

17. Let him eat that day his favourite food.

18. To his teacher he shall give (that) pair of garments, the turban, ear-rings and jewel, staff and shoes, and the parasol.

KHANDA 2.

1. If he wishes to have a house built, he draws with an Udumbara branch three times a line round (the building-ground) with (the words), ' Here I include the dwellings for the sake of food,' and sacrifices in (its) centre on an elevated spot,

2. (With the texts,) 'Who art thou? Whose art

---

12. Pratilîna evidently means the same thing that is so often expressed in the Buddhist texts by pa/isallîna.

18. The pair of garments are those referred to in Sûtra 6; on the turban see Sûtra 8. On staff and shoes comp. Sûtras 10, 11; on the parasol, Sûtra 9.

2, 1 seqq. On the house of the Vedic Indians, comp. Zimmer, Altindisches Leben, pp. 148 seqq.

thou? To whom do I sacrifice thee, desirous of (dwelling in the) village? Svâhâ!

'Thou art the gods' share on this (earth). From here have sprung the fathers who have passed away. The ruler has sacrificed, desirous of (dwelling in the) village, not omitting anything that belongs to the gods. Svâhâ!'

3. Having had the pits for the posts dug,

4. He pours water-gruel into them,

5. And with (the verse), 'This branch of the immortal one I erect, a stream of honey, promoting wealth. The child, the young one, cries to it; the cow shall low to it, the unceasingly fertile one'—he puts an Udumbara branch which has been besmeared with ghee into the pit for the right door-post.

6. 'This branch of the world I establish, a stream of honey, promoting wealth. The child, the young one, cries to it; the cow shall low to it that has a young calf'—thus to the left.

7. In the same way at the two (pits) to the south, to the west, and to the north.

8. With (the verse), 'This branch of this tree, that drops ghee, I erect in the immortal. The child, the young one, cries to it; cows shall flock to it, unceasingly fertile ones'—he erects the chief post.

9. 'May the young child come to it, may the calf . . . . ; may they come to it with a cup of Parisrut, with pots of curds.

---

9. On parisrut, see Zimmer, Altindisches Leben, p. 281. The words bhuvanas pari give no sense; Pâraskara probably gives the true reading, â vatso *gagadaih* saha (III, 4, 4; comp. Sûtra 8: Vasû*ms* *ka* Rudrân Âdityân Îsâna*m* *gagadaih* saha; *gagada* is explained in *Gaya*râma's commentary by anuga, anu*k*ara). The word *gagada* of course was exposed to all sorts of corruptions;

1. 'Stand here, O post, firm, rich in horses and cows, ...; stand safely, dropping ghee; stand here, fixed in the ground, prosperous, long-lasting (?), amid the prosperity of people who satiate themselves. May the malevolent ones not reach thee!

'Hither are called the cows; hither are called goats and sheep; and the sweet essence (?) of food is called hither to our house.

'Stand fast in the Rathantara; recline on the Vâmadevya; establish thyself on the Brihat'—with (these texts) he touches the chief post.

2. When the house has been built conformably (to its proper dimensions), he touches the posts.

3. The two (posts) to the east with (the words), 'Truth and faith!'

4. Those to the south with (the words), 'Sacrifice and gift!'

5. Those to the west with (the words), 'Strength and power!'

6. Those to the north with (the words), 'The Brahman and the Kshatra!

7. 'Fortune the pinnacle, law the chief post!

---

thus the text of Âsvalâyana has *gâyatâm* saka; the Atharva-veda (III, 12, 7) *gagatâ* saha; and from this *gagat* to the bhuvana found in our text the way is not very long.

3, 1. According to Nârâyana the verse given in chap. 2, 9 forms one Mantra with those in 3, 1. The meaning of sîlamâvatî is uncertain. The word reoccurs in Rig-veda X, 75, 8. Pâraskara (III, 4, 4) has sûnritâvatî. On tilvila, comp. Rig-veda V, 62, 7. The following word is quite uncertain both as to its reading and its meaning. Comp. p. 143 seq. of the German edition. On kîlâla, comp. Zimmer, loc. cit. p. 281.

7. Comp. Pâraskara III, 4, 18.

8. 'Day and night the two door-jambs!'

9. 'The year the roof!'

10. With (the verse), 'A bull, an ocean' (Rig-veda V, 47, 3) let him bury an anointed stone under the pinnacle.

KHANDA 4.

1. At the sacrifice to Vâstoshpati—

2. Having established the (sacred) domestic fire outside with (the words), 'I place (here) Agni with genial mind; may he be the assembler of goods. Do no harm to us, to the old nor to the young; be a saviour to us, to men and animals!'—

3. Having put a new water-pot on fresh eastward-pointed Kusa-grass,

4. And spoken over it (the words), 'Unhurt be our men, may our riches not be squandered!'—

5. He sacrifices three oblations in the forenoon with the Stotriya text of the Rathantara with repetition and Kakubh-forming;

6. (Three oblations with the Stotriya) of the Vâmadevya at midday;

7. Of the Brihat in the afternoon;

8. The four Mahâvyâhritis, the three verses, 'Vâstoshpati!' (Rig-veda VII, 54, 1-3), (the single verses,) 'Driving away calamity,' (and) 'Vâstoshpati,

---

4, 1. The sacrifice to Vâstoshpati is celebrated when the sacrificer enters his new house.

2. Comp. above, I, 7, 9.

5-7. On the way of reciting a Pragâtha, so as to form three verses, see Indische Studien, VIII, 25; Zeitschrift der deutschen Morg. Gesellschaft, XXXVIII, 476. The Stotriya of the Rathantara is Rig-veda VII, 32, 22 seq.; that of the Vâmadevya, IV, 31, 1-3; that of the Brihat, VI, 46, 1 seq.

a firm post' (Rig-veda VII, 55, 1; VIII, 17, 14), and
to (Agni) Svish/akrit a tenth oblation of cooked
food at night.

9. Taking with himself his eldest son and his wife,
carrying grain, let him enter (the house with the
words),

'Indra's house is blessed, wealthy, protecting;
that I enter with my wife, with offspring, with cattle,
with increase of wealth, with everything that is
mine.'

KHANDA 5.

1. 'To every able one, to every blissful one, to
you I turn for the sake of safety, of peace. Free
from danger may we be. May the village give me
in charge to the forest. All! give me in charge to
the great one,'—thus (he speaks) when leaving the
village.

2. 'May the forest give me in charge to the village.
Great one! give me in charge to the all'—thus
(he speaks) when entering the village, not without
(carrying) something (with himself, such as fuel,
flowers, &c.)

3. I enter the blessed, joyful house, which does
not bring death to men ; manly (I enter) that which
is rich in men. Bringing refreshment, dropping
ghee (we enter the house) in which I shall joyfully
rest'—this verse is constantly to be pronounced
(when he enters the house).

5, 3. For anyeshv aham we should read perhaps yeshv aham.
Âsvalâyana-Sraut. II, 5, 17 has teshv aham.

KHANDA 6.

1. One who has not set up the (sacred Srauta) fires, when setting out on a journey, looks at his house.

2. (He murmurs the text,) 'Do ye both, Mitra and Varuna, protect this house for me; unscathed, undisturbed, may Pûshan guard it till our return;'

3. And murmurs (the verse), 'Upon the path we have entered' (Rig-veda VI, 51, 16).

KHANDA 7.

1. When he then returns from his journey, he looks at his house (and says),

2. 'House, do not fear, do not tremble; bringing strength we come back. Bringing strength, joyful and wise, I come back to thee, to the house, rejoicing in my mind.

'That of which the traveller thinks, that in which dwells much joy, that I call the house. May it know us as we know it.

'Hither are called the cows; hither are called goats and sheep; and the sweet essence (?) of food is called hither to our house.'

3. Having approached the (sacred) domestic fire with the verse, 'This Agni is glorious to us, this is highly glorious. Worshipping him (?) may we suffer no harm; may he bring us to supremity'—

4. Let him pronounce auspicious words.

5. When accepting the water for washing the feet he says, 'The milk of Virâg art thou; may I obtain

---

7, 2. On kîlâla, see chap. 3, 1.

5. Padyâ virâg is the Virâg metre, so far as it consists of

the milk of Virâg; in me (may) the milk of Padyâ Virâg (dwell)!'

<h2 style="text-align:center">KHANDA 8.</h2>

1. When one who has not set up the (sacred Srauta) fires, is going to partake of the first-fruits (of the harvest), let him sacrifice to the Âgrayana deities with (Agni) Svishtakrit as the fourth, and with the word Svâhâ, on his (sacred) domestic fire.

2. Having recited over (the food) which he is going to eat (the formula), 'To Pragâpati I draw thee, the proper portion, for luck to me, for glory to me, for food to me!'—

3. He thrice eats of it, sprinkling it with water, with (the verse), 'From the good you have led us to the better, ye gods! Through thee, the nourishment, may we obtain thee. Thus enter into us, O potion, bringing refreshment; be a saviour to us, to men and animals!'

4. With (the verse), 'This art thou, breath; the truth I speak. This art thou; from all directions thou hast entered (into all beings). Thou driving away old age and sickness from my body be at home with me. Do not forsake us, Indra!'—he touches the place of the heart;

Pâdas; in this connection, of course, the phrase is intended besides to convey the meaning of 'the splendour which dwells in the feet.' Comp. Pâraskara I, 3, 12 and Professor Stenzler's note there. My German translation of this Sûtra of Sânkhâyana rests on a misunderstanding.

8, 1. The Âgrayaneshti is the corresponding rite of the Srauta ritual. Comp. Indische Studien, X, 343. The deities of that sacrifice are Indra and Agni; the Visve devâs; Heaven and Earth.

3. In the text read for tvayâ gvasena, tvayâ-rvasena.

5. With (the words), 'The navel art thou; do not fear; the knot of the breathing powers art thou; do not loosen thyself,' (he touches) the navel;

6. With the verse, 'Bliss with our ears' (Rig-veda I, 89, 8), (he touches) the limbs as stated (in that verse);

7. Worshipping the sun with the verse, 'Yonder eye' (Rig-veda VII, 66, 16).

KHANDA 9.

1. 'May the noisy (goddesses) keep you away from slaughtering hosts. May the entire share, O cows, that belongs to this lord of cows, suffer no harm among you—(and)

'May Pûshan go after our cows' (Rig-veda VI, 54, 5)—this he shall speak over the cows when they go away (to their pasture-grounds).

2. 'May Pûshan hold' (Rig-veda VI, 54, 10), when they run about.

3. 'May they whose udder with its four holes is full of sweet and ghee, be milk-givers to us; (may they be) many in our stable, rich in ghee'—and, 'The cows have come' (Rig-veda VI, 28), when they have come back.

4. The last (verse) when he puts them in (into the stable).

5. The hymn, 'Refreshing wind' (Rig-veda X, 169), (he recites over the cows), when they are gone into the stable.

KHANDA 10.

1. The new moon that follows after the Phâlguna

___

9, 1. The noisy ones are the winds; comp. the passage of Sânkhâyana-Srauta-sûtra, quoted p. 144 of the German edition.

full moon, falls under (the Nakshatra) Revatî: on
that (new moon day) he shall have the marks made
(on his cattle),

2. With (the words), ' Thou art the world, thousandfold prospering. To Indra may exertion (?)
give thee. Inviolate art thou, unhurt, sap, food,
protection. For as many (cows) I shall do this
now, for more (than these) may I do it in the latest
year.'

3. Of that (cow) that calves first let him sacrifice
the biestings with the two verses, ' Yearly the milk of
the cow' (Rig-veda X, 87, 17. 18).

4. If she brings forth twin-calves, let him sacrifice
with the Mahâvyâhritis, and give the mother of the
twins (to the Brâhmaṇas).

KHANDA 11.

1. Now (follows) the Vrishotsarga (i.e. setting a
bull at liberty).

2. On the Kârttika full moon day or on that
day of the Âsvayuga (month) that falls under (the
Nakshatra) Revatî—

3. He sacrifices, after having kindled amid the
cows a well-inflamed fire, Âgya oblations (with the
words),

4. ' Here is delight; take delight here. Svâhâ!

10, 2. The reading of tvâ sramo dadat is doubtful. See the
Various Readings in the German edition.

11, 1. A part of this chapter is nearly identical with the corre-
sponding section of the Kâṭhaka-grihya; see Jolly's article, Das
Dharma-sûtra des Vishṇu, &c. (Sitzung der philos. philol. Classe der
Bairischen Academie, 7 Juni, 1879), p. 39. Comp. also Pâraskara
III, 9; Vishṇu LXXXVI, and Jolly's remarks, in Deutsche Rund-
schau X, p. 428.

Here is still-standing; here is (your) own still-standing. Svâhâ!

'I have let the calf join its mother. May the calf, sucking its mother's breast, support increase of wealth among us. Svâhâ!'

5. With the verse, 'May Pûshan go after our cows' (Rig-veda VI, 54, 5) he sacrifices from (a mess of sacrificial food) belonging to Pûshan.

6. Having murmured the Rudra-(hymns),

7. (He takes) a one-coloured, two-coloured, or three-coloured (bull),

8. Or one that protects the herd,

9. Or that is protected by the herd,

10. Or it may also be red.

11. It should have all its limbs complete, and be the finest (bull) in the herd.

12. Having adorned that (bull),

13. And the four best young cows of the herd, having adorned those too,

14. (He says,) 'This young (bull) I give you as your husband; sporting with him, your lover, walk about. Do not desert us (?), being joined (with us) from your birth. In increase of wealth, in food may we rejoice. Svâhâ!'

15. When (the bull) is in the midst (of the cows), he recites over (them), ' Refreshing,' &c. (Rig-veda X, 169, 1 seq.) down to the end of the Anuvâka.

16. With the milk of all of them he shall cook milk-rice and feed Brâhmanas with it.

---

6. Rig-veda I, 43. 114; II, 33; VII, 46.

14. The translation 'do not desert us,' rests on the conjecture mâvasthâta; see the Various Readings, and the note on p. 145 of the German edition.

KHANDA 12.

1. After the Âgrahâyani (or the full moon day of the month Mârgasîrsha) (follow) the three Ashtakâs in the second fortnight (of the Mârgasîrsha and of the two following months).

2. At the first of these he sacrifices vegetables,

3. With (the verse), ' She who shone forth first is this (earth) ; she walks, having entered into this (earth). The wife has brought forth (children), the new-creating mother. May the three powers follow her. Svâhâ !'

4. Now (the oblation for Agni) Svishtakrit,

5. With (the verses), 'She in whom Yama, the son of Vivasvat, and all gods are contained, the Ashtakâ whose face is turned to all sides, she has satiated my desires.

'They call thy teeth "the pressing-stones;" thy

12, 1. On the Ashtakâ festivals, of which some texts reckon three, while others have four, comp. Weber, Naxatra (second article), pp. 337, 341 seq.; Bühler, S. B. E., II, p. 214; Ludwig, Rig-veda, vol. iv, pp. 424 seq.; Atharva-veda III, 10. The last Ashtakâ, which is celebrated in the dark fortnight of Mâgha, is called Ekâshtakâ ; this Ashtakâ is called the ' wife of the year,' ' the image of the year,' ' the disposer of the days.' If the Phâlguna month is reckoned as the first of the year, this Ashtakâ precedes the year's beginning only by a few days; there are also some Vedic passages which point to the Ekâshtakâ's following shortly after the beginning of the year; see Weber, loc. cit., p. 342.

3. Instead of navakrit the parallel texts (except the Mantrabrâhmana II, 2, 12) have navagat, which is explained by nûtanavivâhavatî (Ludwig, loc. cit.); the ' three powers ' are understood by Mâdhava (in the commentary on Taitt. Samh. IV, 3, 11) as Agni, Sûrya, and Kandra.

5. After pavamânah there is evidently a word wanting that

udder is (Soma) Pavamâna ; .... are the months and half-months. Adoration to thee, O glad-faced one! Svâhâ!'

KHANDA 13.

1. At the middle (Ash*t*akâ) and in the middle of the rainy season,

2. The four Mahâvyâh*ri*tis (and) the four (verses), 'They who have thirsted' (Rig-veda X, 15, 9 seq.): having quickly recited (these verses) he shall sacrifice the omentum ;

3. Or (he shall do so) with the verse, 'Carry the omentum, *G*âtavedas, to the Manes, where thou knowest them in the world of virtue. May streams of fat flow to them ; may the wishes of the sacrificer be fulfilled. Svâhâ!'

4. (Then follow) the four Mahâvyâh*ri*tis (and) the four (verses), 'They who have thirsted' (see Sûtra 2): (thus is offered) an eightfold oblation of cooked food, together with the cut-off portions.

---

indicated the limb of the Ash*t*akâ's body identified with the months and half-months.

13, 1. On madhyâvarsha, comp. Weber, loc. cit., pp. 331, 337. Nârâya*n*a understands not 'in the middle of the rainy season,' but 'in the middle of the year' (see his note, p. 146 of the German edition). I cannot help thinking that the word madhyâvarshe, given by the MSS. here and in Pâraskara III, 3, 13, and explained by Nârâya*n*a, is a corrupt reading which we should correct into mâghyavarshe ('the festival celebrated during the rainy season under the Nakshatra Maghâs'), or something like that. The MSS. of Â*s*valâyana-G*ri*hya II, 5, 9 have mâghyâvarsha*m*, mâghâvarsha*m*, mâdhyâvarsha*m*. Vish*n*u (LXXVI, 1, comp. LXXVIII, 52, and Professor Jolly's note, Sacred Books of the East, VII, p. 240) mentions 'the three Ash*t*akâs, the three Anvash*t*akâs, a Mâgha day which falls on the thirteenth of the dark half of the month Praush*t*hapada.' Comp. Manu III, 273, varshâsu *k*a maghâsu *k*a ; Yâg*ñ*avalkya I, 260.

5. Or, 'Interposed are the mountains; interposed is the wide earth to me. With the sky and all the points of the horizon I interpose another one instead of the father. To N. N. svâhâ!

'Interposed to me are the seasons, and days and nights, the twilight's children. With the months and half-months I interpose another one instead of the father. To N. N. svâhâ!

'With the standing ones, with the streaming ones, with the small ones that flow about : with the waters, the supporters of all I interpose another one instead of the father. To N. N. svâhâ!

'Wherein my mother has done amiss, going astray, faithless to her husband, that sperm may my father take as his own; may another one fall off from the mother. To N. N. svâhâ!'—these four (verses) instead of the Mahâvyâhritis, if (the sacrificer) is an illegitimate child.

6. Or milk-rice (should be offered).

7. On the next day the Anvashtakya ceremony (i.e. ceremony following the Ashtakâ) in accordance with the rite of the Pindapitriyagña.

KHANDA 14.

1. On the last (Ashtakâ) he sacrifices cakes,

2. With the words, 'The Ukthya and the Atirâtra, the Sadyahkrî together with the metre—Ashtakâ!

---

5. Instead of 'N.N.' (the text has the feminine amushyai) the sacrificer inserts the name of his mother. For mâsâs, ardhamâ-sâs I propose to read, mâsais, ardhamâsais.

7. On Anvashtakya, comp. Bühler, S. B. E., XIV, p. 55; Jolly, loc. cit., p. 59.

Preparer of cakes! Adoration to thee, O glad-faced one. Svâhâ!'

3. A cow or a goat is the animal (to be sacrificed), or a mess of cooked food (should be offered).

4. Or he may optionally offer food to a cow.

5. Or he may optionally burn down brushwood in the forest and say, 'This is my Ash/akâ.'

6. But let him not neglect to do (one of these things). But let him not neglect to do (one of these things).

Here ends the Third Adhyâya.

14, 3–6. This is one of the passages which the author has taken unchanged from a more ancient Sûtra; see Âsv. II, 4, 8–11; Gobhila IV, 1 (end of the chapter). The Sûtras do not refer, as their position would seem to indicate, to the third, but to the second Ash/akâ.

5. Comp. Weber, loc. cit., p. 342, note 1.

1. Let him offer (Srâddha oblations) every month to the fathers.

2. Having invited an uneven number of Brâhmanas, versed in the Veda, at least three, to sit down as (representing) the fathers,

---

1, 1. Khandas 1–4 contain the rules regarding the Srâddha oblations directed to the Manes. The dinners offered in connection with these Srâddha sacrifices to Brâhmanas and also—though of this of course no notice is taken in Vedic texts—to Sramanas stood in the first line among the exhibitions of liberality of lay people towards priests and monks. Thus we find among the stock phrases that constantly reoccur in the Pâli Pitakas, the mention of Samanas and Brâhmanas 'who have eaten the food given to them out of faith' (saddhâdeyyâni bhoganâni bhuñgitvâ)—wherein the 'food given out of faith' (saddhâdeyya) either chiefly or exclusively means the Srâddha dinners, which are so called because the sacrificer gives them 'full of faith' (sraddhâsamanvita, Manu III, 275) to the Brâhmanas and through them to the Manes.

The principal form of Srâddha is that treated of in chap. 1, which is designated in other texts (see, for instance, Âsvalâyana-Grihya IV, 7, 1) as pârvana srâddha. There are, however, besides the parvan of the new moon, other times also considered as admissible for the performing of this monthly Srâddha; see Gautama XV, 2 seq.; Âpastamba II, 16, &c.; and comp. on the Srâddhas in general the passages quoted by Professor Jolly, Das Dharma-sûtra des Vishnu (Sitzung der Bair. Akademie, phil. Classe, 7 Juni, 1879), pp. 46 seq. ; Max Müller, 'India, what can it teach us?' pp. 234 seq., 374 seq.

2. '"As the fathers" means : he invites the youngest, middle-aged, and eldest Brâhmanas to sit down in the place of the father, the grandfather, and the great-grandfather' (Nârâyana). A similar explanation of pitrivat is mentioned by Nârâyana on Âsvalâyana-

3. And having strewn sesamum into an uneven number of water-pots,

4. He shall pour them out over the hands of the Brâhma*n*as, assigning (this gift) to them with the words, ' N. N. ! This to thee!'

5. After this they should be adorned ;

6. And after he has (respectfully) spoken to them, and has put food into the fire,

7. Assigning (the food) to them with the words, ' N. N.! This to thee !' he shall cause them to eat.

8. While they are eating, he shall murmur the Mahâvyâh*ri*tis, the Sâvitrî, the Madhuvâtîya-verses (Rig-veda I, 90, 6 seq.), and verses addressed to the Manes and to (Soma) Pavamâna.

G*ri*hya IV, 7, 2. My German translation of this Sûtra ought to be altered accordingly.

Besides the Brâhma*n*as mentioned in this Sûtra, who represent the fathers, according to all the commentaries, other Brâhma*n*as had to be invited as representing the Vi*s*ve devâs. Nârâya*n*a gives detailed statements as to the number of the pait*ri*ka and of the daivika Brâhma*n*as to be invited, and though at first sight a Euro-pean reader would rather be inclined to doubt whether at the *S*râddha ceremony, as the author of the text intended to describe it, any Brâhma*n*as at all had to be present except the pait*ri*kas, the Sûtra 2, 5 shows that the commentators are quite right in their statements regarding both categories of Brâhma*n*as.

5–7. It would be more natural to alter the division of the Sûtras, so as to bring âmantrya in the fifth, anna*ñ* *k*a in the seventh Sûtra.   In this case we should have to translate : 5. After this, having (respectfully) spoken to them who have been adorned (by him with flowers, ornaments, &c.) ; 6. And having put (food) into the fire, 7. And having assigned the food to them, &c., he shall cause them to eat.—The respectful address mentioned in the fifth Sûtra consists, according to Nârâya*n*a, in the announce-ment, ' Ye Brâhma*n*as, I will put (food) into the fire !' (comp. Â*s*v.-G*ri*hya IV, 7, 18), which he subsequently does with the formulas, ' To Agni Kavyavâhana svâhâ ! To Soma Pit*ri*mat svâhâ ! To Yama Aṅgirasvat Pit*ri*mat svâhâ !' Comp. Baudhâyana II, 14, 8.

9. When they have finished with eating, he shall offer the lumps (of flour).

10. Before (their dinner he shall offer) the lumps, according to some (teachers).

11. Behind (these he places the lumps) for their wives, putting something between (these and the preceding ones).

12. To the Brâhma*n*as he shall announce the remnants.

13. The rites of the putting (of food) into the fire (see Sûtra 6), &c. have been declared (in the *S*rauta-sûtra) by the Pi*nd*apit*ri*yag*ñ*a.

KHA*N*DA 2.

1. Now (follows) the Ekoddish*t*a (i.e. the *S*râddha ceremony directed to a single dead person),

2. With one strainer,

3. One (pot of) Argha-water,

4. One lump (of flour).

5. No inviting (takes place here), nor the putting

---

9. As to the way in which the Pi*nd*as should be offered, Nârâ-ya*n*a refers to the *S*rauta-sûtra (IV, 4).

10, 11. Pi*nd*ân evidently belongs to the tenth Sûtra, not, as the Indian tradition takes it, to the eleventh. Between the Pi*nd*as of the fathers and those belonging to the mothers he puts, according to Nârâya*n*a, for instance, Darbha grass.

13. *S*rauta-sûtra IV, 3 seq.

2, 1. Eka uddish*t*o yasmin *s*râddhe tad ekoddish*t*am (Når.). This is the kind of *S*râddha sacrifice which is to be per-formed for one twice-born during the first year after his death; see Manu III, 247; Yâg*ñ*avalkya I, 250.

3. This rule about the Argha water corresponds to those given with regard to the Pârva*n*a *S*râddha in the Sûtras 3 and 4 of the preceding chapter.

5. 'Because the âvâhana (inviting) is forbidden here, it follows

(of food) into the fire, nor (do) the Visve devâs (take part in this ceremony). 'Relished?'—thus are they to be asked whether they are satiated. 'May it approach (the fathers),' instead of 'imperishable.'
6. 'Be satisfied,' when sending them away.
7. Thus through one year, when one has died.
8. And (then) omission of the fourth one.

KHANDA 3.

1. Now (follows) the Sapindikarana (i.e. reception of a dead person into the community of Pinda-offerings with the other Manes).

that it must take place at the Pârvana Srâddha' (Når.). According to Râmakandra's Paddhati he shall say to the Brâhmanas, 'I will invite hither the fathers;' and when they give their consent, he invites them with Rig-veda X, 16, 12. Comp. Yâgñavalkya I, 232 seq., &c. Regarding the Visve devâs comp. the note on chap. 1, 2; as to the trïptaprasna (the question whether they are satiated) comp. Manu III, 251; Yâgñ. I, 240. At the Pârvana Srâddha, after the Brâhmanas have finished their dinner and rinsed their mouths, and after the Pindas have been offered, the sacrificer says, 'May what has been given at this Srâddha to our father N. N., who belongs to the gotra N. N., be imperishable!' (comp. Yâgñ. I, 242.) This phrase is to be altered at the Ekoddishta Srâddha in the way indicated in this Sûtra.

8. After the Ekoddishta Srâddha has been performed for a dead person during the first year after his death, he is to be admitted, by the Sapindikarana ceremony, among the other Manes, and receives thenceforward his Pinda together with them at the ordinary Pâr-vana Srâddha. As the ritual of this Srâddha requires that the number of the 'fathers' worshipped should be three, the accession of a new person makes necessary the omission of the pra-pra-pitâmaha, who has now become fourth among the fathers.

3, 1. It appears to me that this whole chapter is a later addition to the original text. The last Sûtra of the preceding chapter, treating of the omission of the fourth 'father,' which forms, as shown in the preceding note, a consequence of the Sapindikarana,

2. When one year has elapsed, or three half-months,

3. Or on a day when something good happens,

4. He fills four water-pots with sesamum, scents, and water,

5. Three for the fathers, one for the (newly) dead person,

6. And pours the pot that belongs to the (newly) dead person out into the pots of the fathers with the two verses, 'They who commonly' (Vâgasaneyi Samhitâ XIX, 45. 46).

7. Thus also the lump (of flour).

8. This is the Sapindikarana.

KHANDA 4.

1. Now (follows) the Âbhyudayika (i.e. the Srâddha ceremony referring to good luck).

---

supposes this ceremony to be known and to require no special explanation. Had the intention of the author been to treat of the Sapindikarana, this would have been the right place for mentioning the katurthavisarga, and not, as we really read it, the end of the chapter treating of the Ekoddishta. As pointing in the same direction I will mention that the Sâmbavya-Grihya, while giving the first, second, and fourth chapter of this Adhyâya, omits the third. Finally it seems decisive to me that the fifth (Parisishta) book of the Sâṅkhâyana-Grihya treats of the Sapindikarana in a whole chapter (V, 9), which shows that the text itself, as the author of the Parisishta read it, gave no exposition of this ceremony.

2. Nârâyana says that tripaksha means either three pakshas, i. e. one month and a half, or one paksha deficient by three days, i. e. twelve days. We need not say that the latter explanation is inadmissible; it evidently rests on a wrong conclusion drawn from a passage of another Sûtra quoted by him, in which it is stated that the Sapindikarana should be performed samvatsarânte dvâdasâhe vâ.

4, 1. The Âbhyudayika Srâddha has to be performed on such

2. In the fortnight of the increasing moon, on an auspicious day,

3. After the sacrifice to the mothers has been performed,

4. And an even number of (Brâhma*n*as) versed in the Veda have been invited to sit down ;

5. In the forenoon ;

6. The rite is performed from left to right.

7. The murmuring with the omission of the verses belonging to the Manes.

8. The Darbha blades are straight.

9. Barley is to be used instead of sesamum.

10. The lumps are mixed with curds, jujube fruits, fried grain.

11. On inviting (the Manes, he should say), 'The Nândimukha (glad-faced ?) Manes will I invite.'

12. 'May the Nândimukha Manes be rejoiced,' instead of 'imperishable.'

13. 'The Nândimukha Manes will I make speak,' when he makes (the Brâhma*n*as) speak.

14. '(Was it) well done ?'—thus are they to be asked whether they are satiated.

occasions as the birth of a son, the marriage of a son or a daughter, the performance of ceremonies such as the nâmakarman, *kûd*â-karman, &c. See Yâg*ñ*avalkya I, 249.

3. A *S*râddha ceremony directed to the mothers here precedes that consecrated to the fathers.

6. Professor Stenzler's translation of Yâg*ñ*avalkya, loc. cit. (pra-dakshi*n*âv*ri*tka = die Ehrfurcht beobachtend), has to be corrected according to this Sûtra.

7. See chap. 1, 8.   9. See chap. 1, 3.

11. Concerning the 'invitation' (âvâhana) see the note on chap. 2, 5.

12. See chap. 2, 5 and the note there.

13. 'When he causes them to say Svadhâ.' Nârâya*n*a. Comp. Â*sv*.-G*ri*hya IV, 7, 30.

14. Comp. chap. 2, 5.

15. The rest is the same (as in the other kinds of Srâddha rites), as far as it is not prohihited (by contrary rules).

KHANDA 5.

1. Now (follows) the Upâkarana (i.e. the ceremony by which the annual course of study is opened).

2. When the herbs appear, under the Nakshatra Hasta or Sravana,

3. Let him make oblations of the flour of fried barley and of grains, mixed with curds and ghee, with the (whole) Veda, verse by verse : thus say some (teachers).

4. Or with the first verses of the Sûktas and Anuvâkas.

5. With the first verses of the Adhyâyas and of the sections belonging to the (different) Rishis, according to Mândûkeya.

6. But Kaushîtaki has said :

7. 'I praise Agni the Purohita' (Rig-veda I, 1, 1), this one verse,

8. 'The Kushumbhaka (mungoose?) has said it ;' 'If thou criest, O bird, announce luck to us ;' 'Sung by Gamadagni;' 'In thy abode the whole world rests;'

5, 1. As to the Upâkarana, see the statements of Professor Weber in his second article on the Nakshatras, Abhandlungen der Berliner Akademie, 1861, p. 338, and of Professor Bühler in his notes on Âpastamba, S. B. E., II, pp. 110, 111.

2. The Nakshatra Sravana is evidently considered as particularly fit for this occasion because of its name containing an allusion to sruti, &c.

4. I have followed Nârâyana, but perhaps I ought to have translated, 'Sûktas or Anuvâkas,' and in the fifth Sûtra, 'Adhyâyas or the sections, &c.'

'Come to our sacrifice, O you that are worthy of sacrifice, with care ;' 'Whosoever, be he ours, be he alien ;' 'Look on, look about ;' 'Come here, Agni, the Maruts' friend ;' 'The oblation, O king, cooked for thee :' each time two verses,

9. 'That blessing and bliss we choose'—this one verse (the first and last verse of each Mandala).

10. (Taking something) of the remnants of the sacrificed (food) they partake of that sacrificial food with this (verse), 'I praised Dadhikrâvan' (Rigveda IV, 39, 6).

11. They sip water, sit down,

12. Murmur the Mahâvyâhritis, the Sâvitrî, and the auspicious hymns commencing from the beginning of the Veda,

13. And cause the teacher to pronounce auspicious wishes.

---

9. According to Kaushîtaki, the oblations are made with the first and last rikas of each Mandala. The last rik of the tenth Mandala quoted here, tak kham yor â vrinîmahe, is different from the verse with which our Samhitâ (the Sâkala Samhitâ of the Rig-veda) closes. It is well known that tak kham yor â vrinîmahe is the last verse in the Bâshkala Sâkhâ which was adopted by the Sânkhâyana school (comp. Indische Studien, IV, 431; Weber, Verzeichniss der Berliner Sanskrit-Handschriften, p. 314, &c.; Indische Literaturgeschichte, second edition, Nachtrag, p. 2). It was also known long since that the Bâshkala Sâkhâ of the Rig-veda contains eight hymns more than the Sâkala Sâkhâ. The Karanavyûha Bhâshya (comp. Dr. von Schroeder's Introduction to his excellent edition of the Maitrâyanî Samhitâ, vol. i, p. xxiv), known to me through the kindness of Professor Weber, tells which eight hymns these are. There it is said (folio 22 of Professor Weber's MS.) that in the Bâshkala Samhitâ there followed after VIII, 48 the first two of the Vâlakhilya hymns, after VIII, 94 the Vâlakhilya hymns 3-7, and at the end of the whole collection the so-called samgñâna hymn (see Professor Max Müller's edition, vol. vi, p. 32), which ends with the very verse quoted in our Sûtra, tak kham yor â vrinîmahe.

14. Of this (ceremony) it is also said,

15. 'Desirous (of acquiring) for the hymns in-exhaustible vigour, reverence, and also soundness, the *R*ishis, by the power of their austerities, have discovered the Upâkarman.

16. 'Therefore a constant performer of the six kinds of works should, in order that his Mantras might be successful, perform the Upâkarman—so they say—if he wishes for success of his (holy) works.

17. 'At the time of the Upâkarman and of the Utsarga an interruption (of the Veda-study) shall take place for (three days and) three nights, likewise at the Ash*t*akâs for one day and one night, and so on the last night of each season.'

KHANDA 6.

1. On the first day of the bright fortnight of Mâgha,

2. To the north-east,

3. In a place covered with herbs,

4. Having murmured the hymns sacred to the Sun, 'Upwards that *G*âtavedas' (Rig-veda I, 50), 'The bright face of the gods' (I, 115), 'Adoration to Mitra's (eye)' (X, 37), 'From the sky (where he dwells) may Sûrya protect us' (X, 158),

---

16. The six kinds of works are, performing sacrifices (ya*g*ana), officiating at the sacrifices of others (yâ*g*ana), studying the Veda (adhyayana), teaching the Veda to others (adhyâpana), giving (dâna), and accepting gifts (pratigraha). Nârâya*n*a.

17. Concerning the Utsarga, see chap. 6. This *S*loka occurs also Manu IV, 119 with the reading kshepa*n*am instead of ksha-pa*n*am ('kshapa*n*am *kh*andasâm virâma anadhyâya*h*,' Nârâya*n*a). Kshapa*n*am is correct.

6, 1. This Kha*nd*a treats of the Utsarga, i.e. the ceremony performed at the end of the term.

5. And having thrown clods of earth (on the ground) to the different quarters (of the horizon), from the left to the right, with the hymn, 'A ruler indeed' (Rig-veda X, 152), verse by verse,

6. And having satiated (with water) the *Ri*shis, the metres, the deities, faith and insight, and the fathers man by man,

7. They interrupt (the study of) the hymns for six months and a half,

8. Or for five and a half.

9. But if they (wish to) recite them (nevertheless), let the recitation go on after a pause of one day and one night.

KHANDA 7.

1. Now the interruption (of the Veda recitation):—

2. In the case of prodigies until the same time (next day),

3. And in the case of other miracles;

4. In the case of lightning, thunder, and rains (the recitation shall be interrupted) till the twilight has thrice passed;

5. At a *S*râddha-dinner for one day;

6. If a death (of relations) or birth has happened, for ten days;

7. On the fourteenth days (of the fortnights), the new moon days, and the Ash*t*akâ days,

---

6. On the tarpa*n*a, comp. chaps. 9 and 10.

7, 2. The translation of âkâlam given in my German edition (Während der betreffenden Zeit) is wrong : comp. the commentary there quoted at p. 150; Gautama XVI, 22 ; Professor Stenzler's note on Pâraskara II, 11, 2.

6. Agha*m* sapi*nd*asodakayor mara*n*am. Nârâya*n*a.

7. According to Nârâya*n*a the *k*a at the end of this Sûtra would

8. And on misty days.

9. And when the teacher has died, for ten days;

10. When he has heard of it, for three days;

11. And (on the death) of those whose family-head he is.

12. On receiving (gifts) as at the Srâddha.

13. On (the death of) a fellow-student;

14. When he has followed (the funeral of) a dead person,

15. And when he has laid down the lumps of flour to the fathers.

16. At night;

17. During twilight;

18. On the full and change of the moon;

19. After sunset;

20. In the neighbourhood of a Sûdra;

21. When the sound of a Sâman is heard;

22. On a burial ground;

---

be intended to convey the meaning that on the pratipad days of each fortnight the study should also be interrupted.

8. The translation of nabhya is quite conjectural. Nârâyaṇa gives a different meaning to this word; comp. p. 150 of the German edition.

11. Âkâryaputrâdayaḥ. Nârâyaṇa.

21. The reason why the recitation of the Rig-veda is forbidden when the sound of a Sâman is heard, becomes manifest, for instance, from Âpastamba I, 10, 7, where the discontinuance of the Veda-study is prescribed when the barking of dogs, the braying of asses, the cry of a wolf, &c., the sound of musical instruments, of weeping, and of a Sâman is heard. Loud sounds like these would disturb the recitation of Rik or Yagus texts. A very curious opinion has been recently brought forward by Professor Aufrecht (see his edition of the Rig-veda, second edition, vol. ii, p. xxxviii) that the incompatibility of the recitation of Rik hymns and of Sâmans 'beruht auf der Kenntniss von der Willkür und der zum Theil unwürdigen Weise, in welcher der alte Text des Rig-veda in diesem Gesangbuche (i. e. the Sâmavedârkika) behandelt ist.'

23. In a wilderness which belongs to the village;

24. In a village where a corpse is;

25. On seeing forbidden sights;

26. On hearing what is forbidden;

27. On smelling a foul smell;

28. If a high wind blows;

29. If a cloud emits (heavy) rain;

30. On a carriage road;

31. And while the sound of a lute is heard;

32. While being on a chariot;

33. (In the neighbourhood) of a dog as (in that) of a Sûdra;

34. Having climbed up a tree;

35. Having descended into a pit;

36. (Immersed) in water;

37. While anybody cries;

38. While suffering bodily pain;

39. While he is naked;

40. Whilst impure with the remnants of food;

41. On a bridge;

42. On the occasion of the shaving of the hair and the beard until the bath;

43. While being rubbed;

44. While bathing;

45. When having sexual intercourse;

46. While being anointed;

47. (In the neighbourhood) of a man who has to touch corpses (a corpse-bearer, &c.), of a woman that has recently been confined, or that has her courses, as (in the neighbourhood) of a Sûdra;

---

23. Grâmâranye grâmam (read, grâma?) evâranyam vanam tatra nâdhîyîta. Nârâyana.

29. Except during the rainy season. Nârâyana.

45. Nârâyana also understands maithuna, and I think that the German translation ought to be corrected accordingly.

48. With veiled hands;

49. In an army;

50. In presence of a Brâhmana who has not had his meal, and of cows (that have eaten nothing);

51. When (these impediments) have passed, let them (continue to) recite (the Veda).

52. Should any of these cases arise against his will, let him (continue to) recite after having held his breath and looked at the sun.

53. (The same rules hold good,) except (those regarding) lightning, thunder, and rain, for (the study of) the Kalpa. During the five months and a half (they have to behave) as while it rains.

54. Thereof it is also said,

55. 'Food, water, roots and fruits, and whatsoever else Srâddha-food there may be: even when he has (only) accepted thereof, the study should be interrupted; the Brâhmana's hand is his mouth; so it is taught.'

---

53. I think that this Sûtra contains two different rules which have to be separated, viz. 1. vidyutstanayitnuvarshavargam kalpe; 2. varshavad ardhashashtheshu. The first of these rules would extend the cases of anadhyâya mentioned in this chapter to the study of the Kalpa-sûtra, except the cases of lightning, rain, &c. The second would refer to the five months and a half following on the Utsarga ceremony (comp. chap. 6, 8), and would imply that during this time the same texts are to be studied or not, according as their study is allowed or forbidden during rainfall: i. e. the study of the Samhitâ is to be discontinued, while that of the Kalpa is allowed to go on. Râmakandra and Nârâyana differ from this interpretation; see p. 151 of the German edition.

55. Comp. Manu IV, 117; Vasishtha XIII, 16.

1. And to (students) who have been duly initiated he shall set forth (the Veda) ;

2. The teacher sitting to the east or to the north, the other one to the south, with his face turned to the north.

3. Or two (students shall be so seated).

4. But more (than two) as there is room (for them).

5. He should not sit on a high seat in presence of a Guru,

6. Nor on the same seat (with him),

7. Nor with outstretched feet,

8. Nor stretching his arms under his knees,

9. Nor leaning his body (against a support),

10. Nor forming with his feet a lap,

11. Nor holding his feet like an axe.

12. After (the student) has said, 'Recite, sir!' the teacher shall cause him to pronounce the syllable OM.

13. 'OM,' replies the other.

14. Thereafter let him recite uninterruptedly.

15. When he has recited, he embraces (his teacher's feet),

16. Says, 'We have finished, sir!' and (goes away) according to his business.

8, 1. Nyâyena sishyadharmena upetâh prâptâs tebhyah sishyebhyo vartayed adhyayanam âkâryah pravartayet. Nârâyana.

11. Karanam kuthârikârûpam kritvâ na pathed ity arthah. Nârâyana.

12. The words adhîhi bho (recite, sir!) are pronounced by the student ; this follows from the passages quoted in the note on II, 5, 10. Nârâyana states that those words are pronounced by the teacher (âkâryo guruh sishyam adhyâpanârtham adhihi bho 3 iti sabdam uktvâ . . .).

17. (He shall say,) 'Leave! Pause meanwhile!' according to some (teachers).

18. Let no one step between (a teacher and students) who study.

19. Let no one change his place during the recitation.

20. Should any fault be committed, let him fast three days, or one day and one night, repeat the Sâvitrî as long as he can, and give something to the Brâhma*n*as; then after an interruption of one day and one night the study should go on.

KHA*ND*A 9.

1. Having bathed,

2. And having submerged himself at the time prescribed for the bath, he satiates the deities :

---

19. The translation of âtmâna*m* viparihâret is conjectural; comp. also Nârâya*n*a's note, p. 151 of the German edition.

9, 1. It is not expressly stated in our text for what occasion the tarpa*n*a (i. e. satiating of deities, *R*ishis, &c. with water-offerings), which is treated of in chap. 9–10, shall be prescribed. The comparison of Baudhâyana II, 9 might perhaps lead us to believe that the ceremony in question is to be performed whenever the sacrificer takes a bath. But the two texts which are most closely connected with ours, the *S*âmbavya and Âsvalâyana G*ri*hyas, seem to point clearly to another conclusion. The *S*âmbavya-sûtra transposes the rules about the tarpa*n*a to the place which would correspond to Sûtra II, 7, 28 of our text. The passage of the *S*âmbavya-sûtra runs thus: mûle ku*nd*a*m* k*ri*tvâ yathoktam adbhi*h* parishi*ñk*aty athemâs (so the MS.) tarpayati Agni*h* Pragâpatir Virûpâksha*h*, &c. It ends: pitara*h* pitâmahâ*h* prapitâmahâ*h* Paila*h* Kaho*l*a*h* Kaushîtaka*h* (sic) Kaho*l*âya Kaushîtakaye svadhâstv iti pratipurusha*h* (sic) pit*ri*m̐s tarpayitvâ. The last words are taken from the Sûtra IV, 6, 6 of our text. Thus there can be no doubt that *S*âmbavya intended to prescribe the tarpa*n*a for the conclusion of the

3. 'Agni may satiate himself; Vâyu may satiate himself; Sûrya may satiate himself; Vishnu may satiate himself; Pragâpati may satiate himself; Virûpâksha may satiate himself; Sahasrâksha may satiate himself; Soma, Brahman, the Vedas, the gods, the *Ri*shis, and all the metres, the word Om, the word Vashat, the Mahâvyâh*ri*tis, the Sâvitrî, the sacrifices, heaven and earth, the Nakshatras, the air, days and nights, the numbers, the twilights, the oceans, the rivers, the mountains, fields, herbs, trees, Gandharvas and Apsaras, the serpents, the birds, the Siddhas, the Sâdhyas, the Vipras, the Yakshas, the Rakshas, the beings that have these (Rakshas, &c.) at their end, may satiate themselves.

'I satiate the *S*ruti; I satiate the Sm*ri*ti; I satiate the firmness; I satiate the delight; I satiate

---

vedâdhyayana. The same can be said of Âsvalâyana, who also by the position which he assigns to the tarpana sections (III, 4) brings it into a similar connection with the vedâdhyayana (see Nârâyana's commentary on Âsv., loc. cit.). We may also refer to the treatise about the study of the Âranyaka, which is appended to the Sânkhâyana-Gri*h*ya as its sixth book; there the tarpana is mentioned quite in the same connection (VI, 6, 10 seq.). I believe, therefore, that in our text, chapters 9 and 10 have found their place here as a sort of supplementary addition to chap. 6, 6, just as in the first book the list of Nakshatras seems likewise appended to the Sûtra I, 25, 5.

According to Nârâyana, snâta*h* in the first Sûtra would refer to the bath which forms part of the Samâvartana ceremony (see III, 1, 1), so that it would be the Gri*h*astha, who has taken the Samâvartana bath, to whom the following rules refer.

3. Comp. the similar lists of Âsvalâyana, Gri*h*ya III, 4; Sâmbavya, quoted in my German edition of Sânkhâyana, p. 153; and Baudhâyana II, 9 (S. B. E., vol. xiv, pp. 252 seq.). The last seems to be the most modern.

It should be observed that the section of the list contained in this Sûtra, as well as that given below, chap. 10, 3, is divided into

the success ; I satiate the thought ; I satiate belief
and insight, and the memory, cows and Brâhma*n*as,
movable and immovable things.   All beings may
satiate themselves !'—so far with the sacrificial cord
suspended over the left shoulder.

KHANDA 10.

1. Now with the sacrificial cord suspended over
the right shoulder,

2. Looking in the direction that belongs to the
Manes (i.e. the south):

3. 'The (*R*ishis) of the hundred (*Ri*k*as), the
(*R*ishis) of the middle (Ma*nd*alas), G*ri*tsamada,
Vi*s*vâmitra, *G*amadagni, Vâmadeva, Atri, Bharad-
vâ*g*a, Vasish*th*a, the Pragâthas, the (*R*ishis) of the
Pavamâna hymns, the (*R*ishis) of the short hymns
and of the long hymns, Sumantu, *G*aimini, Vai-
*s*ampâyana, Paila, the Sûtras, the Bhâshyas, Gârgya,
Babhru, Bâbhravya, Ma*nd*u, Mâ*nd*avya, Gârgî Vâ-

---

two parts, in the first of which the name of the being to be worshipped is given in the nominative case, with the verb t*ri*py a t u,
while in the second it stands in the accusative, with the verb tarpayâmi. The first part of this section contains the names of gods
and of divine beings, such as the rivers, the mountains, &c.; in the
second part are found abstract qualities or notions, such as m a t i,
dh*ri*ti, *s*ruti. Similarly in chapter 10, 3 the Vedic poets, a few
ancient teachers, and wise women, such as Gârgî or Sulabhâ, form
the first part of the list, and then follow, in the accusative case, the
names of such doctors as *S*âṅkhâyana, Â*s*valâyana, *S*âkalya. In
Â*s*valâyana's Sûtra of the first of our two sections only the first
part reoccurs, the second is omitted, while the second section is
found there in its entirety, with the same difference of names
given in the nominative and accusative cases. The conjectures,
however, which I had once based on this difference (see my German
edition, pp. 152, 153) as to the distinction of a more ancient part of
the list, and of later supplements, are perhaps too hazardous.

*k*aknavî, Va*d*avâ Prâtitheyî, Sulabhâ Maitreyî (may satiate themselves).

'(I satiate) Kahola Kaushîtaki, Mahâkaushîtaki, Suya*gñ*a *S*âṅkhâyana, Â*s*valâyana, Aitareya, Mahaitareya, Bhâradvâ*g*a, *G*âtûkar*n*ya, Paiṅgya, Mahâpa'ṅgya, Bâshkala, Gârgya, *S*âkalya, Mâ*nd*ûkeya, Mahâdamatra, Audavâhi, Mahaudavâhi, Sauyâmi, *S*aunaki, *S*âkapû*n*i, Gautami; and whatsoever other teachers there are, may they all satiate themselves.

4. ' The fathers man by man.

5. ' The ancestry of the father may satiate itself.

6. ' The ancestry of the mother may satiate itself.'

KHA*ND*A 11.

1. Let him not look at a naked woman, except during sexual intercourse,

2. Nor (look) at the sun while it rises or sets,

3. At an enemy,

4. At an evil-doer,

5. At a person that has to touch dead bodies.

6. Let him not talk with a woman who has recently been confined or who has her courses,

7. Nor with those (mentioned before).

8. Let him not eat food from which its strength is taken away.

9. Let him not do his work with implements wasted by use.

10. Let him not eat together (with his wife),

11, 1 seq. Rules of conduct for a Snâtaka, i.e. a man who has completed his studentship.

7. Etai*h* pûrvoktai*h* anâptâdibhir na sa*m*vadet. Nârâya*n*a.

10. Nârâya*n*a states that ' with his wife ' is to be supplied to this Sûtra, which indeed is rendered probable through the comparison of Gautama IX, 3=; Manu IV, 43, &c.

11. Nor remnants (of food).

12. Remnants of (food belonging to the) Manes, gods, guests, and servants he may eat.

13. Gleaning ears of corn, receiving alms unasked for, or for which he has asked the good, performing sacrifices for others, are the means of livelihood ;

14. (Of these) each preceding one is the more respectable.

15. Or if (his livelihood) cannot be gained (in one of the ways mentioned), let him follow the occupation of a Vaisya.

16. (He shall be) careful about his duties towards Manes and gods.

17. In due time (he shall) have intercourse with his wife.

18. He shall not lie down (to sleep) in the day-time,

19. Nor during the first or the last watch of the night.

20. Let him not sit on the bare ground.

21. He shall constantly perform the prescribed duties regarding the use of water.

22. (And constantly) have his sacrificial cord suspended over his left shoulder.

23. Let him not abandon his teacher,

24. Except on (his teacher's) command,

25. Or with (his) permission.

KHANDA 12.

1. Every day he shall respectfully salute his teacher,

---

11. Here also Nârâyana understands bhâryâyâ bhukta-sesham.

15. Comp. Professor Bühler's note on Gautama X, 5, S. B. E., vol. ii, p. 225.

19. Râtreh pûrvaprahare râtreh paskimaprahare ka. Nârâyana.

2. And his Gurus,

3. A *S*rotriya when meeting him,

4. When he returns from a journey, (also) one who is not a *S*rotriya.

5. In the words, 'I am N.N., sir!' pronouncing his own name, crossing his hands (so as to seize with his right hand the right foot, and with his left hand the left of the other person).

6. (The person who has been thus saluted, in reply addressing him with his name,) 'N.N.!' and seizing his hands, pronounces a wish to him.

7. Let him not go to a sacrifice without being chosen (thereto).

8. And let him beware of (doing) wrong.

9. Let him not go to assemblies of people.

10. If he has come upon (such assemblies), let him not point out (anything evil) against (anybody).

11. He shall not be a reviler, nor slanderous, nor a wanderer from house to house, nor a prattler.

12. He shall not walk alone,

13. Nor naked,

14. Nor with veiled hands.

15. Gods'-houses (he shall walk round) keeping the right side turned to them.

12, 5. Nârâya*n*a : 'As to how that respectful salutation (abhi-vâdana) should be performed, he says . . . with his own right hand he touches the right foot of the Â*k*ârya or other person (whom he salutes), and with his left hand the left foot (comp. Manu II, 72) (and says), "I am N. N. (amuka*s*arman) of the Gotra N. N., sir ! I offer my respectful salutation !"'

6. 'The Â*k*ârya or other person seizes the hands of the saluting person,' &c. Nârâya*n*a.

10. See Nârâya*n*a's commentary, p. 154 of the German edition.

16. Let him not run.

17. Let him not spit.

18. Let him not scratch himself.

19. Let him not look on urine and excrements.

20. Let him sit with veiled head,

21. Not on the bare (ground),

22. If he has only one garment, suspending his sacrificial cord on his ear,

23. Not turning his face to the sun,

24. Nor his rump,

25. In the day-time with his face to the north, at night to the south.

26. He shall not (eject) phlegm into water, nor in the neighbourhood (of water).

27. He shall not climb up a tree.

28. He shall not look down into a well.

29. He shall not go to an execution-place,

30. And in no case to a cemetery.

31. Let him bathe day by day with his clothes on.

32. When he has bathed, let him put on another garment before he is dry.

KHANDA 13.

1. Under (the Nakshatra) Rohinî he shall have the ploughing done.

2. Before it is done, he shall offer at the eastern boundary of his field a Bali to Heaven and Earth.

3. With a verse sacred to Heaven and Earth and with the words, 'Adoration to Heaven and Earth!' (he performs his) worship (to Heaven and Earth).

---

16. According to Nârâyana we should have to supply, 'while it is raining,' which is countenanced by a number of parallel texts, for instance, Âsv.-Grihya III, 9, 6.

4. When the plough is being put into motion first, let a Brâhmana touch the plough reciting this (verse), 'For luck may us the plough-shares' (Rig-veda IV, 57, 8).

5. 'Through the lord of the field'—with (this hymn) (Rig-veda IV, 57), verse by verse, to the different directions (of the sky), from left to right, worship is done.

KHANDA 14.

1. When going to cross water, he performs the Svastyayana (ceremony for lucky progress).

2. He sacrifices thrice with his joined hands full of water into the waters, with the words, 'Adoration to the Sea, the child of the reed! Adoration to Varuna, the lord of righteousness! Adoration to all rivers!'—

3. Murmuring, ' May Visvakarman, the father of them all, relish the food offered.'

4. Against the stream for flowing (waters); up into the air for standing ones.

5. Should he while crossing apprehend any danger, let him murmur the hymn of Vasishtha, ' The eldest of which is the sea' (Rig-veda VII, 49); this (will serve to him as) a boat.

KHANDA 15.

1. The Sravana (oblation) he offers on the full moon day that falls under (the Nakshatra) Sravish-thâs, of the flour of fried barley, or of cooked food,

2. With (the words), ' To Vishnu svâhâ! To (the Nakshatra) Sravana svâhâ! To the full moon of Srâvana svâhâ! To the rainy season svâhâ!'

3. Having established the (sacred) domestic fire outside, and having mixed together fried grain and the flour of fried barley with butter, he sacrifices—

4. With (the words), 'To the Lord of the celestial Serpents svâhâ! To the celestial Serpents svâhâ!'

5. Having placed to the north of the fire a new water-pot on eastward-pointed, fresh Kusa grass,

6. With (the words), 'May the Lord of the celestial Serpents wash himself! May the celestial Serpents wash themselves!'—he pours water into it.

7. With (the words), 'May the Lord of the celestial Serpents comb himself! May the celestial Serpents comb themselves!'—he makes movements with a comb.

8. With (the words), 'May the Lord of the celestial Serpents paint himself! May the celestial Serpents paint themselves!'—he pours out portions of paint.

9. With (the words), 'May the Lord of the celestial Serpents tie (this) to (himself)! May the celestial Serpents tie (this) to themselves!'—he offers flowers.

10. With (the words), 'May the Lord of the celestial Serpents clothe himself! May the celestial Serpents clothe themselves!'—he offers a thread.

11. With (the words), 'May the Lord of the celestial Serpents anoint (his eyelashes)! May the celestial Serpents anoint (their eyelashes)!'—he spirts out (small portions of collyrium) with a young Kusa shoot.

12. With (the words), 'May the Lord of the celestial Serpents look (at himself)! May the celestial Serpents look (at themselves)!'—he makes them look in a mirror.

15, 7. For this signification of pha*n*a, comp. *K*ullavagga V, 2, 3.

13. With (the words), 'Lord of the celestial Serpents, this is thy Bali! Celestial Serpents, this is your Bali!'—he makes a Bali-offering.

14. In the same way for the aërial (Serpents).

15. For those dwelling in the directions (of the horizon).

16. For the terrestrial ones.

17. (He repeats these Mantras) thrice each time, the first (part) with higher voice each time,

18. The second (part) with lower voice each time.

19. In this way he shall offer day by day with the spoon, in small portions, a Bali of the flour of fried barley with water, down to the Pratyavarohana (or the ceremony of the 'redescent'), at night, keeping silence.

20. And (his wife) shall put (it) down silently.

21. The close of the ceremony is the same as the beginning.

22. With (the verse), 'The good protectress' (Rig-veda X, 63, 10), let him ascend the (high) couch.

17, 18. The text has ukkaistarâm—ukkaistarâm, and nik-aistarâm—nikaistarâm. Nârâyana (comp.the text of his scholion, p. 155 of the German edition) understands this in a different way; he says that in the water-pot mentioned in the fifth Sûtra two different sthânas are to be distinguished, a higher part of it and a lower (uttarâdharatayâ). Now when the sacrificer, for instance, as prescribed in Sûtra 6, invites the Lord of the celestial Serpents, and the celestial Serpents to wash themselves, the pouring out of water would have to be performed first thrice for the Lord of the celestial Serpents in the higher place, then thrice for the celestial Serpents in the lower place.

19. On the Pratyavarohana see chap. 17.

20. Nârâyana : vâgyamayuktâ yagamânapatnî evam balidravyâdikam upasâdayet.

22. 'From the Srâvanî till the Âgrahâyanî (see chap. 17, 1) one shall not sleep on the ground out of fear of the snakes.' Nârâyana.

KHANDA 16.

1. On the full moon day of Âsvayuga a milk-rice oblation to Indra.

2. Having sacrificed Âgya with (the words), ' To the two Asvins svâhâ! To the two Asvayug svâhâ! To the full moon of Âsvayuga svâhâ! To the autumn svâhâ! To Pasupati svâhâ! To the tawny one svâhâ!'—

3. He shall sacrifice a mixture of curds and butter with this hymn, 'The cows came hither' (Rig-veda VI, 28), verse by verse.

4. That night they let the calves join their mothers.

5. Then feeding of the Brâhmanas.

KHANDA 17.

1. On the Âgrahâyanî full moon day he shall re-descend,

2. (Or) under (the Nakshatra) Rohinî, or under the Proshthapadâs.

3. In the morning, having taken a handfull of Samî leaves, Madhûka flowers, reeds, Apâmârga plants, and of Sirîsha, Udumbara, Kusa shoots, and jujube fruits, and an earth-clod (taken) out of a furrow,

4. Having put (all that) into a water-pot,

16, 3. Ghritamisram dadhi prishâtakam.   Nârâyana.   Comp. the Grihya-samgraha II, 59.

17, 1. The Pratyavarohana (i. e. redescent) here described is the ceremony performed at the end of the time during which sleeping on high bedsteads is prescribed (chap. 15, 22). Beginning from the Srâvanî full moon till the Pratyavarohana, the offerings to the Serpents mentioned above have to be repeated every day (chap. 15, 19); the Pratyavarohana is the concluding ceremony of these rites devoted to the Serpents.

5. And, after he has quickly repeated the Mahâ-vyâh*r*itis and the Sâvitrî, having repeatedly immersed (it) therein with this hymn, 'May he burn away from us pain' (Rig-veda I, 97), he shall drive away the evil from the persons standing under his protection, from left to right, and pour out (the water) to the north.

6. A Madhuparka is the fee for the sacrifice.

KHANDA 18.

1. 'May summer, winter and spring, autumn and rainy season be well-ordered to us. May we be under the safe protection of these seasons, and may they last (to us) through a hundred years. Svâhâ!

'Beat away, O white one, with thy foot, with the fore-foot and with the hind-foot, these seven daughters of Varu*n*a and all that belong to the king's tribe. Svâhâ!

'To the white one, the son of Vidârva svâhâ! To Vidârva svâhâ! To Takshaka Vaisâleya svâhâ! To Visâla svâhâ!'—with (these words) he sacrifices (oblations) of Â*g*ya.

2. 'May a good winter, a good spring, a good summer be bestowed (on us). May the rains be to us happy rains; may the autumns be blessed to us.'

3. With (the verse), 'Blessing on us, Mitra' (Rig-veda I, 90, 9), he sweeps (the floor) with a Palâ*s*a branch,

---

5. Sara*n*yebhyo g*r*ihebhya*h* (read, g*r*ihyebhya*h*) sarvebhya*h* sakâsât, &c. Nârâya*n*a.

18, 1. This chapter continues the description of the Pratyavaro-ha*n*a begun in the preceding chapter.

Râ*g*abândhavai*h*, as our text has, should be corrected into râ*g*abândhavî*h*; comp. Âsv. II, 3, 3.

4. Sprinkles (it with water) with (the verse), 'From the sea the wave' (Rig-veda IV, 58, 1),

5. And spreads out a layer (of straw) with (the verse), 'Be soft, O earth' (Rig-veda I, 22, 15).

6. They then lie down on their sides, the eldest one to the right hand—

7. With (the words), 'In the Brahman I establish myself, in the Kshatra,' on (their) right (sides);

8. With (the words), 'Among the horses I establish myself, among the cows,' on (their) left (sides);

9. With (the words), 'Among the cattle I establish myself, in prosperity,' on (their) right (sides);

10. With (the words), 'Among offspring I establish myself, in food,' on (their) left (sides).

11. With (the verse), 'Arise, the living' (Rig-veda I, 113, 16), they arise.

12. During that night they lie on that layer.

13. Afterwards where they like.

KHANDA 19.

1. On the full moon day of Kaitra,

2. (Taking) jujube leaves, and making of meal (images) of couples of animals as it happens.

3. A figure with prominent navel to Indra and Agni.

4. Balls to Rudra.

5. According to custom the Nakshatras and (their ?) images (?). According to custom the Nakshatras and (their ?) images (?).

Here ends the Fourth Adhyâya.

19, 2–5. Several points in the translation of these Sûtras are uncertain. See the extracts from the commentary of Nârâyana, pp. 156 seq. of the German edition.

1. Now when he intends to set out on a journey, he makes (his sacred) fire enter into himself, (or) into the two kindling sticks, or into (an ordinary) log of wood,

2. Once with (the text), 'Come, enter into my Prâ*n*as,' twice silently.

3. Or with (the verse), 'This is thy womb' (Rigveda III, 29, 10) he warms the two kindling sticks,

4. Or an (ordinary log of) wood.

5. And before sunset the kindling (by attrition),

6. And at the time of the Vai*s*vadeva sacrifice.

7. Having carried a common fire to a place that has been smeared (with cowdung), which is elevated, and

1, 1. The ceremony of Samâroha*n*a, by which the duties towards the sacred fire are suspended, by causing the fire to 'enter' into the sacrificer's body, or into the two Ara*n*is, or into another piece of wood, is already mentioned in several passages of the Brâhma*n*a texts; comp. the quotations given by Professor Weber, Indische Studien, IX, 311. Comp. besides Âsvalâyana-*S*rauta-sûtra III, 10; *S*âṅkhâyana-*S*raut. II, 17. The Samâroha*n*a into the sacrificer's own body is done by warming the hands at the sacred fire; see Âsv., loc. cit., Sûtra 6. In the *S*âṅkhâyana-*S*rauta-sûtra the corresponding rule, which regards there of course the Âhitâgni, runs thus, 'If he performs the Samâroha*n*a, he warms his hands at the Gârhapatya fire, and then touches his Prâ*n*as with the words, "Come, enter into my Prâ*n*as."' On the two other cases, see the Sûtras 3 and 4. Sûtras 2, 3, 5 are taken word for word from the *S*rauta-sûtra.

2. This Sûtra refers only to the case where he causes the fire to enter into himself.

5. Comp. the commentary on Âsv.-*S*raut., loc. cit. 8. He makes the fire redescend from his body or from the Ara*n*is by performing the Manthana (kindling the fire by attrition of the Ara*n*is).

7. The Mantra alluded to here is given in the *S*rauta-sûtra. It

which has been sprinkled (with water), he makes (the
sacred fire) redescend (from its receptacle, with the
formula), ' Redescend !'

8. If the fire goes out, he sacrifices the two
Sarvaprâya*s*kitta oblations (oblations for general
expiation) and (other oblations) with (the formulas),
' Protect us, Agni, that we may prosper. Svâhâ!
Protect us that we may obtain all wealth. Svâhâ!
The sacrifice protect, O resplendent one! Svâhâ!
Protect everything, O hundredfold wise one.
Svâhâ!'

9. In the case of a breach of his vow let him fast
and sacrifice (an oblation) of Âg*y*a with (the verse),
' Thou, Agni, art the lord of the vow' (Rig-veda
VIII, 11, 1).

KHANDA 2.

1. Now about (the consecration of) ponds, wells,
and tanks.

2. In the bright fortnight, or on an auspicious
Tithi,

3. Having cooked barley-grains with milk,

4. He shall sacrifice with the two (verses), ' Thou

---

runs thus, ' Redescend, O G*â*tavedas; carry again offerings to the
gods, knowing us. Long life, offspring, wealth bestow on us;
uninjured shine in our dwelling !'

8–9. These Sûtras stand in no connection with the Samârohana
treated of before.

On the two Sarvaprâya*s*kitta oblations see above, I, 9, 12 and the
note there.

The vow spoken of in Sûtra 9 Nârâyana refers to the restrictions
regarding the food which the sacrificer and his wife are to eat on
the Upavasatha days, connected with the festivals of the full and
new moon.

2, 1 seq. Comp. Âsvalâyana-Parisish*t*a IV, 9.

hast us, Agni' (Rig-veda IV, 1, 4. 5), (and with the
verses), 'We propitiate thy wrath' (I, 24, 14), 'This
my prayer, Varu*n*a' (I, 25, 19), 'Loosen the highest,
Varu*n*a' (I, 24, 15), 'This prayer of the man who
exercises himself' (VIII, 42, 3),

5. (And with the words), 'The domestic one, he
who goes away from the house, the refreshing one,
he who goes into the kennel, he who dwells in the
kennel, he who comes out of it, the greedy one, the
destroyer of enemies'—to the different directions (of
the horizon), beginning with that belonging to Varu*n*a (i. e. the west), from left to right.

6. In the centre he makes oblations with milk with
(the verses), 'Having eyes all around' (Rig-veda
X, 81, 3), 'This has Vish*n*u' (Rig-veda I, 22, 17),

7. Plunging (into the water) with (the verse),
'Whatever here' (Rig-veda VII, 89, 5).

8. A cow and a pair of clothes is the fee for the
sacrifice.

9. Then feeding of the Brâhma*n*as.

KHANDA 3.

1. Now at (the consecration of) a garden : having
established the (sacred) fire (in that garden),

2. (And) having prepared a mess of cooked food,

3. He shall sacrifice with (the formulas), 'To

---

5. These are names of Agni dwelling in the waters; see
Pâraskara II, 6, 10 ; Mantrabrâhma*n*a I, 7, 1. Several of the
names are here misspelled ; thus Gr*i*hya, Apagr*i*hya should be, no
doubt, Gohya, Upagohya, which is the reading given in Pâraskara,
loc. cit.

3, 1 seqq. Comp. Âsvalâyana-Pari*s*ish*t*a IV, 10. Nârâya*n*a uses
for the ceremony here described the expressions Ârâmapratish*th*â,
Ârâmotsarga.

Vish*n*u svâhâ! To Indra and Agni svâhâ! To
Visvakarman svâhâ!' (and with the verses), 'Whom
the men' (Rig-veda III, 8, 6 seq.), verse by verse.

4. He recites over (the garden), 'O tree with thy
hundred branches' (Rig-veda III, 8, 11).

5. The fee for the sacrifice is gold.

KHANDA 4.

1. Now if a half-monthly sacrifice has not been
performed, one or the other of them, then a mess of
rice (is to be offered as an expiation),

2. With (the words), 'To Agni Vaisvânara svâhâ!
To Agni Tantumat svâhâ!'

3. In the case of an intermission of the (morning
or evening) oblations—

4. (He shall make expiatory oblations), in the
evening with (the formula), 'Enlightener of the
darkness, adoration! Svâhâ!'

5. In the morning with (the formula), 'Enlightener
of the morning, adoration! Svâhâ!'

6. After he has sacrificed as many oblations as there
had been sacrifices (left out), the sacrifice (itself goes
on) as (stated) above.

KHANDA 5.

1. If a dove or an owl sits down (on his house),

2. Let him sacrifice with (the hymn), 'O gods, the
dove' (Rig-veda X, 165), verse by verse.

4, 6. Nârâya*n*a: 'After he has thus taken and sacrificed as many
Sruvas full of Âgya as there were sacrifices omitted through his
guilt, the morning and evening sacrifices have to be performed as
(stated) above (I, 3, 10) with oblations of rice or barley.'

3. If he has seen a bad dream or an occurrence boding misfortune,

4. Or when the cawing of a crow is heard in (the dead of) night,

5. And in the case of other prodigies,

6. Let him cook rice-grains with milk,

7. With the milk of a cow that has a calf of the same colour (with her own),

8. But in no case of a black (cow),

9. And let him sacrifice with the night-hymn (Rig-veda X, 127), verse by verse.

10. Having eaten the remnants of those oblations with the Mahâvyâhritis,

11. And having recited over his ears (the verse), 'Blessing with our ears' (Rig-veda I, 89, 8),

12. And over himself (the verse), 'May a hundred autumns be before us, ye gods' (ibid. 9),

13. He shall give something to the Brâhmanas.

KHANDA 6.

1. When a disease has befallen him,

2. Let him offer boiled rice-grains with Gave-dhukâ-grass with (the hymn), 'These (prayers) to Rudra, the strong one, with braided hair' (Rig-veda I, 114), verse by verse.

KHANDA 7.

1. If (his wife) gives birth to a child, without the Sîmantonnayana having been performed,

2. (Or if) the Gâtakarman has not been performed (for the child),

---

7, 1. On the Sîmantonnayana, see 1, 22.
2. The Gâtakarman has been described I, 24.

3. He places, when ten days have elapsed since (the delivery), the little child in the mother's lap,

4. And after he has sacrificed with the Mahâvyâh*ri*tis, the sacrifice (that had been omitted, is performed) as (stated) above.

KHANDA 8.

1. If a post puts forth shoots,

2. Let him prepare a mess of cooked food and offer the boiled rice with the two (verses), ' In that way bringing forth deeds' (*S*rauta-sûtra III, 17, 1), ' Of tawny shape, weighty, a giver of vigour' (Rigveda II, 3, ·9).

3. Should the pot for the Pra*n*îtâ water, the Â*g*ya-pot, or any other earthen (vessel) be damaged and leak,

4. He sacrifices the two Sarvaprâya*s*itta oblations and recites the three verses, ' He who without' (Rig-veda VIII, 1, 12 seq.), over the broken (vessel).

5. Should the two (Ku*s*a blades which are used as) strainers be spoiled before the completion of the sacrifice,

6. Let him sacrifice the Sarvaprâya*s*itta and make new ones with (the verse), ' In the water, Agni' (Rigveda VIII, 43, 9).

KHANDA 9.

1. Now (follows) the Sapi*nd*ikara*n*a.

---

3. On the ten days, comp. I, 25, 1 and the note there.
8, 3. On the Pra*n*îtâ water, see above, I, 8, 8. 25.
4. Comp. I, 9, 12 and the note there.
5. See I, 8, 14 seqq.   6. See Sûtra 4.
9, 1 seqq. Comp. above, IV, 3 and the notes there.

2. Let him fill four water-pots (for the Manes) from the father upwards,

3. And prepare in the same way lumps (of flour),

4. And let him distribute the first lump on the (other) three with (the verses), ' They who commonly, concordantly (dwell) in Yama's realm, the fathers : for them be space, freedom, adoration, sacrifice established among the gods.

' They who commonly, harmoniously (dwell), the living among the living, mine : may their prosperity fall to my lot in this world through a hundred years '—

And with the two (verses), 'Equal the design' (Rig-veda X, 191, 3. 4).

5. In the same way the vessels with Argha water.

6. In the same way for the mother, for a brother, and for a wife that has died before (her husband), adding (the lump belonging to that person) to those (other) lumps.

KHANDA 10.

1. If the bees make honey in his house,

2. Let him fast and sacrifice a hundred and eight pieces of Udumbara wood, which are besmeared with curds, honey, and ghee, with the two (verses), ' No (harm) to us in our offspring' (Rig-veda I, 114, 8. 9).

3. And let him murmur the hymn, ' For welfare may Indra and Agni' (Rig-veda VII, 35); and (the same hymn should be used) at all (ceremonies), such

---

2. On these four vessels, see IV, 3, 4 seq.

5. These are the vessels mentioned in the second Sûtra.

10, 3. This is a supplementary rule belonging to the exposition of the general type of sacrifice. On the ' Pratisruta' sacrifice, see I, 7, 1 seqq.; I, 9, 19.

as that of the sacrifice after assent has been declared (see above, I, 7, 1).

4. After he has sacrificed seventeen one span long pieces of Palâsa wood, he then seizes the Sruva.

5. Fifteen at the full and new moon sacrifices.

6. At the Ash*t*akâ ceremony in the middle of the rainy season there may optionally be three (pieces of wood); the sacrifice as at the Pit*ri*ya*gñ*a.

KHA*ND*A 11.

1. If an anthill arises in his house, the house should be abandoned.

2. Then, after having fasted three nights (and days), he should perform the great expiation.

Here ends the Fifth Adhyâya.

---

4. See I, 9, 1. 3.

6. Comp. III, 13, 1 with the note.

11, 2. Nârâya*n*a understands the 'great expiation' as a rite directed to Gane*s*a and to the planets (comp. Yâ*gñ*avalkya I, 276 seq., 292, &c.); that this ceremony was known already to the author of this Sûtra seems very doubtful. Another 'mahâsânti' is frequently mentioned in the Kau*s*ika-sûtra (quoted in Böhtlingk-Roth's Dictionary); comp. my German edition of *S*ânkhâyana, p. 159.

1. Now, after having paid reverence to Brahman, to the Brahmarishi, to (those who descend from) Brahman's womb, to Indra, Pragâpati, Vasishtha, Vâmadeva, Kahola Kaushîtaki, Mahâkaushîtaki, Suyagña Sânkhâyana, Âsvalâyana, Aitareya, Mahaitareya, Kâtyâyana, Sâtyâyana, Sâkalya, Babhru, Bâbhravya, Mandu, Mândavya, and to all the teachers of the past, we will henceforth explain the rules for the Âranyaka as forming the subject of Svâdhyâya (private recitation of a text).

2. The teacher abstains through one day and one night from sexual intercourse and from eating flesh.

3. Raw flesh, a Kandâla, a woman that has lately been confined, or that has her courses, seeing blood or persons whose hands have been cut off: (these persons and things he shall know form) impediments for the study.

4. And of the corpse-like (animals?).

5. Those which enter (their dens?) with the mouth first (?).

1, 1 seqq. Comp. the general remarks on this sixth book in the Introduction, p. 11.

For the names in the opening invocation, comp. above, IV, 10; on the Vratas and the study of the different Âranyaka sections chiefly treated of in this book, see above, II, 11. 12, and the Introduction, p. 8.

2. Comp. II, 11, 6.

3–5. Comp. II, 12, 10, and the note of Nârâyana, p. 160 of the German edition.

6. When he has vomited, or when his beard has been shaved,

7. When he has eaten flesh or partaken of a *S*râddha or birth dinner,

8. During the days that immediately follow on (days of) study in the village,

9. Three nights (and days), if (he has been) put out of order,

10. (Or has been violently) seized by others,

11. And during the second half of the days that precede (?) the Parvan days,

12. And if fire-flames, lightning, thunder, (heavy) rains, and great clouds appear,

13. And if a storm (blows) that carries away pebbles, as long as that lasts.

2, 1. During four months after the full moon of Âshâ*dh*a let him not study.

2. Especially the *S*akvarî verses (are concerned by what has been declared). Such are the rules.

KHANDA 2.

3. Let them go to a clean spot in the north-eastern direction, that receives its light from the east.

4. The drawing of water (should be done) before sunrise,

---

6. Comp. IV, 7, 42. See also Ait. Âra*n*yaka V, 3, 9.

7. Comp. IV, 7, 5.

2, 2. It seems to me that this Sûtra should be divided into two (after *s*akvarya*h*), so that the words iti niyamâ*h* would correspond to iti bhâshikam, chap. 2, 13.

3. Comp. II, 12, 11. Perhaps the Petersburg Dictionary is right in proposing for prâg*g*yotisham the translation, vor Anbruch des Lichtes. Nârâya*n*a says, prâk purastât *g*yotir yasmin tam ... pradesam.

5. And the entering into the circle with this verse, 'She who smells of salve' (Rig-veda X, 146, 6).

6. The circle should have its entrance to the east or to the north; it should be (praised as) excellent among the people, not too spacious, not too narrow.

7. The final expiation (should extend) to the Vâmadevya.

8. And the invitation to resume the recitation (is done in the following way):

9. After they have sipped water that stands outside the circle,

10. Let them resume the recitation, having performed the expiation.

11. If the vessel used in the expiation is damaged, sprinkling (with water forms) the expiatory act (to be performed for it).

12. (That) sprinkling, however, (one should perform) holding gold or a bunch of Darbha grass in his hand.

13. So far what pertains to the general rules.

KHANDA 3.

1. Now after they have entered the circle—

2. The teacher sits down with his face to the east, the others, according to their rank, (sit down) towards the south, with their faces to the north.

---

5. The Mandala is a circular space marked by a line of water.

6. I am doubtful whether we should read vâ ganâgrîyam and translate as I have done in accordance with the note of Nârâyana, or if the reading should be vâ ganâgrîyam, 'not in the presence of people,' so that ganâgriya would mean ganânâm agre.

7. On the expiation (sânti) comp. chap. 3, 12.

3, 2, 3. Comp. IV, 8, 2-4.

3. If that is impossible, with their faces to all directions.

4. Let them expect the rising of the sun,

5. And when they behold it in its splendour,

6. Let them with (the words), 'Recite, sir!' seize with their hands, holding the right hand uppermost, the feet of the teacher, which have been washed, with the right (hand) the right (foot), with the left the left,

7. And having then put (the hands) into the vessel used for the expiation, into water in which pieces of Dûrvâ stalks are, let them begin their study, when their hands have ceased to drip.

8. This is the rite. But when they are tired, let one of them bring it about that the vessel used for the expiation be not empty.

9. And all (should do so) at the beginning and the end of (each) Adhyâya.

10. (All) that is done continuously, without interruption.

11. Now the expiation.

12. The syllable OM, the Mahâvyâhritis, the Sâvitrî, the Rathantara, the Brihat, the Vâmadevya; Brihat and Rathantara with repetition and Kakubh-forming.

---

6. Comp. above, II, 5, 10, &c.

7. The translation of apinvamânaih pânibhih is conjectural. Nârâyana's explanation of apinvamâna by asamsrishta is inadmissible.

10. Nârâyana explains this Sûtra in the following way. If it is impossible, for any reason, to recite the whole text, only the beginning and the concluding words of each Adhyâya (see Sûtra 9) are to be repeated; and these should be recited without interruption so as to form one continual text.

12. Comp. above, III, 4, 5.

13. These (holy words and verses) are (thus) made to attain (the number of) ten.

14. 'Of decades consists the Virâg'—thus says the Brâhmana.

KHANDA 4.

1. 'Unerring mind, vigorous eye (is) the sun, the noblest of the stars. Inauguration, do no harm to me!'—with (these words) they look at Savitri (i. e. the sun).

---

13. The Gâyatrî is one verse; the Rathantara and the Brihat are Pragâthas which are changed in the usual way into Trikas; the Vâmadevya is one Trika: thus the number of ten is obtained.

14. Kaush. Brâhmana 17, 3; 19, 5.

4, 1. The formula 'Adabdham manah,' &c. has to be recited before each of the single Âranyaka texts (the Sakvarî verses, the Mahâvrata, &c.); to this formula are added, before or after it, as the case may be, other texts specified in the Sûtras 2-8. Of these there can be no doubt about the meaning of Sûtras 7, 8, treating of the introductory formulas of the Samhitâ section (Kaush. Âr. VII-VIII) and of the Mantha section (ibid. IX): before the text adabdham, &c. are to be added, in the first case the formula ritam vadishyâmi, &c., in the second case two Rikas addressed to Savitri. These formulas and verses have been received into the Âranyaka text and are found there in the order here stated, at the beginning of books VII and IX. The meaning of the words samhitânâm tu pûrvam (Sûtra 7) having thus been established, I can see no reason why we should not interpret the words sakvarînâm tu pûrvam (Sûtra 3) quite in the same way. Thus the introductory benediction for the recital of the Sakvarî verses would consist, firstly of the verses stated in Sûtra 4, then of the formula adabdham, &c.; those verses would have to be repeated again after the Sakvarî verses (end of Sûtra 4). The recitation of the Mahâvrata (Sûtras 1, 2) and of the Upanishads (Sûtra 5) is preceded by adabdham, &c., and then by the four verses stated in Sûtra 2. The interpretation which Nârâyana gives of this Sûtra is not quite the same as that which I have here proposed; see p. 163 of the German edition.

2. One (verse), 'You both the gladdening one'
(Rig-veda X, 131, 4), and the three (verses), 'Blessing to us on the paths' (Rig-veda X, 63, 15-17)
(are to be repeated before the recitation) of the
Mahâvrata (chapter).

3. But (at that) of the Sakvarî (verses) before
(the formula mentioned in the first Sûtra):

4. The three Trikas, 'To him, the thirsty one'
(Rig-veda VI, 42, 1-3), 'The wealthiest (Soma), O
wealthy one' (VI, 44, 1-3), 'Him who does no harm
to you' (VI, 44, 4-6), (the verse), 'To him, to him
the sap of the herb' (VI, 42, 4), (and the verse),
'Verily thou art a hero' (VIII, 81, 28)—thus for the
Sakvarî (verses) before and afterwards.

5. Now for the Upanishad (texts)—

6. The same (recitation) as for the Mahâvrata.

7. For the Saṃhitâs, however, before (the text
given in the first Sûtra the formula has to be
recited), 'I shall speak right, I shall speak truth
(&c.)'—this is the difference (in the case of the
Saṃhitâs).

8. Now for the Mantha the two verses (have to
be recited) before (the formula given in the first
Sûtra), 'This we entreat of Savitar,' 'That glorious
(splendour) of Savitar' (Rig-veda V, 82, 1; III,
62, 10).

---

4. According to the reading of some MSS. we should have to
translate, or (the verse), 'Verily,' &c.

7. On the Saṃhitâs (Kaush. Âr. VII, VIII) see Max Müller, Rig-
veda Prâtisâkhya, pp. 4 seq.; Ait. Âraṇyaka III (pp. 305 seqq., ed.
Bibl. Ind.; Sacred Books of the East, I, pp. 247 seq.).

8. Regarding the description of the Mantha sacrifice (Kaush. Âr.
IX) which has to be performed by one who wishes to attain great-
ness, comp. Satap. Brâhmaṇa XIV, 9, 2; Khând. Up. V, 2, 4;
Sacred Books of the East, I, p. 75.

9. With (the formula), 'Unerring mind' (see Sûtra 1), then follow the expiatory formulas that belong to the (different) sections.

10. (All) this on one day.

KHANDA 5.

Khanda 4, 11. Now if the time for rising has come, they drive away (all) evil,

12. Perform the standing expiation,

13. And look at the sun with (the words), 'From here I take out the brightness(?).'

Khanda 5, 1. 'That (I place) within myself'— with (these words they turn their thoughts to the universal) Self that is placed (within themselves?)— three times repeated(?).

2. With (the formula), 'May happiness rejoice in me and glory; may happiness rejoice with me and glory;—

3. 'Together with Indra, with the hosts, with power, with glory, with strength I will rise'—he rises up.

11, 12. Nârâyana has the following note : 'The evil which is attached to their body, such as dirt, they drive away, i. e. they remove it by means of their reciting (of the sacred texts), and then they perform the standing expiation which has been declared above, which begins with the syllable Om and with the Mahâvyâhritis' (see chap. 3, 12).

5, 1. Nârâyana says that dadhe is supplied to this Mantra from the preceding Sûtra, and so indeed the Mantra is given in the Aitareya recension. The translation of abhinihitam trir hitam is merely tentative; see Nârâyana's note, p. 165, of the German edition. Perhaps abhinihitam should be taken in its grammatical value, and the Sûtra should be translated, '"That (I place) into myself (âtmani)"—with these words (they look) at themselves, pronouncing (the word âtmani) with Abhinidhâna, three times repeated (?).' On abhinidhâna, comp. Professor Max Müller's edition of the Rig-veda Prâtisâkhya, pp. cxvii seqq.

4. 'May happiness rise to me; may glory rise to me'—when he has risen.

5. 'Hereby I shake off the hater, the rival, the evil one, and the bringer of misfortune'—with (this formula) having shaken the end of the garment,—

6. The hymn, 'Away those to the east' (Rig-veda X, 131), the two (verses), 'And may Indra have mercy upon us' (II, 41, 11. 12), the one (verse), 'Of what we are in fear, O Indra' (VIII, 50, 13)—(when these texts have been murmured), they look with (the verse), 'A ruler indeed, great art thou' (X, 152, 1) to the east; with (the verse), 'The giver of bliss' (X, 152, 2) to the south, turned to the right; with (the verse), 'Away the Rakshas' (X, 152, 3) to the west; with (the verse), 'Destroy, O Indra, our' (X, 152, 4) to the north, turned to the left; with (the verse), 'Away, O Indra' (X, 152, 5) to the sky, turned to the right.

KHANDA 6.

1. Having worshipped the Sun with (the verses), 'Savitrî from the west,' 'This eye' (Rig-veda X, 36, 14; VII, 66, 16),

2. They turn away, come back, sit down.

3. With (the words), 'As the water is appeased'— they draw water out of the vessel used for the expiation,

4. Pour it out on the ground,

5. Spread (some) of that (water over the ground) with (the words), 'As the earth (is appeased),'—

6, 2. Nârâyana explains vyâvartamânâh by parâvartamânadharmayuktâh.

5. Perhaps we should read asyâm (scil. prithivyâm) abhi-

6. He (then) smears it on his right shoulder with (the words), ' Thus may peace dwell in me.'

7. In the same way a second time.

8. In the same way a third time.

9. ' Piece by piece thou art produced ; piece by piece thou risest up; bring welfare to us, O house !'— with (this text they) take pieces of Dûrvâ stalks (out of the vessel of water), put them on their heads,

10. (And make water-offerings with the formulas), ' May Agni satiate himself ; may Vâyu satiate himself; may Sûrya satiate himself; may Vishnu satiate himself; may Pragâpati satiate himself; may Virû-pâksha satiate himself; may Sahasrâksha satiate himself ; may all beings satiate themselves.'

11. (Then) Sumantu, Gaimini, Vaisampâyana, Paila, and the other teachers (receive their offerings).

12. (Then) every one (worships in the same way) his fathers.

13. With (the text), ' To the sea you' (Sraut. IV, 11, 11) they pour out the water,

14. Murmur the Vâmadevya,

15. And separate according to their pleasure.

16. (The final benedictory formula runs thus), ' Through the power of wisdom, of Sruti and Smriti, as handed down by tradition, through (that power) which has its measure in (the Vedic texts) that have been gone through (?), and which is possessed of

---

karshanti, and translate, ' they draw (lines of that water) on this (earth).'

6. Nârâyana says that all the students are to do so.

10. Comp. above, IV, 9. On the way in which this Tarpana is to be performed, Nârâyana refers to the Sûtra II, 7, 5.

11. Comp. above, IV, 10.

12. Comp. above, IV, 10, 4-6.

undisputed firmness, may peace be with us in welfare.
Adoration be to gods, *Ri*shis, Manes, and men! May
they whom we have adored, make happy life, beauty,
health, peace, incolumity, imperishableness, vigour,
splendour, glory, power, holy lustre, renown, age,
offspring, cattle, adoration, increase.   From wrongly
spoken, wrongly used (prayer), from everything that
is deficient or excessive, for the good of gods and
*Ri*shis, may the Brahman and Truth protect me;
may the Brahman and Truth protect me!'

End of the Sixth Adhyâya.

End of the *S*ânkhâyana - G*ri*hya.

ÂSVALÂYANA-GRIIIYA-SÛTRA.

ÂSVALÂYANA-GR/HYA-SÛTRA.

MOST of the questions referring to the Gṛihya-sûtra of
Âsvalâyana will be treated of more conveniently in connection with the different subjects which we shall have to
discuss in our General Introduction to the Gṛihya-sûtras.
Here I wish only to call attention to a well-known passage
of Sha*d*guruṣishya, in which that commentator gives some
statements on the works composed by Âsvalâyana and by
his teacher Saunaka. As an important point in that
passage has, as far as I can see, been misunderstood by
several eminent scholars, I may perhaps be allowed here to
try and correct that misunderstanding, though the point
stands in a less direct connection with the Gṛihya-sûtra than
with another side of the literary activity of Âsvalâyana.

Sha*d*guruṣishya[1], before speaking of Âsvalâyana, makes
the following statements with regard to Âsvalâyana's
teacher, Saunaka. 'There was,' he says, 'the Sâkala
Sa*m*hitâ (of the Rig-veda), and the Bâshkala Sa*m*hitâ;
following these two Sa*m*hitâs and the twenty-one Brâhma*n*as, adopting principally the Aitareyaka and supple-
menting it by the other texts, he who was revered by
the whole number of great *R*ishis composed the first
Kalpa-sûtra.' He then goes on to speak of Âsvalâyana —
'Saunaka's pupil was the venerable Âsvalâyana. He who
knew everything he had learnt from that teacher, composed a Sûtra and announced (to Saunaka that he had
done so)[2].' Saunaka then destroyed his own Sûtra, and

---

[1] See Max Müller's History of Ancient Sanskrit Literature, pp. 230 seqq.;
Indische Studien, I, 102.

[2] This seems to me to be the meaning of sûtra*m* kṛitvâ nyavedayat;

determined that Âsvalâyana's Sûtra should be adopted by
the students of that Vedic *S*âkhâ. Thus, says Sha*d*guru-
*s*ishya, there were twelve works of *S*aunaka by which a
correct knowledge of the Rig-veda was preserved, and three
works of Âsvalâyana. *S*aunaka's da*s*a granthâs were,
the five Anukrama*n*is, the two Vidhânas, the Bârhaddai-
vata, the Prâtisâkhya, and a Smârta work[1]. Âsvalâyana,
on the other hand, composed the *S*rauta-sûtra in twelve
Adhyâyas, the G*ri*hya in four Adhyâyas, and the fourth
Âra*n*yaka : this is Âsvalâyana's great Sûtra composition[2].

Here we have an interesting and important statement by
which the authorship of a part of the Aitareyâra*n*yaka,
which would thus be separated from the rest of that text,
is ascribed, not to Mahidâsa Aitareya, but to an author of
what may be called the historical period of Vedic antiquity,
to Âsvalâyana.

But what is the fourth Âra*n*yaka to which this passage
refers? Is it the text which is now set down, for instance,
in Dr. Râ*g*endralâla Mitra's edition, as the fourth Âra-
*n*yaka of the Aitareyins?

Before we give an answer to this question, attention must
be called to other passages referring, as it could seem, to
another part, namely, the fifth part of the Âra*n*yaka.

Sâya*n*a, in his great commentary on the Rig-veda, very
frequently quotes the pa*nk*amâra*n*yaka as belonging
to *S*aunaka. Thus in vol. i, p. 112, ed. Max Müller, he says :
pa*nk*amâra*n*yaka aush*n*ihat*ri*kâsîtir iti kha*nd*e *S*aunakena
sûtrita*m* surûpak*ri*tnum ûtaya iti trî*n*y endra sânasi*m* rayim
iti dve iti. There is indeed in the fifth Âra*n*yaka a chapter
beginning with the words aush*n*ihi t*ri*kâsîti*h*, in which the
words quoted by Sâya*n*a occur[3]. Similar quotations, in

---

the case is similar to that where a pupil goes on his rounds for alms and
announces (nivedayati) to his teacher what he has received. Prof. Max Müller
translates these words differently; according to him they mean that Âsvalâyana
'made a Sûtra and taught it.'
    [1] Comp. Prof. Bühler's article in the Journal As. Soc. of Bengal, 1866,
pp. 149 seqq.
    [2] Dvâda*s*âdhyâyaka*m* sûtra*m* *k*atushka*m* g*ri*hyam eva *k*a *k*aturthâra*n*yaka*m*
*k*eti hy Âsvalâyanasûtrakam.
    [3] See p. 448 of Dr. Râ*g*endralâla Mitra's edition in the Bibliotheca Indica.

which the fifth Âra*n*yaka is assigned to *S*aunaka, are found in Sâya*n*a's commentary on the Âra*n*yaka itself; see, for instance, p. 97, line 19, p. 116, line 3.

Thus it seems that the authorship of both the fourth and the fifth Âra*n*yaka was ascribed to teachers belonging to the Sûtra period of Vedic literature, viz. to *S*aunaka and to Â*s*valâyana respectively. And so we find the case stated by both Professor Weber, in his 'Vorlesungen über indische Literaturgeschichte[1],' and Dr. Râ*g*endralâla Mitra, in the Introduction to his edition of the Aitareya Âra*n*yaka[2].

But we must ask ourselves: Are the two books of the Âra*n*yaka collection, ascribed to those two authors, really two different books? It is a surprising fact that Sha*d*guru*s*ishya, while speaking of Â*s*valâyana's authorship of the fourth book, and while at the same time intending, as he evidently does, to give a complete list of *S*aunaka's compositions, does not mention the fifth Âra*n*yaka among the works of that author. In order to account for this omission the conjecture seems to suggest itself that Sha*d*guru*s*ishya, when speaking of the fourth Âra*n*yaka as belonging to Â*s*valâyana, means the same work which Sâya*n*a sets down as the fifth, and which he ascribes to *S*aunaka. At first sight this conjecture may seem perhaps rather hazardous or unnatural; however I believe that, if we compare the two texts themselves which are concerned, we shall find it very probable and even evident. What do those two Âra*n*yaka books contain? The fourth is very short: it does not fill more than one page in the printed edition. Its contents consist exclusively of the text of the Mahânâmnî or *S*ak-varî verses, which seem to belong to a not less remote

---

[1] 2nd edition, p. 53: Obwohl wir für das vierte Buch des letztern (i.e. of the Aitareya Âra*n*yaka) sogar die directe Nachricht haben, dass es dem Â*s*valâyana, dem Schüler eines *S*aunaka angehört, so wie auch ferner für das fünfte Buch desselben dieser *S*aunaka selbst als Urheber gegolten zu haben scheint, nach dem was Colebrooke Misc. Ess. I, 47 n. darüber berichtet.

[2] P. 11: If this assumption be admitted, the proper conclusion to be arrived at would also be that the whole of the fifth Book belongs to *S*aunaka, and the whole of the fourth Book to Â*s*valâyana. P. 12: The writings of both Â*s*valâyana and *S*aunaka which occur in the Âra*n*yaka, etc.

antiquity than the average of the Rig-veda hymns. They
can indeed be considered as forming part of the Rig-veda
Sa*m*hitâ, and it is only on account of the peculiar mystical
holiness ascribed to these verses, that they were not studied
in the village but in the forest[1], and were consequently
received not into the body of the Sa*m*hitâ itself, but into
the Âra*n*yaka. They are referred to in all Brâhma*n*a texts,
and perhaps we can even go so far as to pronounce our
opinion that some passages of the Rig-veda hymns themselves allude to the *S*akvarî verses :

ya*k kh*akvarîshu b*r*ihatâ rave*n*endre *s*ushmam ada-
dhâtâ Vasish*thâh* (Rig-veda VII, 33, 4).

*r*ik*â*m tva*h* posham âste pupushvân gâyatra*m* tvo gâyati
*s*akvarîshu (Rig-veda X, 71, 11).

So much for the fourth Âra*n*yaka. The fifth contains a
description of the Mahâvrata ceremony. To the same subject also the first book is devoted, with the difference that
the first book is composed in the Brâhma*n*a style, the fifth
in the Sûtra style[2].

Now which of these two books can it be that Sha*d*guru*s*ishya reckons as belonging to the 'Âsvalâyanasûtraka?'
It is impossible that it should be the fourth, for the Mahânâmnî verses never were considered by Indian theologians
as the work of a human author; they shared in the a p a u-
r u s h e y a t v a of the Veda, and to say that they have been
composed by Âsvalâyana, would be inconsistent with the
most firmly established principles of the literary history of
the Veda both as conceived by the Indians and by ourselves. And even if we were to admit that the Mahânâmnî verses can have been assigned, by an author like
Sha*d*guru*s*ishya, to Âsvalâyana,—and we cannot admit

---

[1] See *S*ânkhâyana-G*r*ihya II, 12, 13.
[2] Thus Sâya*n*a, in his note on V, 1, 1, says : Nanu prathamâra*n*yake ≈ pi atha
mahâvratam Indro vai Vr*i*tra*m* hatvetyâdinâ mahâvratapr ayogo ≈ bhihita*h*,
pa*nk*ame ≈ pi tasyaivâbhidhâne punarukti*h* syât. nâya*m* dosha*h*, sûtrabrâhma*n*a-
rûpe*n*a tayor vibhedât. pa*nk*amâra*n*yakam *r*ishiprokta*m* sûtra*m*, prathamâra*n*yakan tv apaurusheya*m* brâhma*n*am. ata eva tatrârthavâdaprapa*nk*ena
sahitâ vidhaya*h* *s*rûyante, pa*nk*ame tu na ko py arthavâdo ≈ sti . . . . ara*n*ya
evaitad adhyeyam ity abhipretyâdhyetâra âra*n*yakâ*nde* ≈ ntarbhâvyâdhîyate.

this,—there is no possibility whatever that he can have used the expression 'Âsvalâyanasûtrakam' with regard to the Mahânâmnis; to apply the designation of a Sûtra to the Mahânâmnî hymn would be no less absurd than to apply it to any Sûkta whatever of the *Rik*-Sa*m*hitâ. On the other hand, the fifth book of the Âra*n*yaka is a Sûtra ; it is the only part of the whole body of the Âra*n*yaka collection which is composed in the Sûtra style. And it treats of a special part of the Rig-veda ritual the rest of which is embodied in its entirety, with the omission only of that very part, in the two great Sûtras of Âsvalâyana. There seems to me, therefore, to be little doubt as to the fifth Âra*n*yaka really being the text referred to by Sha*dg*uru*s*ishya, though I do not know how to explain his setting down this book as the fourth. And I may add that there is a passage, hitherto, as far as I know, unnoticed, in Sâya*n*a's Sâma-veda commentary, in which that author directly assigns the fifth Âra*n*yaka not, as in the Rig-veda commentary, to *S*aunaka, but to Âsvalâyana. Sâya*n*a there says[1]: yathâ bahv*rik*âm adhyâpakâ mahâvratapra*yoga*pratipâdakam Âsvalâyananirmita*m* kalpasûtram ara*n*ye‧dhîyamânâ*h* pa*nk*amam âra*n*yakam iti vedatvena vyavaharanti.

Instead of asserting, therefore, that of the two last Âra*n*yakas of the Aitareyinas the one is ascribed to *S*aunaka, the other to Âsvalâyana, we must state the case otherwise : not two Âra*n*yakas were, according to Sâya*n*a and Sha*dg*uru*s*ishya, composed by those Sûtrakâras, but one, viz. the fifth, which forms a sort of supplement to the great body of the Sûtras of that *K*ara*n*a, and which is ascribed either to *S*aunaka or to Âsvalâyana. Perhaps further research will enable us to decide whether that Sûtra portion of the Âra*n*yaka, or we may say quite as well, that Âra*n*yaka portion of the Sûtra, belongs to the author of the *S*rauta-sûtra, or should be considered as a remnant of a more ancient composition, of which the portion studied in the forest has survived, while the portion

---

[1] Sâma-veda (Bibl. Indica), vol. i, p. 19.

which was taught in the village was superseded by the more recent Âsvalâyana-sûtra.

There would be still many questions with which an Introduction to Âsvalâyana would have to deal; thus the relation between Âsvalâyana and Saunaka, which we had intended to treat of here with reference to a special point, would have to be further discussed with regard to several other of its bearings, and the results which follow therefrom as to the position of Âsvalâyana in the history of Vedic literature would have to be stated. But we prefer to reserve the discussion of these questions for the General Introduction to the Grihya-sûtras.

ÂSVALÂYANA-GR/HYA-SÛTRA.

1. The (rites) based on the spreading (of the three sacred fires) have been declared; we shall declare the Gr/hya (rites).

2. There are three (kinds of) Pâkayagñas, the hutas, (i. e. the sacrifices) offered over the fire; over something that is not the fire, the prahutas; and at the feeding of Brâhmaнas, those offered in the Brahman.

3. And they quote also R/kas, 'He who with a piece of wood or with an oblation, or with knowledge ("veda").'

1, 1. The spreading (vitâna or, as it is also called, vihâra or vistâra) of the sacred fires is the taking of two of the three sacrificial fires, the Âhavanîya fire and the Dakshinâgni, out of the Gârhapatya fire (see, for instance, Weber's Indische Studien, IX, 216 seq.). The rites based on, or connected with the vitâna, are the rites forming the subject of the Srauta ritual, which are to be performed with the three fires.

2. Comp. Sânkhâyana-Gr/hya I, 5, 1; 1, 10. 7. The division here is somewhat different from that given by Sânkhâyana; what Sânkhâyana calls ahuta, is here prahuta ('sacrificed up'); the prahutas of Sânkhâyana form here no special category; the prâsitas of Sânkhâyana are the brahmaнi hutâs of Âsvalâyana. Thus Âsvalâyana has three categories, while Sânkhâyana (and quite in the same way Pâraskara I, 4, 1) gives four. Nârâyaнa mentions as an example of prahuta sacrifices the baliharaнa prescribed below, I, 2, 3.

3. Rig-veda VIII, 19, 5, 'The mortal who with a piece of wood, or with an oblation, or with knowledge worships Agni, who with adoration (worships him) offering rich sacrifices,' &c.

4. Even he who only puts a piece of wood (on the
fire) full of belief, should think, ' Here I offer a sacrifice ; adoration to that (deity) !'

(The *Rik* quoted above then says), ' He who with
an oblation'—and, ' He who with knowledge;' even by
learning only satisfaction is produced (in the gods).

Seeing this the *Ri*shi has said, ' To him who does
not keep away from himself the cows, to him who longs
for cows, who dwells in the sky, speak a wonderful
word, sweeter than ghee and honey.' Thereby he
means, ' This my word, sweeter than ghee and honey,
is satisfaction (to the god) ; may it be sweeter.'

(And another *Ri*shi says), ' To thee, O Agni, by
this *Rik* we offer an oblation prepared by our heart ;
may these be oxen, bulls, and cows.' (Thereby he
means), ' They are my oxen, bulls, and cows (which
I offer to the god), they who study this text, reciting
it for themselves (as their Svâdhyâya).'

(And further on the *Rik* quoted above says), ' He
who (worships Agni) with adoration, offering rich
sacrifices.' ' Verily also by the performing of adoration (the gods may be worshipped) ; for the gods are
not beyond the performing of adoration ; adoration
verily is sacrifice'—thus runs a Brâhma*n*a.

---

4. The words of the *Rik*, ' with an oblation,' are here repeated,
the Vedic instrumental âhutî being replaced and explained by the
regular form âhutyâ.

The following *Rik* is taken from the eighth Ma*nd*ala, 24, 20.
The god compared there with a rutting bull is Indra.

The following verse is Rig-veda VI, 16, 47 ; we may doubt as to
the correctness of the explanation given in our text, by which te te
is referred to the persons studying the hymns of the *Ri*shi. All these
quotations of course are meant to show that the knowledge of the
Veda and the performing of namas (adoration) is equivalent to a
real sacrifice.

KANDIKÂ 2.

1. Now he should make oblations in the evening and in the morning of prepared sacrificial food,

2. To the deities of the Agnihotra, to Soma Vanaspati, to Agni and Soma, to Indra and Agni, to Heaven and Earth, to Dhanvantari, to Indra, to the Visve devâs, to Brahman.

3. He says Svâhâ, and then he offers the Balis—

4. To those same deities, to the waters, to the herbs and trees, to the house, to the domestic deities, to the deities of the ground (on which the house stands),

5. To Indra and Indra's men, to Yama and Yama's men, to Varuna and Varuna's men, to Soma and Soma's men—these (oblations he makes) to the different quarters (of the horizon, of which those are the presiding deities).

6. To Brahman and Brahman's men in the middle,

2, 1. This is the Vaisvadeva sacrifice; comp. Sânkhâyana-Grihya II, 14, &c.

2. The deities of the Agnihotra are Sûrya, Agni, and Pragâpati.

On Soma Vanaspati see the quotations given in Böhtlingk-Roth's Dictionary s. v. vanaspati, 2.

3. I think the division of the Sûtras should be altered, so that svâheti would belong to Sûtra 2, and the third Sûtra would consist only of the words atha baliharanam. In this case we should have to translate,

(1) Now he should make oblations, &c.

(2) With the words, 'To the deities of the Agnihotra (i. e. to Agni, to Sûrya, to Pragâpati), to Soma Vanaspati, &c., svâhâ!'

(3) Then (follows) the offering of the Balis.

Comp. Sânkh.-Grihya II, 14, 4. 5, which passage seems to confirm the view expressed here.

5. Manu III, 87.

7. To the Vi*s*ve devâs, to all day-walking beings—
thus by day;

8. To the night-walking (beings)—thus at night.

9. To the Rakshas—thus to the north.

10. 'Svadhâ to the fathers (i. e. Manes)'—with
these words he should pour out the remnants to the
south, with the sacrificial cord suspended over the
right shoulder.

KA*ND*IKÂ 3.

1. Now wherever he intends to perform a sacrifice,
let him besmear (with cowdung) a surface of the
dimension at least of an arrow on each side; let him
draw six lines thereon, one turned to the north, to
the west (of the spot on which the fire is to be
placed); two (lines) turned to the east, at the two
different ends (of the line mentioned first); three
(lines) in the middle (of those two); let him sprinkle
that (place with water), establish the (sacred) fire
(thereon), put (two or three pieces of fuel) on it, wipe
(the ground) round (the fire), strew (grass) round (it),
to the east, to the south, to the west, to the north,
ending (each time) in the north. Then (follows)
silently the sprinkling (of water) round (the fire).

2. With two (Ku*s*a blades used as) strainers the
purifying of the Â*g*ya (is done).

3. Having taken two Ku*s*a blades with unbroken
tops, which do not bear a young shoot in them, of
the measure of a span, at their two ends with his

3, 1. Comp. *S*ânkh.-G*ri*hya I, 7, 6 seq., where the statements
regarding the lines to be drawn are somewhat different, and the note
there.

3. Comp. the description of this act of purifying the Â*g*ya, which
is in some points more detailed, in *S*ânkh.-G*ri*hya I, 8, 14–21.

thumbs and fourth fingers, with his hands turned
with the inside upwards, he purifies (the Âgya, from
the west) to the east, with (the words), 'By the
impulse of Savit*ri* I purify thee with this uninjured
purifier, with the rays of the good sun'—once with
this formula, twice silently.

4. The strewing (of grass) round (the fire) may be
done or not done in the Âgya offerings.

5. So also the two Âgya portions (may optionally
be sacrificed) in the Pâkaya*gñ*as.

6. And the (assistance of a) Brahman (is optional),
except at the sacrifice to Dhanvantari and at the
sacrifice of the spit-ox (offered to Rudra).

7. Let him sacrifice with (the words), 'To such
and such a deity svâhâ!'

8. If there is no rule (as to the deities to whom
the sacrifice belongs, they are) Agni, Indra, Pra*gâ*-
pati, the Vi*s*ve devâs, Brahman.

9. (Different Pâkaya*gñ*as, when) offered at the
same time, should have the same Barhis (sacrificial
grass), the same fuel, the same Âgya, and the same
(oblation to Agni) Svish*t*ak*ri*t.

10. With reference thereto the following sacrificial
stanza is sung :

'He who has to perform (different) Pâkaya*gñ*as,
should offer them with the same Âgya, the same

---

4. Comp. *S*ânkh.-G*ri*hya I, 8, 12.

5. On the two Âgyabhâgas offered to Agni and Soma comp.
below, chap. 10, 13 ; *S*ânkh.-G*ri*hya I, 9, 5 seq.

6. Comp. on these exceptions the Sûtras below, I, 12, 7 ; IV,
8, 15.

7. Comp. *S*ânkh.-G*ri*hya I, 9, 18.

9. On the oblation to Agni Svish*t*ak*ri*t, see Indische Studien,
IX, 217.

Barhis, and the same Svish/akr/t, even if the deity
(of those sacrifices) is not the same.'

KANDIKÂ 4.

1. During the northern course of the sun, in the
time of the increasing moon, under an auspicious
Nakshatra the tonsure (of the child's head), the
initiation (of a Brahma/ârin), the cutting of the
beard, and marriage (should be celebrated).

2. According to some (teachers), marriage (may
be celebrated) at any time.

3. Before those (ceremonies) let him sacrifice four
Âgya oblations—

4. With the three (verses), 'Agni, thou purifiest
life' (Rig-veda IX, 66, 10 seq.), and with (the one
verse), ' Pragâpati, no other one than thou' (Rig-veda
X, 121, 10).

5. Or with the Vyâhr/tis.

6. According to some (teachers), the one and the
other.

7. No such (oblations), according to some (teachers).

8. At the marriage the fourth oblation with the
verse, 'Thou (O Agni) art Aryaman towards the girls'
(Rig-veda V, 3, 2).

KANDIKÂ 5.

1. Let him first examine the family (of the intended
bride or bridegroom), as it has been said above,

4, 1. Sânkh.-Gr/hya I, 5, 2–5.
5. With the words, bhû/, bhuva/, sva/, and with the three
words together.
6. Thus eight oblations are offered, four with the four R/kas
quoted in the fourth Sûtra, and four with the Vyâhr/tis.
7. Neither the oblations with the R/kas nor those with the
Vyâhr/tis.
5, 1. Srauta-sûtra IX, 3, 20, ' Who on their mother's as well as

'Those who on the mother's and on the father's side.'

2. Let him give the girl to a (young man) endowed with intelligence.

3. Let him marry a girl that shows the characteristics of intelligence, beauty, and moral conduct, and who is free from disease.

4. As the characteristics (mentioned in the preceding Sûtra) are difficult to discern, let him make eight lumps (of earth), recite over the lumps the following formula, ' Right has been born first, in the beginning; on the right truth is founded. For what (destiny) this girl is born, that may she attain here. What is true may that be seen,' and let him say to the girl, ' Take one of these.'

5. If she chooses the (lump of earth taken) from a field that yields two crops (in one year), he may know, ' Her offspring will be rich in food.' If from a cow-stable, rich in cattle. If from the earth of a Vedi (altar), rich in holy lustre. If from a pool which does not dry up, rich in everything. If from a gambling-place, addicted to gambling. If from a place where four roads meet, wandering to different directions. If from a barren spot, poor. If from a burial-ground, (she will) bring death to her husband.

---

on their father's side through ten generations are endowed with knowledge, austerity, and meritorious works,' &c.

4. I prefer the reading of the Bibliotheca Indica edition, countenanced by Nârâya*n*a's commentary, durvig*ñ*eyâni laksha*n*ânîti, &c. The lumps are to be taken from the eight places mentioned in Sûtra 5.

5. No doubt the correct reading is not that given by Nârâya*n*a and accepted by Professor Stenzler, dvipravrâginî, but vipravrâ*g*inî, as four of Professor Stenzler's MSS. read (see his Variae Lectiones, p. 48, and the Petersburg Dictionary s.v. vipravrâ*g*in).

KANDIKÂ 6.

1. (The father) may give away the girl, having decked her with ornaments, pouring out a libation of water: this is the wedding (called) Brâhma. A son born by her (after a wedding of this kind) brings purification to twelve descendants and to twelve ancestors on both (the husband's and the wife's) sides.

2. He may give her, having decked her with ornaments, to an officiating priest, whilst a sacrifice with the three (Srauta) fires is going on : this (is the wedding called) Daiva. (A son) brings purification to ten descendants and to ten ancestors on both sides.

3. They fulfil the law together : this (is the wedding called) Prâgâpatya. (A son) brings purification to eight descendants and to eight ancestors on both sides.

4. He may marry her after having given a bull and a cow (to the girl's father): this (is the wedding called) Ârsha. (A son) brings purification to seven descendants and to seven ancestors on both sides.

5. He may marry her, after a mutual agreement has been made (between the lover and the damsel) : this (is the wedding called) Gândharva.

6. He may marry her after gladdening (her father) by money : this (is the wedding called) Âsura.

6, 1. Comp. Vasish/ha I, 30; Âpastamba II, 11, 17; Baudhâyana I, 20, 2.

2. Vasish/ha I, 31; Âpastamba II, 11, 19; Baudhâyana I, 20, 5.

3. Baudhâyana I, 20, 3.

4. Vasish/ha I, 32; Âpastamba II, 11, 18; Baudhâyana I, 20, 4.

5. Vasish/ha I, 33; Âpastamba II, 11, 20; Baudhâyana I, 20, 6.

6. Vasish/ha I, 35 (where this rite is designated as Mânusha); Âpastamba II, 12, 1; Baudhâyana I, 20, 7.

7. He may carry her off while (her relatives) sleep or pay no attention: this (is the wedding called) Paisâka.

8. He may carry her off, killing (her relatives) and cleaving (their) heads, while she weeps and they weep: this (is the wedding called) Râkshasa.

KANDIKÂ 7.

1. Now various indeed are the customs of the (different) countries and the customs of the (different) villages: those one should observe at the wedding.

2. What, however, is commonly accepted, that we shall state.

3. Having placed to the west of the fire a mill-stone, to the north-east (of the fire) a water-pot, he should sacrifice, while she takes hold of him. Standing, with his face turned to the west, while she is sitting and turns her face to the east, he should with (the formula), 'I seize thy hand for the sake of happiness' seize her thumb if he desires that only male children may be born to him;

4. Her other fingers, (if he is) desirous of female (children);

5. The hand on the hair-side together with the

7. Baudhâyana I, 20, 9.

8. Vasishtha I, 34 (where this rite is called Kshâtra); Âpastamba II, 21, 2; Baudhâyana I, 20, 8. The text of this Sûtra seems to be based on a hemistich hatvâ bhittvâ ka sirshâni rudadbhyo rudatim haret; comp. Manu III, 33.

7, 3. Professor Stenzler is evidently right in taking asmânam as in apposition to drishadam. Nârâyana says, drishat prasiddhâ asmâ tatputrakah. tatrobhayoh pratishthâpanam siddham.

The sacrifice is that prescribed in Sânkh.-Grihya I, 12, 11. 12. Regarding the rite that follows, comp. Sânkh.-Grihya I, 13, 2.

thumb, (if) desirous of both (male and female children).

6. Leading her three times round the fire and the water-pot, so that their right sides are turned towards (the fire, &c.), he murmurs, 'This am I, that art thou; that art thou, this am I; the heaven I, the earth thou; the Sâman I, the *Rik* thou. Come! Let us here marry. Let us beget offspring. Loving, bright, with genial mind may we live a hundred autumns.'

7. Each time after he has lead her (so) round, he makes her tread on the stone with (the words), 'Tread on this stone; like a stone be firm. Overcome the enemies; tread the foes down.'

8. Having 'spread under' (i.e. having first poured Âgya over her hands), her brother or a person acting in her brother's place pours fried grain twice over the wife's joined hands.

9. Three times for descendants of *G*amadagni.

10. He pours again (Âgya) over (what has been left of) the sacrificial food,

11. And over what has been cut off.

12. This is the rule about the portions to be cut off.

13. 'To god Aryaman the girls have made sacrifice,

---

6. Sânkhâyana-Grihya I, 13, 4. 9. 13.
7. Sânkhâyana-Grihya I, 13, 12.
8. Sânkhâyana-Grihya I, 13, 15. 16.
9. The two portions of fried grain poured over the bride's hands, together with the first (upastarana) and the second (pratyabhighâ-rana) pouring out of Âgya, constitute the four Avattas, or portions cut off from the Havis. The descendants of *G*amadagni were pañ*k*âvattinas, i.e. they used to cut off five such portions (see Kâtyâyana I, 9, 3; Weber, Indische Studien, X, 95); so they had to pour out the fried grain three times.
13. Sânkhâyana-Grihya I, 18, 3; 13, 17; 14, 1.

to Agni ; may he, god Aryaman, loosen her from this,
and not from that place, Svâhâ!

'To god Varuna the girls have made sacrifice, to
Agni ; may he, god Varuna, &c.

'To god Pûshan the girls have made sacrifice, to
Agni ; may he, god Pûshan, &c.'—with (these verses
recited by the bridegroom) she should sacrifice (the
fried grain) without opening her joined hands, as if
(she did so) with the (spoon called) Sruk.

14. Without that leading round (the fire, she sacrifices grain) with the neb of a basket towards herself
silently a fourth time.

15. Some lead the bride round each time after the
fried grain has been poured out : thus the two last
oblations do not follow immediately on each other.

16. He then loosens her two locks of hair, if they
are made, (i.e. if) two tufts of wool are bound round
her hair on the two sides,—

17. With (the Rik), 'I release thee from the band
of Varuna' (Rig-veda X, 85, 24).

18. The left one with the following (Rik).

19. He then causes her to step forward in a north-
eastern direction seven steps with (the words), 'For
sap with one step, for juice with two steps, for thriving of wealth with three steps, for comfort with four
steps, for offspring with five steps, for the seasons

14, 15. According to those teachers whose opinion is related in
Sûtras 6–14, the leading round the fire, the treading on the stone,
and the offering of fried grain (with the three parts of the Mantra,
Sûtra 13) are repeated thrice ; then follows the offering prescribed in
Sûtra 14, so that the last two offerings follow immediately on each
other. This is not the case, if in the first three instances the order
of the different rites is inverted, as stated in Sûtra 15.

In Sûtra 14 Nârâyana explains sûrpapula by kona.

19. Sânkhâyana-Grihya I, 14, 5. 6; 13, 2; Pâraskara I, 8, 1.

with six steps. Be friend with seven steps. So be
thou devoted to me. Let us acquire many sons
who may reach old age!'

20. Joining together their two heads, (the bridegroom? the Âkârya?) sprinkles them (with water)
from the water-pot.

21. And she should dwell that night in the house
of an old Brâhmana woman whose husband is alive
and whose children are alive.

22. When she sees the polar-star, the star Arun-
dhatî, and the seven Rishis (ursa major), let her
break the silence (and say), 'May my husband live
and I get offspring.'

KANDIKÂ 8.

1. If (the newly-married couple) have to make a
journey (to their new home), let him cause her to
mount the chariot with the (verse), 'May Pûshan
lead thee from here holding thy hand' (Rig-veda X,
85, 26).

2. With the hemistich, 'Carrying stones (the river)
streams; hold fast each other' (Rig-veda X, 53, 8)
let him cause her to ascend a ship.

3. With the following (hemistich) let him make
her descend (from it).

4. (He pronounces the verse), 'The living one
they bewail' (Rig-veda X, 40, 10), if she weeps.

5. They constantly carry the nuptial fire in front.

---

20. Sânkhâyana-Grihya I, 14, 9; Pâraskara I, 8, 5.
22. Sânkhâyana-Grihya I, 17, 2 seq.; Pâraskara I, 8, 19.
8, 1. Sânkhâyana-Grihya I, 15, 13.
2. Sânkhâyana-Grihya I, 15, 17. 18.
4. Sânkhâyana-Grihya I, 15, 2.

6. At lovely places, trees, and cross-ways let him murmur (the verse), 'May no waylayers meet us' (Rig-veda X, 85, 32).

7. At every dwelling-place (on their way) let him look at the lookers on, with (the verse), 'Good luck brings this woman' (Rig-veda X, 85, 33).

8. With (the verse), 'Here may delight fulfil itself to thee through offspring' (Rig-veda X, 85, 27) he should make her enter the house.

9. Having given its place to the nuptial fire, and having spread to the west of it a bull's hide with the neck to the east, with the hair outside, he makes oblations, while she is sitting on that (hide) and takes hold of him, with the four (verses), 'May Pragâpati create offspring to us' (Rig-veda X, 85, 43 seq.), verse by verse, and with (the verse), 'May all the gods unite' (Rig-veda X, 85, 47), he partakes of curds and gives (thereof) to her, or he besmears their two hearts with the rest of the Âgya (of which he has sacrificed).

10. From that time they should eat no saline food, they should be chaste, wear ornaments, sleep on the ground three nights or twelve nights;

11. Or one year, (according to) some (teachers); thus, they say, a *Ri*shi will be born (as their son).

12. When he has fulfilled (this) observance (and has had intercourse with his wife), he should give the bride's shift to (the Brâhma*n*a) who knows the Sûryâ hymn (Rig-veda X, 85);

13. Food to the Brâhma*n*as;

---

6. *S*âṅkhâyana-G*ri*hya I, 15, 14.
8. *S*âṅkhâya*n*a-G*ri*hya I, 15, 22; 16, 12.
9. *S*âṅkhâyana-G*ri*hya I, 16, 1. 2.
12. *S*âṅkhâyana-G*ri*hya I, 14, 12.

14. Then he should cause them to pronounce auspicious words.

KANDIKÂ 9.

1. Beginning from the seizing of (the bride's) hand (i. e. from the wedding), he should worship the domestic (fire) himself, or his wife, or also his son, or his daughter, or a pupil.

2. (The fire) should be kept constantly.

3. When it goes out, however, the wife should fast : thus (say) some (teachers).

4. The time for setting it in a blaze and for sacrificing in it has been explained by (the rules given with regard to) the Agnihotra,

5. And the sacrificial food, except meat.

6. But if he likes he may (perform the sacrifice) with rice, barley, or sesamum.

7. He should sacrifice in the evening with (the formula), 'To Agni svâhâ!' in the morning with (the formula), 'To Sûrya svâhâ!' Silently the second (oblations) both times.

KANDIKÂ 10.

1. Now the oblations of cooked food on the (two) Parvan (i. e. the new and full moon) days.

2. The fasting (which takes place) thereat has been declared by (the corresponding rules regarding) the Darsapûrnamâsa sacrifices.

9, 1. Comp. Sânkhâyana-Grihya II, 17, 3.

4. Sânkhâyana-Grihya I, 1, 12 ; Âsvalâyana-Srauta II, 2.

5. Âsvalâyana-Srauta II, 3, 1 seq. Nârâyana: By the prohibition of meat which is expressed in the words 'Except meat,' it is to be understood that the food to be sacrificed, as stated in other Sâstras, may likewise be chosen.

3. And (so has been declared) the binding together of the fuel and of the Barhis,

4. And the deities (to whom those oblations belong), with the exception of the Upâ*ms*uyâ*g*a (offerings at which the formulas are repeated with low voice), and of Indra and Mahendra.

5. Other deities (may be worshipped) according to the wishes (which the sacrificer connects with his offerings).

6. For each single deity he pours out four handsful (of rice, barley, &c.), placing two purifiers (i. e. Ku*s*a blades, on the vessel), with (the formula), 'Agreeable to such and such (a deity) I pour thee out.'

7. He then sprinkles them (those four portions of Havis with water) in the same way as he had poured them out, with (the formula), 'Agreeable to such and such (a deity) I sprinkle thee.'

8. When (the rice or barley grains) have been husked and cleansed from the husks three times, let him cook (the four portions) separately,

9. Or throwing (them) together.

10. If he cooks them separately, let him touch the grains, after he has separated them, (and say,) 'This to this god ; this to this god.'

11. But if he (cooks the portions) throwing (them) together, he should (touch and) sacrifice them, after he has put (the single portions) into different vessels.

12. The portions of sacrificial food, when they

10, 3. See Â*s*valâyana-*S*rauta I, 3, 28 Scholion ; Kâty.-*S*rauta II, 7, 22.

4. See Hillebrandt, Das altindische Neu- und Vollmondsopfer, p. 111 ; my note on Sânkhâyana-G*r*ihya I, 3, 3.

12. In the Mantra we have a similar play upon words (iddha,

have been cooked, he sprinkles (with Âgya), takes
them from the fire towards the north, places them
on the Barhis, and sprinkles the fuel with Âgya
with the formula, 'This fuel is thy self, Gâtavedas;
thereby burn thou and increase, and, O burning
One, make us increase and through offspring, cattle,
holy lustre, and nourishment make us prosper.
Svâhâ!'

13. Having silently poured out the two Âghâras
(or Âgya oblations poured out with the Sruva, the
one from north-west to south-east, the other from
south-west to north-east), he should sacrifice the two
Âgya portions with (the formulas), 'To Agni
svâhâ! To Soma svâhâ!'—

14. The northern one belonging to Agni, the
southern one to Soma.

15. It is understood (in the Sruti), 'The two eyes
indeed of the sacrifice are the Âgya portions,

16. 'Therefore of a man who is sitting with his
face to the west the southern (i. e. right) eye is
northern, the northern (i. e. left) eye is southern.'

17. In the middle (of the two Âgya portions he

lit, or burning, and samedhaya, make us prosper) as in Sânkh.-
Grihya II, 10, 4.

13. Pâraskara I, 5, 3; Sânkh.-Grihya I, 9, 5 seq.

14. Sânkh.-Grihya I, 9, 7.

15. Professor Stenzler here very pertinently refers to Satapatha
Brâhmana I, 6, 3, 38.

16. It is doubtful whether this paragraph should be considered
as forming part of the quotation from the Sruti. The object of
this passage is, in my opinion, to explain why the southern Âgyabhâga belongs to Soma, who is the presiding deity of the north,
and the northern Âgyabhâga to Agni, the presiding deity of the
south-east. Professor Stenzler's opinion about this paragraph is
somewhat different.

17. Sânkh.-Grihya I, 9, 8.

sacrifices the other) Havis, or more to the west, finishing (the oblations) in the east or in the north.

18. To the north-east the oblation to (Agni) Svish*t*ak*ri*t.

19. He cuts off (the Avadâna portions) from the Havis from the middle and from the eastern part ;

20. From the middle, the eastern part and the western part (the portions have to be cut off) by those who make five Avadânas ;

21. From the northern side the portion for Svish*t*ak*ri*t.

22. Here he omits the second pouring (of Âg*y*a) over (what is left of) the sacrificial food.

23. 'What I have done too much in this ceremony, or what I have done here too little, all that may Agni Svish*t*ak*ri*t, he who knows it, make well sacrificed and well offered for me. To Agni Svish*t*ak*ri*t, to him who offers the oblations for general expiation, so that they are well offered, to him who makes us succeed in what we desire! Make us in all that we desire successful! Svâhâ !'

24. He pours out the full vessel on the Barhis.

25. This is the Avabh*ri*tha.

19, 20. See above, the note on I, 7, 9 about the Avadâna portions and the peculiar custom of the descendants of *G*amadagni with regard to them.

22. Comp. above, I, 7, 10. 'Here' means, at the Svish*t*ak*ri*t oblation.

23. Comp. Pâraskara I, 2, 11 ; *S*atapatha Brâhma*n*a XIV, 9, 4, 24. On the oblations for general expiation (sarvaprâya*sk*ittâhuti) comp. *S*ânkh.-G*ri*hya I, 9, 12, and the note.

24. 'A full vessel which has been put down before, he should now pour out on the Barhis.' Nârâya*n*a.

25. This pouring out of the vessel holds here the place of the Avabh*ri*tha bath at the end of the Soma sacrifice. See Weber, Indische Studien, X, 393 seq.

26. This is the standard form of the Pâkayagñas.

27. What has been left of the Havis is the fee for the sacrifice.

KANDIKÂ 11.

1. Now (follows) the ritual of the animal sacrifice.

2. Having prepared to the north of the fire the place for the Sâmitra fire, having given drink (to the animal which he is going to sacrifice), having washed the animal, having placed it to the east (of the fire) with its face to the west, having made oblations with the two Rikas, 'Agni as our messenger' (Rig-veda I, 12, 1 seq.), let him touch (the animal) from behind with a fresh branch on which there are leaves, with (the formula), 'Agreeable to such and such (a deity) I touch thee.'

3. He sprinkles it from before with water in which rice and barley are, with (the formula), 'Agreeable to such and such (a deity) I sprinkle thee.'

4. Having given (to the animal) to drink of that (water), he should pour out the rest (of it) along its right fore-foot.

5. Having carried fire round (it), performing that act only (without repeating a corresponding Mantra), they lead it to the north.

6. In front of it they carry a fire-brand.

11, 2. The Sâmitra fire (literally, the fire of the Samitri, who prepares the flesh of the immolated animal) is the one mentioned below in Sûtras 7 and 10. Comp. Indische Studien, X, 345. 'I touch thee' is upâkaromi; comp. Kâtyâyana-Srauta-sûtra VI, 3, 19. 26.

6. It seems that this fire-brand is the same which had been carried round the animal, according to Sûtra 5. Comp. Kâtyâyana-Srauta-sûtra VI, 5, 2–5.

7. This is the Sâmitra (fire).

8. With the two Vapâsrapanî ladles the 'performer' touches the animal.

9. The sacrificer (touches) the performer.

10. To the west of the Sâmitra (fire) he (the Samitri) kills (the animal), the head of which is turned to the east or to the west, the feet to the north; and having placed a grass-blade on his side of the (animal's) navel, (the 'performer') draws out the omentum, cuts off the omentum, seizes it with the two Agnisrapanîs, sprinkles it with water, warms it at the Sâmitra (fire), takes it before that fire, roasts it, being seated to the south, goes round (the two fires), and sacrifices it.

11. At the same fire they cook a mess of food.

12. Having cut off the eleven Avadânas (or portions which have to be cut off) from the animal, from all its limbs, having boiled them at the Sâmitra (fire),

---

7. Comp. Sûtra 2.

8. On the two Vapâsrapanîs, comp. Kâtyâyana-Srauta-sûtra VI, 5, 7; Indische Studien, X, 345. The act which is here attributed to the kartrî ('performer'), belongs in the Srauta ritual to the incumbencies of the Pratiprasthâtrî.

10. On the way in which animals had to be killed at sacrifices, see Weber's Indische Studien, IX, 222 seq.

On the position of the head and the feet of the victim, comp. Kâtyâyana-Srauta-sûtra VI, 5, 16. 17.

According to Kâtyâyana VI, 6, 8 seq. a grass-blade is placed on the dead animal's body before the navel (agrena nâbhim); through that grass-blade he cuts into the body and draws out the omentum.

'That fire' is, according to Nârâyana, not the Sâmitra but the Aupâsana fire. In the same way in the Srauta ritual the warming of the omentum is performed at the Sâmitra, the boiling at the Âhavanîya fire. Kâtyâyana VI, 6, 13. 16.

11. The Aupâsana fire is referred to.

12. The eleven portions are indicated by Kâtyâyana, Srauta-sûtra VI, 7, 6.

[29]　　　　　　N

and having warmed the heart on a spit, let him sacrifice first from the mess of cooked food (mentioned in Sûtra 11);

13. Or together with the Avadâna portions.

14. From each of the (eleven) Avadânas he cuts off two portions.

15. They perform the rites only (without corresponding Mantras) with the heart's spit (i.e. the spit on which the heart had been; see Sûtra 12).

KANDIKÂ 12.

1. At a Kaitya sacrifice he should before the Svish*t*ak*ri*t (offering) offer a Bali to the Kaitya.

2. If, however, (the Kaitya) is distant, (he should send his Bali) through a leaf-messenger.

---

14. 'A Pañkâvattin cuts off three portions. Having performed the Upastarana and the Pratyabhighârana (the first and second pouring out of Âgya) he sacrifices (the cut-off portions).' Nârâyana.

15. On the rites regarding the spit, see Kâtyâyana VI, 10, 1 seq.; Indische Studien, X, 346.

12, 1. There seems to be no doubt that Professor Stenzler is right in giving to kaitya in this chapter its ordinary meaning of religious shrine ('Denkmal'). The text shows that the Kaitya sacrifice was not offered like other sacrifices at the sacrificer's home, but that in some cases the offering would have to be sent, at least symbolically, to distant places. This confirms Professor Stenzler's translation of kaitya. Nârâyana explains kaitya by kitte bhava, and says, 'If he makes a vow to a certain deity, saying, "If I obtain such and such a desire, I shall offer to thee an Âgya sacrifice, or a Sthâlîpâka, or an animal"—and if he then obtains what he had wished for and performs that sacrifice to that deity : this is a kaitya sacrifice.' I do not know anything that supports this statement as to the meaning of kaitya.

2. ' He should make of a leaf a messenger and a carrying-pole.' Nârâyana.

It is not clear whether besides this image of a messenger there was also a real messenger who had to carry the Bali to the Kaitya,

3. With the *Rik*, 'Where thou knowest, O tree' (Rig-veda V, 5. 10), let him make two lumps (of food), put them on a carrying-pole, hand them over to the messenger, and say to him, 'Carry this Bali to that (*K*aitya).'

4. (He gives him the lump) which is destined for the messenger, with (the words), 'This to thee.'

5. If there is anything dangerous between (them and the *K*aitya), (he gives him) some weapon also.

6. If a navigable river is between (them and the *K*aitya, he gives him) also something like a raft with (the words), 'Hereby thou shalt cross.'

7. At the Dhanvantari sacrifice let him offer first a Bali to the Purohita, between the Brahman and the fire.

KANDIKÂ 13.

1. The Upanishad (treats of) the Garbhalambhana, the Pu*m*savana, and the Anavalobhana (i. e. the ceremonies for securing the conception of a child, the male gender of the child, and for preventing disturbances which could endanger the embryo).

2. If he does not study (that Upanishad), he

---

or whether the whole rite was purely symbolical, and based on the principle: In sacris ficta pro veris accipiuntur.

3. Comp. Pâraskara III, 11, 10.

6. Pâraskara III, 11, 11,

7. Comp. above, chap. 3, 6.

13, 1. Nârâya*n*a evidently did not know the Upanishad here referred to; he states that it belongs to another *S*âkhâ. Comp. Professor Max Müller's note on B*ri*had Âra*n*yaka VI, 4, 24 (S. B. E., vol. xv, p. 222).

2. 'He should give her the two beans as a symbol of the testicles, and the barley grain as a symbol of the penis.' Nârâya*n*a.

should in the third month of her pregnancy, under
(the Nakshatra) Tishya, give to eat (to the wife),
after she has fasted, in curds from a cow which has
a calf of the same colour (with herself), two beans
and one barley grain for each handful of curds.

3. To his question, 'What dost thou drink?
What dost thou drink?' she should thrice reply,
'Generation of a male child! Generation of a male
child!'

4. Thus three handfuls (of curds).

5. He then inserts into her right nostril, in the
shadow of a round apartment, (the sap of) an herb
which is not faded,

6. According to some (teachers) with the Pragâvat
and Gîvaputra hymns.

7. Having sacrificed of a mess of cooked food
sacred to Pragâpati, he should touch the place of
her heart with the (verse,) 'What is hidden, O thou
whose hair is well parted, in thy heart, in Pragâpati,
that I know; such is my belief. May I not fall
into distress that comes from sons.'

---

5. Nârâyana (comp. also the Prayogaratna, folio 40; Âsvalâya-
nîya-Grihya-Parisish/a I, 25; MS. Chambers 667) separates this
rite from the ceremony described in Sûtras 2–4. He says that
Sûtras 2–4—as indeed is evidently the case—refer to the Pumsa-
vana, and in Sûtra 5 begins the Anavalobhana (comp. garbharaksha*na, Sânkh. I, 21). To me it seems more probable that the
text describes one continuous ceremony. There is no difficulty in
supposing that of the Anavalobhana, though it is mentioned in
Sûtra 1, no description is given in the following Sûtras, the same
being the case undoubtedly with regard to the Garbhalambhana,
of which a description is found in the Âsv.-Parisish/a I, 25.

6. Two texts commencing â te garbho yonim etu and Agnir
etu prathama*h. See Stenzler's Various Readings, p. 48, and the
Bibliotheca Indica edition, p. 61.

KAṆḌIKÂ 14.

1. In the fourth month of pregnancy the Símantonnayana (or parting of the hair, is performed).

2. In the fortnight of the increasing moon, when the moon stands in conjunction with a Nakshatra (that has a name) of masculine gender—

3. Then he gives its place to the fire, and having spread to the west of it a bull's hide with the neck to the east, with the hair outside, (he makes oblations,) while (his wife) is sitting on that (hide) and takes hold of him, with the two (verses), 'May Dhâtri give to his worshipper,' with the two verses, 'I invoke Râkâ' (Rig-veda II, 32, 4 seq.), and with (the texts), 'Ne_g_amesha,' and, 'Pra_g_âpati, no other one than thou' (Rig-veda X, 121, 10).

4. He then three times parts her hair upwards (i. e. beginning from the front) with a bunch containing an even number of unripe fruits, and with a porcupine's quill that has three white spots, and with three bunches of Ku_s_a grass, with (the words), 'Bhûr, bhuva_h_, svar, om!'

5. Or four times.

6. He gives orders to two lute-players, 'Sing king Soma.'

7. (They sing,) 'May Soma our king bless the human race. Settled is the wheel of N.N.'—(here they name) the river near which they dwell.

14, 3. Comp. above, chap. 8, 9. Regarding the two verses Dhâtâ dadâtu dâ_s_ushe, see _S_âṅkh.-G_ri_hya I, 22, 7. The Neg_amesha hymn is Rig-veda Khailika sûkta, vol. vi, p. 31, ed. Max Müller.

7. Comp. Pâraskara I, 15, 8. The Gâthâ there is somewhat different. I cannot see why in the Â_s_valâyana redaction of it nivish_ta_kakrâsau should not be explained, conformably to the

8. And whatever aged Bráhma*n*a woman, whose husbands and children are alive, tell them, that let them do.

9. A bull is the fee for the sacrifice.

KA*ND*IKÂ 15.

1. When a son has been born, (the father) should, before other people touch him, give him to eat from gold (i. e. from a golden vessel or with a golden spoon) butter and honey with which he has ground gold(-dust), with (the verse), 'I administer to thee the wisdom ('veda') of honey, of ghee, raised by Savit*ri* the bountiful. Long-living, protected by the gods, live a hundred autumns in this world!'

2. Approaching (his mouth) to (the child's) two ears he murmurs the 'production of intelligence:' 'Intelligence may give to thee god Savit*ri*, intelligence may goddess Sarasvatî, intelligence may give to thee the two divine A*s*vins, wreathed with lotus.'

3. He touches (the child's) two shoulders with (the verse), 'Be a stone, be an axe, be insuperable gold. Thou indeed art the Veda, called son; so live a hundred autumns'—and with (the verses), 'Indra, give the best treasures' (Rig-veda II, 21, 6), 'Bestow on us, O bountiful one, O speedy one' (Rig-veda III, 36, 10).

4. And let them give him a name beginning with

---

regular Sandhi laws, as nivish/a*k*akrâ asau. The wheel of course means the dominion.

15, 1. Comp. Â*sv*.-Gr*i*hya-Pari*s*ish/a I, 26. I follow Professor Stenzler, who corrects maghonâm into maghonâ; comp. *S*âṅkh.-Gr*i*hya I, 24, 4.

3. Vedo may as well be the nominative of veda as that of vedas ('property').

a sonant, with a semivowel in it, with the Visarga at its end, consisting of two syllables,

5. Or of four syllables;

6. Of two syllables, if he is desirous of firm position; of four syllables, if he is desirous of holy lustre;

7. But in every case with an even number (of syllables) for men, an uneven for women.

8. And let him also find out (for the child) a name to be used at respectful salutations (such as that due to the Â*k*ârya at the ceremony of the initiation); that his mother and his father (alone) should know till his initiation.

9. When he returns from a journey, he embraces his son's head and murmurs, 'From limb by limb thou art produced; out of the heart thou art born. Thou indeed art the self called son; so live a hundred autumns!'—(thus) he kisses him three times on his head.

10. The rite only (without the Mantra is performed) for a girl.

KA*ND*IKÂ 16.

1. In the sixth month the Annaprâ*s*ana (i.e. the first feeding with solid food).

2. Goat's flesh, if he is desirous of nourishment,

3. Flesh of partridge, if desirous of holy lustre,

4. Boiled rice with ghee, if desirous of splendour:

5. (Such) food, mixed with curds, honey and ghee he should give (to the child) to eat with (the verse), 'Lord of food, give us food painless and strong;

16, 1 seq. Comp. Sânkh.-G*ri*hya I, 27, 1 seq. The two texts are nearly word for word identical.

bring forward the giver; bestow power on us, on
men and animals.'

6. The rite only (without the Mantra) for a girl.

KANDIKÂ 17.

1. In the third year the Kaula (i.e. the tonsure
of the child's head), or according to the custom of
the family.

2. To the north of the fire he places vessels which
are filled respectively, with rice, barley, beans, and
sesamum seeds;

3. To the west (the boy) for whom the ceremony
shall be performed, in his mother's lap, bull-dung in
a new vessel, and Sami leaves are placed.

4. To the south of the mother the father (is
seated) holding twenty-one bunches of Kusa grass.

5. Or the Brahman should hold them.

6. To the west of (the boy) for whom the ceremony is to be performed, (the father) stations himself and pours cold and warm water together with
(the words), 'With warm water, O Vâyu, come
hither!'

7. Taking of that (water), (and) fresh butter, or
(some) drops of curds, he three times moistens (the
boy's) head, from the left to the right, with (the
formula), 'May Aditi cut thy hair; may the waters
moisten thee for vigour!'

8. Into the right part (of the hair) he puts each

---

4. He cuts off the hair four times on the right side (Sûtras 10–
14), three times on the left side (Sûtra 15); each time three Kusa
bunches are required. This is the reason why twenty-one bunches
are prescribed.

8. Each of the four times and of the three times respectively that
he cuts off the hair; see the preceding note.

time three Kusa bunches, with the points towards (the boy) himself, with (the words), ' Herb! protect him!'

9. (With the words,) 'Axe! do no harm to him!' he presses a copper razor (on the Kusa blades),

10. And cuts (the hair) with (the verse), ' The razor with which in the beginning Savit*ri* the knowing one has shaved (the beard) of king Soma and of Varu*n*a, with that, ye Brâhma*n*as, shave now his (hair), that he may be blessed with long life, with old age.'

11. Each time that he has cut, he gives (the hairs) with their points to the east, together with *S*amî leaves, to the mother. She puts them down on the bull-dung.

12. 'With what Dhât*ri* has shaven (the head) of B*ri*haspati, Agni and Indra, for the sake of long life, with that I shave thy (head) for the sake of long life, of glory, and of welfare'—thus a second time.

13. ' By what he may at night further see the sun, and see it long, with that I shave thy (head) for the sake of long life, of glory, and of welfare'—thus a third time.

14. With all (the indicated) Mantras a fourth time.

15. Thus three times on the left side (of the head).

16. Let him wipe off the edge of the razor with (the words), ' If thou shavest, as a shaver, his hair with the razor, the wounding, the well-shaped, purify his head, but do not take away his life.'

---

13. Instead of yena bhûyas *k*a râtryâm, Pâraskara (II, 1, 16) has, yena bhûri*s* *k*arâ divam.

16. Comp. Pâraskara II, 1, 19 ; Atharva-veda VIII, 2, 17.

17. Let him give orders to the barber. 'With luke-warm water doing what has to be done with water, without doing harm to him, arrange (his hair) well.'

18. Let him have the arrangement of the hair made according to the custom of his family.

19. The rite only (without the Mantras) for a girl.

KANDIKÂ 18.

1. Thereby the Godânakarman (i.e. the ceremony of shaving the beard, is declared).

2. In the sixteenth year.

3. Instead of the word 'hair' he should (each time that it occurs in the Mantras) put the word 'beard.'

4. Here they moisten the beard.

5. (The Mantra is), 'Purify his head and his face, but do not take away his life.'

6. He gives orders (to the barber with the words), 'Arrange his hair, his beard, the hair of his body, and his nails, ending in the north.'

7. Having bathed and silently stood during the rest of the day, let him break his silence in the presence of his teacher, (saying to him,) 'I give an optional gift (to thee).'

8. An ox and a cow is the sacrificial fee.

---

18. On these family customs, see Grihya-samgraha-parisishta II, 40; Roth, Zur Literatur und Geschichte des Weda, p. 120; Max Müller, History of A. S. L., p. 54 seq.; Weber, Indische Studien, X, 95.

18, 4. See above, chap. 17, 7.

5. See chap. 17, 16.

6. According to Nârâyana, he says to the barber (chap. 17, 17), 'With lukewarm water doing what has to be done with water, without doing harm to him, arrange his hair, his beard, the hair of his body, and his nails, ending in the north.'

7, 8. On restrictions like that contained in the eighth Sûtra as to the object in which the vara (optional gift) had to consist, see Weber, Indische Studien, V, 343.

9. Let (the teacher) impose (on the youth the observances declared below) for one year.

KANDIKÂ 19.

1. In the eighth year let him initiate a Brâhmana,
2. Or in the eighth year after the conception ;
3. In the eleventh a Kshatriya ;
4. In the twelfth a Vaisya.
5. Until the sixteenth (year) the time has not passed for a Brâhmana ;
6. Until the twenty-second for a Kshatriya ;
7. Until the twenty-fourth for a Vaisya.
8. After that (time has passed), they become patitasâvitrîka (i.e. they have lost their right of learning the Sâvitrî).
9. No one should initiate such men, nor teach them, nor perform sacrifices for them, nor have intercourse with them.
10. (Let him initiate) the youth who is adorned and whose (hair on the) head is arranged, who wears a (new) garment that has not yet been washed, or an antelope-skin, if he is a Brâhmana, the skin of a spotted deer, if a Kshatriya, a goat's skin, if a Vaisya.
11. If they put on garments, they should put on dyed (garments) : the Brâhmana a reddish yellow one, the Kshatriya a light red one, the Vaisya a yellow one.
12. Their girdles are : that of a Brâhmana made of Munga grass, that of a Kshatriya a bow-string, that of a Vaisya woollen.

9. See below, chap. 22, 22.

19, 10. By the 'arranging of the hair' the cutting of the hair is implied, as is seen from chap. 22, 22.

13. Their staffs are : that of a Brâhma*n*a of Palâsa wood, that of a Kshatriya of Udumbara wood, that of a Vaisya of Bilva wood.

KA*N*DIKÂ 20.

1. Or all (sorts of staffs are to be used) by (men of) all (castes).

2. While (the student) takes hold of him, the teacher sacrifices and then stations himself to the north of the fire, with his face turned to the east.

3. To the east (of the fire) with his face to the west the other one.

4. (The teacher then) fills the two hollows of (his own and the student's) joined hands with water, and with the verse, ' That we choose of Savit*ri*' (Rig-veda V, 82, 1) he makes with the full (hollow of his own hands the water) flow down on the full (hollow of) his, (i.e. the student's hands.) Having (thus) poured (the water over his hands) he should with his (own) hand seize his (i.e. the student's) hand together with the thumb, with (the formula), ' By the impulse of the god Savit*ri*, with the arms of the two Asvins, with Pûshan's hands I seize thy hand, N.N.!'

5. With (the words), ' Savit*ri* has seized thy hand, N.N.!' a second time.

6. With (the words), ' Agni is thy teacher, N.N.!' a third time.

7. He should cause him to look at the sun while the teacher says, ' God Savit*ri*, this is thy Brahma-*k*ârin ; protect him ; may he not die.'

20, 2. He offers the oblations prescribed above, chap. 1, 4, 3 seq.

8. (And further the teacher says), 'Whose Brahma*k*ârin art thou? The breath's Brahma*k*ârin art thou. Who does initiate thee, and whom (does he initiate)? To whom shall I give thee in charge?'

9. With the half verse, 'A youth, well attired, dressed came hither' (Rig-veda III, 8, 4) he should cause him to turn round from the left to the right.

10. Reaching with his two hands over his (i.e. the student's) shoulders (the teacher) should touch the place of his heart with the following (half verse).

11. Having wiped the ground round the fire, the student should put on a piece of wood silently. 'Silence indeed is what belongs to Pra*g*âpati. The student becomes belonging to Pra*g*âpati'—this is understood (in the *S*ruti).

KANDIKÂ 21.

1. Some (do this) with a Mantra: 'To Agni I have brought a piece of wood, to the great *G*âtavedas. Through that piece of wood increase thou, O Agni; through the Brahman (may) we (increase). Svâhâ!'

2. Having put the fuel (on the fire) and having

---

11. On the wiping of the ground round the fire, comp. above, chap. 3, 1 ; *S*ânkhâyana-G*ri*hya I, 7, 11. Nârâya*n*a here has the following remarks, which I can scarcely believe to express the real meaning of this Sûtra : ' Here the wiping of the ground round the fire is out of place, because the Sa*m*skâras for the fire have already been performed. As to that, it should be observed that the wiping is mentioned here in order that, when fuel is put on the fire in the evening and in the morning, the sprinkling of water and the wiping may be performed. But on this occasion (at the Upanayana) the student does not perform the wiping, &c., and silently puts a piece of wood on that fire.'

touched the fire, he three times wipes off his face
with (the words), 'With splendour I anoint myself.'

3. 'For with splendour does he anoint himself'—
this is understood (in the *S*ruti).

4. 'On me may Agni bestow insight, on me
offspring, on me splendour.

'On me may Indra bestow insight, on me offspring,
on me strength (indriya).

'On me may Sûrya bestow insight, on me offspring,
on me radiance.

'What thy splendour is, Agni, may I thereby become resplendent.

'What thy vigour is, Agni, may I thereby become
vigorous.

'What thy consuming power is, Agni, may I thereby
obtain consuming power'—with (these formulas) he
should approach the fire, bend his knee, embrace
(the teacher's feet), and say to him, 'Recite, sir!
The Sâvitrî, sir, recite!'

5. Seizing with his (i.e. the student's) garment and
with (his own) hands (the student's) hands (the
teacher) recites the Sâvitrî, (firstly) Pâda by Pâda,
(then) hemistich by hemistich, (and finally) the whole
(verse).

6. He should make him recite (the Sâvitrî) as far
as he is able.

7. On the place of his (i.e. the student's) heart (the
teacher) lays his hand with the fingers upwards, with
(the formula), 'Into my will I take thy heart; after
my mind shall thy mind follow; in my word thou
shalt rejoice with all thy will; may B*r*ihaspati join
thee to me.'

1. Having tied the girdle round him and given him the staff, he should impose the (observances of the) Brahmakarya on him—

2. (With the words), 'A Brahmakârin thou art. Eat water. Do the service. Do not sleep in the day-time. Devoted to the teacher study the Veda.'

3. Twelve years lasts the Brahmakarya for (each) Veda, or until he has learnt it.

4. Let him beg (food) in the evening and in the morning.

5. Let him put fuel on (the fire) in the evening and in the morning.

6. Let him beg first of a man who will not refuse,

7. Or of a woman who will not refuse.

8. (In begging he should use the words), 'Sir, give food!'

9. Or, '(Sir, give) Anupravakanîya (food).'

10. That (which he has received) he should announce to his teacher.

11. He should stand the rest of the day.

12. After sunset (the student) should cook the Brâhmaudana (or boiled rice with which the Brâhmanas are to be fed) for the Anupravakanîya sacrifice (the sacrifice to be performed after a part of the Veda has been studied), and should announce to the teacher (that it is ready).

22, 9. Food for the Anupravakanîya offering; see Sûtra 12.

10. Sânkhâyana-Grihya II, 6, 7; Pâraskara II, 5, 8.

12. 'The student should, according to the rules for the Pâkayagñas, cook the Anupravakaniya food and announce it to the teacher in the words, " The food is cooked." ' Nârâyana.

13. The teacher should sacrifice, while the student takes hold of him, with the verse, 'The wonderful lord of the abode' (Rig-veda I, 18, 6).

14. A second time with the Sâvitrî—

15. And whatever else has been studied afterwards.

16. A third time to the Rishis.

17. A fourth time (the oblation) to (Agni) Svishtakrit.

18. Having given food to the Brâhmanas he should cause them to pronounce the end of the Veda (study).

19. From that time (the student) should eat no saline food; he should observe chastity, and should sleep on the ground through three nights, or twelve nights, or one year.

20. When he has fulfilled those observances, (the teacher) performs (for him) the 'production of intelligence,' (in the following way) :

21. While (the student) towards an unobjectionable direction (of the horizon) sprinkles thrice (water) from the left to the right with a water-pot round a

15. Nârâyana mentions as such texts especially those belonging to the Âranyaka, viz. the Mahânâmnyas, the Mahâvrata, and the Upanishad. But there is no reason why we should not think quite as well of the Rig-veda Samhitâ itself.

18. 'He should say, "Sirs! Pronounce the end of the Veda (study)." And they should reply, " May an end of the Veda (study) be made." ' Nârâyana.

20. Comp. above, chap. 15, 2.

21. 'The objectionable directions are three, the south, the south-east, the south-west.' Nârâyana.

Susravas, which I have translated by 'glorious,' at the same time means, 'endowed with good hearing,' i.e. successful in study. The student therefore by the same word prays for glory and for success in Vedic learning.

Palâsa (tree) with one root, or round a Kusa bunch,
if there is no Palâsa, (the teacher) causes him to say,
'O glorious one, thou art glorious. As thou, O
glorious one, art glorious, thus, O glorious one, lead
me to glory. As thou art the preserver of the
treasure of sacrifice for the gods, thus may I become
the preserver of the treasure of the Veda for men.'

22. Thereby, beginning with his having the hair
cut, and ending with the giving in charge, the imposing of observances has been declared.

23. Thus for one who has not been initiated
before.

24. Now as regards one who has been initiated
before :

25. The cutting of the hair is optional,

26. And the 'production of intelligence.'

27. On the giving in charge there are no express
rules (in this case);

28. And on the time.

29. (He should recite to him) as the Sâvitrî (the
Rik), 'That we choose of god Savit*ri*' (Rig-veda V,
82, 1).

KANDIKÂ 23.

1. He chooses priests (for officiating at a sacrifice)
with neither deficient nor superfluous limbs, 'who on

---

22. The rules stated above for the Upanayana, beginning with
the prescription regarding the cutting of the hair (given chap. 19,
10 in the words, 'whose [hair on the] head is arranged ;' see the
note there), and ending with the ceremony prescribed chap. 20, 8,
are to be extended also to other cases of the imposing of a vow,
such, for instance, as that mentioned chap. 18, 9.

25. See chap. 19, 10.   26. See above, Sûtra 20.
27. See chap. 20, 8.   28. See chap. 4. 1.
29. Instead of the ordinary Sâvitrî, Rig-veda III, 62, 10.
23, 1. Comp. Srauta-sûtra IX, 3, 20 ; Grihya-sûtra I, 5, 1.

the mother's and on the father's side (&c.),' as it has been said above.

2. Let him choose young men as officiating priests : thus (declare) some (teachers).

3. He chooses first the Brahman, then the Hot*ri*, then the Adhvaryu, then the Udgât*ri*.

4. Or all who officiate at the Ahîna sacrifices and at those lasting one day.

5. The Kaushîtakinas prescribe the Sadasya as the seventeenth, saying, 'He is the looker-on at the performances.'

6. This has been said in the two *Rik*as, ' He whom the officiating priests, performing (the sacrifice) in many ways' (Rig-veda VIII, 58, 1. 2).

7. He chooses the Hot*ri* first.

8. With (the formula), 'Agni is my Hot*ri*; he is my Hot*ri*; I choose thee N. N. as my Hot*ri*' (he chooses) the Hot*ri*.

---

4. The Ahîna sacrifices are those which last more than one day, but not more than twelve days. (Indische Studien, IX, 373 ; X, 355.) The priests officiating at such sacrifices are the sixteen stated in the *Srauta*-sûtra IV, 1, 6. 7. Those besides the sixteen, though they are chosen (saty api vara*n*e) for taking part in the sacred performances, have not the rank of *ri*tvi*g*as (officiating priests) ; such are the Sadasya, the *Samitri*, and the *K*amasâdhvaryava*h* (schol. *Srautas*. loc. cit.). See Max Müller's History of A. S. L., pp. 450, 469 seq. As to the Sadasya, however, there was some difference of opinion (see the next Sûtra).

5. On the office of the Sadasya, see Indische Studien, X, 136, 144.

6. The two *Rik*as quoted here belong to the tenth among the Vâlakhilya hymns, a hymn omitted in many of the Rig-veda MSS. They give no special confirmation to the rules stated in our text, but contain only a general allusion to the unity of the sacrifice, which the various priests perform in many various ways.

7. 'If the four (chief) priests have to be chosen, the choosing of the Brâhma*n*a stands first in order (see above, Sûtra 3) ; if all (the sixteen), then the choosing of the Hot*ri* stands first in order.' Nârâya*n*a.

9. With (the formula), 'Kandramas (the moon) is my Brahman; he is my Brahman; I choose thee N. N. as my Brahman' (he chooses) the Brahman.

10. With (the formula), 'Âditya (the sun) is my Adhvaryu; (he is my Adhvaryu, &c.)'—the Adhvaryu.

11. With (the formula), 'Parganya is my Udgâtri; (he is my Udgâtri, &c.)'—the Udgâtri.

12. With (the formula), 'The waters are my reciters of what belongs to the Hotrakas'—the Hotrakas.

13. With (the formula), 'The rays are my Kamasâdhvaryus'—the Kamasâdhvaryus.

14. With (the formula), 'The ether is my Sadasya'—the Sadasya.

15. He whom he has chosen should murmur, 'A great thing thou hast told me; splendour thou hast told me; fortune thou hast told me; glory thou hast told me; praise thou hast told me; success thou hast told me; enjoyment thou hast told me; satiating thou hast told me; everything thou hast told me.'

16. Having murmured (this formula), the Hotri declares his assent (in the words), 'Agni is thy Hotri; he is thy Hotri; thy human Hotri am I.'

17. 'Kandramas (the moon) is thy Brahman; he is thy Brahman (&c.)'—thus the Brahman.

18. In the same way the others according to the prescriptions (given above).

19. And if (the priest who accepts the invitation)

---

12. The twelve priests of the sixteen (see § 4 note) who do not stand at the head of one of the four categories. Those at the head are enumerated in the Sutras 8–11.

13, 14. See above, § 4 note.

19. Priests who only perform the Agnyâdheya for a person, are, according to Nârâyana's note on this Sûtra, not considered as

is going to perform the sacrifice (for the inviting person, he should add), 'May that bless me; may that enter upon me ; may I thereby enjoy (bliss).'

20. The functions of an officiating priest are not to be exercised, if abandoned (by another priest), or at an Ahîna sacrifice with small sacrificial fee, or for a person that is sick, or suffering, or affected with consumption, or decried among the people in his village, or of despised extraction : for such persons (the functions of a *Ritvig* should not be exercised).

21. He (who is chosen as a *Ritvig*) should ask the Somapravâka, 'What sacrifice is it ? Who are

performing a sacrifice for him; consequently the formula given here is only to be used by priests who are elected for a Soma sacrifice. Stenzler translates, ' So spricht er, wenn er das Opfer durch sie vollziehen lassen will.' But this would be yakshya-mâ*na*h, not yâ*ga*yishyan.

20. The tradition takes nî*k*adakshi*na*sya as in apposition to ahînasya, and I have translated accordingly. But I cannot help thinking that the two words should be separated, so that we should have to translate, ' or at an Ahîna, or for a person that gives small sacrificial fee.' Thus the Brâhma*na* quoted by Âpastamba (see the commentary on the Pañ*k*avi*m*sa Brâhma*na*, vol. i, p. 6, ed. Bibl. Indica) gives the following questions which the *Ritvig* to be chosen should ask, ' Is it no Ahîna sacrifice ? Is the *Ritvig* office not abandoned by others? Is the sacrificial fee plentiful ?' It is a very singular fact, that on the one hand the assistance of a number of *Ritvigas* was unanimously declared necessary for the perform-ance of an Ahîna sacrifice, while on the other hand it was considered objectionable, at least among some of the Vedic schools, to officiate at such a sacrifice. See Weber's Indische Studien, X, 150, 151.

On anude*s*yabhi*s*asta Nârâya*na* says, sade*s*inâbhi*s*astasyaivam eke. anye tu *s*râddhe pratishiddhasyety âhu*h*. It seems to me that anude*s*ya (or rather ânude*s*ya ?) in Sâṅkhâyana-*S*raut. V, 1, 10 (Indische Studien, X, 147) means the same, though the commentary on that Sûtra ascribes a different meaning to that word.

21. The Somapravâka is the messenger who invites the priests on behalf of the sacrificer to officiate at his intended Soma sacrifice. Comp. Indische Studien, IX, 308.

the priests officiating? What is the fee for the sacrifice?'

22. If (all the conditions) are favourable, he should accept.

23. Let (the officiating priests) eat no flesh nor have intercourse with a wife until the completion of the sacrifice.

24. 'By this prayer, O Agni, increase' (Rig-veda I, 31, 18)—with (this verse) let him offer (at the end of the sacrifice) an oblation of Âgya in (his own) Dakshinâgni, and go away where he likes;

25. In the same way one who has not set up the (Srauta) fires, in his (sacred) domestic fire with this *Rik*, 'Forgive us, O Agni, this sin' (Rig-veda I, 31, 16).

KANDIKÂ 24.

1. When he has chosen the *Ritvigas*, he should offer the Madhuparka (i. e. honey-mixture) to them (in the way described in Sûtras 5 and following);

2. To a Snâtaka, when he comes to his house;

3. And to a king;

4. And for a teacher, the father-in-law, a paternal uncle, and a maternal uncle.

5. He pours honey into curds,

6. Or butter, if he can get no honey.

7. A seat, the water for washing the feet, the Arghya water (i. e. perfumed water into which flowers have been thrown), the water for sipping, the honey-

---

24, 1 seqq. Comp. Sâṅkhâyana-Grihya II, 15. The second Sûtra is paraphrased by Nârâyana thus, 'To a person that has performed the Samâvartana (see below, III, 8), when he comes on that day to his house with the intention of forming a matrimonial alliance.'

mixture, a cow: every one of these things they
announce three times (to the guest).

8. With (the verse), 'I am the highest one among
my people, as the sun among the thunderbolts. Here
I tread on him whosoever infests me'—he should
sit down on the seat (made of) northward-pointed
(grass).

9. Or (he should do so) after he has trodden
on it.

10. He should make (his host) wash his feet.

11. The right foot he should stretch out first to a
Brâhmana,

12. The left to a Sûdra.

13. When his feet have been washed, he receives
the Arghya water in the hollow of his joined hands
and then sips the water destined thereto, with (the
formula), 'Thou art the first layer for Ambrosia.'

14. He looks at the Madhuparka when it is
brought to him, with (the formula), 'I look at thee
with Mitra's eye.'

15. He accepts it with his joined hands with (the
formula), 'By the impulse of the god Savitri, with
the arms of the two Asvins, with the hands of Pûshan
I accept thee.' He then takes it into his left hand,
looks at it with the three verses, 'Honey the winds
to the righteous one' (Rig-veda I, 90, 6 seqq.), stirs
it about three times from left to right with the fourth
finger and the thumb, and wipes (his fingers) with
(the formula), 'May the Vasus eat thee with the
Gâyatrî metre'—to the east;

16. With (the formula), 'May the Rudras eat thee
with the Trishtubh metre'—to the south;

17. With (the formula), 'May the Âdityas eat
thee with the Gagatî metre'—to the west;

18. With (the formula), ' May the Vi*s*ve devâs eat thee with the Anush*t*ubh metre'—to the north.

19. With (the formula), ' To the beings thee'—he three times takes (some of the Madhuparka substance) out of the middle of it.

20. With (the formula), 'The milk of Virâ*g* art thou '—he should partake thereof the first time,

21. With, ' The milk of Virâ*g* may I obtain'—the second time,

22. With, ' In me (may) the milk of Padyâ Virâ*g* (dwell) '—the third time.

23. (He should) not (eat) the whole (Madhuparka).

24. He should not satiate himself.

25. To a Brâhma*n*a, to the north, he should give the remainder.

26. If that cannot be done, (he should throw it) into water.

27. Or (he may eat) the whole (Madhuparka).

28. He then makes a rinsing of his mouth follow (on the eating of the Madhuparka) with the water destined thereto, with (the formula), ' Thou art the covering of Ambrosia.'

29. With (the formula), ' Truth! Glory! Fortune! May fortune rest on me!'—a second time.

30. When he has sipped water, they announce to him the cow.

31. Having murmured, 'Destroyed is my sin ; my sin is destroyed,' (he says,) ' Om, do it.' if he chooses to have her killed.

32. Having murmured, ' The mother of the Rudras, the daughter of the Vasus ' (Rig-veda VIII,

22. On Padyâ Virâ*g*, see the note on Sânkhâyana-G*ri*hya III, 7, 5.
28. Comp. above, Sûtra 13.

101, 15), (he says,) ' Om, let her loose,' if he chooses to let her loose.

33. Let the Madhuparka not be without flesh, without flesh.

End of the First Adhyâya.

33. Comp. *Sânkhâyana-Grihya* II, 15, 2.

1. On the full moon day of the *Srâvana* month the *Srâvana* ceremony (is performed).

2. Having filled a new jug with flour of fried barley, he lays (this jug) and a spoon for offering the Balis on new strings of a carrying pole (and thus suspends them).

3. Having prepared fried barley grains, he smears half of them with butter.

4. After sunset he prepares a mess of cooked food and a cake in one dish and sacrifices (the cooked food) with the four verses, ' Agni, lead us on a good path to wealth ' (Rig-veda I, 189, 1 seqq.), verse by verse, and with his hand the (cake) in one dish with (the formula), ' To the steady One, the earth-demon, svâhâ !'

5. (The cake) should be (entirely) immersed (into the butter), or its back should be visible.

6. With (the verse), ' Agni, do not deliver us to evil' (Rig-veda I, 189, 5) he sacrifices over it (the butter) in which it had lain.

7. With (the verse), ' May the steeds at our invocation be for a blessing to us ' (Rig-veda VII, 38, 7) (he sacrifices) the besmeared grains with his joined hands.

8. The other (grains) he should give to his people.

9. Out of the jug he fills the spoon with flour,

1, 1. Nârâyana's observation that the *Srâvana* full moon can fall also under certain other Nakshatras than *Sravana* itself, furnishes no reason why we should think here of solar months, as Prof. Stenzler proposes.

7, 8. See above, Sûtra 3.   9. See above, Sûtra 1.

goes out (of the house) to the east, pours water on
the ground on a clean spot, sacrifices with (the
formula), ' To the divine hosts of the serpents
svâhâ!' and does reverence to them with (the
formula), ' The serpents which are terrestrial, which
are aerial, which are celestial, which dwell in the
directions (of the horizon)—to them I have brought
this Bali; to them I give over this Bali.'

10. Having gone round (the Bali) from left to
right, he sits down to the west of the Bali with (the
words), ' The serpent art thou; the lord of the
creeping serpents art thou; by food thou protectest
men, by cake the serpents, by sacrifice the gods.
To me, being in thee, the serpents being in thee
should do no harm. I give over the firm one
(i. e. the spoon) to thee.'

11. ' Firm one, (I give) N. N. (in charge) to thee!
Firm one, (I give) N. N. (in charge) to thee!'—
with (these words he gives) his people, man by man,
(in charge to the serpent god);

12. ' Firm one, I give myself in charge to thee!'—
with these words himself at the end.

13. Let no one step between it (i. e. the Bali, and
the sacrificer), until the giving in charge has been
performed.

14. With (the formula), ' To the divine hosts of
the serpents svâhâ!'—let him offer the Bali in the
evening and in the morning, till the Pratyavarohana
(i. e. the ceremony of the ' redescent').

15. Some count (the days till the Pratyavarohana)

---

14. On the Pratyavarohana, see the third chapter of this
Adhyâya.

15. I.e. two Bali offerings for each day, one for the morning and
one for the evening.

and offer the corresponding number of Balis already
on that day (on which the Sravaṇâ ceremony is
performed).

KANDIKÂ 2.

1. On the full moon day of Âsvayuga the Âsvayugî
ceremony (is performed).

2. Having adorned the house, having bathed and
put on clean garments, they should pour out a mess
of cooked food for Pasupati, and should sacrifice it
with (the formula), ' To Pasupati, to Siva, to Saṃkara,
to Prishâtaka svâhâ!'

3. He should sacrifice with his joined hands a
mixture of curds and butter (prishâtaka) with (the
formula), 'May what is deficient be made full to me;
may what is full not decay to me. To Prishâtaka
svâhâ!'

4. 'United with the seasons, united with the
manners, united with Indra and Agni, svâhâ!

' United with the seasons, united with the manners,
united with the Visve devâs, svâhâ!

' United with the seasons, united with the manners,
united with Heaven and Earth, svâhâ!'—with (these
formulas) a mess of cooked food is offered at the

2, 2. ' The plural " They should sacrifice it " means, that while
the sacrifice is performed by the householder, his sons and the
other persons belonging to the house should touch him.' Nârâyaṇa.

4. The Âgrayaṇa sacrifice, which is offered when the sacrificer is
going to partake of the first-fruits of the harvest, is treated of, with
relation to a sacrificer who keeps the Srauta fires, in the Srauta-
sûtra II, 9. This Sûtra in my opinion should be understood as a
supplementary addition to that chapter. Nârâyaṇa refers the rule
here given to the case of any incident or danger (âpad) which pre-
vents the sacrificer from performing the ceremony in its fuller
form, as prescribed in the Srauta-sûtra.

Âgrayana sacrifice by one who has set up the (sacred
Srauta) fires.

5. Also by one who has not set up the (Srauta)
fires (the same offering is performed) in the (sacred)
domestic fire.

KANDIKÂ 3.

1. On the full moon of Mârgasîrsha the 'redescent' (is performed)—on the fourteenth (Tithi),

2. Or on (the Tithi of) the full moon (itself).

3. Having again renovated the house by (giving a
new) coating (to the walls), by spreading out (a new
roof), and by levelling (the floor), they should sacrifice
after sunset (oblations) of milk-rice with (the texts),
' Beat away, O white one, with thy foot, with the fore-
foot and with the hind-foot, these seven daughters
of Varuna and all that belong to the king's tribe.
Svâhâ!

'Within the dominion of the white one no serpent
has killed anything. To the white one, the son of
Vidârva, adoration! Svâhâ!'

4. Here no oblation to (Agni) Svishtakrit (is
made).

5. 'May we be secure from Pragâpati's sons'—
thus he murmurs while looking at the fire.

3, 1. On the ceremony of ' redescent,' comp. Sânkhâyana-Grihya
IV, 17; Pâraskara III, 2. The fourteenth Tithi of the bright fortnight, preceding the full moon, is referred to.

3. 'Again' refers to chap. 2, 2. As to the words ' they should
sacrifice,' comp. the note on the same Sûtra. The first Mantra
reoccurs in Sânkhâyana-Grihya IV, 18, 1. The text of the second
should be, na vai svetasyâdhyâkâre, &c.; comp. Pâraskara II,
14, 5.

5. The serpents are the children of Kasyapa (i.e. Pragâpati) and
Kadrû; see Mahâbhârata I, 1074 seqq.

6. (Saying), 'Be happy and friendly to us'—he should think in his mind of the winter.

7. To the west of the fire is a well-spread layer (of straw); on that he should sit down, murmur (the verse), 'Be soft, O earth' (Rig-veda I, 22, 15), and lie down (on that layer) with his people, with the head to the east and the face to the north.

8. The others, as there is room.

9. Or following on each other from the eldest to the youngest.

10. Those who know the Mantras, should murmur the Mantras.

11. Arising (they should) three times (murmur the verse), 'From that place may the gods bless us' (Rig-veda I, 22, 16).

12. The same (verse) a fourth time with their faces to the south, to the west, and to the north.

13. Having arisen, having murmured the hymns sacred to the Sun and the auspicious hymns, having prepared food and given to the Brâhmaṇas to eat, he should cause (them) to pronounce auspicious words.

KANDIKÂ 4.

1. On the eighth days of the four dark fortnights of (the two seasons of) winter and Sisira the Ashtakâs (are celebrated).

---

10. ' The Mantras beginning from " Be soft, O earth " (Sûtra 7) down to the auspicious hymns (Sûtra 13).' Nârâyaṇa.

11. It follows from Sûtra 12 that they are to turn here their faces to the east.

12. They mutter one Pâda of that verse, which is in the Gâyatri metre, turned towards each of the three directions.

4, 1. Comp. Sânkhâyana-Grihya III, 12 seqq. The four

2. Or on one (of these days).

3. The day before, he should offer to the Fathers (i. e. Manes)—

4. Boiled rice, boiled rice with sesamum seeds, rice-milk—

5. Or cakes made of four Saravas (of ground grain)—

6. Sacrificing with the eight (verses), 'May the lower (Fathers) and the higher arise' (Rig-veda X, 15, 1 seqq.), or with as many (verses) as he likes.

7. Then on the next day the Ash/akâs (are celebrated) with an animal (sacrifice) and with a mess of cooked food.

8. He may also give grass to an ox,

9. Or he may burn down brushwood with fire—

10. With (the words), 'This is my Ash/akâ.'

11. But he should not omit celebrating the Ash-/akâ.

12. This (Ash/akâ) some state to be sacred to the Visve devâs, some to Agni, some to the Sun, some to Pragâpati, some state that the Night is its deity, some that the Nakshatras are, some that the Seasons are, some that the Fathers are, some that cattle is.

13. Having killed the animal according to the

months of Hemanta and Sisira are Mârgasirsha, Pausha, Mâgha, and Phâlguna.

2. The statement of the Prayogaratna that in case the sacrificer should celebrate only one Ash/akâ festival, the Ash/akâ of the Mâgha month is to be selected, well agrees with the designation of this Ash/akâ as 'the one Ash/akâ' (ekâsh/akâ); see Weber, Naxatra II, 341 seq.; Indische Studien, XV, 145.

7 seqq. Comp. the nearly identical passage in Sânkhâyana-Grihya III, 14, 3 seqq. and the note there. Âsvalâyana evidently gives these rules not as regarding one special Ash/akâ but all of them.

13. Comp. above, I, 11, 1. 2. 10. As to the Mantra, comp. Sânkhâyana III, 13, 3.

ritual of the animal sacrifice, omitting the sprinkling (with water) and the touching of the animal with a fresh branch, he should draw out the omentum and sacrifice it with (the verse), 'Carry the omentum, Gâtavedas, to the Fathers, where thou knowest them resting afar. May streams of fat flow to them ; may all these wishes be fulfilled. Svâhâ !'

14. Then (follow oblations) of the Avadâna portions and the cooked food, two with (the two verses), ' Agni, lead us on a good path to wealth ' (Rig-veda I, 189, 1 seq.), (and other oblations with the texts), ' May summer, winter, the seasons be happy to us, happy the rainy season, safe to us the autumn. The year be our lord who gives breath to us ; may days and nights produce long life. Svâhâ !

' Peaceful be the earth, happy the air, may the goddess Heaven give us safety. Happy be the quarters (of the horizon), the intermediate quarters, the upper quarters ; may the waters, the lightnings protect us from all sides. Svâhâ !

' May the waters, the rays carry our prayers (to the gods); may the creator, may the ocean turn away evil ; may the past and the future, (may) all be safe to me. Protected by Brahman may I pour forth songs. Svâhâ !

' May all the Âdityas and the divine Vasus, the Rudras, the protectors, the Maruts sit down (here). May Pragâpati, the abounding one, the highest ruler, bestow vigour, offspring, immortality on me. Svâhâ !

' Pragâpati, no other one than Thou (Rig-veda X, 121, 10).'

---

14. I read, as Prof. Stenzler and the Petersburg Dictionary do, svârâ ksharâni. Comp. Pâraskara III, 3, 6.

15. The eighth (oblation) is that to (Agni) Svi-sh/akr*it*.

16. He should give to the Brâhma*n*as to eat: this has been said.

KA*N*DIKÂ 5.

1. On the following day the Anvash/akya (i. e. the ceremony following the Ash/akâ, is performed).

2. Having prepared (a portion) of that same meat, having established the fire on a surface inclined towards the south, having fenced it in, and made a door on the north side of the enclosure, having strewn round (the fire) three times sacrificial grass with its roots, without tossing it, turning the left side towards the fire, he should put down the things to be offered, boiled rice, boiled rice with sesamum seeds, rice-milk, meal-pap with curds, and meal-pap with honey.

3. (The ceremony should be performed) according to the ritual of the Pi*nd*apit*ri*ya*gñ*a.

4. Having sacrificed (of those sorts of food) with the exception of the meal-pap with honey, let him give (lumps of those substances) to the Fathers.

5. And to (their) wives, with the addition of rum and the scum of boiled rice.

6. Some (place the lumps to be offered) into pits, into two or into six.

16. See above, chap. 3, 13.

5, 2. The meat is that of the animal killed on the Ash/akâ day; see chap. 4, 13.

3. This ritual is given in the *S*rauta-sûtra II, 6 seq.

4. He sacrifices the two oblations prescribed in the *S*rauta-sûtra II, 6, 12, to Soma pit*ri*mat and to Agni kavyavâhana.

7. In those situated to the east he should give (the offerings) to the Fathers.

8. In those to the west, to the wives.

9. Thereby the ceremony celebrated in the rainy season on the Mâgha day, in the dark fortnight after the full moon of Praush*th*apada (has been declared).

10. And thus he should offer (a celebration like the Anvash*t*akya) to the Fathers every month, observing uneven numbers (i. e. selecting a day with an uneven number, inviting an uneven number of Brâhma*n*as, &c.).

11. He should give food at least to nine (Brâhma*n*as),

12. Or to an uneven number;

13. To an even number on auspicious occasions or on the performance of meritorious deeds (such as the consecration of ponds, &c.);

14. To an uneven number on other (occasions).

15. The rite is performed from left to right. Barley is to be used instead of sesamum.

KANDIKÂ 6.

1. When going to mount a chariot he should touch the wheels with his two hands separately with (the words), ' I touch thy two fore-feet. Thy two wheels are the B*ri*hat and the Rathantara (Sâmans).'

9. Comp. the note on Sânkhâyana-Gr*i*hya III, 13, 1.
10. Comp. Sânkhâyana-Gr*i*hya IV, 1, 1.
13. Sânkhâyana-Gr*i*hya IV, 4, 4.
15. Sânkhâyana-Gr*i*hya IV, 4, 6. 9.
6, 1. ' He should touch at the same time the right wheel with his right hand, the left wheel with his left hand.' Nârâya*n*a.

2. 'Thy axle is the Vâmadevya'—with (these words he touches) the two (naves) in which the axle rests.

3. He should mount (the chariot) with the right foot first, with (the words), 'With Vâyu's strength I mount thee, with Indra's power and sovereignty.'

4. He should touch the reins, or if the horses have no reins, (he should touch) the horses with a staff, with (the words), 'With Brahman's splendour I seize you. With truth I seize you.'

5. When (the horses) put themselves in motion, he should murmur, 'Go forward to thousandfold successful vigour, divine chariot, carry us forward!' —(and the verse), 'Free, strong be thy limbs!' (Rigveda VI, 47, 26.)

6. With this (verse he should touch also) other articles of wood.

7. 'May the two oxen be strong, the axle firm' (Rig-veda III, 53, 17)—with (this verse) he should touch (each) part of the chariot (alluded to in that verse).

8. With (the verse), 'The earth, the good protectress, the unattained heaven' (Rig-veda X, 63, 10) (he should ascend) a ship.

9. With a new chariot he should drive round a widely known tree or round a pool that does not dry up, with his right side turned towards it, and then should fetch branches which bear fruits,

---

2. On the Vedic form of the chariot and of the wheels, comp. Zimmer, Altindisches Leben, p. 247.

6. According to Nârâyana this Sûtra would refer only to other vehicles of wood, which he is directed to touch with that *Rik* when going to mount them. Perhaps the commentator is right; the wording of the *Rik* is well in keeping with his explanation.

10. Or something else that belongs to the household.

11. (He then) should drive (in that chariot) to an assembly.

12. Having murmured, while looking at the sun, (the verse), 'Make our renown highest' (Rig-veda IV, 31, 15), he should descend.

13. 'To the bull among my equals' (Rig-veda X, 166, 1)—(this verse he should murmur) while approaching (that assembly?).

14. 'May we be called to-day Indra's best friends' (Rig-veda I, 167, 10)—when the sun is setting.

15. 'Thus I address you, O daughters of heaven, while you arise' (Rig-veda IV, 51, 11)—when day appears.

KANDIKÂ 7.

1. Now the examination of the ground (where he intends to build a house).

2. (It must be) non-salinous soil of undisputed property,

3. With herbs and trees,

4. On which much Kuśa and Vîraṇa grass grows.

5. Plants with thorns and with milky juice he should dig out with their roots and remove them—

6. And in the same way the following (sorts of plants), viz. Apâmârga, potherbs, Tilvaka, Parivyâdha.

7. A spot where the waters, flowing together from all sides to the centre of it, flow round the resting-place, having it on their right side, and then flow off to the east without noise—that possesses all auspicious qualities.

8. Where the waters flow off, he should have the provision-room built.

9. Thus it becomes rich in food.

10. On a spot which is inclined towards the south, he should have the assembly-room constructed; thus there will be no gambling in it.

11. (But others say that) in such (an assembly-room) the young people become gamblers, quarrelsome, and die early.

12. Where the waters flow together from all directions, that assembly-room (situated on such a spot) brings luck and is free from gambling.

KA*N*DIKÂ 8.

1. Now he should examine the ground in the following ways.

2. He should dig a pit knee-deep and fill it again with the same earth (which he has taken out of it).

3. If (the earth) reaches out (of the pit, the ground is) excellent; if it is level, (it is) of middle quality; if it does not fill (the pit, it is) to be rejected.

4. After sunset he should fill (the pit) with water and leave it so through the night.

5. If (in the morning) there is water in it, (the ground is) excellent; if it is moist, (it is) of middle quality; if it is dry, (it is) to be rejected.

6. White (ground), of sweet taste, with sand on the surface, (should be elected) by a Brâhma*n*a.

7. Red (ground) for a Kshatriya.

8. Yellow (ground) for a Vai*s*ya.

9. He should draw a thousand furrows on it and should have it measured off as quadrangular, with equal sides to each (of the four) directions;

10. Or as an oblong quadrangle.

11. With a *Sami* branch or an Udumbara branch he sprinkles it (with water), going thrice round it, so that his right side is turned towards it, reciting the *Santâtiya* hymn.

12. And (so he does again three times) pouring out water without interruption, with the three verses, 'O waters, ye are wholesome' (Rig-veda X, 9, 1 seqq.).

13. In the interstices between the bamboo staffs he should have the (single) rooms constructed.

14. Into the pits in which the posts are to stand, he should have an Avakâ, i. e. (the water-plant called) *Sipâla* put down; then fire will not befall him: thus it is understood (in the *Sruti*).

15. Having put (that plant) into the pit in which the middle-post is to stand, he should spread (on it) eastward-pointed and northward-pointed Kusa grass and should sprinkle (on that grass) water into which rice and barley have been thrown, with (the words), 'To the steady one, the earth-demon, svâhâ!'

16. He then should, when (the middle-post) is being erected, recite over it (the two verses),

'Stand here, fixed in the ground, prosperous, long-

8, 11. The hymn of which all verses (except a few) commence with, and frequently contain, the word *sam* (Rig-veda VII, 35).

13. The bamboo staffs (vamsa) rest on the chief posts (sthûnâ); see chap. 9, 1. 2.

15. Comp. chap. 1, 4.

16. Comp. *Sânkhâyana-Grihya* III, 3, 1 and the note there. How stâmirâvatîm should be corrected and translated is quite uncertain. Instead of poshasva Prof. Stenzler proposes to read poshasya, as *Sânkhâyana* has; I have adopted this correction.— In the second verse *gâyatâm* saha seems to be corrupt; comp. my note on *Sânkhâyana* III, 2, 9. Instead of parisritah we should read, as *Sânkhâyana*, Pâraskara, and the Atharva-veda (III, 12, 7) have, parisrutah.

lasting (?), standing amid prosperity. May the malevolent ones not attain thee!

'To thee (may) the young child (come), to thee the calf. . . ; to thee (may) the cup of Parisrut (come); (to thee) may they come with pots of curds.'

KANDIKÂ 9.

1. (Over) the bamboo staff, when it is put on (the middle-post, he recites the hemistich),

2. 'Rightly ascend the post, O staff, bestowing on us long life henceforward.'

3. On four stones, on which Dûrvâ grass has been spread, he should establish the water-barrel with (the words), 'Arise on the earth'—

4. Or with (the verse), 'The Arangara sounds, three times bound with the strap. It praises the welfare; may it drive away ill.'

5. He then should pour water into it with (the verse), 'Hither may king Varuna come with the plentiful (waters); at this place may he stay contented; bringing welfare, dropping ghee may they lie down together with Mitra.'

6. He then 'appeases' it (in the following way).

7. He puts gold into water into which rice and barley have been thrown, and (with that water) he sprinkles it three times, going round it with his right side turned towards it, with the Santâtîya hymn.

8. And (so he does again three times) pouring out

9, 4. The meaning of Arangara is unknown to me; it seems to be a musical instrument. Comp. Atharva-veda XX, 135, 13.

6. The ground on which the house is to be built.

7. On the Santâtîya hymn, see above, chap. 8. 11.

8. This Sûtra is identical with chap. 8, 12.

water without interruption, with the three verses, 'O
waters, ye are wholesome' (Rig-veda X, 9, 1 seqq.).

9. In the middle of the house he should cook a
mess of food, sacrifice (therefrom) with the four
verses, 'Vâstoshpati, accept us' (Rig-veda VII, 54,
1 seqq.), verse by verse, should prepare food, should
give to the Brâhma*n*as to eat, and should cause them
to say, 'Lucky is the ground! Lucky is the ground!'

KANDIKÂ 10.

1. It has been declared how he should enter the
house (when returning from a journey).

2. The house, when he enters it, should be provided with seed-corn.

3. He should have his field ploughed under the
Nakshatras Uttarâ*h* Prosh*tht*apadâs, (Uttarâ*h*) Phâl-
gunyas, or Rohi*n*i.

4. In order that the wind may blow to him from
the field, he should offer oblations with the hymn,
'Through the lord of the field' (Rig-veda IV, 57),
verse by verse, or he should murmur (that hymn).

5. He should speak over the cows when they go
away, the two verses, 'May refreshing wind blow
over the cows' (Rig-veda X, 169, 1 seq.).

6. When they come back, (he should recite the
following verses,)
'May they whose udder with its four holes is full

9. Comp. above, chap. 3, 13.
10, 1. See *S*rauta-sûtra II, 5, 17 seqq. It is there expressly
stated that these rules refer also to an Anâhitâgni.
3. *S*ânkhâyana IV, 13, 1.
5. *S*ânkhâyana-G*ri*hya III, 9.
6. *S*ânkhâyana, loc. cit.—Should the reading upa maitu be corrected into upa maita?

of honey and ghee, be milk-givers to us; (may they be) many in our stable, rich in ghee.

'Come hither to me, giving refreshment, bringing vigour and strength. Giving inexhaustible milk, rest in my stable that I may become the highest one'—

And, 'They who have raised their body up to the gods'—the rest of the hymn (Rig-veda X, 169, 3. 4).

7. Some recite (instead of the texts stated in Sûtra 6) the Âgâvîya hymn.

8. He should approach their herds, if the cows do not belong to his Guru, with (the words), 'Prospering are ye; excellent are ye, beautiful, dear. May I become dear to you. May you see bliss in me.'

End of the Second Adhyâya.

---

7. The hymn commencing â gâvo agman (hither came the cows) is Rig-veda VI, 28.

8. Perhaps the last words (which are repeated twice in order to mark the end of the Adhyâya) should be written sa*m* mayi *g*ânîdhvam, 'live with me in harmony together.'

1. Now (follow) the five sacrifices :

2. The sacrifice to the Gods, the sacrifice to the Beings, the sacrifice to the Fathers, the sacrifice to Brahman, the sacrifice to men.

3. Here now, if he makes oblations over the (sacred) fire, this is the sacrifice to the Gods.

If he makes Bali offerings, this is the sacrifice to the Beings.

If he gives (Pinda offerings) to the Fathers, this is the sacrifice to the Fathers.

If he studies (Vedic) texts, this is the sacrifice to Brahman.

If he gives to men, this is the sacrifice to men.

4. These (five kinds of) sacrifices he should perform every day.

KANDIKÂ 2.

1. Now the rules how one should recite (the Vedic texts) for one's self.

2. He should go out of the village to the east or to the north, bathe in water, sip water on a clean spot, clad with the sacrificial cord; he should spread out, his garment being not wet, a great quantity of Darbha grass, the tufts of which are directed towards the east, and should sit down thereon with his face turned to the east, making a lap, putting together his hands in which he holds purifiers (i. e. Kusa blades), so that the right hand lies uppermost.

1, 1 seqq. Comp. Satapatha Brâhmana XI, 5, 6, 1 seqq.

It is understood (in the *S*ruti), 'This is what
Darbha grass is: it is the essence of waters and
herbs. He thus makes the Brahman provided with
essence.'
Looking at the point where heaven and earth
touch each other, or shutting his eyes, or in whatever
way he may deem himself apt (for reciting the Veda),
thus adapting himself he should recite (the sacred
texts) for himself.

3. The Vyâh*ri*tis preceded by (the syllable) Om
(are pronounced first).

4. He (then) repeats the Sâvitrî (Rig-veda III, 62,
10), (firstly) Pâda by Pâda, (then) hemistich by
hemistich, thirdly the whole.

KA*ND*IKÂ 3.

1. He then should recite for himself (the following
texts, viz.) the *Ri*kas, the Ya*g*us, the Sâmans, the
Atharvan and A*n*giras hymns, the Brâhma*n*as, the
Kalpa (Sûtras), the Gâthâs, the (texts in honour of
kings and heroes, called) Nârâ*sa*msîs, the Itihâsas
and Purâ*n*as.

2. In that he recites the *Ri*kas, he thereby satiates
the gods with oblations of milk—in that (he recites)
the Ya*g*us, with oblations of ghee—the Sâmans, with
oblations of honey—the Atharvan and A*n*giras
hymns, with oblations of Soma—the Brâhma*n*as,
Kalpas, Gâthâs, Nârâ*sa*msîs, Itihâsas and Purâ*n*as,
with oblations of ambrosia.

3, 1. On this and the following paragraphs comp. chiefly *S*atapatha
Brâhma*n*a XI, 5, 6. Other enumerations, contained in the Veda
itself, of the texts that were considered as forming the Veda or as
attached to the body of the Veda, are found in the *S*atapatha
Brâhma*n*a XIV, 5, 4, 10 (Sacred Books, XV, 111), and in the
*Kh*ândogya Upanishad VII, 1 (Sacred Books, I, 109).

3. In that he recites the *Rik*as, rivers of milk flow, as a funeral oblation, to his Fathers. In that (he recites) the Ya*g*us, rivers of ghee—the Sâmans, rivers of honey—the Atharvan and Angiras hymns, rivers of Soma—the Brâhma*n*as, Kalpas, Gâthâs, Nârâ*s*a*m*sîs, Itihâsas and Purâ*n*as, rivers of ambrosia.

4. After he has recited (those texts) as far as he thinks fit, he should finish with the following (verse), 'Adoration to Brahman! Adoration be to Agni! Adoration to the Earth! Adoration to the Herbs! Adoration to the Voice! Adoration to the Lord of the Voice! Adoration I bring to great Vish*n*u!'

KANDIKÂ 4.

1. He satiates the deities: 'Pra*g*âpati, Brahman, the Vedas, the gods, the *R*ishis, all metres, the word Om, the word Vasha*t*, the Vyâh*ri*tis, the Sâvitrî, the sacrifices, Heaven and Earth, the air, days and nights, the numbers, the Siddhas, the oceans, the rivers, the mountains, the fields, herbs, trees, Gandharvas and Apsaras, the snakes, the birds, the cows, the Sâdhyas, the Vipras, the Yakshas, the Rakshas, the beings that have these (Rakshas, &c.) at their end.'

2. Then the *R*ishis: 'The (*R*ishis) of the hundred (*Rik*as), the (*R*ishis) of the middle (Ma*n*dalas), G*ri*t-

---

4, 1. Comp. Sânkhâyana-G*ri*hya IV, 9. Nârâya*n*a: 'Having finished (the Svâdhyâya) he satiates with water oblations these deities.'

Pra*g*âpati and the following words stand in the nominative; the verb to be supplied is tr*i*pyatu (tr*i*pyantu), 'may he (they) satiate himself (themselves).'

2. Sânkhâyana-G*ri*hya IV, 10. Sânkhâyana has pâvamânâ*h*, 'the (*R*ishis) of the Pavamâna hymns,' but pra*g*âthâ*h* as Âsvalâyana has, and not as we should expect, prâgâthâ*h*.

samada, Viśvâmitra, Vâmadeva, Atri, Bharadvâ*g*a, Vasish*th*a, the Pragâthas, the Pavamâna hymns, the (*Ri*shis) of the short hymns, and of the long hymns.'

3. (Then) with the sacrificial cord suspended over the right shoulder :

4. 'Sumantu, *G*aimini, Vaiśampâyana, Paila, the Sûtras, the Bhâshyas, the Bhârata, the Mahâbhârata, the teachers of law, *G*ânanti, Bâhavi, Gârgya, Gautama, *S*âkalya, Bâbhravya, Mâ*nd*avya, Mâ*nd*ûkeya, Gârgî Vâ*k*aknavî, Va*d*avâ Prâtîtheyî, Sulabhâ Maitreyî, Kahola Kaushîtaka, Mahâkaushîtaka, Paiṅgya, Mahâpaiṅgya, Suya*gñ*a *S*âṅkhâyana, Aitareya, Mahaitareya, the *S*âkala (text), the Bâshkala (text), Su*g*âtavaktra, Audavâhi, Mahaudavâhi, Sau*g*âmi, *S*aunaka, Âśvalâyana—and whatsoever other teachers there are, may they all satiate themselves.'

5. After he has satiated the Fathers man by man, and has returned to his house, what he gives (then), that is the sacrificial fee.

6. And it is also understood (in the *S*ruti), 'May he be standing, walking, sitting, or lying, (the texts belonging to) whatsoever sacrifice he repeats, that sacrifice indeed he has offered.'

7. It is understood (in the *S*ruti), ' Regarding this (Svâdhyâya) there are two cases in which the study (of the sacred texts) is forbidden: when he is impure himself, and when the place is.'

---

4. The names from Kahola Kaushîtaki down to Âśvalâyana stand in the accusative ; tarpayâmi, ' I satiate N. N.' is to be supplied.

5. Nârâya*n*a : 'He satiates his father, grandfather, and greatgrandfather, and goes to his house. What he then gives, for instance, food offered to guests, or given as alms (to religious beggars), is considered as the sacrificial fee for the Brahmayâ*gñ*a.'

6. Comp. *S*atapatha Brâhma*n*a XI, 5, 7, 3. 4.

KAṆḌIKÂ 5.

1. Now (follows) the Adhyâyopâkaraṇa (i. e. the ceremony by which the annual course of study is opened);

2. When the herbs appear, (when the moon stands in conjunction) with Sravaṇa, in the Srâvaṇa month,

3. Or on the fifth (Tithi of that month), under (the Nakshatra) Hasta.

4. Having sacrificed the two Âgya portions, he should offer Âgya oblations (to the following deities, viz.) Sâvitrî, Brahman, Belief, Insight, Wisdom, Memory, Sadasaspati, Anumati, the metres, and the Ṛishis.

5. He then sacrifices grains with curds (with the following texts):

6. 'I praise Agni the Purohita'—this one verse (Rig-veda I, 1, 1),

7. 'The Kushumbhaka (mungoose?) has said it'— 'If thou criest, O bird, announce luck to us'—'Sung by Gamadagni'—'In thy abode the whole world rests'

5, 2, 3. Perhaps the division of these Sûtras should be altered, so that srâvaṇasya would belong to Sûtra 2. In this case we should have to translate, '2. When the herbs appear, (on a day on which the moon stands in conjunction) with Sravaṇa. 3. Or on the fifth (Tithi) of the Srâvaṇa month, under (the Nakshatra) Hasta.' Comp. srâvaṇasya pañkamîm, Pâr. II, 10, 2. If we count the month beginning with the bright fortnight, and assume that the full moon day of Srâvaṇa falls, as the name of the month implies, on Sravaṇa, the fifth Tithi of that month will fall indeed on Hasta. Comp. on the dates of the Upâkaraṇa, Prof. Weber's remarks, Die vedischen Nachrichten von den Naxatra II, 322, and on the special symbolical signification of the Nakshatra Sravaṇa in this connection, my note on Sâṅkhâyana IV, 5, 2.

4. On the two Âgya portions, comp. above, I, 3, 5; 10, 13 seqq.

7. Comp. Sâṅkhâyana IV, 5, 8. The verses with which the oblations are performed, are the first and last verses of each Maṇḍala.

—' Come to our sacrifice, O you that are worthy of sacrifice, with care '—' Whosoever, be he ours, be he alien '—' Look on, look about '—' Come here, Agni, the Maruts' friend '—' The oblation, O king, cooked for thee '—each time two verses ;

8. ' United is your will ' (Rig-veda X, 191, 4)—this one verse ;

9. ' That blessing and bliss we choose '—this one verse.

10. When he intends to study (the Veda together with pupils), he should, while the pupils take hold of him, sacrifice to those deities, and sacrifice to (Agni) Svish/akr/t, and partake of the grains with curds ; then (follows) the ' cleaning.'

11. Sitting down to the west of the fire on Darbha grass, the tufts of which are directed towards the east, he should put Darbha blades into a water-pot, and making a Brahmâñgali (i. e. joining his hands as a sign of veneration for the Brahman), he should murmur (the following texts):

12. The Vyâhritis preceded by (the syllable) Om (stand first) ; (these) and the Sâvitrî he should repeat three times and then recite the beginning of the Veda.

9. This is the last verse of the Rik-Samhitâ in the Bâshkala Sâkhâ. See my note on Sânkhâyana IV, 5, 9.

10. The expression, ' Those deities' would, according to Nârâyana, refer not only to the deities stated in Sûtra 4, but also to the deities of the first and last verses of the Mandalas (Sûtras 6 seqq.). On the grains with curds, comp. Sûtra 5. The technical sense of the ' cleaning' is explained in the Srauta-sûtra I, 8, 2 ; comp. Hillebrandt, Das altindische Neu- und Vollmondsopfer, p. 130, note 1. The sacrificer covers his joined hands with the Kusa grass spread out round the fire, and has water sprinkled on them.

11. On the term brahmâñgali, comp. Manu II, 71.

13. In the same way at the Utsarga (i. e. at the ceremony performed at the end of the term of Vedic study).

14. He should study six months.

15. One who has performed the Samâvartana (should live during that time) according to the regulations for Brahmakârins.

16. The others according to the rules.

17. Some say that he should have intercourse with his wife.

18. That (is a practice) sacred to Pragâpati.

19. This (Upâkarana) they call vârshika (i. e. belonging to the rainy season).

20. On the middle Ashtakâ they offer food to those deities, and descend into water.

21. They satiate those same deities (with water oblations),

22. (And besides) the Âkâryas, the Rishis, and the Fathers.

23. This is the Utsargana.

KANDIKÂ 6.

1. Instead of the Kâmya ceremonies (i. e. the ceremonies, prescribed in the Srauta-sûtra, by which

---

15. On the Samâvartana, see below, chap. 8 seq. The restrictions referred to consist in the interdiction of eating honey and meat, of having sexual intercourse, of sleeping in a bedstead and in the day-time, &c. Nârâyana.

16. I.e. the Brahmakârins.

17. I.e. one who has performed the Samâvartana.

20. After the six months (Sûtra 14) have elapsed, on the Ashtakâ of Mâgha.

23. Or Utsarga, see Sûtra 13.

6, 1. Nârâyana divides this Sûtra into two: 1. atha kâmyânâm sthâne kâmyâh; 2. karavah.

2242 ÂSVALÂYANA-GR/HYA-SÛTRA.

special wishes are attained, oblations of) boiled (rice)
grains, for the attainment of those wishes, (should be
made by the Gr*i*hya sacrificer).

2. He attains (thereby) those same wishes.

3. For a person that is sick, or suffering, or
affected with consumption, a mess of boiled (rice)
grains in six oblations (should he offered)—

4. With this (hymn), 'I loosen thee by sacrificial
food, that thou mayst live' (Rig-veda X, 161).

5. If he has seen a bad dream, he should worship
the sun with the two verses, 'To-day, god Savit*ri*'
(Rig-veda V, 82, 4, 5), and with the five verses,
'What bad dreams there are among the cows' (Rig-
veda VIII, 47, 14 seqq.),

6. Or with (the verse), 'Whosoever, O king, be
it a companion or a friend' (Rig-veda II, 28, 10).

7. When he has sneezed, yawned, seen a disagreeable sight, smelt a bad smell, when his eye
palpitates, and when he hears noises in his ears, he
should murmur, 'Well-eyed may I become with my
eyes, well-vigoured with my face, well-hearing with
my ears. May will and insight dwell in me!'

8. If he has gone to a wife to whom he ought
not to go, or if he has performed a sacrifice for a
person for whom he ought not to do so, or has eaten
forbidden food, or accepted what he ought not to
accept, or pushed against a piled-up (fire altar) or

---

8. Nârâya*na* is evidently wrong in explaining *k*aity a*m* yûpa*ñ*
*k*a by agni*k*ayanastha*m* yûpa*m* (which is not, as Prof. Stenzler
takes it, der Opferpfahl auf einem Bestattungsplatze).
Comp. Gobhila III, 3, 34 ; Gr*i*hya-sa*m*graha-pari*s*ish*t*a II, 4.

I have translated the second verse in Sûtra 8, as if the text had
kalpantâm. The MSS. give kalpatâm. Atharva-veda VII, 67 has
kalpayantâm.

against a sacrificial post, he should sacrifice two
Âgya oblations with (the verses),

'May my faculties return into me, may life return,
may prosperity return ; may my goods return to
me ; may the divine power return into me.   Svâhâ !

'These fires that are stationed on the (altars
called) Dhish*n*yâs, may they be here in good order,
each on its right place. (Agni) Vai*s*vânara, grown
strong, the standard of immortality, may he govern
my mind in my heart.   Svâhâ !'

9. Or (he may sacrifice) two pieces of wood,

10. Or murmur (the same two verses without any
oblation).

KAN̄DIKÂ 7.

1. If the sun sets while he is sleeping without
being sick, he should spend the rest of the night
keeping silence, without sitting down, and should
worship the sun (when it rises) with the five
(verses), 'The light, O sun, by which thou de-
stroyest darkness' (Rig-veda X, 37, 4 seq.).

2. If (the sun) rises (while he is sleeping without
being sick), being fatigued without having done any
work, or having done work that is not becoming, he
should keep silence, &c., as before, and perform his
worship (to the sun) with the following four (verses,
Rig-veda X, 37, 9 seq.).

3. Invested with the sacrificial cord, constantly
fulfilling the prescribed duties regarding the use of

7, 2. Perhaps we should correct the text, akarma*s*rântam ana-
bhirûpe*n*a karma*n*â vâ vâgyata iti, &c.

3 seq. See *S*ânkhâyana-Gr*i*hya II, 9.   There the same word
anvash*t*amade*s*a occurs.

water, he should perform the Sandhyâ (or twilight devotion), observing silence.

4. In the evening he should, turning his face to the north-west, to the region between the chief (west) point and the intermediate (north-western) point (of the horizon), murmur the Sâvitrî, (beginning) when the sun is half set, until the stars appear.

5. In the same way in the morning—

6. Standing, with his face turned to the east, until the disk (of the sun) appears.

7. If a dove flies against his house or towards it, he should sacrifice with (the hymn), ' O gods, the dove' (Rig-veda X, 165), verse by verse, or should murmur (that hymn).

8. ' We have thee, O Lord of the path ' (Rig-veda VI, 53)—if he is going out for doing some business.

9. ' Bring us together, Pûshan, with a knowing one ' (Rig-veda VI, 54)—if he wishes to find something lost, or if he has strayed.

10. ' Journey over the ways, Pûshan' (Rig-veda I, 42)—if he is going out on a long or dangerous way.

KANDIKÂ 8.

1. Now when returning (home from his teacher) he should get the following things, viz. a jewel (to be tied round the neck), two ear-rings, a pair of garments, a parasol, a pair of shoes, a staff, a wreath, (pounded seed of the Karañga fruit) for rubbing with, ointment, eye salve, a turban ; (all that) for himself and for the teacher.

---

9. Mû/ha may either mean, ' having lost his way,' or ' bewildered in his mind.' Nârâya/na prefers the latter explanation (' pragñâ-hina/h ').

2. If he cannot get it for both, only for the teacher.

3. He then should get a piece of wood of a tree which is sacrificially pure, in a north-eastern direction —

4. Sappy (wood) if he wishes for the enjoyment of food, or for prosperity, or for splendour ; dry (wood), if for holy lustre,

5. (Wood) which is both (sappy and dry, in its different parts), if (he wishes) for both.

6. Having put the piece of wood on high, and having given a cow and food to the Brâhmaṇas, he should perform the ceremony of shaving the beard.

7. He should alter the texts so that they refer to himself.

8. With Ekaklîtaka (he should perform the rub-bing).

9. Having washed himself with lukewarm water, and having put on two (new) garments which have not yet been washed, with (the verse), ' Garments with fat splendour you put on, (Mitra and Varuṇa)' (Rig-veda I, 152, 1), he should anoint his eyes with (the words), ' The sharpness of the stone art thou ; protect my eye.'

10. With (the words), ' The sharpness of the stone

8, 6. ' On high ' means ' not on the ground ' (Nârâyaṇa). On the gaudânikam karma (the shaving of the beard), comp. above, Adhyâya I, Kaṇḍikâ 18. The word ' ceremony ' would mean here, according to Nârâyaṇa, that he should perform the rite alone, without observing such prescriptions as stated above, I, 18, 7.

7. Thus, instead of ' Herb ! protect him !' (I, 17, 8) he is to say, ' Herb ! protect me !' and so on.

8. Ekaklîtaka is, according to Nârâyaṇa and the Prayogaratna, the seed of such a Karaṅga fruit (Pongamia Glabra, Vent.) which contains only one grain of seed. Such grains are pounded before he rubs himself therewith.

art thou ; protect my ear '—he should tie on the two
ear-rings.

11. After having salved his two hands with
ointment, a Brâhma*n*a should salve his head first,

12. A Râ*g*anya his two arms,

13. A Vai*s*ya the belly,

14. A woman her secret parts,

15. Persons who gain their livelihood by running,
their thighs.

16. With (the formula), 'Free from pain art thou,
free from pain may I become'—he should put on
the wreath.

17. Not (such a wreath) which is called mâlâ.

18. If they call it mâlâ, he should cause them to
call it sra*g*.

19. With (the formula), ' The standing-places of
the gods are you ; protect me from all sides'—he
steps into the shoes, and with (the formula), ' The
heaven's covering art thou '—he takes the parasol.

20. With (the formula), ' Reed thou art ; from
the tree thou descendest ; protect me from all
sides'—(he takes) a staff of reed.

21. Having with the hymn ' Giving life ' tied the
jewel to his neck and arranged the turban (on his
head), he should standing put the piece of wood (on
the fire).

---

21. On the hymn beginning with the words 'Giving life,' see
Prof. Stenzler's note on this Sûtra. Its first verse is identical with
Vâ*g*asaneyi Sa*m*hitâ XXXIV, 50 (comp. also *S*âṅkhâyana-Gr/hya
III, 1, 7), and so are most of its verses found in that Sa*m*hitâ or in the
Atharva-veda ; the whole of it occurs among the Rig-veda Khilas
(vol. vi, p. 25, 2–12).

KANDIKÂ 9.

1. (He says), ' Memory and reproach and knowledge, faith, and wisdom as the fifth, what is sacrificed,
and what is given, and what is studied, and what is
done, truth, learning, vow—
' The vow which belongs to Agni together with
Indra, with Pragâpati, with the Rishis, with the
royal ones among the Rishis, with the Fathers, with
the royal ones among the Fathers, with the human
beings, with the royal ones among the human beings,
with shine, over-shine, after-shine, counter-shine, with
gods and men, with Gandharvas and Apsaras, with
wild animals and domestic animals,—the vow, belonging to my own self, dwelling in my own self,
that is my universal vow. Hereby, O Agni, I become addicted to the universal vow. Svâhâ!'

2. With (the hymn), ' Mine, Agni, be vigour '
(Rig-veda X, 128, 1), verse by verse, he should put
pieces of wood (on the fire).

3. He should pass that night at a place where
they will do honour to him.

9, 1. ' "My memory and my non-memory, that is my double
vow "—in this way the twelve (parts of which the first section of
the Mantra consists) should be recited.' Nârâyana. I think the
commentator is wrong here, and that section should rather be
recited as it is given in the text without any alteration ; it forms a
regular Sloka. Agneh instead of Agne is a conjecture of Prof.
Stenzler, which I have adopted.

2. According to Nârâyana the hymn should be recited including
the Khila, so that ten pieces of wood are offered. Now the hymn
consists of nine verses ; there can be, consequently, only one
Khailika verse, which is, I suppose, the first verse of the Khila
quoted above, p. 228.

3. By a Madhuparka (Nârâyana). Compare Sânkhâyana-Grihya
III, 1, 14.

4. When, after having finished his (task of) learning, he has offered something to the teacher, or has received his permission, he should take a bath (which signifies the end of his studentship).

5. He (i.e. the Snâtaka) has to keep the following observances :

6. He shall not bathe in the night-time; he shall not bathe naked; he shall not lie down naked; he shall not look at a naked woman, except during sexual intercourse; he shall not run during rain; he shall not climb up a tree; he shall not descend into a well; he shall not swim with his arms across a river; he shall not expose himself to danger. 'A great being indeed is a Snâtaka'—thus it is understood (in the Sruti).

KA*ND*IKÂ 10.

1. If (a student) wishes to be dismissed (by his teacher), he should pronounce before the teacher his (i. e. the teacher's ?) name—

2. (And should say), 'Here we will dwell, sir!'

4. Nârâya*n*a : He makes an offer to the teacher in the words, 'What is it that I can do for you?'—and what the teacher tells him, that he does.

10, 1. Nârâya*n*a refers this rule to a student who has performed the Samâvartana and wishes to go away. But a comparison of Sâṅkhâyana-Gr*i*hya II, 18 seems to make it probable that the ceremony described here has nothing to do with the Samâvartana. I take this chapter rather for a description of the way in which a student has to take leave of his teacher when setting out on a journey. 'His name' is the teacher's name, according to Nârâya*n*a.

2. Sâṅkhâyana II, 18, 1. Sâṅkh. has aha*m* vatsyâmi; Âsvalâyana, ida*m* vatsyâma*h*. The commentator says that instead of ida*m* the Âsrama is to be named which the student chooses to enter upon, for instance, 'Devadatta, we will dwell in the state of a householder, sir!'

3. With a loud voice (the words) following after the name.

4. 'Of inhalation and exhalation'—(this he says) with a low voice,

5. And (the verse), 'Come hither, Indra, with thy lovely-sounding, fallow-coloured (horses)' (Rig-veda III, 45, 1).

6. The aged one then murmurs, 'To inhalation and exhalation I, the wide-extended one, resort with thee. To the god Savit*ri* I give thee in charge'— and the verse.

7. When he has finished (that verse), and has muttered, 'Om! Forwards! Blessing!' and recited (over the student the hymn), 'The great bliss of the three' (Rig-veda X, 185)—(he should dismiss him).

8. On one who has been thus dismissed, danger comes from no side—thus it is understood (in the *S*ruti).

9. If he hears (on his way) disagreeable voices of birds, he should murmur the two hymns, 'Shrieking, manifesting his being' (Rig-veda II, 42, 43), and (the verse), 'The divine voice have the gods created' (Rig-veda VIII, 100, 11).

10. 'Praise the renowned youth who sits on the war-chariot' (Rig-veda II, 33, 11)—if (he hears disagreeable voices) of deer.

11. From the direction, or from the (being) from which he expects danger, towards that direction he should throw a fire-brand, burning on both sides, or having twirled about a churning-stick from the right to the left, with (the words), 'Safety be to me, Mitra

---

6. I have translated, as Prof. Stenzler has also done, according to *S*ânkhâyana's reading, pr*â*ñâpânâ ... tvayâ. The 'aged one' is the teacher, the verse that which is quoted in Sûtra 5.

and Varu*n*a; encounter the foes and burn them up
with your flame. May they find none who knows
them and no support; divided by discord may they
go to death'—

12. He turns the churning-stick downwards with
(the verse), 'The combined wealth of both, heaped
together' (Rig-veda X, 84, 7).

KA*ND*IKÂ 11.

1. If unknown danger from all sides (menaces him),
he should sacrifice eight Â*g*ya oblations with (the
formulas),

'P*ri*thivî (the earth) is covered; she is covered by
Agni. By her, the covered one, the covering one,
I ward off the danger of which I am in fear. Svâhâ!

'Antariksha (the air) is covered; it is covered by
Vâyu. By it, the covered, the covering, I ward off
the danger of which I am in fear. Svâhâ!

'Dyaus (the heaven) is covered; she is covered by
Âditya (the sun). By her, &c.

'The quarters (of the horizon) are covered;
they are covered by *K*andramas (the moon). By
them, &c.

'The waters are covered; they are covered by
Varu*n*a. By them, &c.

'The creatures are covered; they are covered by
Prâ*n*a (the breath). By them, &c.

'The Vedas are covered; they are covered by the
metres. By them, &c.

'All is covered; it is covered by Brahman. By
it, &c. Svâhâ!'

11, 1. 'Covered' is v*ri*ta; 'I ward off' is the causative of the
same verb, vâraye.

2. Then, stationing himself towards the north-east, he murmurs the Svasti-Âtreya and, 'Of what we are in fear, Indra' (Rig-veda VIII, 61, 13 seqq.), down to the end of the hymn.

KANDIKÂ 12.

1. When a battle is beginning, (the royal Purohita) should cause the king to put on his armour (in the following way).

2. (The Purohita) stations himself to the west of (the king's) chariot with (the hymn ?), 'I have brought thee hither; be here' (Rig-veda X, 173).

3. With (the verse), 'Like a thunder-cloud is his countenance' (Rig-veda VI, 75, 1), he should tender the coat of mail to him.

4. With the following (verse) the bow.

5. The following (verse) he should cause him to repeat.

6. He should murmur himself the fourth.

7. With the fifth he should tender the quiver to him.

8. When (the king) starts, the sixth.

9. The seventh (he recites) over the horses.

10. The eighth he should cause (the king) to repeat while looking at the arrows;

2. The Svasti-Âtreya is the part of the hymn V, 51, which very frequently contains the word svasti (vv. 11-15). There is a Khila appended to that hymn (Rig-veda, vol. iii, p. 30), which, according to Nârâyana, is also to be murmured on this occasion.

12, 2. According to Nârâyana the Pratîka here signifies not the verse, but the whole hymn, though a whole Pâda is given (comp. Srauta-sûtra I, 1, 17).

11. (The verse), 'Like a serpent it encircles the arm with its windings' (Rig-veda VI, 75, 14), when he ties to his arm the leather (by which the arm is protected against the bow-string).

12. He then mounts up to (the king on his chariot), while he is driving, and causes him to repeat the Abhîvarta hymn (Rig-veda X, 174) and the two verses, 'He who, Mitra and Varuna' (Rig-veda VIII, 101, 3 seq.).

13. He then should look at him with the Apratiratha, Sâsa, and Sauparna hymns.

14. The Sauparna is (the hymn), 'May the streams of honey and ghee flow forwards.'

15. (The king) should drive (in his chariot successively) to all quarters (of the horizon).

16. He should commence the battle in the line of battle invented by Âditya or by Usanas.

17. He should touch the drum with the three verses, 'Fill earth and heaven with thy roar' (Rig-veda VI, 47, 29 seqq.).

18. With (the verse), 'Shot off fall down' (Rig-veda VI, 75, 16), he should shoot off the arrows.

---

12. The Abhîvarta hymn begins with the word abhîvartena, and is ascribed to Abhîvarta Âṅgirasa.

13. The Apratiratha hymn is Rig-veda X, 103 (ascribed to Apratiratha Aindra); the Sâsa, X, 152 (ascribed to Sâsa Bhâradvâga). On the Sauparna, see the next Sûtra.

14. This hymn is not found in any Vedic Samhitâ, as far as I know, nor does it occur in the Suparnâdhyâya. I have followed Prof. Stenzler's conjecture pra dhârâ yantu instead of pradhârayantu, which is confirmed by Sâyana's note on Aitareya Brâhmana VI, 25, 7; VIII, 10, 4 (pp. 365, 399, ed. Aufrecht).

17, 18. According to Nârâyana the subject is the king.

19. 'Where the arrows fly' (l. l. v. 17)—this (verse) he should murmur while they are fighting.

20. Or he should teach (the king the texts mentioned). Or he should teach (the king).

End of the Third Adhyâya.

***

19. Here the subject is the Purohita.

1. If disease befalls one who has set up the (sacred Srauta) fires, he should leave his home (and go away) to the eastern, or northern, or north-eastern direction.

2. 'The sacred fires are fond of the village'—thus it is said.

3. Longing for it, desirous of returning to the village they might restore him to health—thus it is understood (in the Sruti).

4. Being restored to health, he should offer a Soma sacrifice, or an animal sacrifice, or an ordinary sacrifice, and take his dwelling (again in the village).

5. Or without such a sacrifice.

6. If he dies, one should have a piece of ground dug up to the south-east or to the south-west—

7. At a place which is inclined towards the south or towards the south-east.

8. According to some (teachers), inclined towards south-west.

9. (The piece of ground dug up should be) of the length of a man with upraised arms,

10. Of the breadth of one Vyâma (fathom),

1, 1. Comp. Srauta-sûtra VI, 9, 1. The funeral rites according to the Grihya-sûtras have been treated of by Prof. Max Müller, Zeitschrift der Deutschen Morgenländischen Gesellschaft, vol. ix.

3. I. e. longing for the village. I here differ from Prof. Stenzler's translation, 'Indem sie, um nach dem Dorfe zu kommen, ihm Gutes wünschen.' Prof. Stenzler here follows Nârâyana, who has the following note, grâmam âgantum ikkhanto·gnaya enam âhitâgnim âsamsante, ayam agado bhaved iti.

4. Comp. Srauta-sûtra VI, 9, 7.

5. Srauta-sûtra VI, 10, 1.

11. Of the depth of one Vitasti (span).

12. The cemetery should be free from all sides.

13. It should be fertile in herbs.

14. But plants with thorns and with milky juice, &c., as stated above.

15. From which the waters flow off to all sides : this is a characteristic required for the cemetery (*smasâna*) where the body is to be burned.

16. 'They cut off (from the dead body) the hair, the beard, the hairs of the body, and the nails'— this has been stated above.

17. (They should provide) plenty of sacrificial grass and of butter.

18. They here pour clarified butter into curds.

19. This is the 'sprinkled butter' used for the Fathers (i. e. Manes).

KANDIKÂ 2.

1. (The relations of the dead person) now carry (his sacred) fires and (his) sacrificial vessels in that direction.

---

12. Nârâyana : By the word *smasâna* (cemetery) two different *smasânas* are designated here, because below (Sûtra 15) a distinction is added (to the word *smasâna*), in the words, 'This is a characteristic required for the *smasâna* where the body is to be burned.' Thus the place where the body is burned, and the place where the gathered bones are deposited, both are called *smasâna*.

14. See above, II, 7, 5.

15. See the note on Sûtra 12.

16. See the *Srauta-sûtra* VI, 10, 2.

17. Dvigulpha*m* barhir âgyañ *ka*. Nârâya*na* explains dvigulpha by prabhûta. Comp. bahula*tri*na, Kâtyâyana XXV, 7, 15.

18. 'Here' means, at a ceremony directed to the Manes. Nârâya*na*.

2, 1. In the direction stated above, chap. 1, 6.

2. After them aged persons forming an odd number, men and women not going together, (carry) the dead body.

3. Some (say) that (the dead body should be carried) in a cart with a seat, drawn by cows.

4. (Some prescribe) a she-animal for covering (the dead body with its limbs):

5. A cow,

6. Or a she-goat of one colour.

7. Some (take) a black one.

8. They tie (a rope) to its left fore-foot and lead it behind (the dead body).

9. Then follow the relations (of the dead person), wearing their sacrificial cords below (round their body), with the hair-locks untied, the older ones first, the younger ones last.

10. When they have thus arrived at the place, the performer (of the rites) walks three times round the spot with his left side turned towards it, and with a Sami branch sprinkles water on it, with (the verse), 'Go away, withdraw, and depart from here' (Rig-veda X, 14, 9).

11. To the south-east, on an elevated corner (of that place), he places the Âhavanîya fire,

12. To the north-west the Gârhapatya fire,

13. To the south-west the Dakshina fire.

14. After that a person that knows (how to do it), piles up between the fires a pile of fuel.

---

4. See chap. 3, 20–25.

10. Kartodakena (i. e. kartâ udakena) is evidently the right reading, not gartodakena.

12, 13. The words, 'on an elevated corner' (Sûtra 11) have to be supplied.

14. As to the pronoun enam, which refers, with an irregular

15. After sacrificial grass and a black antelope's skin with the hair outside has been spread out there, they place the dead body thereon, which they have carried so as to pass by the Gârhapatya fire on its north-side, turning its head towards the Âhavanîya.

16. To the north (of the body they place) the wife (of the deceased),

17. And a bow for a Kshatriya.

18. Her brother-in-law, being a representative of her husband, or a pupil (of her husband), or an aged servant, should cause her to rise (from that place) with (the verse), 'Arise, O wife, to the world of life ' (Rig-veda X, 18, 8).

19. The performer (of the rites) should murmur (that verse), if a Sûdra (makes her rise from the pile).

20. With (the verse), ' Taking the bow out of the hand of the deceased' (Rig-veda X, 18, 9), (he takes away) the bow.

21. It has been stated (what is to be done) in case a Sûdra (should perform this act).

22. Having bent the bow, he should, before the piling up (of the things mentioned below, which are put on the dead body) is done, break it to pieces, and throw it (on the pile).

---

construction, to the dead person, comp. Satapatha Brâhmana XII, 5, 2, 7.

16. The wife is made to lie down on the pile.

18. Possibly the words devarah and patisthânîyah refer to two different persons, so that we should have to translate, ' Her brother-in-law, (or some other) representative of her husband, &c.'

19. This refers to the case of the aged servant. The word for which we have put Sûdra here and in Sûtra 21, is vrishala.

22. See Sûtra 19.

KANDIKÂ 3.

1. He should then put the following (sacrificial) implements (on the dead body).

2. Into the right hand the (spoon called) *G*uhû.

3. Into the left the (other spoon called) Upabh*ri*t.

4. On his right side the (wooden sacrificial sword called) Sphya, on his left (side) the Agnihotrahavanî (i. e. the ladle with which the Agnihotra oblations are sacrificed).

5. On his chest the (big sacrificial ladle called) Dhruvâ. On his head the dishes. On his teeth the pressing-stones.

6. On the two sides of his nose the two (smaller sacrificial ladles called) Sruvas.

7. Or, if there is only one (Sruva), breaking it (in two pieces).

8. On his two ears the two Prâ*s*itrahara*n*as (i. e. the vessels into which the portion of the sacrificial food belonging to the Brahman is put).

9. Or, if there is only one (Prâ*s*itrahara*n*a), breaking it (in two pieces).

10. On his belly the (vessel called) Pâtrî,

11. And the cup into which the cut-off portions (of the sacrificial food) are put.

12. On his secret parts the (staff called) *S*amyâ.

13. On his thighs the two kindling woods.

3, 1. On the different implements mentioned in the following Sûtras, comp. Prof. Max Müller's paper in the Zeitschrift der Deutschen Morgenländischen Gesellschaft, vol. ix, pp. vii seqq.; lxxviii seqq.

8. On the Prâ*s*itra and the Prâ*s*itrahara*n*as, comp. Hillebrandt, Neu- und Vollmondsopfer, pp. 119 (with note 6), 120, 131.

14. On his legs the mortar and the pestle.

15. On his feet the two baskets.

16. Or, if there is only one (basket), tearing it (in two pieces).

17. Those (of the implements) which have a hollow (into which liquids can be poured), are filled with sprinkled butter.

18. The son (of the deceased person) should take the under and the upper mill-stone for himself.

19. And the implements made of copper, iron, and earthenware.

20. Taking out the omentum of the she-animal he should cover therewith the head and the mouth (of the dead person) with the verse, ' Put on the armour (which will protect thee) against Agni, by (that which comes from) the cows' (Rig-veda X, 16, 7).

21. Taking out the kidneys (of the animal) he should lay them into the hands (of the dead body) with the verse, ' Escape the two hounds, the sons of Saramâ' (Rig-veda X, 14, 10), the right (kidney) into the right (hand), the left into the left.

22. The heart (of the animal he puts) on the heart (of the deceased).

23. And two lumps (of flour or rice), according to some (teachers).

17. Nârâyana explains âsekanavanti by bilavanti. On prishadâgya ('sprinkled butter') comp. the two last Sûtras of the first chapter.

19. The statement in Satapatha Brâhmana XII, 5, 2, 14 is somewhat different.

20. Anustaranyâ vapâm. See chap. 2, 4.

23. Nârâyana states that these lumps are not put, as one would be inclined to believe, on the heart, but into the hands of the deceased. Sûtra 24 shows that this interpretation is correct.

24. (Only) if there are no kidneys, according to some (teachers).

25. Having distributed the whole (animal), limb by limb (placing its different limbs on the corresponding limbs of the deceased), and having covered it with its hide, he recites, when the Pra*n*îta water is carried forward, (the verse), ' Agni, do not overturn this cup' (Rig-veda X, 16, 8).

26. Bending his left knee he should sacrifice Â*g*ya oblations into the Dakshi*n*a fire with (the formulas), ' To Agni svâhâ ! To Kâma svâhâ ! To the world svâhâ ! To Anumati svâhâ !'

27. A fifth (oblation) on the chest of the deceased with (the formula), ' From this one verily thou hast been born. May he now be born out of thee, N. N. ! To the heaven-world svâhâ !'

KA*ND*IKÂ 4.

1. He gives order, 'Light the fires together.'

2. If the Âhavanîya fire reaches (the body) first, he should know, ' It has reached him in the heaven-world. He will live there in prosperity, and so will this one, i. e. his son, in this world.'

3. If the Gârhapatya fire reaches (the body) first, he should know, ' It has reached him in the air-world. He will live there in prosperity, and so will this one, i. e. his son, in this world.'

---

24. I. e. if there is no Anustara*n*î animal, which is considered as optional (see chap. 2, 4).

25. Comp. Kâtyâyana XXV, 7, 35.

27. He who is born out of the deceased, is Agni. See *S*atapatha Brâhma*n*a II, 3, 3, 5; and also XII, 5, 2, 15.

4, 2. *S*atapatha Brâhma*n*a XII, 5, 2, 10.

3. *S*atapatha Brâhma*n*a 1. 1. § 9.

4. If the Dakshina fire reaches (the body) first, he should know, ' It has reached him in the world of men. He will live there in prosperity, and so will this one, i. e. his son, in this world.'

5. If (the three fires) reach (the body) in the same moment, they say that this signifies the highest luck.

6. While (the body) is burning, he recites over it the same texts, 'Go on, go on, on the ancient paths' (Rig-veda X, 14, 7).

7. Being burnt by a person who knows this, he goes to the heaven-world together with the smoke (of the funeral pile)—thus it is understood (in the Sruti).

8. To the north-east of the Âhavanîya fire he should have a knee-deep pit dug and should have an Avakâ, i. e. (the water-plant called) Sîpâla put down into it. From that (pit) he (i. e. the deceased) goes out and together with the smoke he goes up to the heaven-world—thus it is understood (in the Sruti).

9. After he has recited (the verse), ' These living ones have separated from the dead' (Rig-veda X, 18, 3), they turn round from right to left and go away without looking back.

10. When they have come to a place where standing water is, having once (plunged into it and) emerged

---

4. Satapatha Brâhmana I. 1. § 11.

5. Satapatha Brâhmana I. 1. § 12.

6. 'The same texts' means that the texts indicated in the Srauta-sûtra VI, 10, 19 (twenty-four verses taken from the hymns X, 14, 16, 17, 18, 154) have to be recited.

8. Comp. above, II, 8, 14.

10. 'All the Samânodaka relations (see Manu V, 60), men and women, should pour out one handful of water each. Pronouncing

from it, they pour out one handful (of water), pronounce the Gotra name and the proper name (of the
deceased), go out (of the water), put on other garments, wring out (the old garments) once, lay them
away with their skirts to the north, and sit down
until the stars appear.

11. Or they may enter (their houses), when still (a
part) of the sun-disk is seen,

12. The younger ones first, the older ones last.

13. When they have come to the houses, they
touch a stone, the fire, cow's dung, fried barley,
sesamum seeds, and water.

14. Let them not cook food during that night.

15. Let them subsist on bought or ready-made food.

16. Let them eat no saline food for three nights.

17. Let them optionally for twelve nights avoid
the distribution of gifts and the study (of Vedic texts),
if one of the chief Gurus (has died).

18. Ten days after (the death of) Sapi*nd*as,

---

the Gotra name and the proper name of the deceased, saying, for
instance, " Devadatta, belonging to the Gotra of the Kâ*s*yapas, this
water is for thee !"—they sprinkle it out, with southward-turned
faces.' Nârâya*n*a.

12. Possibly prave*s*yu*h* (they should enter) belongs to this
Sûtra. In Prof. Stenzler's edition and in the commentary of
Nârâya*n*a it is taken as belonging to Sûtra 11.

15. Vasish*th*a IV, 15. Nârâya*n*a here observes, 'Some authorities omit this Sûtra.'

17. 'Father and mother and the teacher who, after having performed the Upanayana for him, has taught him the whole Veda,
are the chief Gurus. When these have died, they should avoid
giving gifts and studying the Veda either for twelve nights, or for
ten nights, this rule standing in correlation with the following one.'
Nârâya*n*a.

18. The Sapi*nd*a relationship is generally defined as the relationship within six degrees, though the statements in the different

19. And of a Guru who is no Sapi*nd*a,

20. And of unmarried female relations.

21. Three nights after (the death of) other teachers,

22. And of a relation who is no Sapi*nd*a,

23. And of married female relations,

24. Of a child that has no teeth,

25. And of a dead-born child.

26. One day, after (the death of) a fellow-pupil,

27. And of a *S*rotriya of the same village.

KA*ND*IKÂ 5.

1. The gathering (of the bones is performed) after the tenth (Tithi from the death), (on a Tithi) with an odd number, of the dark fortnight, under a single Nakshatra.

2. A man into a male urn without special marks, a woman into a female one without special marks.

3. Aged persons of an odd number, not men and women together (gather the bones).

4. The performer of the ceremony walks three times round the spot with his left side turned towards

texts do not exactly agree. See Âpastamba II, 15, 2 ; Manu V, 60 ; Gautama XIV, 13 (with Prof. Bühler's note, Sacred Books, vol. ii, p. 247, &c.).

21. Comp. Sûtras 17, 19.

5, 1. Nârâya*n*a (comp. the Âsvalâyana-Gr*i*hya-Pari*s*ish*t*a III, 7) understands this Sûtra in a different way. 'After the tenth Tithi of the dark fortnight, on a Tithi with an odd number, i. e. on the eleventh, thirteenth, or fifteenth.' The single Nakshatras are those the name of which does not denote two Nakshatras (as, for instance, the two Ashâ*dh*âs). Comp. Kâty.-*S*raut. XXV, 8, 1 ; Manu V, 59.

2. Urns, with or without protuberances like female breasts, are considered as female or male accordingly.

3. See chap. 2, 2.

4. Comp. chap. 2, 10.

it, and sprinkles on it with a *Sami* branch milk mixed with water, with the verse, ' O cool one, O thou that art full of coolness' (Rig-veda X, 16, 14).

5. With the thumb and the fourth finger they should put each single bone (into the urn) without making a noise,

6. The feet first, the head last.

7. Having well gathered them and purified them with a winnowing basket, they should put (the urn) into a pit, at a place where the waters from the different sides do not flow together, except rain water, with (the verse), ' Go to thy mother Earth there' (Rig-veda X, 18, 10).

8. With the following (verse) he should throw earth (into the pit).

9. After he has done so, (he should repeat) the following (verse).

10. Having covered (the urn) with a lid with (the verse), ' I fasten to thee' (Rig-veda X, 18, 13), they then should go away without looking back, should bathe in water, and perform a *Srâddha* for the deceased.

KANDIKÂ 6.

1. They who have lost a Guru by death, or are afflicted by other misfortune, should perform on the new-moon day an expiatory ceremony.

2. Before sunrise they should carry their fire

---

7. Nârâyana explains pavana by *sûrpa.* He says that the ' performer' (kartri) repeats this and the following texts.

10. 'They should give a *Srâddha* to the deceased exclusively, according to the Ekoddish/a rite.' Nârâyana.

6, 2. According to Nârâyana the fire means here not the sacred domestic fire, but a common kitchen fire. I doubt whether the

together with its ashes and with its receptacle to the south with the half-verse, ' I send far away the flesh-devouring Agni' (Rig-veda X, 16, 9).

3. Having thrown that (fire) down at a place where four roads meet or somewhere else, they walk round it three times, turning their left sides towards it, beating their left thighs with their left hands.

4. They then should return home without looking back, bathe in water, have their hair, their beards the hair of their bodies, and their nails cut, and furnish themselves with new jars, pots, vessels for rinsing the mouth, wreathed with garlands of Samî flowers, with fuel of Samî wood, with two pieces of Samî wood for kindling fire, and with branches to be laid round the fire, with bull's dung and a bull's hide, fresh butter, a stone, and as many bunches of Kusa grass as there are young women (in the house).

5. At the time of the Agni(-hotra) he should kindle fire with the hemistich, ' Here may this other Gâtavedas' (Rig-veda X, 16, 9).

commentator is right. The ceremonies described in the following Sûtras seem to point rather to a renewal of the sacred Grihya fire, the old one having proved unlucky to the sacrificer. In the same way, in the Srauta ritual, a sacrificer who, after having performed the Âdhâna, has bad luck, performs the Punarâdheya.

3. Comp. Kâtyâyana-Srauta-sûtra V, 10, 15.

5. The text has agnivelâyâm, which Nârâyana explains by agnihotraviharanakâle aparâhne. He states that the fire should be produced by attrition of two new kindling woods (arani), mentioned in Sûtra 4. The fire thus kindled is to be used, he says, as a kitchen-fire. Herein he seems to me to have misunderstood the meaning of the ceremony; see the note on Sûtra 2. The hemistich quoted in this Sûtra (which is the second half of the same verse of which the first half is prescribed in Sûtra 2) clearly points to the sacred quality of the fire in question : it runs thus, 'Here may this other Gâtavedas carry the offerings to the gods, the knowing one.'

6. Keeping that (fire) burning, they sit till the
silence of the night, repeating the tales of the aged,
and getting stories of auspicious contents, Itihâsas
and Purâ*n*as, told to them.

7. When all sounds have ceased, or when (the
others) have gone to the house or the resting-place,
(the performer of the ceremony) should pour out an
uninterrupted stream of water, beginning at the south
side of the door, with (the verse), ' Spinning the
thread follow the light of the aerial space ' (Rig-veda
X, 53, 6), (going round the house), ending at the
north side of the door.

8. Having then given its place to the fire, and
having spread to the west of it a bull's hide with the
neck to the east, with the hair outside, he should
cause the people belonging to the house to step on
that (hide) with (the verse), 'Arise to long life,
choosing old age' (Rig-veda X, 18, 6).

9. With (the verse), ' This I lay round the living '
(Rig-veda X, 18, 4), he should lay branches round
(the fire).

10. After having with (the words), ' A mountain
(i. e. a stone) they shall place between themselves
and death,' placed a stone to the north of the fire,
and having sacrificed with the four (verses), ' Go
hence, O death, on another way ' (Rig-veda X, 18,

---

7. The person who pours out the water is, as Nârâya*n*a says,
the kart*ri*, i. e. the performer of the whole ceremony. The word
cannot be translated, as Prof. Stenzler does, der Bestatter, no
funeral ceremonies being here treated of.

8. See above, I, 8, 9. Here Nârâya*n*a sees that the fire is the
sacred one. He says, atha*s*abdo *s*min kâle *s* gnyantaram aupâ-
sanam upasamâdadhyâd iti *gñ*âpanârtham.

10. The words, ' A mountain,' &c., stand at the end of the verse
quoted in Sûtra 9.

1–4), verse by verse, he should look at his people
with (the verse), 'As the days follow each other'
(ibid. 5).

11. The young women (belonging to the house)
should, with each hand separately, with their thumbs
and fourth fingers, with young Darbha blades, salve
their eyes with fresh butter, and throw (the Darbha
blades) away, turning their faces away.

12. (The performer of the ceremony) should look
at them, while they are salving themselves, with (the
verse), 'These women, being no widows, having
noble husbands' (Rig-veda X, 18, 7).

13. With (the verse), 'Carrying stones, (the river)
streams forward; take hold of each other' (Rig-veda
X, 53, 8)—the performer (of the ceremony) first
should touch the stone.

14. After that, stationing himself to the north-
east, while (the others) go round with the fire, with
bull's dung, and with an uninterrupted stream of
water, repeating the three verses, 'O waters, ye are
wholesome' (Rig-veda X, 9, 1 seqq.), he should
murmur the verse, 'These have led round the cow'
(Rig-veda X, 155, 5).

15. A tawny-coloured bull should he lead round—
thus they say.

16. They then sit down at a place where they
intend to tarry, having put on garments that have
not yet been washed.

17. (There) they sit, avoiding to sleep, till sunrise.

18. After sunrise, having murmured the hymns
sacred to the sun and the auspicious hymns, having

18. See above, II, 3, 13.

prepared food, having made oblations with (the hymn),
'May he drive evil away from us with his shine'
(Rig-veda I, 97), verse by verse, having given to the
Brâhma*n*as to eat, he should cause (them) to pronounce
auspicious words.

19. A cow, a cup of metal, and a garment that has
not yet been washed, constitute the sacrificial fee.

KA*N*DIKÂ 7.

1. Now at a *S*râddha ceremony, at that which is
celebrated on the Parvan day, or for the attainment
of special wishes, or at the Âbhyudayika *S*râddha
(i. e. the *S*râddha celebrated when some good luck
has happened), or at the Ekoddish*t*a *S*râddha (the
*S*râddha directed to a single dead person)—

2. He causes Brâhma*n*as who are endowed with
learning, moral character, and correct conduct, or
with one of these (characteristics), who have been
invited in time, who have taken a bath, washed their
feet, and sipped water, to sit down, as representa-
tives of the Fathers, with their faces turned to the
north, one for each one of the Fathers, or two for
each, or three for each.

3. The larger their number is, the greater is the
reward (which the sacrificer is entitled to expect).

4. But in no case one (Brâhma*n*a) for all (the
fathers).

7, 1. Comp. on the *S*râddha ceremonies in general the note on
*S*ânkhâyana-Gr*i*hya IV, 1, 1, and the quotations given there. The
Pârva*n*a *S*râddha, which is celebrated on the new-moon day, is
treated of by *S*ânkhâyana IV, 1, the Âbhyudayika *S*râddha, IV,
4, the Ekoddish*t*a *S*râddha, IV, 2.

5. Optionally (he may invite only one Brâhmana) except at the first (Srâddha).

6. By (the exposition of) the Pinda sacrifice (the corresponding rules) have been declared (for the Srâddha ceremonies also).

7. Having given water (to the Brâhmanas),

8. Having given to them double-folded Darbha blades, and a seat,

9. Having (again) given water (to them),

10. Having poured water into three vessels of metal, of stone, and of earthen-ware, or (into three vessels) made of the same substance, over which he has put Darbha grass,

11. And having recited over (that water the verse), ' For luck and help the divine waters ' (Rig-veda X, 9, 4), he pours sesamum seeds into it with (the formula), 'Sesamum art thou; Soma is thy deity; at the Gosava sacrifice thou hast been created by

---

5. Anâdye. Of the different interpretations of this word which Nârâyana gives, it may suffice here to quote two. The first Srâddha may either mean the Pârvana Srâddha, because this stands first among the different kinds of Srâddha ceremonies enumerated in Sûtra 1 ; or it may mean the Sapindikarana (see Sânkhâyana IV, 3). for this is the first occasion on which a dead person receives Srâddha oblations together with two others of the Fathers.

6. The sacrifice to the Manes, as forming part of the Srauta ritual, is explained in the Srauta-sûtra II, 6 seq.

8. Yâgñavalkya I, 229.

9. Yâgñavalkya I, 230. The reading of several words of the Mantra is doubtful, and the parallel texts, as Prof. Stenzler has not failed to observe, differ; especially the words pratnavadbhih prattah seem to me to be corrupt. The word pratnavat is only known to the Petersburg Dictionary as having the meaning, 'containing the word pratna,' which will not do here. Thus, I think that the reading pratnam adbhih priktah should be adopted ; the translation would be, ' Anciently thou hast been mixed with water.'

the gods. By the ancients thou hast been offered.
Through the funeral oblation render the Fathers and
these worlds propitious to us. Svadhâ! Adoration!'

12. (The different rites are performed) from the
right to the left.

13. With (the part) of the other (i. e. left) hand
between the thumb (and the fore-finger), because he
wears the sacrificial cord over his left shoulder, or
with the right hand which he seizes with the left (he
offers the Arghya water to the Fathers with the
words), ' Father, this is thy Arghya. Grandfather,
this is thy Arghya. Great-grandfather, this is thy
Arghya'—having first offered (ordinary) water (to
the Fathers).

14. When he is going to hand over that (Arghya
water to the Brâhmanas who represent the Fathers,
he says once each time), 'Svadhâ! The Arghya
water!'

15. Over (the Arghya water) which has been

<hr />

12. Comp. Sâṅkhâyana-Grihya IV, 4, 6.

13. The part of the hand above the thumb is called the 'Tîrtha
belonging to the Manes;' see, for instance, Baudhâyana's Dharma-
sûtra I, 8, 16. The sacrificer is here understood to wear his sacrificial
cord suspended over the left shoulder (he is 'yâgñopavîtin'). But
as the oblation here treated of is directed to the Manes, it is
required that he should be prâkînâvîtin. Now he is considered
as prâkînâvîtin, according to Nârâyana, not only if the cord is
suspended over his right shoulder (which is the ordinary meaning
of prâkînâvîtin), but also if the hand with which he performs the
rites, and the shoulder over which he wears the sacred cord, are
either both right or both left. Thus here, acting with the left-hand
and wearing the cord over the left shoulder, he becomes prâkînâvîtin.

The last word (appûrvam) is separated by Nârâyana from the
rest, so that it forms a separate Sûtra.

15. The sacrificer gives the water to the Brâhmanas, and these

poured out, he should recite the verse, 'The celestial waters which have been produced on the earth, the aerial waters and the waters which are terrestrial, the gold-coloured ones, apt for sacrifice, may these waters bring us luck and be kind to us.' Pouring together what has been left (in the three Arghya vessels) he moistens his face with that water, if he desires that a son should be born to him.

16. 'He should· not take up the first vessel, into which the Arghya water for the Fathers has been poured. Hidden the Fathers dwell therein : thus Saunaka has said.'

17. In that moment the gifts of perfumes, garlands, incense, lights, and clothes are offered (to the Brâhmanas).

18. Having taken some food (of the Sthâlipâka prepared for the Pindapitriyagña), and having besmeared it with ghee, he asks (the Brâhmanas) for their permission by saying, 'I shall offer it in the fire,' or, 'I will sacrifice my offering in the fire,' or, 'I will offer it in the fire.'

19. The permission (is given in the words). 'It may be offered,' or, 'Sacrifice thy offering,' or, 'Offer it.'

20. He then sacrifices in the fire as stated above,

---

pour it out. Instead of prithivî sambabhûvuh (prithivî being intended as a locative; see Lanman, Noun-inflection in the Veda, p. 389) we should read, no doubt, as the parallel texts have, payasâ sambabhûvuh: 'The celestial waters which have united themselves with milk.'

16. This is a Sloka.

17. Manu III, 209; Yâgñavalkya I, 231.

20. The oblations alluded to in this Sûtra are prescribed in the Srauta-sûtra, II, 6, 12. They are directed to Soma pitrimat and to Agni kavyavâhana.

21. Or, if they give their permission, in the
hands (of the Brâhma*n*as).

22. ' The mouth of the gods verily is the fire, the
mouth of the Fathers is the hand '—thus says the
Brâhma*n*a.

23. If in the hands, he assigns to them other food,
after they have sipped water.

24. The food (is put together) with the food.

25. It is said, 'What is given away and offered,
that brings prosperity.'

26. When he sees that they are satiated, he should
recite (the verses) containing the word m a dh u, and
(the verse), ' They have eaten, they have enjoyed
themselves ' (Rig-veda I, 82, 2).

27. Having asked them, ' Relished ?' and having
taken the food, whatever food he has used, together
with the Sthâlipâka, in order to make lumps thereof,
he should offer the rest (to the Brâhma*n*as).

28. After they have either accepted (that rest of
food), or left it (to him), and have finished eating,
he should, before they have sipped water, put down
the lumps for the Fathers.

---

21. According to Manu (III, 212) this is done only in case there
is no fire. Possibly abhyanug*ñ*âyâm belongs to Sûtra 20, so
that we should have to translate, ' He then sacrifices . . . if they
give their permission. Or in the hands.'

24. ' The food which is left from the oblations he puts with the
food (Sûtra 23) which is to be eaten by the Brâhma*n*as, and has
been put into the vessels.' Nârâya*n*a.

25. Is s*r*ish*t*am to be understood in the sense of vis*r*ish*t*am ?
Nârâya*n*a explains it by prabhûtam.

26. The verses containing the word m a d h u are Rig-veda I, 90,
6–8.

27. On the question, ' Relished ?' compare *S*ânkhâyana-G*r*/*i*hya
IV, 2, 5. For several kinds of *S*râddha ceremonies a Sthâlîpâka is
prescribed, for others it is not; for the *S*râddhas of the last kind
the words ' Together with the Sthâlîpâka ' are not valid.

29. After they have sipped water, according to some (teachers).

30. Having strewn the food on the ground and suspended the sacrificial cord over his left shoulder, he should dismiss the Brâhmanas, (saying to them), ' Say Om! Svadhâ !'

31. Or, ' So be it! Svadhâ !'

KANDIKÂ 8.

1. Now the spit-ox (sacrificed to Rudra).

2. In autumn or in spring, under the (Nakshatra) Ârdrâ.

3. The best of his herd,

4. (An ox) which is neither leprous nor speckled;

5. One with black spots, according to some ;

6. If he likes, a black one, if its colour inclines to copper-colour.

7. He sprinkles it with water, into which he has thrown rice and barley,

8. From head to tail,

9. With (the formula), ' Grow up, agreeable to Rudra the great god.'

10. He should let it grow up. When it has cut its teeth, or when it has become a bull—

11. To a quarter (of the horizon) which is sacrificially pure,

12. At a place which cannot be seen from the village,

---

30. They reply, ' Om ! Svadhâ !'

8, 1. According to Nârâyana, the 'spit-ox' sacrifice is so called because it is offered to Rudra the spit-wearer.

5. Kalmâsho nâma krishnabindukitah. Nârâyana.

10. This Sûtra should rather be divided into two.

11. I. e. to the east or the north.

13. After midnight,

14. According to some, after sunrise.

15. Having caused a Brahman who is versed in
learning and knows the practice (of this sacrifice), to
sit down, having driven a fresh branch with leaves
into the ground as a sacrificial post, (having taken)
two creeping plants or two Ku*s*a ropes as two
girdles, and having wound the one round the sacrificial post, and tied the other round the middle of the
animal's head, he binds it to the sacrificial post or to
the girdle (which he had tied to that post) with (the
formula), ' Agreeable to him to whom adoration (is
brought), I bind thee.'

16. The sprinkling with water and what follows is
the same as at the animal sacrifice.

17. We shall state what is different.

18. Let him sacrifice the omentum with the Pâtri
or with a leaf—thus it is understood (in the *S*ruti)—

19. With (the formulas), ' To Hara, M*ri*da, *S*arva,
*S*iva, Bhava, Mahâdeva, Ugra, Bhîma, Pa*s*upati,
Rudra, *S*ankara, Î*s*âna svâhâ !'

20. Or with the last six (parts of that formula),

21. Or with (the formula), ' To Rudra svâhâ !'

22. Let him make Bali offerings towards the four
quarters (of the horizon), to each on four rings of
Ku*s*a net-work, with (the formulas), ' The hosts,
Rudra, which thou hast towards the eastern direction,

---

15. Round the middle of the head means, between the two horns.
Nârâya*n*a.

16. See above, I, 11.

22. This Bali offering is performed, according to Nârâya*n*a,
before the Svish*t*ak*ri*t oblation of the chief sacrifice. On ku*s*asûna
the commentator has the note, ' Darbhastambais *tri*nais *k*a kalpavad
(or rather, as Prof. Stenzler writes, ka*t*akavad) grathitvâ sarveshâm
agra*m* g*ri*hîtvâ, ekîk*ri*tya grathitâ*h* ku*s*asûnâ u*k*yante.'

to them this (offering is brought). Adoration to
thee! Do no harm to me!' In this way the
assigning (of the offerings is performed) according
to the different quarters (of the horizon).

23. With the following four hymns he should
worship the four quarters, viz. 'What shall we to
Rudra,' 'These prayers to Rudra,' 'To thee, O
father,' 'These songs to Rudra with the strong bow'
(Rig-veda I, 43, 114; II, 33; VII, 46).

24. (This) worship to the quarters (of the horizon)
(is performed) at all sacrifices to Rudra.

25. The husks and chaff (of the rice), the tail, the
skin, the head, the feet (of the sacrificial animal) he
should throw into the fire.

26. He should turn the skin to some use, according
to Sâmvatya.

27. To the north of the fire, on rows of Darbha
grass, or on rings of Kusa net-work, he should pour
out the blood (of the sacrificial animal) with (the
formula), 'Hissing ones! Noisy ones! Searching
ones! Seizing ones! Serpents! What here belongs
to you, take that.'

28. Then, turning to the north, (he assigns it) to
the serpents (in the words), 'Hissing ones! Noisy
ones! Searching ones! Seizing ones! Serpents!
What here belongs to you, take that.'

Then the serpents take whatever has flowed down
there of blood or of the contents of stomach and
entrails.

29. All names, all hosts, all exaltations belong

---

26. Perhaps Sâmvatya is a mis-spelling of the name of the well-
known Grihya teacher Sâmbavya.

27. Darbhavitâ is explained in the commentary by darbharâgi.

to him;—to a sacrificer who knows that, he gives
joy.

30. Even to a man who only with words sets
forth (some part) of that (ceremony), he will do no
harm ; thus it is understood (in the *S*ruti).

31. He should not partake of that (sacrifice).

32. They should not take anything belonging to
it into the village. For this god will do harm to
(human) creatures.

33. He should keep away his people from the
vicinity (of the place where he has sacrificed).

34. On an express injunction, however, he
should partake (of that sacrificial food), for it will
bring luck.

35. This spit-ox sacrifice procures wealth, (open)
space, purity, sons, cattle, long life, splendour.

36. After he has sacrificed, he should let loose
another (animal).

37. He should not be without such an animal.

38. Then he will not be without cattle—thus it is
understood (in the *S*ruti).

39. Muttering the *S*antâtîya hymn, he should go
to his house.

40. If disease befalls his cattle, he should
sacrifice to that same god in the midst of his cow-
stable—

41. A mess of cooked food, which he sacrifices in
its entirety.

---

32. Instead of abhimâruka we ought to read abhimânuka.
See Aitareya Brâhma*n*a III, 34, and the Petersburg Dictionary
s. v. abhimânuka.

36. He should destine another young animal in the way stated
above (Sûtras 7 seqq.) to a new *S*ûlagava sacrifice.

39. Rig-veda VII, 35. Comp. above, II, 8, 11.

42. Having thrown the sacrificial grass and the Âgya into the fire, he should lead his cows through the smoke.

43. Murmuring the Santâtîya hymn, he should go in the midst of his cattle.

44. Adoration to Saunaka! Adoration to Saunaka!

End of the Fourth Adhyâya.

End of the Âsvalâyana-Grihya-sûtra.

PÂRASKARA-GRIHYA-SÛTRA.

INTRODUCTION

TO THE

PÂRASKARA-G*R*IHYA-SÛTRA.

THE G*r*ihya-sûtra of Pâraskara, which belongs to the
White Yagur-veda and forms an appendix to Kâtyâyana's
*S*rauta-sûtra, has been edited, with a German translation,
by the scholar who was the first to make a G*r*ihya text
accessible to Orientalists and to begin to grapple with the
first and most serious difficulties that beset its interpretation, and who has continued since to do more than any-
one else towards elucidating that important branch of Vedic
literature. It would be very unbecoming in any one engaged
in the study of G*r*ihya texts, not to acknowledge most
warmly the debt of gratitude which he owes to Professor
Stenzler. At the same time the respect due to the veteran
editor and interpreter of Â*s*valâyana and Pâraskara not
only allows, but requires that one who proposes to himself
the same task at which Prof. Stenzler has worked with so
much learning, should state as clearly as possible what
that distinguished scholar has left for others to do, and
why one who prepares an English translation of Pâraskara
has a very different task from merely translating into
English the German translation of Prof. Stenzler.

If I may venture to express in one word the difference
between Prof. Stenzler's method, as I understand it, for
getting at the meaning of a doubtful or obscure passage,
and the method which I have endeavoured to follow, I
should say that with Prof. Stenzler the first step and,

I believe, in many cases also the last step is to ask how
Gayarâma and Râmak/ishna understand the passage in
question, while I hold that we ought rather to make ourselves independent from those commentators in the sense
in which Prof. Max Müller once expressed himself [1], 'not
that I ever despise the traditional interpretation which the
commentators have preserved to us, but because I think
that, after having examined it, we have a right to judge for
ourselves.' There exists a commentary on the Pâraskara-
Gr/hya which far surpasses in trustworthiness Gayarâma's
Sagganavallabha and Râmak/ishna's Samskâraganapati,
and which is not composed by an author who, as says
Goethe,
        — im Auslegen ist munter ;
    Legt er nicht aus, so legt er unter.
But the leaves of that commentary are scattered through
a good many volumes. Here we find a few lines of it in the
Satapatha Brâhmana or in Kâtyâyana's Srauta-sûtra ; there
Sânkhâyana or Âsvalâyana has preserved a word or a sentence that belongs to it ; or the law-books of Manu or
Yâgñavalkya help us to understand a difficult or doubtful
aphorism of our text. In one word : the only true commentary on a work like Pâraskara's Gr/hya is that which
the ancient literature itself furnishes. No one will say that
in Prof. Stenzler's translation and notes this commentary
has not been consulted. But it has been consulted perhaps
not quite as much as it ought to have been, and Râmakrishna and Gayarâma have been consulted too much.
They have been consulted and followed in many instances, where a continued consideration of what can be
the meaning of a word and what can not, and of what the
parallel texts say with regard to the subject in question,
would have shown that those commentators, instead of
interpreting Pâraskara's meaning, father on him vague
opinions of their own.
    Perhaps it will not be out of place here .to point our

---

[1] Sacred Books of the East, vol. xv, p. 2, note 2.

criticism, lest it should be deemed unjust, by a few remarks on a single passage of Pâraskara in which the difference of Prof. Stenzler's way of translating and of our own becomes manifest. Of the numerous passages which could be selected for this purpose, I choose Sûtra I, 2, 5, belonging to the description of the setting up of the sacred domestic fire. The text of that Sûtra runs thus :

5. ara*n*ipradânam eke.

Prof. Stenzler translates as follows :

'Einige sagen, es müsse durch Reibhölzer erzeugtes Feuer sein.'

The two Sûtras which precede give a description of that ceremony from which evidently the opinion of the 'eke' mentioned in this Sûtra differs, or to which they find it necessary to add something. Those Sûtras run thus :

3. After he has fetched fire from the house of a Vai*s*ya who is rich in cattle—

4. All ceremonies are performed as at the cooking of the *k*âtushprâ*s*ya food[1].

It seems evident that the Â*k*âryas to whom the opinion spoken of in Sûtra 5 belongs, add, or perhaps substitute, to the fetching of the fire which is to be worshipped as the sacrificer's domestic fire, from a rich Vai*s*ya's house, another rite in which an ara*n*i, i.e. a stick for kindling the fire by attrition, is made use of in some way or other.

Now if this may be accepted as a vague expression of the general purport of the Sûtra, what is the literal meaning of the words? 'Some (teachers),' it says, '(prescribe) the pradâna of the kindling stick (or, of the kindling sticks).'

What does pradâna mean? *G*ayarâma says,

'pra*s*abda upa*s*abdârthe. ara*n*yupâdânakam eka â*k*âryâ i*kkh*anti.'

---

[1] The food which is eaten by the four chief officiating priests of the *S*rauta ritual. For these priests a mess of food is prepared at the ceremony of the âdhâna of the *S*rauta fires.

That is: 'The word pra stands in the sense of the word upa. Some teachers desire that it (i. e. the fire) should have the kindling sticks as its physical basis[1].'

Thus, if Gayarâma is right, Prof. Stenzler's translation would be justified. But can we acquiesce indeed in simply accepting the commentator's opinion? Pradâna is pradâna and not upâdâna, as pradadâti is not upâdatte. Pradadâti means 'he hands over,' and pradâna 'the handing over.' This is an established fact, and an interpreter of a Vedic text should not allow himself to be induced by a statement like that of Gayarâma about the preposition pra standing in the sense of upa, to abate one iota of it. Thus we are obliged, until passages have been discovered which modify our knowledge of what pradâna means—but such passages most certainly will never be discovered—to translate:

5. Some (teachers say that) the handing over of the kindling sticks (takes place).

We should give that translation even if we were not able to find an explanation for it. It appears that Prof. Stenzler, as far as we can judge from his note, has not even thought of the possibility of disregarding the authority of Gayarâma and Râmakrishna, or of looking through the parallel texts to see whether they do not throw light on what that 'handing over of the kindling sticks' signifies. The text to be consulted first is of course Kâtyâyana's Srauta-sûtra. As the Srauta ritual contains a description of an âdhâna which is in some way the prototype of the corresponding Grihya ceremony, we may possibly expect to discover, in the course of that description, the statements regarding the arani-pradâna for which we are searching. Now Kâtyâyana[2], having described the setting up of the fire in the gârhapatyâgâra, states that at sunset the sacrificer and his

---

[1] Râmakrishna also, according to Prof. Stenzler's note, explains pradâna by upâdâna, kârana, utpattisthâna.

[2] IV, 7, 15 seqq. The corresponding passage of the Paddhati is found at p. 358 of Prof. Weber's edition.

wife sit down to the west of the fire which has just been established, and then the Adhvaryu hands over to them the two kindling sticks[1]. The Paddhati, in describing that act, goes into further details. The Adhvaryu hands over to the sacrificer the two Aranis, which, as required by custom, are wrapped up in new clothes. The wife takes the adharârani from his hand and puts it on her lap; the sacrificer puts the uttarârani on his lap, and they do homage to them with flowers, saffron, sandal wood, &c.; then, after the performance of some other ceremonies, they put the two Aranis away on a chair or bench. The two Aranis have to be kept by the sacrificer; if they are lost or burnt or destroyed in any other way, other Aranis must be procured, and by their attrition a new fire must be kindled[2].

Âpastamba likewise mentions, in his description of the Agnyâdhâna[3], the handing over of the two Aranis, and indicates a Mantra which the Adhvaryu recites in giving them to the sacrificer, and two other Mantras with the one of which the sacrificer receives them, while he recites the other over the Aranis, after having taken them into his hands.

Finally we may quote here, as bearing witness to the custom of the Aranipradâna, a passage taken from Nârâyana's commentary on the Sânkhâyana-Grihya. Though the decisive words in that passage rest only on the authority of the commentator and not of the Sûtrakâra himself, they deserve to be taken notice of, as they are not subject to the suspicion that they could be influenced by a misunderstanding of that very Sûtra of Pâraskara of which we are treating. Nârâyana says, in his explanation of Sânkhâyana I, 1, 10[4]: 'To the west of the fire the sacrificer, and southwards (of him) the wife sits down. The

---

[1] IV, 7, 22 : asvatthasamigarbhârani prayakkhati.
[2] See the commentary on IV, 7, 22, and the passages of the Karmapradîpa quoted there.
[3] Srauta-sûtra V, 8, 7 ; vol. i, p. 255, of Prof. Garbe's edition.
[4] Sâyamâhutisamskâro adhvaryupratyaya ity akâryâh.

handing over of the kindling sticks does not take place. For it is a fire fetched (from a Vaisya's house, &c.) which is inaugurated here[1].' Then the commentator goes on to quote a *Sloka*:

'The handing over of the Ara*n*is which the Adhvaryu sometimes performs,

'Is not in accordance with the opinion of Suya*gñ*a[2]; he does not approve of kindling the fire by attrition[3].'

Thus, I think, no doubt can remain as to the real meaning of Pâraskara's Sûtra : it means what its words signify and what is in accordance with Kâtyâyana and Âpastamba, and it does not mean what the commentators most gratuitously would make it mean.

Perhaps I have dwelt here too long on the interpretation of a few words which are of no peculiar interest in themselves. But I venture to hope that the discussion on these words will serve as a specimen, by which the fundamental difference of two methods of handling our texts may be discerned. Let us never forget how much we owe to the scholars who have followed the first of these methods, but for ourselves let us choose the second.

---

[1] Agne*h* pa*sk*âd ya*g*amâno dakshi*n*ata*h* patnî *k*a upavisati. ara*n*ipradâna*m* na kartavya*m*. âh*ri*tasyâgner eva sa*m*skâra*h*.

[2] On this name of *S*âṅkhâyana, see my Introduction to the translation of the *S*âṅkhâyana-G*ri*hya, above, p. 3.

[3]   Atrâra*n*ipradâna*m* yad adhvaryu*h* kurute kva*k*it,
mata*m* tan na Suya*gñ*asya mathita*m* so ≈tra ne*kkh*ati.

PÂRASKARA-GR*I*HYA-SÛTRA.

KÂ*N*DA I, KA*N*DIKÂ 1.

1. Now henceforth the performance of the domestic sacrifices of cooked food (will be explained).

2. Having wiped (around the surface on which he intends to perform a sacrifice), having besmeared it (with cowdung), having drawn the lines thereon, having taken the earth out (of the lines), having besprinkled (the place with water), having established the (sacred) fire, having spread out the seat for the Brahman to the south, having carried forward (the Pra*n*îta water), having spread (Ku*s*a grass) round (the fire), having put down (the different things used at the sacrifice) according as they are wanted, having prepared two (Ku*s*a blades used as) strainers, having consecrated the Proksha*n*î

1, 1. Comp. *S*ânkhâyana-Gr*i*hya I, 1 ; Â*s*valâyana-Gr*i*hya I, 1, &c. It seems to me that Professor Stenzler is not quite right in giving to the opening words of the text athâta*h*, which he translates 'nun also,' the explanation: 'das heisst, nach Beendigung des *S*rauta-sûtra von Kâtyâyana.' I think rather it can be shown that ata*h* does not contain a reference to something preceding ; thus the *S*rauta-sûtra, which forms the first part of the whole Sûtra collection, is opened in the same way by the words athâto*·*dhikâra*h*.

2. The description of the standard form of domestic sacrifice opens with an enumeration of the five so-called bhûsa*m*skâra (parisamuhya, &c.). On the samûhana (for parisamuhya is derived

water, having sprinkled (with that water the sacrificial implements) according to what is needed, having poured out (the Âg*ya* or sacrificial butter into the pot), and having put the sacrificial butter on the fire, he should (lustrate the butter by) moving a fire-brand round it.

3. Having warmed the (sacrificial spoon called) Sruva, having wiped it, having besprinkled it (with water), and warmed it again, he should put it down.

4. Having taken the Âg*ya* from the fire, having purified it, having looked at it, and (having purified) the Proksha*nî* water as above, having taken up the Ku*s*a blades with which he is to take hold (of the Âg*ya* pot) by its under surface, having put pieces of wood on (the fire), and having sprinkled (water round it), he should sacrifice.

5. This is the rite wherever a sacrifice is performed.

KA*ND*IKÂ 2.

1. The setting up of the Âvasathya (or sacred domestic) fire (is performed) at the time of his wedding.

from the root ûh, not from vah; comp. below, II, 4, 2: pâ*n*inâgnim parisamûhati), see *S*ânkhâyana I, 7, 11; G*ri*hya-sa*m*graha-pari*s*ish*ta* I, 37, &c. On the lines drawn on the sacrificial surface, see *S*ânkhâyana I, 7, 6 seq.; Â*s*valâyana I, 3, 1; G*ri*hya-sa*m*graha-pari*s*ish*ta* I, 47 seq.

4. Pûrvavat ('as above') can possibly, as Professor Stenzler understands it, have been said with regard to Kâtyâyana's rule, II, 3, 33: Tâbhyâm (scil. pavitrâbhyâm) utpunâti Savitur va iti. But it is also possible that the expression may refer to the second Sûtra of this chapter, where it is said, proksha*nîh* sa*m*skr*i*tya. On upayamanân ku*s*ân, comp. Kâtyâyana I, 10, 6–8.

2, 1. Comp. *S*ânkhâyana-G*ri*hya I, 1, 3.

2. At the time of the division of the inheritance, according to some (teachers).

3. After he has fetched fire from the house of a Vaisya who is rich in cattle,—

4. All ceremonies are performed as at the cooking of the *k*âtushprâ*s*ya food.

5. Some (say that) the handing over of the kindling sticks (should take place),

6. Because the *S*ruti says, 'There are five great sacrifices.'

7. Having cooked a mess of sacrificial food for the deities of the Agnyâdheya, and having sacrificed the two Â*g*ya portions, he sacrifices (the following) Â*g*ya oblations :

8. 'Thou, Agni' (Vâ*g*. Sa*m*hitâ XXI, 3) ; 'Thus

---

2. Sânkhâyana I, 1, 4. 3. Sânkhâyana I, 1, 8.

4. The *k*âtushprâsya food is prepared, at the time of the setting up of the *S*rauta fires, for the four chief officiating priests of the *S*rauta sacrifices. Comp. *S*atapatha Brâhma*n*a II, 1, 4. Kâtyâyana's corresponding rules with regard to the Âdhâna of the *S*rauta fires are found at IV, 7. 15. 16.

5. Comp. the remarks on this Sûtra, in the Introduction, pp. 263 seq.

6. *S*atapatha Brâhma*n*a XI, 5, 6, 1 : 'There are five great sacrifices which are great Sattras, viz. the sacrifice to living beings, the sacrifice to men, the sacrifice to the Manes, the sacrifice to the gods, the Brahmaya*g*ña.' As the Gr*i*hya ceremonies are included here under the category of mahâya*g*ñas or great sacrifices, they require, according to the teachers whose opinion is stated in Sûtra 5, a form of the Agnyâdhâna (setting up of the sacred fire) analogous to the Agnyâdhâna of the *S*rauta ritual, and containing, like that Âdhâna, the act of the Ara*n*ipradâna or handing over of the kindling woods (Sûtra 5).

7. The deities of the Agnyâdheya, or of the *S*rauta ceremony corresponding to the Gr*i*hya rite here treated of, are Agni pavamâna, Agni pâvaka, Agni *s*u*k*i, Aditi. On the Â*g*yabhâgas, see Sânkhâyana I, 9, 7, &c.

8. The verses Vâ*g*. Sa*m*h. XXI, 3, 4, the two verses quoted

thou, Agni' (Vâg. Sa*m*hitâ XXI, 4); 'This, O
Varu*n*a'(XXI, 1); 'For this I entreat thee' (XXI,
2); 'Thy hundred'(Kâty.-*S*raut. XXV, 1, 11); 'And
quick, Agni' (Kâty. l.l.); 'The highest one' (Vâg.
Sa*m*h. XII, 12); 'Be both to us' (ibid. V, 3)—with
(these verses he sacrifices) eight (oblations) before
(the oblations of cooked food).

9. Thus he sacrifices also afterwards, after he has
made oblations of the mess of cooked food to the
deities of the Agnyâdheya.

10. And to (Agni) Svish*t*ak*ri*t,

11. With (the formulas), 'Into the quick one
(has been put) Agni's (sacrificial portion) over
which the word vasha*t* has been spoken;' 'What I
have done too much;' 'O gods who know the way.'

12. Having sacrificed the Barhis, he partakes (of
the sacrificial food).

13. Then food is given to the Brâhma*n*as.

Kâty. XXV, 1, 11, and fifthly the verse Vâg. Sa*m*h. XII, 12, are
prescribed for the Sarvaprâya*sk*itta (or general expiatory ceremony),
see Kâtyâyana l.l.

11. Professor Stenzler, following *G*ayarâma, takes the whole as
one Mantra, which he translates: 'Ungehemmet sei Agni's Spende,
die durch die That ich überreich machte, bahnschaffende Götter!'
But the words yat karma*n*âtyarîri*k*am are the opening words
of a Mantra quoted *S*atapatha Brâhma*n*a XIV, 9, 4, 24, (comp.
also Â*s*valâyana-G*ri*hya I, 10, 23; the connection in which atyarî-
ri*k*am there stands, shows that the word designates a mistake made in
the sacrificial work by doing too much.) The words devâ gâtu-
vida*h* are the Pratîka of Vâg. Samhitâ VIII, 21. Thus I have no
doubt that also ayâsy Agner vasha*t*k*ri*tam (or possibly ayâsy
Agner (?) and vasha*t*k*ri*tam (?)) is a Pratîka. Of course, the
translation of these words must remain uncertain until the Mantra
to which they belong has been discovered.

12. On the throwing into the fire of the Barhis, comp. Kâtyâyana
III, 8.

KANDIKÂ 3.

1. To six persons the Arghya reception is due : to a teacher, to an officiating priest, to the father-in-law, to the king, to a friend, to a Snâtaka.

2. They should honour them (with the Arghya reception) once a year.

3. But officiating priests (they should receive) whenever they intend to perform a sacrifice.

4. Having ordered a seat to be got (for the guest), he says, 'Well, sir ! sit down ! We will do honour to you, sir !'

5. They get for him a couch (of grass) to sit down on, another for the feet, water for washing the feet, the Argha water, water for sipping, and the honey-mixture, i. e. curds, honey, and ghee, in a brass vessel with a brass cover.

6. Another person three times announces (to the guest) the couch and the other things (when they are offered to him).

7. He accepts the couch.

8. He sits down thereon with (the verse), ' I am the highest one among my people, as the sun among the thunder-bolts. Here I tread on whosoever infests me.'

9. With the feet (he treads) on the other (bundle of grass).

3, 1. On vaivâhya, which I have translated 'father-in-law,' comp. the note on Sânkhâyana II, 15, 1.

2, 3. Comp. below. Sûtra 31, and Sânkhâyana-Grihya II, 15. 10.

6. Âsvalâyana-Grihya I, 24, 7.

8. I have translated according to the reading of Âsvalâyana (l. l. § 8), vidyutâm instead of udyatâm.

9, 10. There is no doubt that these Sûtras should be divided

10. When he is seated on the couch, he washes (for his guest) the left foot and then the right foot.

11. If (the host) is a Brâhma*n*a, the right first.

12. (He does so) with (the formula), 'The milk of Virâ*g* art thou. The milk of Virâ*g* may I obtain. (May) the milk of Padyâ Virâ*g* (dwell) in me.'

13. He accepts the Arghya water with (the words), 'Waters are ye. May I obtain through you all my wishes.'

14. Pouring it out he recites over (the waters the formula), 'To the ocean I send you; go back to your source. Unhurt be our men. May my sap not be shed.'

15. He sips water with (the formula), 'Thou camest to me with glory. Unite me with lustre. Make me beloved by all creatures, the lord of cattle, unhurtful for the bodies.'

16. With (the formula), 'With Mitra's' (Vâ*g*. Sa*m*h., Kâ*n*va*s*âkhâ II, 3, 4) he looks at the Madhuparka.

17. With (the formula), 'By the impulse of the god Savit*ri*' (Vâ*g*. Sa*m*h. l. l.) he accepts it.

18. Taking it into his left hand he stirs it about

thus: pâdayor anya*m*. vish*t*ara âsînâya savya*m* pâda*m* prakshâlya dakshi*n*am prakshâlayati. Thus it is said in the Khâdira-Gr*ih*ya: vish*t*aram âstirya . . . adhyâsita. pâdayor dvitiyayâ (scil. *rik*â) dvau *k*et. Gobhila has the Sûtra: pâdayor anyam.

11. The words brâhma*n*a*s k*et refer to the host, as the comparison of Â*s*valâyana I, 24, 11, shows.

12. Comp. Â*s*valâyana l. l. § 22; *S*ânkhâyana III, 7, 5.

13. The play on words (âpas = waters, avâpnavâni = may I obtain) is untranslatable.

16. Â*s*valâyana-Gr*ih*ya I, 24, 14.

17. Â*s*valâyana-Gr*ih*ya I, 24, 15.

18. Â*s*valâyana-Gr*ih*ya l. l. Anna*s*ane instead of annâ*s*ane is simply a mistake in spelling.

three times with the fourth finger of his right hand with (the formula), 'Adoration to the brown-faced One. What has been damaged in thee, when the food was eaten, that I cut off from thee.'

19. And with the fourth finger and the thumb he spirts away (some part of the Madhuparka) three times.

20. He partakes of it three times with (the formula), 'What is the honied, highest form of honey, and the enjoyment of food, by that honied, highest form of honey, and by that enjoyment of food may I become highest, honied, and an enjoyer of food.'

21. Or with (the verses) that contain the word ' honey,' verse by verse.

22. Let him give the remainder (of the Madhuparka) to a son or a pupil who is sitting to the north.

23. Or let him eat the whole of it (himself).

24. Or he should pour out (the remainder) to the east, at an unfrequented spot.

25. Having sipped water, he touches his bodily organs with (the formula), 'May speech dwell in my mouth, breath in my nose, sight in my eyes, hearing in my ears, strength in my arms, vigour in my thighs. May my limbs be unhurt, may my body be united with my body!'

26. When (the guest) has sipped water, (the host), holding a butcher's knife, says to him three times, 'A cow!'

27. He replies, ' The mother of the Rudras, the daughter of the Vasus, the sister of the Âdityas, the

---

21. These are the three verses, Vâg. Samhitâ XIII. 27-29.
22. Âsvalâyana-Grihya I, 24. 25.   23. Âsvalâyana l.l. § 27.
24. Âsvalâyana l.l. § 26.

navel of immortality. To the people who understand me, I say, "Do not kill the guiltless cow, which is Aditi." I kill my sin and N.N.'s sin,'—thus, if he chooses to have it killed.

28. But if he chooses to let it loose, he should say, 'My sin and N.N.'s sin has been killed. Om! Let it loose! Let it eat grass!'

29. But let the Argha not be without flesh.

30. On the occasion of a sacrifice and of a wedding let (the guest) say, 'Make it (ready).'

31. Even if he performs more than one Soma sacrifice during one year, let only priests who have received (from him) the Arghya reception, officiate for him, not such who have not received it; for this has been prescribed in the *S*ruti.

K*a*ND*I*KÂ 4.

1. There are four kinds of Pâkaya*gñ*as, viz. the huta, the ahuta, the prahuta, and the prâ*s*ita.

2. On the following five occasions, viz. the wedding, the tonsure (of the child's head), the initiation (of the Brahma*k*ârin), the cutting of the beard, and the parting of the hair, (on these occasions) in the outer hall,

3. On a place that has been smeared (with cowdung), which is elevated, and which has been sprinkled (with water), he establishes the fire,

29, 30. These Sûtras are identical with two Sûtras in the *S*ânkhâyana-Gr*i*hya II, 15, 2. 3. See the note there. It seems to me inadmissible to translate § 29, as Professor Stenzler does: Der Argha darf aber nicht immer ohne Fleisch sein.

31. *S*ânkhâyana-Gr*i*hya II, 15, 10.

4. 1–5. See *S*ânkhâyana-Gr*i*hya I, 5, 1–5 and the notes.

4. Having kindled it by attrition, according to some teachers, at his marriage. ·

5. During the northern course of the sun, in the time of the increasing moon, on an auspicious day he shall seize the hand of a girl,

6. Under one of the (three times) three Nakshatras of which a constellation designated as Uttara is first,

7. Or under (the Nakshatras) Svâti, M*ri*ga*s*iras, or Rohi*n*î.

8. Three (wives are allowed) to a Brâhma*n*a, in accordance with the order of the castes,

9. Two to a Râ*g*anya,

10. One to a Vai*s*ya,

11. One *S*ûdra wife besides to all, according to some (teachers), without using Mantras (at the ceremonies of wedding, &c.).

12. He then makes her put on the (under) garment with (the verse), 'Live to old age ; put on the garment ! Be a protectress of the human tribes against imprecation. Live a hundred years full of vigour ; clothe thyself in wealth and children. Blessed with life put on this garment ! '

13. Then the upper garment with (the verse), 'The goddesses who spun, who wove, who spread

6. I. e. under the constellations Uttaraphalgunî or the two constellations following it, Uttarâshâ*dh*â or the two constellations following it, Uttarabhâdrapadâ or the two constellations following it.

12. The words of the Mantra bhavâ k*ri*sh*t*inâm abhi*s*asti-pâvâ no doubt are an imitation of Rig-veda I, 76, 3, bhavâ ya*g*ñâ-nâm abhi*s*astipâvâ (where the words are applied to Agni). Thus the use of the masculine abhi*s*astipâvâ with reference to the bride may be accounted for.

13. Comp. Atharva-veda XIV, 1, 45. This parallel passage shows us the way to correct the text of this very much corrupted Mantra.

out, and who drew out the threads on both sides,
may those goddesses clothe thee for the sake of
long life. Blessed with life put on this garment !'

14. (The bride's father?) anoints the two, (while
the bridegroom recites the verse,) ' May the Visve
devâs, may the waters unite our hearts. May
Mâtarisvan, may Dhât*ri*, may Desh*tri* (the 'showing' goddess) join us.'

15. (The bridegroom), having accepted her who is
given away by her father, takes her and goes away
(from that place) with (the verse), 'When thou
wanderest far away with thy heart to the regions of
the world like the wind, may the gold-winged
Vaikar*na* (i.e. the wind?) grant that thy heart may
dwell with me! N. N.!'

16. He then makes them look at each other
(while the bridegroom repeats the verses), 'With no
evil eye, not bringing death to thy husband, bring
luck to the cattle, be full of joy and vigour. Give
birth to heroes ; be godly and friendly. Bring us
luck, to men and animals.

' Soma has acquired (thee) first (as his wife); after
him the Gandharva has acquired (thee). Thy third
husband is Agni; the fourth is thy human husband.

---

14. The literal translation would be: ' He salves together (samañgayati) the two . . . May the waters salve together (sama*ñ*gantu)
our hearts.' It was a real anointing of the bridegroom and of the
bride, that took place, and we cannot accept Professor Stenzler's
translation (based on *Gayarâma's* note: samañgayati parasparam̐
sammukhîkaroti), by which the proper signification of samañgayati
is effaced : Dann heisst (der Vater der Braut) sie beide zusammentreten. See the note on Sânkhâyana-Gr*ih*ya I, 12, 5. The
parallel passage of the Khâdira-Gr*ih*ya runs thus : apare*n*âgnim
auduko gatvâ pâ*n*igrâha*m* mûrdhany avasi*ñk*ed, vadhû*m* *k*a, samañ-
gantv ity avasikta*h*.

16. Comp. Rig-veda X, 85. 44. 40. 41. 37.

' Soma has given thee to the Gandharva ; the Gandharva has given thee to Agni. Wealth and children Agni has given to me, and besides this wife. ' Pûshan ! Lead her to us, the highly blessed one. Sâ na ûrû u*sat*î vihara, yasyâm u*sant*a*h* praharâma *sepa*m yasyâm u kâmâ bahavo nivish*t*yâ (nivish*t*â ?) iti.'

KANDIKÂ 5.

1. Having led her around the fire, keeping it on his right side, according to some (teachers)—

2. Having pushed with his right foot a bundle of grass or a mat to the west of the fire, he sits down.

3. While (the bride) touches him, (the following oblations are made :) the two Âghâra oblations, the two Âgya portions, the Mahâvyâh*ri*tis, the general expiation, the Prâgâpatya oblation, and the Svish*t*ak*ri*t.

4. These are regular (oblations) at every sacrifice.

5. The Svish*t*ak*ri*t comes before the Mahâvyâ-h*ri*tis, if the sacrificial food is different from Âgya.

6. The place for the insertion (of the peculiar oblations belonging to the different sacrifices) is the interval between the general expiation and the oblation to Pragâpati.

7. At the wedding (he may make oblations) with the Râsh*t*rabh*ri*t formulas (i. e. the formulas procuring royal power), if he likes, and with the Gaya and Abhyâtâna formulas (i. e. the formulas procuring

<hr>

5, 3. See the note on Sânkhâyana-Gr*i*hya I, 9, 12.

6. See the note l. l.—I have altered the division of Sûtras 6 and 7, so as to draw the word vivâhe to the seventh Sûtra. The rule in § 6 has an entirely general character ; the formulas stated in § 7 are given for the particular occasion of the vivâha ceremony.

victory, and aiming [at the hostile powers]), if he
knows them—

8. Because it has been said, ' By what sacrifice he
wishes to attain success.'

9. (The *G*aya formulas run thus) : ' Thought and
thinking. Intention and intending. The understood
and understanding. The mind and the *S*akvarî
(verses). The new moon and the full moon. B*ri*hat
and Rathantara.

' Pra*g*âpati, the powerful one in victorious battles,
has given victories (or, the *G*aya formulas) to manly
Indra. To him all subjects bowed down ; he has
become powerful and worthy of sacrifice. Svâhâ ! '

10. (The Abhyâtâna formulas run thus) : ' May
Agni, the lord of beings, protect me. May Indra,
(the lord) of the noblest, Yama, of the earth, Vâyu,
of the air, the Sun, of heaven, the Moon, of the
Nakshatras, B*ri*haspati, of the Brahman, Mitra, of
truth, Varu*n*a, of the waters, the sea, of the rivers,
food, the lord of royalty, protect me. May Soma, (the
lord) of herbs, Savit*ri*, of impulses, Rudra, of cattle,
Tvash*tri*, of forms, Vish*n*u, of mountains, the Maruts,
the lords of hosts, protect me. May the fathers,

8. Taittirîya Sa*m*hitâ III, 4, 6, 1 : ' By what sacrifice he wishes
to attain success, at that (sacrifice) he should make oblations with
them (i.e. with the Abhyâtâna Mantras) : then he will attain success
by that sacrifice.'

9. Instead of sa i havya*h* we ought to read probably sa u
havya*h*, or, as the Taitt. Sa*m*h. III, 4, 4, 1 gives, sa hi havya*h*.
The Maitr. Sa*m*h. has vihavya*h* (II, 10, 2).

10. The words, ' in this power of holiness . . . svâhâ ! ' are to be
added to each member of the whole formula (comp. Atharva-veda
V, 24). The expressions ' fathers ' and ' grandfathers,' which are
twice identically repeated in the translation, stand the first time for
pitara*h* pitâmahâ*h*, and then for tatâs tatâmahâ*h* of the Sanskrit text.

the grandfathers, the former, the later, the fathers, the grandfathers protect me here in this power of holiness, in this worldly power, in this prayer, in this Purohitaship, in this sacrifice, in this invocation of the gods. Svâhâ!'—this is added each time.

11. (He then makes other oblations with the following texts :)

'May Agni come hither, the first of gods. May he release the offspring of this wife from the fetter of death. That may this king Varu*n*a grant, that this wife may not weep over distress (falling to her lot) through her sons. Svâhâ!

'May Agni Gârhapatya protect this woman. May he lead her offspring to old age. With fertile womb may she be the mother of living children. May she experience delight in her sons. Svâhâ!

'Make, Agni, all ways of heaven and earth blissful to us, O thou who art worthy of sacrifices. What is great, born on this (earth), and praised,(born) in heaven, that bestow on us, rich treasures. Svâhâ!

'Come hither, showing us an easy path. Give us bright, undecaying life. May death go away; may immortality come to us. May Vivasvat's son make us safe from danger. Svâhâ!'

12. And the (verse), 'Another way, O death' (Vâ*g*. Sa*m*h. XXXV, 7), after the eating (of the remnant of the sacrificial food), according to some (teachers).

KA*N*DIKÂ 6.

1. The girl's brother pours out of his joined hands into her joined hands fried grain mixed with *S*ami leaves.

6, 1. Sânkhâyana I, 13, 15; Âsvalâyana I, 7, 8.

2. This she sacrifices, with firmly joined hands, standing, (while the bridegroom recites the verses,)

'To the god Aryaman the girls have made sacrifice, to Agni ; may he, god Aryaman, loosen us from here, and not from the husband. Svâhâ!

'This woman, strewing grains, prays thus, "May my husband live long ; may my relations be prosperous." Svâhâ!

'These grains I throw into the fire : may this bring prosperity to thee, and may it unite me with thee. May Agni grant us that. N. N.! Svâhâ!'

3. He then seizes her right hand together with the thumb, with (the verses),

'I seize thy hand for the sake of happiness, that thou mayst live to old age with me, thy husband. Bhaga, Aryaman, Savit*ri*, Purandhi, the gods have given thee to me that we may rule our house.

'This am I, that art thou ; that art thou, this am I. The Sâman am I, the *Rik* thou ; the heaven I, the earth thou.

'Come! Let us marry. Let us unite our sperm. Let us beget offspring. Let us acquire many sons, and may they reach old age.

'Loving, bright, with genial minds may we see a hundred autumns, may we live a hundred autumns, may we hear a hundred autumns!'

K*AN*DIKÂ 7.

1. He then makes her tread on a stone, to the north of the fire, with her right foot, (repeating the

2. *Sâṅkhâyana* I, 18, 3 ; 14, 1 ; Âsvalâyana I, 7. 13.
3. Rig-veda X, 85, 36 ; *Sâṅkhâyana* I, 13, 4, &c.
7, 1. Âsvalâyana-Gr*i*hya I, 7. 7 ; *Sâṅkhâyana*-Gr*i*hya I, 13, 12.

verse,) 'Tread on this stone ; like a stone be firm.
Tread the foes down ; turn away the enemies.'

2. He then sings a song: 'Sarasvatî! Promote
this (our undertaking), O gracious one, bountiful
one, thou whom we sing first of all that is, in whom
what is, has been born, in whom this whole world
dwells—that song I will sing to-day which will be
the highest glory of women.'

3. They then go round (the fire) with (the verse,
which the bridegroom repeats,)

'To thee they have in the beginning carried round
Sûryâ (the Sun-bride) with the bridal procession.
Mayst thou give back, Agni, to the husbands the
wife together with offspring.'

4. Thus (the same rites are repeated) twice again,
beginning from the fried grain.

5. The fourth time she pours the whole fried
grain by the neb of a basket (into the fire) with (the
words), 'To Bhaga svâhâ!'

6. After he has led her round (the fire) three
times, and has sacrificed the oblation to Pragâpati—

KANDIKÂ 8.

1. Then he makes her step forward in a northern
direction seven steps (with the words),

'One for sap, two for juice, three for the prospering of wealth, four for comfort, five for cattle, six
for the seasons. Friend! be with seven steps (united
to me). So be thou devoted to me.'

---

4. See chap. 6, 1.

5. Comp. Khâdira-Grihya I, 3: sûrpena sishtân agnâv opya prâ-
gudikim utkramayet. See also Gobhila II, 2 ; Âsvalâyana I, 7, 14.

8, 1. The parallel texts have sakhâ and saptapadî for sakhe
and saptapadâ of Pâraskara.

2. (The words), 'May Vish*n*u lead thee' are added
to every part (of the formula).

3. From the moment of their going away a man
who holds a water-pot on his shoulder, stands silent
to the south of the fire;

4. To the north, (according to the opinion) of
some (teachers).

5. From that (pot) he sprinkles her (with water)
on her head (with the formula),

'The blessed, the most blessed waters, the peaceful ones, the most peaceful ones, may they give
medicine to thee'—

6. And with the three (verses), 'Ye waters are'
(Vâ*g*. Sa*m*h. XI, 50–52).

7. He then makes her look at the sun with (the
verse), 'That eye' (Vâ*g*. Sa*m*h. XXXVI, 24).

8. He then touches her heart, (reaching) over her
right shoulder, with (the words), 'Into my will I take
thy heart; thy mind shall follow my mind; in my
word thou shalt rejoice with all thy heart; may
Pra*g*âpati join thee to me.'

9. He then recites over her (the verse),'Auspicious
ornaments does this woman wear. Come up to her
and behold her. Having brought luck to her, go
away back to your houses.'

10. A strong man snatches her up from the

<hr>

3. See above, I, 4, 15. The water mentioned here is designated as sthey*â* âpa*h*; see *S*ânkhâyana-G*ri*hya I, 13, 5 seq.;
G*ri*hya-sa*m*graha II, 26. 35.

8. See the note on *S*ânkhâyana-G*ri*hya II, 3, 3.

9. Rig-veda X, 85, 33.

10. The Atharva-veda (XX. 127, 12) has the reading pra
*g*âyadhvam instead of ni shîdantu (in the first Pâda); the second
hemistich there runs thus: iho sahasradakshi*n*o - pi Pûshâ ni shîdati.

ground, and sets her down in an eastern or northern direction in an out-of-the-way house, on a red bull's hide, with (the words),

'Here may the cows sit down, here the horses, here the men. Here may sacrifice with a thousand gifts, here may Pûshan sit down.'

11. And what (the people in) the village tell them, that they should do.

12. For it is said, 'At weddings and funerals he shall enter the village :'

13. (And) because the Sruti says, 'Therefore on these two occasions authority rests with the village.'

14. To the teacher (who helps at the wedding ceremonies) he gives an optional gift.

15. A cow is the optional gift to be given by a Brâhmana,

16. A village by a Râganya,

17. A horse by a Vaisya.

18. A hundred (cows) with a chariot (he gives to a father) who has only daughters.

19. After sunset he shows her the firm star (i.e. the polar-star) with (the words),

'Firm art thou ; I see thee, the firm one. Firm be thou with me, O thriving one !

---

12. I have ventured, differing from Professor Stenzler (' Bei der Hochzeit und auf der Leichenstätte richte er sich nach dem Dorfe '), to translate pravisatât according to its original meaning. Could this possibly be a rule for Vânaprasthas who live in the forest and enter the village only on exceptional occasions?

15–17. Sânkhâyana I, 14, 13 seqq.

18. Sânkhâyana I, 14, 16. Comp. the note there.

19. In the text the word ' firm' (dhruva) is neuter in the two first instances, and refers to the 'firm star;' the third time it is feminine, referring to the bride. Pâraskara has the vocative poshye for the nominative poshyâ of Sânkhâyana I, 17, 3; comp. above, § 1 sakhe for sakhâ.

'To me B*ri*haspati has given thee; obtaining offspring through me, thy husband, live with me a hundred autumns.'

20. If she does not see (the polar-star), let her say notwithstanding, ' I see,' &c.

21. Through a period of three nights they shall eat no saline food; they shall sleep on the ground; through one year they shall refrain from conjugal intercourse, or through a period of twelve nights, or of six nights, or at least of three nights.

KA*N*DIKÂ 9.

1. Beginning from the wedding the worshipping of the Aupâsana (i. e. sacred domestic) fire (is prescribed).

2. After sunset and before sunrise (the fire should

---

21. Sâṅkhâyana I, 17, 5. 6; Âsvalâyana I, 8, 10. 11.

9, 1. The expression which I have translated 'beginning from the wedding' is upayamanaprabh*ri*ti. The Indian commentators and Professor Stenzler explain the term upayamana as implying a reference to the Sûtra I, 1, 4, upayamanân kusân âdâya ('having taken up the Kusa blades with which he is to take hold of the lower surface of the Âgya pot'). 'The worshipping of the domestic fire,' says Stenzler, following the native authorities, 'consists in the rites which have been prescribed above (I, 1, 4), beginning from the word upayamana, i.e. in the taking up of the Kusa blades, the putting of wood on the fire, the sprinkling and sacrificing. As the rites preceding that word, such as the preparation of the sacrificial spoon (I, 1, 3), are hereby excluded, the oblations are offered with the hand.' It would be easy to show that the upayamanâ*h* kusâ*h* have nothing at all to do with the regular morning and evening oblations of which these Sûtras treat. The comparison of Âsvalâyana-Gr*i*hya I, 9, 1 (see also Manu III, 67, &c.) leaves no doubt that upayamana is to be understood here as derived from upaya*kkh*ati in its very frequent meaning of marrying. I have translated the Sûtra accordingly.

2. On the different statements of Vedic authors with regard to the proper time of the morning oblations, see Weber's Indische Studien, X, 329.

be worshipped) with (oblations of) curds, (rice) grains, or fried grains.

3. (He sacrifices) in the evening with (the formulas), 'To Agni svâhâ! To Pragâpati svâhâ!'

4. In the morning with (the formulas), 'To Sûrya svâhâ! To Pragâpati svâhâ!'

5. 'Men are both Mitra and Varuna; men are both the Asvins; men are Indra and Sûrya. May a man be born in me! Again svâhâ!'—with (this verse) a wife who desires to conceive, (should offer) the first (oblation).

KANDIKÂ 10.

1. If (in the chariot) of a king the axle breaks, or something that is bound loosens itself, or the chariot is overturned, or if another accident happens, or (if one of these same things occurs) when a bride is carried home, he establishes the same fire, prepares Âgya, and sacrifices (two Âgya oblations) separately with the two Mantras, 'Here is joy' (Vâg. Samh. VIII, 51 a).

2. Having got ready another chariot, he (i.e. the Purohita or the bridegroom) should make the king or the woman sit down thereon with (the formula), 'In royal power' down to the word, 'in sacrifice'

---

5. Comp. Sânkhâyana-Grihya I, 17, 9, where the reading and the construction slightly differ. The words punah svâhâ at the end of the Mantra seem to be corrupt; the frequent repetition of pumâmsam and pumân through the whole verse suggests the correction pumse svâhâ, or pumbhyah svâhâ, 'to the man svâhâ!' or 'to the men svâhâ!'

10, 1. 'The same fire' is the senâgni (the fire belonging to the army) in the case of the king, the nuptial fire in the second case. The two Mantras are the two parts of Vâg. Samh. VIII, 51 a.

(Vâg. Sa*m*h. XX, 10), and with the (verse), ' I have seized thee' (ibid. XII, 11).

3. The two beasts that draw the chariot, constitute the sacrificial fee.

4. (This is) the penance.

5. Then (follows) feeding of the Brâhma*n*as.

KA*N*DIKÂ 11.

1. In the fourth night (after the wedding), towards morning, (the husband) establishes the fire within (the house), assigns his seat, to the south (of it), to the Brahman, places a pot of water to the north, cooks a mess of sacrificial food, sacrifices the two Â*g*ya portions, and makes (other) Â*g*ya oblations with (the following Mantras) :

2. ' Agni! Expiation! Thou art the expiation of the gods.   I, the Brâhma*n*a, entreat thee, desirous of protection.   The substance which dwells in her that brings death to her husband, that extirpate in her.   Svâhâ !

' Vâyu ! Expiation ! Thou art the expiation of the gods.   I, the Brâhma*n*a, entreat thee, desirous of protection.   The substance which dwells in her that brings death to her children, that extirpate in her.   Svâhâ !

' Sûrya ! Expiation ! Thou art the expiation of the gods.   I, the Brâhma*n*a, entreat thee, desirous of protection.   The substance which dwells in her that brings death to cattle, that extirpate in her. Svâhâ!

' *K*andra ! Expiation ! Thou art the expiation of the gods.   I, the Brâhma*n*a, entreat thee, desirous

---

11, 2. Comp. *S*ânkhâyana-Gr*i*hya I, 18, 3.

of protection. The substance which dwells in her that brings destruction to the house, that extirpate in her. Svâhâ!

'Gandharva! Expiation! Thou art the expiation of the gods. I, the Brâhmana, entreat thee, desirous of protection. The substance which dwells in her that brings destruction to fame, that extirpate in her. Svâhâ!'

3. He sacrifices of the mess of cooked food with (the words), 'To Pragâpati svâhâ!'

4. Each time after he has sacrificed, he pours the remainder of the oblations into the water-pot, and out of that (pot) he besprinkles her on her head with (the words), 'The evil substance which dwells in thee that brings death to thy husband, death to thy children, death to cattle, destruction to the house, destruction to fame, that I change into one that brings death to thy paramour. Thus live with me to old age, N.N.!'

5. He then makes her eat the mess of cooked food with (the words), 'I add breath to thy breath, bones to thy bones, flesh to thy flesh, skin to thy skin.'

6. Therefore one should not wish for sport with the wife of a Srotriya who knows this; for the other one is a person who knows this (and is thereby enabled to destroy a lover of his wife).

7. After he has led her to his house, he should cohabit with her after each of her monthly periods,

8. Or as he likes, because it has been said, 'May we have intercourse as we like, until a child is born.'

---

4. The water-pot is that mentioned in Sûtra 1.

6. Satapatha Brâhmana I, 6, 1, 18; XIV, 9, 4, 11 (=Brihad Âranyaka VI, 4, 12; Sacred Books of the East, vol. xv, p. 218).

8. Taittirîya Samhitâ II, 5, 1, 5.

9. He then touches her heart, (reaching) over her right shoulder, with (the verse), 'O thou whose hair is well parted! Thy heart that dwells in heaven, in the moon, that I know; may it know me. May we see a hundred autumns; may we live a hundred autumns; may we hear a hundred autumns.'

10. In the same way afterwards.

KAN̄DIKÂ 12.

1. At the beginning of each half-month he cooks a mess of sacrificial food, sacrifices to the deities of the festivals of the new and full moon (as stated in the Srauta ritual), and then sacrifices to the following deities: to Brahman, to Pragâpati, to the Visve devâs, and to Heaven and Earth.

2. To the Visve devâs a Bali is offered, to the domestic deities, and to Âkâsa (i. e. the Ether).

3. From the Vaisvadeva food he makes oblations in the fire with (the formulas), 'To Agni svâhâ! To Pragâpati svâhâ! To the Visve devâs svâhâ! To Agni Svishtakrit svâhâ!'

4. Outside (the house) the wife offers the Bali with (the formulas), 'Adoration to the wife! Adoration to the man! To every time of life, adoration! To the white one with the black teeth, the lord of the bad women, adoration!

'They who allure my offspring, dwelling in the village or in the forest, to them be adoration; I offer

---

9. See above, chap. 8, 8.

12, 1. Comp. Sânkhâyana-Grihya I, 3, 3. The deities of the corresponding Srauta festivals are, at the full moon, Agni and Agni-shomau; at the new moon, Agni, Vishnu, and Indrâgnî.

2. Comp. below, II, 9, 3.

3. Sânkhâyana-Grihya II, 14, 3, 4.

a Bali to them.   Be welfare to me!   May they give me offspring.'

5. The remainder he washes out with water. Then (follows) feeding of the Brâhma*n*as.

KANDIKÂ 13.

1. If she does not conceive, he should, after having fasted, under (the Nakshatra) Pushya, lay down (in his house) the root of a white-blooming Si*m*hî plant, and on the fourth day, after (his wife) has bathed, he should in the night-time crush it in water and insert it into her right nostril with (the verse), 'This herb is protecting, overcoming, and powerful. May I, the son of this great (mother), obtain the name of a father!'

KANDIKÂ 14.

1. Now the Pu*m*savana (i.e. the ceremony to secure the birth of a male child),

2. Before (the child in his mother's womb) moves, in the second or third month (of pregnancy).

3. On a day on which the moon stands in conjunction with a Nakshatra (that has a name) of masculine gender, on that day, after having caused (his wife) to fast, to bathe, and to put on two garments which have not yet been washed, and after having in the night-time crushed in water descending roots and shoots of a Nyagrodha tree, he inserts (that into her right nostril) as above, with the two (verses),

---

13, 1. I have translated according to the reading of a similar Mantra found in the Atharva-veda (VIII, 2, 6), which no doubt is correct, sahasvatî instead of sarasvatî.

14, 3. The words 'as above' refer to chap. 13, 1.

'The gold-child' (Vâ*g*. Sa*m*h. XIII, 4) and 'Formed of water' (ibid. XXXI, 17);

4. A Ku*s*a needle and a Soma stalk, according to some (teachers).

5. And he puts gall of a tortoise on her lap.

If he desires, 'May (the son) become valiant,' he recites over him (i.e. over the embryo), modifying the rite (?), 'The Supar*n*a art thou' (Vâ*g*. Sa*m*h. XII, 4), (the Ya*g*us) before (the formulas called) 'steps of Vish*n*u.'

KA*N*DIKÂ 15.

1. Now the Sîmantonnayana (or parting of the pregnant wife's hair).

2. (It is performed) like the Pu*m*savana ;

3. In her first pregnancy, in the sixth or eighth month.

4. After he has cooked a mess of sacrificial food, containing sesamum and Mudga beans, and has sacrificed to Pra*g*âpati, he parts for the wife, who is seated to the west of the fire on a soft chair, her hair upwards (i.e. beginning from the front) with a bunch containing an even number of unripe Udumbara

---

4. Comp. *S*âṅkhâyana-G*ri*hya I, 20, 3.

5. The commentators state that kûrmapitta (gall of tortoise) means 'a dish with water.' I place no confidence in this statement, though I cannot show at present what its origin is. I am not sure about the translation of vik*ri*tyâ (or vik*ri*tya ?). But it seems impossible to me that it should be the name of the metre Vik*ri*ti. 'Steps of Vish*n*u' is a name for the Ya*g*us following in the Sa*m*hitâ on the one prescribed in this Sûtra. It begins, 'Vish*n*u's step art thou, &c.' (Vâ*g*. Sa*m*h. XII, 5).

15, 2. I.e. the Nakshatra under which the ceremony is performed, should be of male gender; the wife is to fast, &c. (see chap. 14, 3).

4. *S*âṅkhâyana-G*ri*hya I, 22, 8 ; Â*s*valâyana I, 14, 4.

fruits, and with three bunches of Darbha grass, with
a porcupine's quill that has three white spots, with
a stick of Viratara wood, and with a full spindle,
with the words, ' Bhûr bhuva*h* sva*h*.'

5. Or (he parts the hair once) with each of the
(three) Mahâvyâh*ri*tis.

6. He ties (the Udumbara fruits, &c.) to a string
of three twisted threads with (the words), ' Rich in sap
is this tree; like the tree, rich in sap, be thou fruitful.'

7. (The husband) then says to two lute-players,
' Sing ye the king, or if anybody else is still more
valiant.'

8. Here some also prescribe a certain stanza (to be
sung by the lute-players) : ' Soma alone is our king.
May these human tribes dwell on thy banks, O
(river) whose dominion is unbroken, N.N.!'—here he
names the name of the river near which they dwell.

9. Then (follows) feeding of the Brâhma*na*s.

KA*NDI*KÂ 16.

1. Soshyantim adbhir abhyukshaty *e*gatu dasa-
mâsya iti (Vâ*g*. Sa*m*h. VIII, 28) prâg yasyai ta iti
(ibid. 29).

2. Athâvarâvapatanam, avaitu p*ri*sni *s*evala*m* *s*une
*g*arâyv attave, naiva mâ*m*sena pîvari na kasmi*ms*
*k*anâyatam ava *g*arâyu padyatâm iti.

3. When the boy is born, he performs for him,
before the navel-string is cut off, the medhâ*g*ana*n*a

6. *S*âṅkhâyana I, 22, 10.
7. *S*âṅkhâyana l.l. §§ 11, 12 ; Â*s*valâyana l.l. § 6.
8. Â*s*valâyana l.l. § 7.　I take avimukta*k*akre to be the vocative
of the feminine.
16, 1. *S*atapatha Brâhma*na* XIV, 9, 4, 22.
2. Atharva-veda I, 11, 4.

(production of intelligence) and the âyushya (rite
for procuring long life).

4. (The medhâg̃anana is performed in the following way:) With his fourth finger and with (an instrument of) gold he gives (to the child) honey
and ghee, or ghee (alone), to eat with (the formulas),
'Bhû*h* I put into thee; bhuva*h* I put into thee;
sva*h* I put into thee. Bhûr bhuva*h* sva*h* everything
I put into thee.'

5. He then performs the âyushya.

6. Near his navel or his right ear he murmurs:
'Agni is long-lived; through the trees he is long-
lived. By that long life I make thee long-lived.

'Soma is long-lived; through the herbs he is, &c.

'The Brahman is long-lived; through the Brâhma*n*as it is, &c.

'The gods are long-lived; through ambrosia
(am*ri*ta) they are, &c.

'The *Ri*shis are long-lived; through their observances they are, &c.

'The Fathers are long-lived; through the Svadhâ
oblations (or oblations made to the Manes) they
are, &c.

'Sacrifice is long-lived; through sacrificial fee it
is, &c.

'The ocean is long-lived; through the rivers it is
long-lived. By that long life I make thee long-lived;'

7. And three times the verse, 'The threefold age'
(Vâg̃. Sa*m*h. III, 62).

8. If he desires, 'May he live his full term of

---

4. Comp. *S*atapatha Brâhma*n*a XIV, 9, 4, 23 seqq. (Br*i*had
Âra*n*yaka VI, 4, 24 seqq.; S. B. E., XV, 222 seq.). The text has
anâmikayâ suvar*n*ântarhitayâ, which literally is: with the nameless
(or fourth) finger, between which (and the food) gold has been put.

life,' he should touch him with the Vâtsapra hymn (Vâg. Samh. XII, 18-29).

9. From the Anuvâka beginning with 'From heaven' (XII, 18 seqq.) he omits the last Rik (XII, 29).

10. Having placed five Brâhmanas towards the (five) regions, he should say to them, ' Breathe ye upon this (child).'

11. The (Brâhmana placed) to the east should say, ' Up-breathing!'

12. The one to the south, ' Back-breathing!'

13. The one to the west, ' Down-breathing!'

14. The one to the north, ' Out-breathing!'

15. The fifth one, looking upwards, should say, ' On-breathing!'

16. Or (the father) may do that himself, going round (his child), if he can find no (Brâhmanas).

17. He recites over the place at which (the child) is born : ' I know, O earth, thy heart that dwells in heaven, in the moon. That I know ; may it know me. May we see a hundred autumns ; may we live a hundred autumns; may we hear a hundred autumns.'

18. He then touches him with (the verse), ' Be a stone, be an axe, be imperishable gold. Thou indeed art the Self called son ; thus live a hundred autumns.'

---

11 seqq. In translating the technical terms for the different kinds of breath, I adopt the expressions chosen by Professor Max Müller, S. B. E., XV, 94. As to the whole rite, comp. Satap. Br. XI, 8, 3. 6.

17. Comp. above, I, 11, 9. The comparison of the parallel Mantra leaves scarcely any doubt that veda (the first word of the verse) is the first, not the third person, and bhûmi the vocative case. Compare the vocative darvi of the Vâg. Samhitâ, while the Atharva-veda has darve. Lanman, Noun-Inflection, p. 390.

18. Satapatha Brâhmana XIV, 9, 4, 26; Âsvalâyana I, 15, 3.

19. He then recites over his mother (the verse),
' Thou art I*d*â, the daughter of Mitra and Varu*n*a ;
thou strong woman hast born a strong son. Be thou
blessed with strong children, thou who hast blessed
us with a strong son.'

20. He then washes her right breast, and gives it
to the child with (the verse), ' This breast' (Vâ*g*.
Sa*m*h. XVII, 87);

21. The left (breast) with (the verse), ' Thy breast
which ' (ibid. XXXVIII, 5)—with these two (verses).

22. He puts down a pot of water near her head
with (the verse), ' O waters, you watch with the gods.
As you watch with the gods, thus watch over this
mother who is confined, and her child.'

23. Having established near the door the fire
that has been kept from (the wife's) confinement, he
throws into that fire at the time of the morning and
evening twilight, until (the mother) gets up (from
childbed), mustard seeds mixed with rice chaff (pronouncing the following names of demons and goblins):
' May *Sand*a and Marka, Upavîra, *Saund*ikeya,
Ulûkhala, Malimlu*k*a, Dro*n*âsa, *K*yavana vanish
hence. Svâhâ !

' May Âlikhat, Animisha, Ki*m*vadanta, Upa*s*ruti,
Haryaksha, Kumbhin, *S*atru, Pâtrapâ*n*i, N*ri*ma*n*i,
Hantrîmukha, Sarshapâru*n*a, *K*yavana vanish hence.
Svâhâ !'

24. If (the demon bringing disease) Kumâra
attacks the boy, the father covers him with a net

19. *Satapatha Brâhma*n*a l. l. § 27. Comp. Professor Max Müller's
note, S. B. E., XV, 223 seq.
21. *Satapatha Brâhma*n*a l. l. § 28.
23. On the sûtikâgni, comp. *Satap. Br. l. l. § 23; *Sânkhâyana-
Gr/hya I, 25, 4, &c.
24. Kûrkura seems to me, and this is also Professor Stenzler's

or with an upper garment, takes him on his lap,
and murmurs : 'Kûrkura, Sukûrkura, Kûrkura, who
holds fast children. *K*et! *k*et! doggy! let him
loose. Reverence be to thee, the Sisara, barker,
bender.

'That is true that the gods have given a boon to
thee. Hast thou then chosen even this boy?
'*K*et! *k*et! doggy! let him loose. Reverence be
to thee, the Sîsara, barker, bender.

'That is true that (the divine she-dog) Saramâ is
thy mother, Sîsara thy father, the black and the
speckled (two dogs of Yama) thy brothers.
'*K*et! *k*et! doggy! let him loose. Reverence be
to thee, the Sîsara, barker, bender.'

25. He then touches (the boy) with (the words),
'He does not suffer, he does not cry, he is not stiff,
he is not sick, when we speak to him and when we
touch him.'

KANDIKÂ 17.

1. On the tenth day (after the birth of the child)
the father, having made (his wife) get up, and having
fed the Brâhma*n*as, gives a name (to the child),

2. Of two syllables, or of four syllables, beginning
with a sonant, with a semivowel in it, with a long
vowel (or) the Visarga (at its end), with a K*ri*t
(suffix), not with a Taddhita ;

3. With an uneven number of syllables, ending in
â, with a Taddhita (suffix) to a girl.

4. (The name) of a Brâhma*n*a (should end in)

opinion, identical with kurkura, kukkura ('dog'). The Peters-
.burg Dictionary explains it, 'Name eines die Kinder bedrohenden
Dämons (vielleicht eine Personification des Hustens).'
17, 1. Comp. Gobhila II, 8, 14; Âsvalâyana I, 15, 4.

*s*arma n (for inst. Vish*n*u*s*arman), that of a Kshatriya
in varman (for inst. Lakshmîvarman), that of a
Vai*s*ya in gupta (for inst. *K*andragupta).

5. In the fourth month (follows) the going out.

6. He makes (the child) look at the sun, pronouncing (the verse), 'That eye' (Vâ*g*. Sa*m*hitâ
XXXVI, 24).

KA*ND*IKÂ 18.

1. When he returns from a journey, he approaches
his house in the manner stated above.

2. When he sees his son, he murmurs, 'From
limb by limb thou art produced; out of the heart
thou art born. Thou indeed art the Self called son;
so live a hundred autumns!'

3. He then kisses his head with (the words),
'With the hi*m*kâra (the mystical syllable hiñ) of
Pra*g*âpati, which gives thousandfold life, I kiss thee.
N. N.! Live a hundred autumns!'—

4. And three times with (the words), 'With the
hi*m*kâra of the cows.'

5. In his right ear he murmurs, 'Bestow on us,
O bountiful, onward-pressing Indra, plentiful, rich
treasures. Give us a hundred autumns to live;
give us many heroes, strong-jawed Indra;'

6. In the left ear, 'Indra, bestow on us the best
treasures, insight of mind, happiness, increase of
wealth, health of our bodies, sweetness of speech,
and that our days may be good days.'

7. For a girl he only kisses the head silently.

18, 1. See Kâtyâyana, *S*rauta-sûtra IV, 12, 22 seq.: With the
words, 'House, be not afraid,' &c. (Vâ*g*. Sa*m*h. III, 41) he
approaches the house. With. 'For peace you' (III, 43) he
enters it.

5. Rig-veda III, 36, 10.   6. Rig-veda II, 21, 6.

KANDIKÂ 19.

1. In the sixth month the Annaprâsana (or first feeding with solid food).

2. Having cooked a mess of sacrificial food, and sacrificed the two Âgyabhâgas, he offers two Âgya oblations, (the first with the verse,) 'The gods have generated the goddess Speech ; manifold animals speak her forth. May she, the sweet-sounding, the cow that (for milk) gives sap and juice to us, Speech, the highly-praised one, come to us. Svâhâ !'

3. And the second (oblation) with (the verse), 'May vigour us to-day' (Vâg. Samhitâ XVIII, 33).

4. He then sacrifices (four oblations) of cooked food with (the formulas),

'Through up-breathing may I enjoy food. Svâhâ!

'Through down-breathing may I enjoy smells. Svâhâ !

'Through my eye may I enjoy visible things. Svâhâ!

'Through my ear may I enjoy renown. Svâhâ !'

5. After he has eaten (himself), he should set apart food of all kinds, and of all different sorts of flavour, and should give it to him (i. e. to his son) to eat,

6. Silently or with (the word), 'Hanta' (i. e. Well !). For it is said in the Sruti, ' Men (live on) the word hanta.'

7. (He feeds the child) with flesh of (the bird called) Bhâradvâgî, if he wishes (to the child) fluency of speech,

8. With flesh of partridge, if abundance of nourishment,

---

2. Rig-veda VIII, 100, 11.   6. Brihad Âranyaka V, 8.

9. With fish, if swiftness,

10. (With flesh) of (the bird) Krikashâ, if long life,

11. (With flesh) of (the bird) Âti, if desirous of holy lustre,

12. With all, if desirous of all.

13. Or each (sort of) food one by one. Then (follows) feeding of the Brâhmanas, or each (sort of) food one by one. Then feeding of the Brâhmanas.

End of the First Kânda.

KÂNDA II, KANDIKÂ 1.

1. When (the son) is one year old, the *Kûdâkarana* (i.e. the tonsure of his head, should be performed),

2. Or before the lapse of the third (year).

3. When he is sixteen years old, the Kesânta (i.e. the shaving of his beard, is to be done),

4. Or, according as it is considered auspicious by all (the different families).

5. After food has been distributed to the Brâhmanas, the mother takes the boy, bathes him, puts on him an under and an upper garment which have not yet been washed, and putting him on her lap, she sits down to the west of the fire.

6. The father taking hold (of his wife) sacrifices Âgya oblations, and after he has partaken of the (sacrificial) food, he pours warm water into cold water with (the words), 'With warm water come hither, Vâyu! Aditi, cut the hair.'

7. At the Kesânta ceremony (Sûtra 3), 'hair and beard' (instead of 'hair').

8. He throws a piece of fresh butter, or of ghee, or some curds into it (i.e. into the water, Sûtra 6).

9. Taking some (water) he moistens the hair near the right ear with (the formula), 'On the impulse of Savitri may the divine waters moisten

1, 6. I see no reason why we should not take Aditi for the name of the goddess. Comp. Atharva-veda VI, 68, 2 : Aditih smasru vapatu. Âsvalâyana-Grihya I, 17, 7. Stenzler translates: Ungebundener, die Haare schneide.

9. The text has, dakshinam godânam undati. The commentary on Kâtyâyana V, 2, 14 explains dakshina godâna : dakshinakarnasamîpavartinam sirahpradesam. Sâyana on Satapatha Brâhmana III, 1, 2, 4 (p. 323, ed. Weber) : godânam nâma karnasyopari pradesah. The Mantra reoccurs in Kâtyâyana, loc. cit.—Savitrâ

thy body in order that long life and splendour may
be thine.'

10. Having unravelled (the hair) with a porcupine's
quill that has three white spots, he puts three young
Ku*s*a shoots into it with (the formula), 'Herb' (Vâ*g*.
Sa*m*h. IV, 1).

11. Taking up a copper razor with (the formula),
'Friendly by name' (Vâ*g*. Sa*m*h. III, 63 a), he cuts
(the hair) with (the formula), 'I cut off' (ibid. 63 b),
(and with the formula,) 'The razor with which
Savit*ri*, the knowing one, has shaven (the beard) of
king Soma and Varu*n*a, with that, ye Brâhma*n*as,
shave his (head), in order that he may be blessed
with long life and may reach old age.'

12. Cutting off (the Ku*s*a shoots) together with
the hair, he throws them on a lump of bull's dung
which they keep northwards of the fire.

13. In the same way two other times silently.

14. The moistening and the other rites are repeated
with the two other (tufts of hair).

15. Behind with (the verse), 'The threefold age'
(Vâ*g*. Sa*m*h. III, 62).

16. Then on the left side with (the verse), 'With
that prayer by which mayst thou, a mighty one, go
to heaven, and long mayst thou see the sun : with
that prayer I shave thee for the sake of life, of
existence, of glory, of welfare.'

prasûtâ*h* should not be translated as Prof. Stenzler does: von
Sav. erzeugt, but : von Sav. angetrieben.

10. This Sûtra is identical with Kâtyâyana-*S*raut. V, 2, 15.

11. Compare Kâtyâyana l. l. § 17. The Mantra, Vâ*g*. Sa*m*h.
III, 63 b, is that given by Kâtyâyana, the following one is that
which the other G*ri*hya texts prescribe.

16. See the various readings of the Mantra given by Professor
Stenzler, p. 53 of his critical annotations, and compare Â*s*valâyana-
G*ri*hya I, 17, 13.

17. Three times he shaves round the head, from left to right;

18. Including the face, at the Kesânta ceremony.

19. (He recites the verse,) 'When the shaver shaves his hair with the razor, the wounding, the well-shaped, purify his head, but do not take away his life.'

20. He adds (the word), 'his face' at the Kesânta ceremony.

21. With that water (Sûtras 6, 8) he moistens his head, and gives the razor to the barber with (the words), 'Without wounding him, shave him.'

22. The locks of hair which are left over, are to be arranged as it is considered auspicious (in his family).

23. Having put away that lump of dung with the hair so that it is hidden in a cow-stable, or in a small pond, or in the vicinity of water, he gives an optional gift to the teacher;

24. A cow at the Kesânta ceremony.

25. After the Kesânta has been performed, (the youth) should observe chastity and should not be shaven through one year, or twelve nights, or six nights, or at least three nights.

KA*ND*IKÂ 2.

1. He should initiate a Brâhma*n*a, when he is eight years old, or in the eighth year after the conception,

2. A Râganya, when he is eleven years old,

---

19. Âsvalâyana I. l. § 16; Atharva-veda VIII, 2, 17.

20. He repeats the Mantra, given in Sûtra 19, in this form: 'When the shaver shaves his hair and his face,' &c.

23. See above, Sûtra 12.

3. A Vaisya, when he is twelve years old.

4. Or according as it is considered auspicious by all (the different families).

5. He should feed the Brâhma*n*as. And they lead him (i. e. the boy who is to be initiated) on, with his head shaven all round, and decked with ornaments.

6. (The teacher) makes him place himself to the west of the fire and say, ' I have come hither for the sake of studentship (brahma*k*arya).' And, ' I will be a student (brahma*k*ârin).'

7. He then makes him put on a garment with (the verse), ' In the way in which B*ri*haspati put the garment of immortality on Indra, thus I put (this garment) on thee, for the sake of long life, of old age, of strength, of splendour.'

8. He ties round him the girdle with (the verse which the youth recites), ' Here has come to me, keeping away evil words, purifying my kind as a purifyer, clothing herself, by (the power of) inhalation and exhalation, with strength, this sisterly goddess, this blessed girdle.'

9. Or, ' A youth, well attired, dressed, came hither. He, being born, becomes glorious. Wise sages extol him, devout ones, turning their minds to the gods.'

10. Or silently.

11. He gives him the staff.

---

6 seqq. Comp. *S*atapatha Brâhma*n*a XI, 5, 4.

8. The commentators differ as to whether the Â*k*ârya or the youth should recite the verse. The comparison of *S*ânkhâyana II, 2, 1 would rather tend to show that it is the teacher, but Gobhila II, 10 says expressly : athainam tri*h* pradakshi*n*am mu*ñ*gamekhalâm pariharan vâ*k*ayatîyam duruktât paribâdhamânety r*i*tasya goptrîti vâ.

9. Rig-veda III, 8, 4. The verse is originally addressed to Agni.

12. (The student) accepts it with (the verse), 'My staff which fell down to the ground in the open air, that I take up again for the sake of long life, of holiness, of holy lustre.'

13. According to some (teachers he accepts the staff) in the way prescribed for the inauguration, because it is said, 'He enters upon a long Sattra (or sacrificial period).'

14. (The teacher) then with his joined hands fills (the student's) joined hands with water with the three (verses), 'Ye waters are' (Vâg. Samh. XI, 50 seqq.).

15. He then makes him look at the sun with (the verse), 'That eye' (Vâg. Samh. XXXVI, 24).

16. He then touches his heart, (reaching) over his right shoulder, with (the words), 'Into my will I take thy heart, &c.'

17. He then seizes (the student's) right hand and says, 'What is thy name?'

18. He replies, 'I am N. N., sir!'

19. He then says to him, 'Whose pupil (brahma-kârin) art thou?'

20. After (the student) has said, 'Yours!'—(the

---

13. *Satapatha* Brâhmana XI, 3, 3, 2: 'He enters upon a long Sattra, who enters upon Brahmakarya.' The student, when being initiated, ought to behave, consequently, in the same way as those who receive the inauguration (dîkshâ) for a long Sattra. This is the meaning of this Sûtra. The rules regarding the staff handed over by the Adhvaryu to the Yagamâna at the dîkshâ ceremony are given by Kâtyâyana, *Srauta-sûtra* VII, 4, 1–4.

15. See above, I, 8, 7.

16. See above, I, 8, 8.

17 seqq. Comp. *Satapatha* Brâhmana XI, 5, 4, 1 seqq.

20. The words 'I am thy teacher' are omitted in one of Professor Stenzler's MSS. and in his translation. But they are given in the parallel passage of the *Satapatha* Brâhmana. The

teacher replies,) ' Indra's pupil art thou ; Agni is thy
teacher ; I am thy teacher, N. N. ! '

21. He then gives him in charge to living beings
with (the formulas), ' To Pra*g*âpati I give thee in
charge. To the god Savit*ri* I give thee in charge.
To the waters, the herbs I give thee in charge. To
Heaven and Earth I give thee in charge. To the
Vi*s*ve devâs I give thee in charge. To all beings I
give thee in charge for the sake of freedom from
harm.'

KA*N*DIKÂ 3.

1. Having walked round the fire with his right
side turned towards it, he sits down.

2. Taking hold (of the student), he sacrifices the
Â*g*ya oblations, and after having partaken (of the
remains of the sacrificial food) he instructs him, ' A
student art thou. Take water. Do the service. Do
not sleep in the day-time. Keep silence. Put fuel
on (the fire). Take water.'

3. He then recites the Sâvitrî to him, who is
seated to the north of the fire, with his face to the
west, sitting near the teacher, and looks (at the
teacher), while (the teacher) looks at him ;

4. Some say, to (the student) who is standing or
seated to the south (of the fire) ;

5. Pâda by Pâda, (then) hemistich by hemistich,
and the third time the whole (verse), reciting it
together (with the student) ;

---

parallel passage in *S*ânkhâyana (G*ri*hya II, 3, 1) also runs thus :
Agnir â*k*âr*y*as tava, asâv, aha*m k*obhau.

3, 1 seqq. Comp. the corresponding section of the *S*atapatha
Brâhma*n*a XI, 5, 4, 6 seqq.

4. *S*atapatha Brâhma*n*a l. l. § 14.

6. After one year, or after six months, or after twenty-four days, or after twelve days, or after six days, or after three days.

7. To a Brâhma*n*a, however, he should recite a (Sâvitrî) verse in the Gâyatrî metre immediately. For it is said in the *S*ruti, 'To Agni indeed belongs the Brâhma*n*a.'

8. A Trish*t*ubh verse to a Râ*g*anya,

9. A *G*agatî to a Vai*s*ya,

10. Or a Gâyatrî to (persons of) all (castes).

KA*ND*IKÂ 4.

1. Now the putting on of fuel.

2. He wipes with his hand (the ground) round the fire with (the formula), 'Agni, glorious one, make me glorious. As thou, glorious Agni, art glorious, thus, O glorious one, bring me to glory. As thou, Agni, art the preserver of the treasure of sacrifice for the gods, thus may I become the preserver of the treasure of the Veda for men.'

3. Having sprinkled (water) round the fire from left to right, he stands up and puts a piece of wood on (the fire) with (the texts),

'To Agni I have brought a piece of wood, to the great *G*âtavedas. As thou, Agni, art inflamed by wood, thus I am inflamed by life, insight, vigour, offspring, cattle, holy lustre.

'May my teacher be the father of living sons; may I be full of insight, not forgetful (of what I have learned); may I become full of glory, of splendour, of holy lustre, an enjoyer of food. Svâhâ!

---

7. *S*atapatha Brâhma*n*a I. I. § 12.
4. 2. Comp. Âsvalâyana-G*r*/hya I, 22, 21.
3. As to anirâkarish*n*u, comp. anirâkara*n*a below, III, 16.

4. In the same way (he puts on) a second (piece of wood) ; and thus a third.

5. Or (each piece) with (the verse), ' Thine is this ' (Vâg. Samh. II, 14).

6. Or (he uses) both (this verse and the formulas given in Sûtra 3).

7. The wiping and sprinkling (of water) round (the fire are repeated) as above.

8. Having warmed his two hands, he wipes his mouth with (the formulas) :

' Agni, thou art the protector of bodies. Protect my body. Agni, thou art the giver of life. Give me life. Agni, thou art the giver of vigour. Give me vigour.

' Agni, what is deficient in my body, that restore to fulness.

' May the god Savitrî bestow insight on me, may the goddess Sarasvatî, may the two divine Asvins, wreathed with lotus, (bestow) insight (on me).'

KANDIKÂ 5.

1. Here (follows the student's) going the rounds for alms.

2. A Brâhmana should beg, addressing (the woman from whom he begs alms) with the word ' Lady ' put at the beginning (of his request),

3. A Râganya, with the word ' Lady ' inserted in the middle,

4. A Vaisya, with the word ' Lady ' put at the end.

5. (He should beg) from three women who will not refuse ;

---

7. See above, Sûtras 2, 3.

5, 2–4. Comp. Âpastamba I, 3, 28 seqq. (S. B. E., II, p. 12); Manu II, 49, &c. The Brâhmana says, 'Lady, give alms;' the Kshatriya, 'Give, lady, alms ;' the Vaisya, 'Give alms, lady.'

5. Âsvalâyana-Grihya I, 22, 7.

6. From six, twelve, or an indefinite number.

7. From his own mother first, according to some (teachers).

8. Having announced the alms received to his teacher, he should stand, keeping silence, through the rest of the day, according to some.

9. Having fetched fire-wood out of the forest without damaging (trees), he should put them on that fire as above, and should abandon his silence.

10. He should sleep on the ground and eat no pungent or saline food.

11. Wearing the staff, worshipping the fire, being obedient to his Guru, going the rounds for alms— (these are the standing duties of students).

12. He should avoid honey or flesh, bathing (for pleasure), sitting on high seats, going to women, falsehood, and taking what is not given to him.

13. Let him live forty-eight years as a student for the (four) Vedas,

14. Or twelve years for each Veda,

15. Or until he has learnt it.

16. The garment (of a student) should be made of hemp, flax, or wool (accordingly as he is a Brâhmana, a Kshatriya, or a Vaisya).

17. The upper garment of a Brâhmana should be an antelope-skin,

18. That of a Râganya the skin of a spotted deer,

---

8. Âsvalâyana I. l. §§ 10, 11.

9. The meaning is, he should not break off branches, but only gather such as have fallen off. The words 'as above' refer to chap. 4.

12. Gautama II, 13; Âpastamba I, 2, 23. 28–30. 21. 26.

13–15. Comp. Âpastamba I, 2, 12 seqq.; Âsvalâyana I, 22, 3.

19. That of a Vai*s*ya a goat's or cow's skin.

20. Or if (the prescribed sort of garment) is not to be had, a cow's hide (should be worn) by all, because to that belongs the first place (among all kinds of garments).

21. The girdle of a Brâhma*n*a should be of Mu*ñ*ga grass,

22. That of a Kshatriya should be a bowstring,

23. That of a Vai*s*ya, made of Mûrvâ (i. e. Sanseveria Roxburghiana).

24. If there is no Mu*ñ*ga (or the other articles prescribed in §§ 22, 23, the girdles should be made) of Ku*s*a grass, of the plant A*s*mantaka, or of Balba*g*a grass (respectively).

25. The staff of a Brâhma*n*a is of Palâ*s*a wood,

26. That of a Râ*g*anya of Bilva wood,

27. That of a Vai*s*ya of Udumbara wood.

28. Or all (sorts of staffs may be used) by all.

29. If the teacher calls him, he shall rise and then answer.

30. If (the teacher calls him) while he is lying down, (he should answer) sitting; if sitting, standing; if standing, walking up (to the teacher); if walking up, running up.

31. If he behaves thus, his fame when he has become a Snâtaka (i. e. when he has taken the bath at the end of his studentship) will be (such that people will say of him), ' To-day he stays there; to-day he stays there.'

32. There are three (kinds of) Snâtakas: a Vidyâ-snâtaka (i. e. a Snâtaka by knowledge), a Vrata-

---

24. Manu II, 43.

32–35. Comp. Âpastamba I, 30, 1–3; Manu IV, 31. The term of the vows extends through forty-eight (or thirty-six, &c.)

snâtaka (i. e. a Snâtaka by the completion of his vows), and a Vidyâ-vrata-snâtaka (i. e. a Snâtaka both by knowledge and by the completion of his vows).

33. He who performs the Samâvartana ceremony, after having finished the study of the Veda, but before the time of his vows has expired, is a Vidyâ-snâtaka.

34. He who performs the Samâvartana, after his vows have expired, but before he has finished the study of the Veda, is a Vrata-snâtaka.

35. He who performs the Samâvartana, after having finished both, is a Vidyâ-vrata-snâtaka.

36. Until the sixteenth year the time (for being initiated) has not passed for a Brâhmana,

37. Until the twenty-second for a Râganya,

38. Until the twenty-fourth for a Vaisya.

39. After that (time has passed), they become patitasâvitrika (or persons who have lost the right of learning the Sâvitrî).

40. No one should initiate such men, nor teach them, nor perform sacrifices for them, nor have intercourse with them.

41. After the time has passed, (they should do) as has been prescribed.

42. A person whose ancestors through three generations have been patitasâvitrikas, is excluded

years; see above, Sûtras 13 and 14, and below, chap. 6, 2. 3. The Samâvartana is the returning home of the student at the end of his studentship.

36–40. Âsvalâyana-Grihya I, 19, 5 seqq. &c.

41. The general rule here alluded to is, according to the commentators, that given by Kâtyâyana, Srauta-sûtra XXV, 1, 12. 13. There it is stated which expiatory oblations have to precede, when a rite that has not been performed, or that has been incorrectly performed, is to be performed for good.

42. Those who have not been initiated in due time, may act as

from the sacrament (of initiation) and from being taught the Veda.

43. Of such persons those who desire to receive the sacrament, may perform the sacrifice of Vrâtya-stoma and then study the Veda, if they like. For (of persons who have done that) it is said, 'Intercourse with them is permitted.'

KAṆDIKÂ 6.

1. When he has finished the Veda, he should take the bath (by which he becomes a Snâtaka);

2. Or when (he has gone through) a studentship of forty-eight years;

3. Or also after (a studentship) of twelve years, according to some (teachers).

4. (Let him take the bath only) if his Guru has given his permission.

5. Rules (regarding the performance of sacrifices), (texts) to be used (at the sacrifices according to those rules), and reasoning (on the meaning of the rites and texts): that is the Veda.

6. Some say (that the Veda should be studied) with its six Aṅgas;

---

stated in Sûtra 41. But if the omission has been perpetuated through three generations, the descendant of such persons is subject to the rules stated in Sûtras 42 and 43.

43. Kâtyâyana, after having given the rules on the Vrâtyastoma sacrifice (see Weber, Indische Literaturgeschichte, 2nd edition, pp. 73 seq.), says: 'Intercourse with them (who have performed that sacrifice) is permitted' (Sraut. XXII, 4, 28).

6, 2. See above, chap. 5, 13.

3. See chap. 5, 14.

5. The expressions of the text for the three categories are, vidhi, vidheya, tarka.

6. I. e. with the supplementary treatises on ritual, grammar, astronomy, etymology, pronunciation of the Mantras, and metrics.

7. Not so that he only knows the ceremonial.

8. But optionally by one who knows the sacrifices (the bath may be taken).

9. (The student) after having embraced (the feet of) his teacher, and put the pieces of wood on the fire, places himself northwards of an enclosure, on eastward-pointed Ku*s*a grass, to the east of eight vessels with water.

10. 'The fires that dwell in the waters; the fire which must be hidden, the fire which must be covered, the ray of light, the fire which kills the mind, the unwavering one, the pain-causing one, the destroyer of the body, the fire which kills the organs—those I leave behind. The shining one, that I seize here'—with (this formula) he draws water out of one (of the eight vessels);

11. With that he besprinkles himself with (the words), 'Therewith I besprinkle myself for the sake of prosperity, of glory, of holiness, of holy lustre.'

12. (A second time he draws water out of a second of the eight vessels with the formula given in Sûtra 10, putting instead of the words, 'The shining one, &c.,' the verse): 'By which you have created prosperity, by which you have touched surâ, with which you have anointed the eyes, which is your glory, O A*s*vins.'

---

10. As to the names of the eight hostile powers of Agni, comp. *S*âṅkhâyana-G*ri*hya V, 2; Atharva-veda XIV, 1, 38; XVI, 1; Mantrabrâhma*n*a I, 7, 1.

12. The reading of the Mantra seems to be corrupt. Compare the form in which it is given by Bhavadeva, quoted in Professor Stenzler's note on this Sûtra. Instead of *s*riyam we have probably to read, as Bhavadeva has, striyam; instead of akshyau, akshân. Professor Stenzler very pertinently compares Atharva-veda XIV, 1, 35. 36. Comp. also Mantrabrâhma*n*a I, 7, 5.

13. (And he draws water out of three other vessels) with (the three verses), 'Ye waters are' (Vâg. Sa*m*h. XI, 50–52), verse by verse.

14. With (water drawn out of) the three other (vessels he besprinkles himself) silently.

15. Having loosened his girdle with (the verse), 'The highest band' (Vâg. Sa*m*h. XII, 12), having put it down, having put on another garment, he worships the sun—

16. With (the formulas), 'Rising, bearing a shining spear, Indra stands with the Maruts; he stands with the gods who walk in the morning. Thou art a ten-fold winner; make me a tenfold winner. Make me attain to renown.

'Rising, bearing a shining spear, Indra stands with the Maruts; he stands with the gods who walk in day-time. Thou art a hundredfold winner; make me a hundredfold winner. Make me attain to renown.

'Rising, bearing a shining spear, Indra stands with the Maruts; he stands with the gods who walk in the evening. Thou art a thousandfold winner; make me a thousandfold winner. Make me attain to renown.'

17. Having eaten curds or sesamum seeds, and having had his matted hair, the hair of his body, and his nails cut, he should cleanse his teeth with an Udumbara branch with (the verse), 'Array your-selves for the enjoyment of food. Here has come king Soma : he will purify my mouth with glory and fortune.'

---

16. In the Mantra the Pâraskara MSS. give bhrâ*g*abhr*i*sh*n*u*h* and bhrâgabhr*i*sh*t*ih, and the Gobhila MSS. (Gr*i*hya III, 4) bhrâ*g*a-bhr*i*sh*t*ibhi*h*. Possibly the instrumental case is right. Böhtlingk and Roth propose to read bhrâ*g*adr*i*sh*t*i*h*.

18. Having anointed himself and bathed again, he takes up the salve for nose and mouth with (the words), 'Satiate my up-breathing and down-breathing; satiate my eye; satiate my ear!'

19. Having poured out to the south the water with which he has washed his hands, with (the words), 'Ye fathers, become pure,' he should salve himself and murmur, 'May I become well-looking with my eyes, well-shining with my face, well-hearing with my ears.'

20. He then should put on a garment which has not yet been washed, or not been soaked in lie, with (the formula), 'For the sake of putting on, of bringing fame, of long life I shall reach old age. I live a hundred long autumns. For the sake of the increase of wealth I will clothe myself.'

21. Then the upper garment with (the verse), 'With glory (come) to me, Heaven and Earth. With glory, Indra and B*ri*haspati! May glory and fortune come to me! may glory be my lot!'

22. If (he has only) one (garment), he should cover himself (with a part of that garment as if it were an upper garment) with the second part of the former (Mantra; Sûtra 20).

23. He takes flowers with (the formula), '(The

---

20. Comp. Kâtyâyana, *S*rauta-sûtra VII, 2, 18, to which Sûtra Professor Stenzler refers.

22. I give this translation merely as tentative. Professor Stenzler translates: Wenn er nur Ein Gewand hat, so bedecke er sich (noch einmal) mit dem oberen Theile des zuerst angelegten. *G*ayarâma (MS. Chambers 373) says: eka*m* *k*et tatrâpi paridhâna-mantra*m* pa*dh*itvâ vastrârdham paridhâya dvir â*k*amya uttarârdhe g*ri*hîtvâ uttarîya*m* [sic] mantra*m* pa*dh*itvottarîya*m* k*ri*tvâ punar dvir â*k*amed ity artha*h*.

23. Hira*ny*.-G*ri*hya I, 3, 11, 4.

flowers) which *G*amadagni has brought for the sake
of faith (has brought to *S*raddhâ?), of love, of the
senses, them I take with glory and with fortune.'

24. He then ties them (to his head) with (the
verse), 'The high, wide glory, which Indra has
created for the Apsarases, the flowers bound up
with that, I tie on to me, to bring me glory!'

25. He binds a turban to his head with (the
verse), 'A youth, well attired.'

26. (He puts on) the two ear-rings with (the
words), 'An ornament art thou; may more ornaments be mine.'

27. He salves his two eyes with (the formula),
'V*ri*tra's' (Vâ*g*. Sa*m*h. IV, 3 b).

28. With (the words), 'Brilliant art thou,' he looks
at his image in a mirror.

29. He takes a parasol with (the words), 'Thou
art B*ri*haspati's covering. Shelter me from evil.
Do not shelter me from splendour and glory.'

30. With (the words), 'You are supports; protect
me from all sides,' he puts on the two shoes.

31. With (the words), 'From all powers of destruction protect me on all sides,' he takes a bamboo staff.

32. (For) the tooth-cleaner, &c. (the Mantras
stated above are to be used) in every case; (for)
the garment, the parasol, and the shoes, the Mantra
(should only be recited) if they have not been used
before.

KA*ND*IKÂ 7.

1. We shall state the rules of conduct for a
Snâtaka.

2. Another (may observe those rules) optionally.

---

25. See above, chap. 2, 9.

3. Dancing, singing, and playing musical instruments, let him neither perform himself nor go (to see or hear it).

4. Sing, however, he may at his pleasure, for there is another saying, 'He sings either or he rejoices in (other people's) singing.'

5. If everything goes well, he shall not go by night to another village, and shall not run.

6. He shall avoid looking into a well, climbing up a tree, gathering fruits, crawling through narrow openings, bathing naked, jumping over uneven ground, using harsh language, looking at the sun while it is rising or setting, and begging. For there is a Sruti: 'After he has bathed, he should not beg. For he who bathes, drives away from himself begging.'

7. If it rains, he shall go without an upper garment, and shall say, 'May this, my thunderbolt, drive away evil.'

8. He shall not look at himself in water.

9. Agâtalomnîm vipumsîm shandham ka nopahaset.

10. Let him call a pregnant woman 'viganyâ' (one who will give birth to a child);

11. An ichneumon (nakula), sakula ;

12. A skull (kapâla), bhagâla ;

---

7. 3. Comp. the similar rule given in the Buddhist Vinaya, Mahâvagga I, 56.

4. Satapatha Brâhmana VI, 1, 1, 15.

5. If no accident happens that makes his going to another village necessary.

6. The passage of the Sruti quoted is found in the Satapatha Brâhmana XI, 3, 3, 7. Comp. Vasishtha XII, 2, 10, 25; Gautama IX, 32, 61, &c.

12. Gautama IX, 21.

13. A rainbow (Indra-dhanu, Indra's bow), mani-dhanu (the jewelled bow).

14. A cow that suckles (her calf) he should not point out to another (person).

15. Let him not void urine or excrements on a ploughed field, on uncovered ground, or while rising up or standing.

16. He shall wipe himself with wood that has fallen off by itself.

17. He should not wear a dyed garment.

18. He should be fixed in his intentions, protect everybody's life, and be everybody's friend, as it were.

KANDIKÂ 8.

1. Through a period of three nights (after the Samâvartana) he should keep (the following) observances.

2. He shall eat no flesh and not drink out of an earthen vessel.

3. He shall avoid seeing women, Sûdras, dead bodies, black birds, and dogs, and shall not talk to (such beings).

4. He shall not eat funeral food, or food of a

---

13. Gautama IX, 22; Vasishtha XII,32.33; Âpastamba I, 31, 18.

14. Gautama IX, 23; Âpastamba I, 31, 10.

15. Gautama IX, 38; Vasishtha XII, 13; Âpastamba I, 30, 15. 18. Before easing himself, he shall first cover the ground with grass or the like.

17. Gautama IX, 4; Âpastamba I, 30, 10.

8, 1. The words of this Sûtra are repeated from Satapatha Brâhmana XIV, 1, 1, 28 (only for karati it is said here karet).

2. Satapatha Brâhmana I. 1. § 30.

3. Satapatha Brâhmana I. 1. § 31. Black birds, according to the commentators, mean crows.

4. Funeral food is such food as described below, III, 10, 26.

Sûdra, or of a woman lying-in (during the period of her impurity).

5. He shall not void urine or excrements, or spit out in the sun-shine, and shall not cover himself against the sun.

6. He shall take warm water for (the rites) in which water is wanted.

7. At night he shall eat by the light (of a lamp or a fire-brand).

8. Or only speaking the truth (suffices instead of the other observances).

9. Also a person who has received the dikshâ (or inauguration for a Soma sacrifice), should observe these rules beginning from (that which regards) the sun-shine (Sûtra 5), if he performs the Pravargya ceremony.

KANDIKÂ 9.

1. Now (follow) the five great sacrifices.

2. Of the Vaisvadeva food he should, after having sprinkled (water) round (the sacred fire), make oblations, with the word Svâhâ (each time repeated), to Brahman, to Pragâpati, to the (deities) of the house, to Kasyapa, and to Anumati.

3. To the domestic deities (he offers) three

---

9. The Pravargya ceremony, one of the preparatory ceremonies of the Soma sacrifice (Indische Studien, X, 363), was not performed at every Soma sacrifice, but there were certain restrictions regarding its performance; see Indische Studien, IX, 219 seq.

9, 1. The five Mahâyagñas are, the sacrifice to the gods, the sacrifice to living Beings, the sacrifice to the Fathers, the sacrifice to the Brahman, the sacrifice to men. As to the meaning of the five categories, see Âsvalâyana-Gr*i*hya III, 1.

2. Compare above, I, 12, 3.

3. Compare above, I, 12, 2.

(Balis) in the water-pot : to Par*g*anya, to the waters, to the Earth ;

4. To Dhât*ri* and Vidhât*ri* at the two door-posts ;

5. To the different quarters (of the horizon), to Vâyu and (to the presiding deities) of the quarters ;

6. In the middle three (Balis) to Brahman, to the Air, to the Sun.

7. To the north of those (he offers Balis) to the Vi*s*ve devâs and to all the beings ;

8. Further on to Ushas and to the Lord of beings ;

9. To the south (to the Fathers) with (the words), ' To the Fathers, Svadhâ ! Adoration !'

10. Having rinsed out the vessel, he should pour it out towards the north-west with (the words), 'Consumption ! this to thee !'

11. Taking the Brâhma*n*a's portion (of the food which he is going to distribute), he should give it to a Brâhma*n*a, after he has made him wash himself, with (the words), ' Well ! (this) to thee !'

12. To (religious) mendicants and to guests they should apportion (food) as due to them.

13. The persons belonging to the house, the young and the old, should eat what is due to them ;

14. Afterwards the householder and his wife.

15. Or the householder (should eat) first, because

---

11. What I have translated ' the Brâhma*n*a's portion ' is a g r a. See on this word the remark of Nîlaka*nth*a quoted by Böhtlingk-Roth s.v. agrahâra : agra*m* brâhma*n*abho*g*ana*m*, tadartha*m* hriyante râ*g*adhanât pr*i*thakkriyante te · grahârâ*h* kshetrâdaya*h*. According to different commentators and lexicographers one Agra is equal to four or to sixteen mouthfuls of food.

15. I cannot indicate any more than Professor Stenzler could, where the passage here quoted occurs in a Brâhma*n*a.

the *Sruti* says, ' Therefore the householder should eat the sweetest food before his guests.'

16. Every day he should sacrifice with the word sváhâ. If he has no food (to offer, he should make his offering) with something else, be it even a piece of wood (only), to the gods, or be it (only) a water-pot, to the Fathers and to men.

KANDIKÂ 10.

1. Now (follows) the Adhyâyopâkarman (or open-ing ceremony at the beginning of the annual course of study).

2. When the herbs appear, (when the moon stands in conjunction) with *Sravana*, on the full-moon day of the *Srâvana* month, or on the fifth (Tithi) of the *Srâvana* month under (the Nakshatra) Hasta ;

3. Having sacrificed the two Âgya portions, he offers two Âgya oblations, (namely,)

4. To the Earth and to Agni, if (he studies) the *Rig*-veda,

5. To the Air and to Vâyu, if the Yagur-veda,

6. To the Heaven and to the Sun, if the Sâma-veda,

7. To the quarters (of the horizon) and to the Moon, if the Atharva-veda;

8. (Besides) to the Brahman, to the metres in every case,

9. And to Pragâpati, to the gods, to the *Rishis*, to Faith, to Insight, to Sadasaspati, to Anumati.

10. The same (oblations are made) when the

16. Comp. *Sânkhâyana-Grihya* II, 17, 2 ; *Satapatha Brâhmana* XI, 5, 6, 2.

10, 2. Comp. *Âsvalâyana-Grihya* III, 5, 2. 3 and my note.

10. On the different vratas (observances) connected with the

observances are imposed (on a student) or given up (by him, after having been kept through the prescribed period of time).

11. With (the verse), 'Sadasaspati' (Vâ*g*. Sa*m*h. XXXII, 13) (the teacher) three times (sacrifices) fried grains.

12. All should repeat (that verse after him).

13. After each oblation they should each time put on the fire three pieces of Udumbara wood, fresh branches with leaves, anointed with ghee, reciting the Sâvitrî.

14. And the students (should put wood on the fire) in the manner stated above.

15. With (the verse), 'Luck may bring us' (Vâ*g*. Sa*m*h. IX, 16) they should eat the fried grains without chewing them.

16. With the verse, 'Of Dadhikrâvan' (Vâ*g*. Sa*m*h. XXIII, 32) they should eat curds.

17. As many pupils as he wishes to obtain, so many sesamum grains should he sacrifice with a dice-board, with the Sâvitrî or with the Anuvâka, 'Bright-resplending' (Vâ*g*. Sa*m*h. XVII, 80 seqq.).

18. After they have eaten (the remainder of the sacrificial food, the teacher) should pronounce the word Om and then repeat the Sâvitrî three times, and the beginnings of the Adhyâyas to (the students) who are seated facing the west:

---

study of the Veda, such as the *S*ukriya-vrata, the *S*âkvara-vrata, &c., comp. especially *S*ânkhâyana-Gr*i*hya II, 11. 12 and the notes there.

14. See above, chap. 4.

17. Âkarshaphalakena. Râmak*ri*sh*n*a states that this is a board of Udumbara wood, of the length of an arm, and of the shape of a serpent. (See Professor Stenzler's note.)

18. The following Sûtras clearly show that this rule is intended for students of the Ya*g*ur-veda only.

19. The beginnings of the sections belonging to the (different) *Ri*shis, if they are Bahv*ri*kas (i. e. if they study the *Ri*g-veda),

20. The Parvans, if they are *Kh*andogas (i. e. if they study the Sâma-veda),

21. The Sûktas, if they are Atharvans.

22. All murmur: 'May it be ours in common; may it bless us in common; may this Brahman be powerful with us together. Indra knows that through which, and in which way, no hatred may spring up amongst us.'

23. Through a period of three nights they should not study (the Veda).

24. And they should not cut the hair of their bodies and their nails.

25. Some say (that this should not be done) till the Utsarga (i. e. the concluding ceremony of the annual course of study).

KANDIKÂ 11.

1. If (a strong) wind is blowing, and on the new-moon day there is an entire interruption of study.

2. If one has partaken of a *S*râddha dinner, if a meteor falls, or distant thundering is heard, or if the earth quakes, or if fiery apparitions are seen, and when a new season begins, (the study shall be interrupted) until the same time next day.

3. If the Utsarga ceremony has been performed,

---

20. On the division of the Sâma-veda into Parvans, comp. Weber, Indische Literaturgeschichte, 2nd edition, p. 72.

11, 1. 'Entire interruption' means, according to the commentators, that not only the study of the Veda itself, but also that of the Vedângas, or even all sorts of worldly instruction are forbidden.

3. I have left the words sarvarûpe *k*a untranslated. Evidently

if clouds appear, ... , (it shall be interrupted) through a period of three nights or till twilight has thrice passed.

4. After he has eaten, until he has (washed and) dried his hands; while being in water; at night-time; at the time of the morning and evening twilight; while a dead body or a Kandâla is in the village.

5. While running, while seeing a person of bad fame or who has lost his caste, if a miraculous or happy event happens, as long as (that which occasions the interruption of study) endures.

6. If hoar-frost (lies on the ground), if a musical instrument is heard, or the cry of a person in pain, at the border of the village, in a burial ground, or if a dog, an ass, an owl, a jackal, or a Sâman song is heard, or if a learned person approaches, as long as (that occasion) endures.

7. If his Guru has died, let him go down into water (for offering water-oblations) and interrupt (the study) for ten nights.

8. If one who has performed with him the Tânû-naptra ceremony, or a fellow-pupil (has died), for three nights.

9. If one who is not his fellow-pupil, (has died,) for one night.

---

sarvarûpa is identical with the doubtful word savarûpa which twice occurs in the Sânkhâyana-Grihya. See the discussion on that word in the note on Sânkhâyana II, 12, 10.

4. On antardivâkîrtye, comp. Manu V, 85. Gautama XVI, 19.

8. The Tânûnaptra is an invocation directed to Tanûnaptri (i.e. the wind) by which the officiating priests and the Yagamâna at a Soma sacrifice pledge their faith to do no harm to each other. See Indische Studien, X, 362.

10. After having studied five months and a half, they should celebrate the Utsarga,

11. Or six months and a half.

12. They then mutter this *Rik*: 'Ye two young sages! The relation which has expired among us, the friendship we dissolve, (turning away) from the condition of friendship.'

13. After having remained together through a period of three nights, they separate.

KANDIKÂ 12.

1. In (the month) Pausha, under (the Nakshatra) Rohinî, or at the middle Ash/akâ let them celebrate the conclusion of the study (of the Veda).

2. Let them go to the brink of water and make water oblations to the gods, the metres, the Vedas, the *Ri*shis, the ancient teachers, the Gandharvas, the other teachers, the year with its divisions, and to their own ancestors and teachers.

3. After having four times quickly recited the Sâvitrî, they should say, 'We have finished.'

4. Interruption (of the study) and (continuation of the) teaching as stated above.

---

12. The reading of the Mantra is doubtful. I think it should stand as Professor Stenzler has printed it, except that I should propose to correct yuvâ into yuvânâ (comp. Âsvalâyana-Srauta VI, 12, 12). It is probable that the gods addressed are the two Asvins, who are called kavî and yuvânâ in several passages of the Vedas.

12, 1. See Âsvalâyana-Grihya III, 5, 20; Sânkhâyana-Grihya IV, 6. On the three Ash/akâs, see below, III, 3, 1.

4. Sânkhâyana-Grihya IV, 5, 17. where the same expression kshapana for interruptions of the study is used. The words 'as above' refer to chap. 10, 23, 24.

KA*ND*IKÂ 13.

1. On an auspicious day the harnessing to the plough. Or under (the Nakshatra) *G*yesh*thâ*, (because that rite is) sacred to Indra.

2. To Indra, Par*g*anya, the two A*s*vins, the Maruts, Udalâkâ*s*yapa, Svâtikârî, Sîtâ, and Anumati, he offers curds, rice grains, perfumes, and fried grains, and then makes the bullocks eat honey and ghee.

3. He should put them to the plough with (the verse), 'They harness to the ploughs' (Vâ*g*. Sa*m*h. XII, 67).

4. With (the verse), 'For luck may us the plough-shares' (Vâ*g*. Sa*m*h. XII, 69) let him plough or touch the plough-share.

5. Or (he may) not (do so), because (that verse) has been prescribed for (the erection of) the Agni (-altar), and the act of sowing stands in connection (with it).

6. After the front-bullock has been sprinkled (with water), they then should plough unploughed ground.

13, 1. Indra is the presiding deity over the constellation *G*yesh*thâ*; see *S*ânkhâyana-Gr*i*hya I, 26, 16, &c.

2. The names of the genius Udalâkâ*s*yapa and of the female genius Svâtikârî occur, as far as I know, only here. Böhtlingk-Roth propose to read Sphâti*m*kârî ('the goddess who gives abundance').

5. At the Agni-*k*ayana ceremony furrows are drawn with the plough on the Agni-kshetra with the verses Vâ*g*. Sa*m*h. XII, 69-72. Afterwards grains of different kinds are sown. See Kâtyâyana XVII, 2, 12 ; 3, 8 ; Indische Studien, XIII, 244 seq. Thus in the *S*rauta ritual the verse Vâ*g*. Sa*m*h. XII, 69 stands in a connection which does not conform to the occasion for which it would be used here.

7. He should make oblations of cooked sacrificial food to the same deities as above, when sowing both rice and barley, and at the sacrifice to Sîtâ.

8. Then (follows) feeding of the Brâhmaṇas.

KAṆDIKÂ 14.

1. Now (follows) the Sravaṇâ ceremony,

2. On the full-moon day of the Srâvaṇa month.

3. He cooks a mess of sacrificial food, fried grains, and a cake in one dish, pounds the greater part of the grains, sacrifices the two Âgya portions, and two (other) Âgya oblations (with the following verses):

4. 'Beat away, O white one, with thy foot, with the fore-foot and with the hind-foot, these seven [children] of Varuṇa and all (daughters) of the king's tribe. Svâhâ!

5. 'Within the dominion of the white one, the Serpent has seen nobody. To the white one, the son of Vidarva, adoration! Svâhâ!'

6. He makes oblations of the mess of cooked sacrificial food to Vishṇu, to Sravaṇa, to the full moon of Srâvaṇa, and to the rainy season,

7. (And oblations) of the grains with (the verse), 'Accompanied with grains' (Vâg. Saṃh. XX, 29).

---

7. 'As above' refers to Sûtra 2. On the Sîtâ-yagña, see below, chap. 17.

14, 1 seqq. Comp. Sânkhâyana IV, 5; Âsvalâyana II, 1; Gobhila III, 7.

4. Âsvalâyana II, 3, 3; Sânkhâyana IV, 18, 1. For Varuṇaiḥ and râgabândhavaiḥ I read Varuṇîḥ, râgabândhaviḥ. Pragâḥ is an interpolation.

5. Âsvalâyana, loc. cit. One is rather tempted to correct ahir dadaṃsa kaṅkana, but Râmakandra's Paddhati on Sânkhâyana gives the reading dadarṣa, as the Pâraskara MSS. do.

8. He sacrifices flour, over which ghee has been poured, to the serpents (with the following Mantras):

9. 'To the lord of the serpents belonging to Agni, of the yellowish, terrestrial ones, svâhâ!

'To the lord of the white serpents belonging to Vâyu, of the aerial ones, svâhâ!

'To the lord of the overpowering serpents belonging to Sûrya, of the celestial ones, svâhâ!

10. The (cake) in one dish he offers entirely (without leaving a remainder for the sacrificer) with (the formula), 'To the firm one, the son of the Earth, svâhâ!'

11. After he has eaten (of the sacrificial food), he throws a portion of the flour into a basket, goes out, besmears an elevated spot outside the hall (with cowdung), says, while a fire-brand is held (before him), 'Do not step between (myself and the fire),' and without speaking (anything except the Mantras), he causes the serpents to wash themselves, (pouring out water for them, with the formulas:)

12. 'Lord of the serpents belonging to Agni, of the yellowish, terrestrial ones, wash thyself!

'Lord of the white serpents belonging to Vâyu, of the aerial ones, wash thyself!

'Lord of the overpowering serpents belonging to Sûrya, of the celestial ones, wash thyself!'

13. Each time after the washing has been done, he offers to the serpents a Bali of flour, picking out

---

11. The ceremony with the fire-brand seems to stand in connection with the rule given by Âsvalâyana, II, 1, 13, that before the sacrificer has 'given himself in charge' to the serpents, nobody is allowed to step between him and the Bali destined for the serpents. Comp. also below, Sûtra 23.

13. I have translated upaghâtam by 'picking out.' On the full

(portions of it) with (the spoon called) Darvî (with the formulas) :

14. 'Lord of the serpents belonging to Agni, of the yellowish, terrestrial ones, this is thy Bali!

'Lord of the white serpents belonging to Vâyu, of the aerial ones, this is thy Bali!

'Lord of the overpowering serpents belonging to Sûrya, of the celestial ones, this is thy Bali!'

15. After he has made them wash themselves as above, he combs them with combs (with the formulas) :

16. 'Lord of the serpents belonging to Agni, of the yellowish, terrestrial ones, comb thyself!

'Lord of the white serpents belonging to Vâyu, of the aerial ones, comb thyself!

'Lord of the overpowering serpents belonging to Sûrya, of the celestial ones, comb thyself!'

17. (He offers) collyrium, ointment, and garlands with (the same formulas), putting at their end, respectively, the words, 'Salve thy eyes!' 'Anoint thyself!' 'Put on garlands!'

18. The remainder of the flour he pours out on the elevated spot (mentioned in Sûtra 11), pours water on it out of a water-pot, and worships the

---

technical meaning of the term, which implies the omission of the upastarana and abhighârana, see Bloomfield's note on Grihya-samgraha I, 111 (Zeitschrift der deutschen Morgenländischen Gesellschaft, XXXV, 568).

15. The words 'as above' refer to Sûtra 11. Pralikhati, which I have translated 'he combs them,' is the same act for which Sânkhâyana (IV, 15, 7) says, phanena keshayati. I think Professor Stenzler is wrong in translating : Er scharrt (das Mehl) mit Kämmen zusammen. Gayarâma says: pralekhanam ka kramena pratimantram balikandûyanam kankataih. tâni ka vaikankatiyâni prâdesamâtrâny ekatodantâni kâshthâni bhavanti.

serpents with the three (verses), 'Adoration be to the serpents' (Vâg. Samh. XIII, 6 seqq.).

19. At that distance in which he wishes the serpents not to approach (the house), he should three times walk round the house, sprinkling an uninterrupted stream of water round it, with the two (verses), 'Beat away, O white one, with thy foot' (Sûtras 4 and 5).

20. He gives away the (spoon called) Darvî (Sûtra 13) and the basket (Sûtra 11), having washed and warmed them.

21. Near the door (of the house) they clean themselves with the three (verses), 'O waters, ye are' (Vâg. Samh. XI, 50 seqq.).

22. Having put away that remainder of flour in a hidden place, he should from that time daily till the Âgrahâyanî, after sunset, when he has performed the service to the fire, offer to the serpents a Bali of flour, picking out (portions of it) with the Darvi (spoon).

23. When he is offering (the Bali), let no one step between (the sacrificer and the Bali).

24. With the Darvi (spoon) he rinses his mouth. Having washed it, he puts it away.

---

20. According to the commentators he gives these things to the man who holds the fire-brand (Sûtra 11).

22. The Âgrahâyanî is the full-moon day of Mârgasîrsha, on which the Pratyavarohana ceremony is celebrated. See below, III, 2; Weber, die vedischen Nachrichten von den Naxatra, II, 332. The expression darvyopaghâtam is the same that has occurred above in Sûtra 13.

23. Comp. Âsvalâyana-Grihya II, 1, 13, and see above, Sûtra 11.

24. Prakshâlya seems to me to refer to the Darvî; see Sûtra 20.

25. They eat the (rice) grains which must not form one coherent mass.

26. Then (follows) the feeding of the Brâhma*n*as.

KA*N*DIKÂ 15.

1. On the full-moon day of Praush*th*apada the sacrifice to Indra.

2. Having cooked milk-rice for Indra and cakes, and having put cakes round (the fire), he sacrifices the two Â*g*ya portions and Â*g*ya oblations to Indra, to Indrâ*n*î, to A*g*a Ekapad, to Ahi Budhnya, and to the Prosh*th*apadâs.

3. After he has eaten (his portion of the sacrificial food), he offers a Bali to the Maruts. For the *S*ruti says, 'The Maruts eat what is not-sacrificed.'

4. (This Bali he offers) in A*s*vattha leaves, because it is said, 'The Maruts stood in the A*s*vattha tree.'

---

25. A sa*m*syûtâ*h*. Comp. Böhtlingk-Roth s.v. sa*m*-sîv.

15, 2. After these Â*g*ya oblations follows the chief oblation of the whole sacrifice, the oblation of milk-rice to Indra. In one of Professor Stenzler's MSS. there is a special Sûtra inserted after Sûtra 2, 'Of the cooked food he makes an oblation with (the formula), "To Indra svâhâ."' I do not, however, think it right to receive this Sûtra into the text, as the other MSS. do not support it, and the commentators did not find it in the text which they read.

3. Professor Stenzler's translation, 'Die Maruts essen kein Opfer,' seems to me not quite exact. I should prefer to say, 'Die Maruts essen Nicht-Opfer.' This passage, taken from *S*atapatha Brâhma*n*a IV, 5, 2, 16, is quoted as supporting the rule that a Bali offering should be made to the Maruts; for in the technical language the term ahuta is applied to Bali offerings (Sânkhâyana-G*ri*hya I, 10, 7, huto-gnihotrahomena, ahuto balikarma*n*î).

4. When Indra called them to his help against V*ri*tra. *S*atapatha Brâhma*n*a IV, 3, 3, 6.

5. (He offers it) with (the texts), 'Brilliantly resplendent' (Vâg. Samh. XVII, 80–85), Mantra by
Mantra,

6. And with the (Mantra called) Vimukha.

7. (This Mantra he repeats only) in his mind.

8. For the *Sruti* says, 'These are their names.'

9. He murmurs, 'To Indra the divine' (Vâg.
Samh. XVII, 86).

10. Then (follows) the feeding of the Brâhmanas.

KANDIKÂ 16.

1. On the full-moon day of Âsvayuga the (offerings of) Prishâtakas (are made).

2. Having cooked milk-rice for Indra he sacrifices
it, mixed with curds, honey, and ghee, to Indra, Indrânî, the two Asvins, the full moon of Âsvayuga,
and to the autumn.

3. After he has eaten (his portion of the sacrificial
food), he sacrifices with his joined hands a Prishâtaka prepared with curds, with the words, 'May
what is deficient be made full to me; may what is
full not decay to me.   Svâhâ!'

4. The inmates of the house look at the mixture of curds, honey, and ghee, with the Anuvâka,

---

5. This Sûtra is identical with the last words of Kâty. XVIII, 4, 23.
6. This is the first part of Vâg. Samh. XVII, 86.
8. Satapatha Brâhmana IX, 3, 1, 26. There it is said that
sukragyotis ('brilliantly resplendent') &c. (the words used in Vâg.
Samh. XVII, 80) are names of the Maruts.
9. This Sûtra is identical with Kâty. XVIII, 4, 25.
16, 1. Prishâtaka means a mixture of curds and butter.   Comp.
Sânkhâyana IV, 16, 3; Âsvalâyana II, 2, 3; Grihya-samgraha-
parisishta II, 59.
3. Âsvalâyana II, 2, 3.

'May Indra come hither' (Vâg. Samh. XX, 47 seqq.).

5. They let the calves join their mothers that night and the Âgrahâyani night.

6. Then (follows) the feeding of the Brâhmanas.

KANDIKÂ 17.

1. Now (follows) the sacrifice to Sîtâ.

2. Wherever he sacrifices, be it (on a field) of rice or of barley, of that grain he should prepare a mess of cooked food.

3. One who has sacrificed may, if he likes, prepare elsewhere also a mess of cooked food, either of rice or of barley.

4. (There should be) no doubt (as to whether rice or barley is to be taken), as a rule thereon has been stated above.

5. If it is impossible (to take one of the two species of corn), (that) is excluded.

6. To the east or to the north of the field, on a

5. Sânkhâyana IV, 16, 4.

17, 1. The goddess Sîtâ is, as her name indicates, the rustic deity of the furrow.

3. Perhaps the meaning is that a person who has already once performed the Sîtâ-yagña on the field, is allowed, when repeating the sacrifice another time, to celebrate it elsewhere, and to choose at his will between rice and barley.

4. A rule has been given in the Srauta-sûtra (Kâty. I, 9, 1: 'Rice or barley, if a Havis [is prescribed] ') which shows that it is indifferent whether rice or barley is taken. Thus the sacrificer is free to elect the one or the other. At least this is the traditional meaning of this Sûtra. But possibly we had better understand it otherwise. The sacrificer should offer, according to Sûtra 3, rice or barley. Whether he has to take the one or the other, there can be no doubt, as the rule given above (Sûtra 2) shows that rice should be cooked, if the ceremony is performed for a rice-field, and barley, if for a barley-field.

clean spot that has been ploughed, so that the crop
be not damaged,

7. Or in the village, because (there) both (rice and
barley) are united, and because no obstacle is there.

8. Where he intends to cook (the sacrificial food),
he establishes the fire on a place that has been
smeared (with cowdung), which is elevated, and
which has been sprinkled (with water), strews (round
the fire) Darbha grass mixed with (stalks of) that
(sort of corn to which the sacrifice refers), sacrifices
the two Âgya portions and Âgya oblations (with the
following Mantras):

9. 'For whom earth and heaven, the intermediate
points and the chief points (of the horizon) are veiled
with light, that Indra I invoke here. May his
weapons be friendly towards us. Svâhâ!

'Whatsoever it be that I wish for at this sacrifice,
O killer of Vritra, may all that be fulfilled to me,
and may I live a hundred autumns. Svâhâ!

'May success, prosperity, earth, rain, eminence,
excellence, luck here protect the creatures. Svâhâ!

'In whose substance dwells the prosperity of all
Vedic and worldly works, Indra's wife Sitâ I invoke.
May she not abandon me in whatever work I do.
Svâhâ!

'Her, who rich in horses, rich in cows, rich in
delight indefatigably supports living beings, Urvarâ
(i. e. the field) who is wreathed with threshing-floors,
I invoke at this sacrifice, the firm One. May she
not abandon me. Svâhâ!'

10. He makes oblations of the cooked sacrificial
food to Sîtâ, Yagâ (the goddess of sacrifice), Samâ
(the goddess of zealous devotion), Bhûti (the goddess
of welfare).

11. Some say that the giving (of the sacrificial food to the deities) accompanies the Mantras.

12. But this is excluded, as the Sruti says, 'The giving (of the oblation to the deity) accompanies the word Svâhâ.'

13. On the Kusa grass which is left over from the strewing (of grass round the fire), he offers a Bali to the protecting demons of the furrow with (the Mantra), 'They who are sitting towards the east with strong bows and quivers, may they protect thee from the east, and be vigilant and not abandon thee. To them I bring adoration, and I offer this Bali to them.'

14. Then to the south with (the Mantra), 'They who are sitting towards the south, not winking the eyes, wearing armour, may they protect thee from the south, and be vigilant and not abandon thee. To them I bring adoration, and I offer this Bali to them.'

15. Then to the west with (the Mantra), 'The powerful ones, the excellent ones, prosperity, earth, Pârshni, Sunamkuri, may they protect thee from the west, and be vigilant and not abandon thee. To them I bring adoration, and I offer this Bali to them.'

16. Then to the north with (the Mantra), 'The fearful ones, like to Vâyu in speed, may they protect

12. The quotation has not been as yet identified in the Sruti itself, but the words quoted are found in Kâty.-Sraut. I, 2, 7.

14. Some words in the beginning of the Mantra are lost. We should probably write: atha dakshinatah. ye dakshinato＊nimishâh ... varmina âsate, &c. Of course it is impossible? to say which is the word that is wanting before (or perhaps after) varminah.

15. Pârshni, which means 'heel,' stands here, of course, as the name of a protecting demon.

thee from the north, on the field, on the threshing-floor, in the house, on the way, and be vigilant and not abandon thee. To them I bring adoration, and I offer this Bali to them.'

17. Of another (sort of food) as the chief (food used at this sacrifice), and with the remainder of Âgya, he distributes Balis as above.

18. And the women should make accompanying oblations, because such is the custom.

19. When the ceremony is finished, he should feed the Brâhmaṇas. He should feed the Brâhmaṇas.

End of the Second Kâṇḍa.

---

17. See above, chap. 13, 2.

1. (Now shall be explained) the partaking of the first-fruits (of the harvest), of a person who has not set up the (sacred *Srauta*) fires.

2. He cooks a mess of fresh sacrificial food, sacrifices the two Âgya portions, and two Âgya oblations, (with the formulas),

'To the hundredfold armed, hundredfold valiant, hundredfold blissful one, the vanquisher of enemies —he who may create a hundred autumns for us. Indra,—may he lead us across (the gulf of) misfortune. Svâhâ !

'The four paths that go between heaven and earth, trodden by the gods—of these (paths) lead us to that which may bring us freedom from decay and decline, O all ye gods. Svâhâ !'

3. Having made oblations of the mess of cooked food to the Âgrayana deities, he makes another oblation to (Agni) Svish/akrit with (the verse), 'Agni, make this (sacrifice) full, that it may be well offered. And may the god destroy all hostile powers. Come hither, showing us a good path. Bestow on us long life, full of splendour and free from decay. Svâhâ !'

4. He then eats (of the fresh fruits with the

_____

1, 1. The corresponding ceremony of the *Srauta* ritual is treated of in Kâty. IV, 6.

2. A fresh Sthâlîpâka means probably a Sthâlîpâka prepared from the fresh grain of the new harvest.

3. The deities of the Âgrayana ceremony, which occupies in the *Srauta* ritual the place corresponding to the rite described here, are Indra and Agni, the Visve devâs, Heaven and Earth.

verses), ' May Agni eat first, for he knows how the
Havis (is fit for sacrifice) ; may he, the friend of all
human tribes, make the herbs blessed to us.

' From the good you have led us to the better, ye
gods! Through thee, the nourishment, may we
obtain thee. Thus enter into us, O potion, bringing
refreshment, for the good of our children and of ourselves, and pleasant.'

5. Or with the (verse) sacred to Annapati (the
Lord of food).

6. For barley, however, (he uses the Mantra),
' This barley, mixed with honey, they have ploughed
through Sarasvatî under Manu. Indra was lord of
the plough, the hundredfold wise one ; ploughers
were the Maruts, the exuberant givers.'

7. Then (follows) the feeding of the Brâhma*n*as.

KA*N*DIKÂ 2.

1. On the full-moon day of Mârga*s*irsha the
Âgrahâya*n*î ceremony (is performed).

2. He cooks a mess of sacrificial food, sacrifices
two Â*g*ya oblations as at the *S*rava*n*â sacrifice, and
other oblations with (the following verses) :

' The night whom men welcome like a cow that
comes to them, (the night) which is the consort of
the year, may that (night) be auspicious to us.
Svâhâ !

---

5. The Annapatîya verse is Vâ*g*. Sa*m*h. XI, 83.

6. Comp. manâv adhi, Rig-veda VIII, 72, 2.

2, 2. The two oblations belonging to the *S*rava*n*â ceremony are
those stated above, II, 14, 4. 5.

2. The first verses in which the Âgrahâya*n*î night is called the
consort of the year, or the image of the year, occur elsewhere with
reference to the Ekâsh*t*akâ night. See Atharva-veda III, 10; Taitt.

'The night which is the image of the year, that we worship. May I reach old age, imparting strength to my offspring. Svâhâ!

'To the Sa*m*vatsara, to the Parivatsara, to the Idâvatsara, to the Idvatsara, to the Vatsara bring ye great adoration. May we, undecayed, unbeaten, long enjoy the favour of these (years) which are worthy of sacrifices. Svâhâ!

'May summer, winter and spring, the rains be friendly, and may autumn be free of danger to us. In the safe protection of these seasons may we dwell, (and) may (they) last (to us) through a hundred years. Svâhâ!'

3. He makes oblations of the cooked food to Soma, to (the Nakshatra) M*ri*ga*s*iras, to the full moon of Mârga*s*îrsha, and to the winter.

4. After he has eaten (of the sacrificial food), he throws the remainder of the flour into a basket, (and then follow the same rites that have been stated above) from (the sacrificer's) going out down to their cleaning themselves.

5. After the cleaning he says, 'The Bali offering is finished.'

6. After they have spread out to the west of the fire a layer (of straw) and a garment that has

---

Sa*m*hitâ V, 7, 2, 1. See also below, Pâraskara III, 3, 5. Sa*m*vatsara, Parivatsara, Idâvatsara, &c. are terms designating the different years of the quinquennial period of the Yuga. See Zimmer, Altindisches Leben, 369, 370.

4. See above, II, 14, 11–21 (not 19–21 as indicated by Professor Stenzler).

6. 'Redescending' means that they do not sleep any longer on high bedsteads, which they did from the *S*râva*n*î day till the Âgrahâya*n*î, on account of the danger from the snakes, but on the ground. See the notes on *S*âṅkh.-G*ri*hya IV, 15, 22; 17, 1.

not yet been washed, they 'redescend,' having bathed, wearing garments which have not yet been washed : the master (of the house) southward, his wife to the north (of her husband, and then the other persons belonging to the house) so that each younger one lies more to the north.

7. Having caused the Brahman to sit down southward, and having placed to the north a water-pot, a Samî branch, an earth-clod taken out of a furrow, and a stone, he murmurs, looking at the fire : ' This Agni is most valiant, he is most blessed, the best giver of a thousand boons, highly powerful. May he establish us both in the highest place.'

8. To the west of the fire he joins his hands (and holds them) towards the east.

9. With the three (verses), 'The divine ship' (Vâg. Samh. XXI, 6–8) they ascend the layer (of straw).

10. He addresses the Brahman : ' Brahman, we will redescend.'

11. The Brahman having given his permission, they redescend with (the words), ' Life, fame, glory, strength, enjoyment of food, offspring !'

12. Those who have received the initiation murmur, 'May a good winter, a good spring, a good summer be bestowed on us. Blessed may be to us the rains ; may the autumns be blessed to us.'

13. With (the verse), ' Be soft to us, O earth' (Vâg. Samh. XXXV, 21), they lie down on their right sides, their heads turned towards the east.

10, 11. See the note on § 6.

12. On upeta, which means a person for whom the Upanayana has been performed, see my note, Sânkhâyana-Grihya II, 1, 1.

14. They arise with (the verse), ' Up! with life, with blessed life. Up! with Pargʹanya's eye, with the seven spaces of the earth.'

15. This (they repeat) two other times, with the Brahman's permission.

16. Let them sleep on the ground four months (after the Pratyavarohaʹna), or as long as they like.

KAʹNDIKÂ 3.

1. After the Âgrahâyaʹnî (full moon follow) the three Ashʹakâs.

2. (The Ashʹakâ is) sacred to Indra, to the Viʹsve devâs, to Pragʹâpati, and to the Fathers.

3. (The oblations are made) with cakes, flesh, and vegetables, according to the order (of the three Ashʹakâs).

4. The first Ashʹakâ (is celebrated) on the eighth day of the fortnight.

5. Having cooked a mess of sacrificial food and having sacrificed the two Âgʹya portions, he sacrifices Âgʹya oblations with (the texts):

(a) ' Thirty sisters go to the appointed place,

---

14. The verse occurs, with a few differences, in the Kâʹnva Sâkhâ of the Vâgʹ. Saʹmhitâ, II, 7, 5.

3, 1. On the Ashʹakâs, celebrated on the eighth days of the three dark fortnights following after the Âgrahâyaʹnî full moon, see Sâṅkhâyana III, 12 seqq.; Âsvalâyana II, 4; Gobhila III, 10.

2. As there are four deities named, I think it probable that they are referred to all Ashʹakâs indiscriminately; comp. Âsvalâyana II, 4, 12. Thus in the Mantras prescribed for the first Ashʹakâ (Sûtras 5 and 6), Indra, the Viʹsve devâs, and Pragʹâpati are named; to the Fathers belongs the Anvashʹakya ceremony.

3. With regard to the order of these substances the Grʹihya texts differ.

5. Comp. Taitt. Saʹmhitâ IV, 3, 11; Atharva-veda III, 10.

(a) The thirty sisters seem to be the days of the month. As to

putting on the same badge. They spread out the
seasons, the knowing sages; having the metres in
their midst they walk around, the brilliant ones.
Svâhâ!

(b) 'The shining one clothes herself with clouds,
with the ways of the sun, the divine night: manifold animals which are born, look about in this
mother's lap. Svâhâ!

(c) 'The Ekâsh*t*akâ, devoting herself to austerities,
has given birth to a child, to the majesty of Indra.
Through him the gods have conquered the hostile
tribes; he became the killer of the Asuras through
his (divine) powers. Svâhâ!

(d) 'You have made me who am not the younger
(sister), the younger; speaking the truth I desire
this: may I be in his (i.e. the sacrificer's?) favour,
as you are; may none of you supplant the other in
her work.

(e) 'In my favour dwelt the omniscient one; he
has found a firm standing; he has got a footing.
May I be in his (i.e. the sacrificer's?) favour, as you
are; may none of you supplant the other in her
work.

(f) 'On the five dawns follows the fivefold
milking; on the cow with the five names, the five
seasons. The five regions (of the sky) are estab-

madhye*khh*andas, comp. Taitt. Sa*m*h. loc. cit. § 1: *kh*andasvati
ushasâ pepisâne; § 2: *k*atush*t*omo abhavad yâ turîyâ ya*gñ*asya
pakshâv *ri*shayo bhavantî, gâyatrî*m* trish*t*ubha*m* *g*agatîm anush*t*u-
bham b*ri*had arka*m* yu*ñg*ânâ*h* suvar â ·bharann idam.

(d) Probably one Ash*t*akâ addresses the others, her sisters, as
*G*ayarâma explains this verse.

(f) The explanation by which the 'fivefold milking' is referred
to what is called in Taitt. Brâhma*n*a II, 2, 9, 'the milkings of
Pra*g*âpati,' seems to me more than doubtful, for 'the milkings

lished through the fifteenfold (Stoma); with one common face (they look over) the one world. Svâhâ!

(g) 'She who shone forth as the first, is the child of truth. One (of them) bears the majesty of the waters; one wanders in the courses of the sun; one (in those) of the heat; Savitri shall govern one. Svâhâ!

(h) 'She who shone forth as the first has become a cow in Yama's realm. Give us milk, thou who art rich in milk, year by year. Svâhâ!

(i) 'She, the owner of bright bulls, has come to us with clouds and with light, she who has all shapes, the motley one, whose banner is fire. Carrying on the common work, leading us to old age, come to us thou who art exempt from old age, Ushas! Svâhâ!

(k) 'The consort of the seasons, the first one has come to us, the leader of days, the producer of offspring. Being one, thou shinest manifold, Ushas. Being free from old age, thou leadest to old age everything else. Svâhâ!'

6. He makes offerings of the mess of cooked food with (the verses):

'May the earth be peaceful, the air friendly to us;

of Pragâpati' are only four: viz. the dark night, the moonlight, the twilight, and the day.

(i) Sukra-rishabhâ cannot be translated, as Professor Stenzler does, 'die schönste unter den Lichtern' (Mâdhava: sukreshu nakshatrâdishu sreshthâ), for this meaning of rishabhâ occurs only in later texts. The word is a Bahuvrîhi compound, as the Petersburg Dictionary explains it.

6. In the first verse I have omitted vyasnavai, which impedes the construction and violates the metre. The word has found its way into the text, no doubt, in consequence of the phrase dîrgham âyur vyasnavai occurring in chap. 2, 2. In the second verse

may the heavens give us bliss and safety. May the
points (of the horizon), the intermediate points,
the upper points give us bliss, and may day and
night create long life for us. Svâhâ!

'May the waters, the rays protect us from all
sides; may the creator, may the ocean turn away
evil. The present and the future, may all be safe
for me. Protected by Brahman, may I be well
guarded. Svâhâ!

'May all Âdityas and the divine Vasus, may the
Rudras and Maruts be our protectors. May Praga-
pati, the highest lord, bestow on us vigour, offspring,
immortality, long life. Svâhâ!'

7. And with (the formula), 'To the Ash/akâ
Svâhâ!'

8. The middle Ash/akâ (is celebrated) with (the
sacrifice of) a cow.

9. He sacrifices the omentum of that (cow) with
(the verse), 'Carry the omentum, O Gâtavedas, to
the fathers' (Vâg. Samh. XXXV, 20).

10. On the day following each (Ash/akâ), the
Anvash/akâ day, (he brings a sacrifice) with the left
ribs and the left thigh, in an enclosure, according to
(the ritual of) the Pindapitriyagña.

11. Also to the female (ancestors he makes Pinda
offerings) and pours (for them) strong liquor and water
oblations into pits, and (offers) collyrium, salves, and
garlands.

12. (He may also make oblations), if he likes, to
the teacher and to the pupils who have no children.

---

akritad is corrupt. I have translated abhayam; comp. Âsvalâyana II, 4, 14. In the third verse I have left out mayi, as
Professor Stenzler has done in his translation.

13. And in the middle of the rainy season (there is) a fourth Ash/akâ on which vegetables are offered.

KANDIKÂ 4.

1. Now the building of the house.

2. Let him have his house built on an auspicious day.

3. Into the pits (in which the posts shall be erected) he pours an oblation with (the words), 'To the steady one, the earth-demon, svâhâ!'

4. He erects the post.

'This navel of the world I set up, a stream of wealth, promoting wealth. Here I erect a firm house ; may it stand in peace, dropping ghee.

'Rich in horses and cows, rich in delight be set up, for the sake of great happiness. To thee may the young calf cry, to thee the lowing cows, the milk-cows.

'To thee (may) the young child (go), to thee the calf with its companions, to thee the cup of Parisrut, to thee (may they go) with pots of curds.

---

13. I have stated in the note on Sânkhâyana III, 13, 1 my reasons for believing that the true reading of this Sûtra is not madhyâvarshe (in the middle of the rainy season), but mâghyavarshe (the festival celebrated during the rainy season under the Nakshatra Maghâs). There are no express rules given with regard to the third Ash/akâ, but I think we should understand this Sûtra as involving a statement on that Ash/akâ : (The third Ash/akâ) and the fourth, on the Mâghyavarsha day, are Sâkâsh/akâs (Ash/akâs on which vegetables are offered). Sânkhâyana (Gr/hya III, 13, 1) declares that the ritual of the fourth Ash/akâ is identical with that of the second.

4, 3. Âsvalâyana-Gr/hya II, 8, 15.

4. On gagadaih saha (in the third verse) see my note on Sânkhâyana-Gr/hya III, 2, 9.

'The consort of Peace, the great one, beautifully attired—bestow on us, O blessed one, wealth and manly power, which may be rich in horses and cows, full of sap like a tree's leaf. May our wealth increase here, clothing itself with prospering'—with (these four Mantras) he approaches the four (posts).

5. Having established the fire inside (the house), having made the Brahman sit down towards the south, having placed a water-pot to the north, and cooked a mess of sacrificial food, he goes out (of the house), and standing near the door, he addresses the Brahman, 'Brahman, I enter (the house)!'

6. When the Brahman has given his consent, he enters with (the formula), 'To right I advance, to luck I advance!'

7. Having prepared Âgya and sacrificed two Âgya oblations with (the two parts of the Mantra), 'Here is joy' (Vâg. Samh. VIII, 51 a), he sacrifices other oblations with (the verses):

(a) 'Vâstoshpati! Receive us (into thy protection); give us good entering and drive away from us evil. For what we ask thee, with that favour us: be a saviour to us, to men and animals. Svâhâ!

(b) 'Vâstoshpati! Be our furtherer; make our wealth increase in cows and horses, O Indu (i.e. Soma). Free from decay may we dwell in thy friendship; give us thy favour, as a father to his sons. Svâhâ!

(c) 'Vâstoshpati! Let us be in a fellowship with thee, which may be valiant, joyful, and well proceeding. Protect our wishes when we rest and

7. Rig-veda VII, 54; 55, 1.

when we do our work. Protect us always, ye (gods), and give us welfare. Svâhâ!

(d) ' Driving away calamity, Vâstoshpati, assuming all shapes, be a kind friend to us. Svâhâ!'

8. He makes offerings of the mess of cooked food (with the following Mantras) :

(a) 'Agni, Indra, Br̥haspati, the Viçve devâs I invoke, Sarasvatî and Vâg̱î. Give me a dwelling-place, ye vigorous ones. Svâhâ!

(b) ' To all the divine hosts of serpents, to the Himavat, the Sudarṣana (mountain), and the Vasus, Rudras, Âdityas, Îṣâna with his companions, to all these I apply. Give me a dwelling-place, ye vigorous ones. Svâhâ!

(c) 'To forenoon and afternoon both together with noon, to evening and midnight, to the goddess of dawn with her wide path, to all these I apply. Give me a dwelling-place, ye vigorous ones. Svâhâ!

(d) ' To the Creator and the Changer, to Viçva-karman, to the herbs and trees, to all these I apply. Give me a dwelling-place, ye vigorous ones. Svâhâ!

(e) ' To Dhâtr̥ and Vidhâtr̥, and to the Lord of treasures together with them, to all these I apply. Give me a dwelling-place, ye vigorous ones. Svâhâ!

(f) ' As a lucky, a happy (place), give me this dwelling-place, Brahman and Prag̱âpati, and all deities. Svâhâ!'

9. After he has partaken (of the sacrificial food), let him put into a brass vessel the different things which he has brought together, Udumbara leaves with strong liquor, green turf, cowdung, curds,

---

8 a. Vâg̱î is, as the name shows, the goddess of quick vigour. Gayarâma explains Vâg̱î, a name of Sîtâ, as a personification of food.

b. Comp. Âçvalâyana II, 1, 14. On g̱agada, comp. above, § 4.

honey, ghee, Kusa grass, and barley, and let him
besprinkle the seats and shrines (for the images of
the gods).

10. He touches (the wall and the posts) at their
eastern juncture with (the words), 'May luck and
glory protect thee at thy eastern juncture.'

11. He touches (them) at their southern juncture
with (the words), 'May sacrifice and sacrificial fee
protect thee at thy southern juncture.'

12. He touches (them) at their western juncture
with (the words), 'May food and the Brâhma*na* protect thee at thy western juncture.'

13. He touches (them) at their northern juncture
with (the words), 'May vigour and delight protect
thee at thy northern juncture.'

14. He then goes out (of the house) and worships
the quarters (of the horizon, the east) with (the
formulas), 'May Ketâ (i.e. will?) and Suketâ (i.e.
good-will?) protect me from the east.

'Agni is Ketâ; the Sun is Suketâ: to them I
apply; to them be adoration; may they protect me
from the east.'

15. Then to the south: 'May that which protects
and that which guards, protect me from the south.

'The Day is that which protects; the Night is
that which guards; to them I apply; to them be
adoration; may they protect me from the south.'

16. Then to the west: 'May the shining one
and the waking one protect me from the west.

'Food is the shining one; Breath is the waking
one; to them I apply; to them be adoration; may
they protect me from the west.'

17. Then to the north: 'May the sleepless one and
the not-slumbering one protect me from the north.

' The Moon is the sleepless one ; the Wind is the not-slumbering one ; to them I apply; to them be adoration ; may they protect me from the north.'

18. When (the house) is finished, he enters it with (the formulas),

' Law, the chief post! Fortune, the pinnacle! Day and night, the two door-boards!

' Indra's house is wealthy, protecting ; that I enter with my children, with my cattle, with everything that is mine.

' Hither is called the whole number (of relatives), the friends whose coming is good. Thus (I enter) thee, O house. May our dwellings be full of in-violable heroes from all sides ! '

19. Then (follows) feeding of the Brâhma*n*as.

KA*N*DIKÂ 5.

1. Now (follows) the putting up of the water-barrel.

2. To the north-east he digs a pit like (the pit for) a sacrificial post, strews into it Ku*s*a grass, fried grains, fruits of the soap-tree, and other auspicious things, and therein he establishes the water-barrel with (the words), ' The sea art thou.'

3. He pours water into it with (the verse), ' Ye

---

18. Comp. *S*ânkhâyana-G*ri*hya III, 3, 7 seq.; chap. 4, 10. The comparison of *S*ânkhâyana shows that we have to divide saha pra*g*ayâ pa*s*ubhi*h*, saha yan me ki*n*ki*d* asty, upahûta*h*, &c. Sâdhu-sa*m*v*ri*ta*h* (if the reading is correct) seems to me to be the nom. plur. of sâdhusa*m*v*ri*t. I understand this to be a Bahuvrihi com-pound, in which sa*m*v*ri*t means ' the approaching.' In Atharva-veda VII, 60, 4 we have sakhâya*h* svâdusa*m*muda*h*. After *s*âle a verb meaning 'I enter,' or something like that, has been lost.

5, 3. Rig-veda X, 30, 12.

waters, rich in wealth, ye possess goods. Ye bring
us good insight and immortality. Ye are the rulers
over wealth and blessed offspring. May Sarasvati
give strength to him who praises her!'—

4. And with the three (verses), 'O waters, ye are'
(Vâg. Sa*m*hitâ XI, 50 seqq.).

5. Then (follows) feeding of the Brâhma*n*as.

KA*N*DIKÂ 6.

1. Now the cure for headache.

2. Having moistened his hands, he passes them
over his eye-brows with (the verse), 'From the eyes,
from the ears, from the whiskers, from the chin,
from the forehead, I drive away this disease of the
head.'

3. If (only) one side (of the head aches, he recites
the verse), 'Cleaver! Thou with the disfigured
eyes! White-wing! Renowned one! And thou
with the various-coloured wing! Let his head not
ache.'

4. Then it will get better.

KA*N*DIKÂ 7.

1. (Now will be declared) the making water round
about a servant who is disposed to run away.

2. While (the servant) is sleeping, he should dis-
charge his urine into the horn of a living animal, and
should three times walk round him, turning his left
side towards him, and sprinkle (the urine) round him,

7, 1. Uṭûla-parimcha*h*. It is probable that uṭûla, as meaning
a slave who habitually runs away, is connected with the use of that
word as the name of a tribe in the north-west of India.

with (the verse), ' From the mountain (on which thou art born), from thy mother, from thy sister, from thy parents and thy brothers, from thy friends I sever thee.

' Run-away servant, I have made water round thee. Having been watered round, where wilt thou go ? '

3. Should he run away (nevertheless, his master) should establish a fire that has been taken from a wood that is on fire, and should sacrifice (in that fire) Kusa plates (used for protecting the hands when holding a hot sacrificial pan) that have been anointed with ghee, with (the formula), ' May the stumbler stumble round thee, ... may he tie thee with Indra's fetter, loosen thee for me, and may he lead another one up (to me).'

4. Then he will quietly remain (in his master's house).

KANDIKÂ 8.

1. The spit-ox (sacrificed to Rudra).

2. It procures (to the sacrificer) heavenly rewards, cattle, sons, wealth, renown, long life.

3. Having taken the sacred domestic fire to the

---

3. Ukhâ yâbhyâm grihyate tâv indvau.　Comm. on Kâtyâyana, Sraut. XVI, 4, 2.

In the Mantra I propose to read, pari tvâ hvalano, &c.　Nivritiendravirudhah seems to be corrupt; it seems to be a compound of nivritta, a second member which is doubtful, and virudh (the plant).　The meaning may have been ' giving it up to consume the plants.'

4. This Sûtra is word for word identical with chap. 6, 4.

8, 1. Âsvalâyana-Grihya IV, 8.

2. Âsvalâyana, loc. cit. § 35.

3. The ' outspreading ' is the establishing of the three sacred Srauta fires, so that the Grihya fire is considered as the Gârhapatya, and the Âhavanîya and Dakshinâgni are taken from it.

forest, and having performed the 'outspreading,' he
should sacrifice the animal to Rudra.

4. One that is not gelded.

5. Or (it may be) a cow, on account of the
designation.

6. Having cooked the omentum, a mess of sacrificial food, and the portions cut off (of the victim),
he sacrifices the omentum to Rudra, the fat to the
Air, and the cut-off portions together with the mess
of cooked food to Agni, Rudra, Sarva, Pasupati,
Ugra, Asani, Bhava, Mahâdeva, Îsâna.

7. (Then follows a sacrifice to) Vanaspati.

8. (To Agni) Svishtakrit at the end.

9. Then (follows) the sprinkling round to the
different quarters (of the horizon).

10. After the sprinkling has been performed, they
sacrifice the Patnî-samyâga offerings to Indrânî,
Rudrânî, Sarvânî, Bhavânî, and Agni Grihapati.

11. The blood he offers in leaves, on (grass-)
bunches, as a Bali to Rudra and to his hosts, with
(the Mantras),

'The hosts, Rudra, which thou hast to the east,
to them this Bali (is given). To them and to thee
be adoration!

'The hosts, Rudra, which thou hast to the south
. . . to the west . . . to the north . . . upwards . . .

---

5. On account of the designation of the sacrifice as sûla-gava.

6. Âsvalâyana, loc. cit. § 19.

9. Gayarâma: disâm vyâghâranam kartavyam iti sûtraseshah.
tak ka vasayâ bhavati yathâgnishomiye.

10. On the Patnî-samyâga offerings, so called because they are
chiefly directed to the wives of the gods, see Hillebrandt, Neu- und
Vollmondsopfer, pp. 151 seqq.

11. Âsvalâyana, loc. cit. § 22.

downwards, to them this Bali (is given). To them and to thee be adoration!'

12. The contents of the stomach and of the entrails, besmeared with blood, he throws into the fire or buries them in the earth.

13. Having placed the animal so that the wind blows from himself to it, he approaches it with the Rudra hymns, or with the first and last Anuvâka.

14. They do not take anything of that animal to the village.

15. Thereby (also) the cow-sacrifice has been declared.

16. (It is combined) with (the offering of) milk-rice ; (the rites) not corresponding (to that special occasion) are omitted.

17. The sacrificial fee at that (sacrifice) is a cow of the same age (as the victim).

KANDIKÂ 9.

1. Now the letting loose of the bull.

2. (The ceremony) has been declared in the cow-sacrifice.

3. (It is performed) on the full-moon day of Kârttika, or on the (day on which the moon stands in conjunction with) Revatî in the Âsvayuga month.

4. Having set a fire in a blaze in the midst of the

12. As to ûvadhya, comp. Âsvalâyana, § 28.
13. The Rudra hymns form the sixteenth Adhyâya of the Vâgasaneyi Samhitâ. Either that whole Adhyâya or the first and last Anuvâka of it is recited.
15. Gobhila III, 6.
9, 1 seqq. Comp. Sânkhâyana III, 11.
2. See above, chap. 8, 15.   3. Sânkhâyana, loc. cit. § 2.
4. Sânkhâyana, § 3. Of course, in Professor Stenzler's translation, 'in der Mitte der Küche' is a misprint for 'in der Mitte der Kühe.'

cows, and having prepared Âgya, he sacrifices six
(oblations) with (the Mantras), ' Here is delight'
(Vâg. Sa*m*h. VIII, 51).

5. With (the verses), ' May Pûshan go after our
cows ; may Pûshan watch over our horses ; may
Pûshan give us strength '—he sacrifices of (the sacrificial food) destined for Pûshan.

6. After murmuring the Rudra hymns they adorn
a one-coloured or a two-coloured (bull) who protects
the herd or whom the herd protects.   Or it should
be red, deficient in no limb, the calf of a cow that
has living calves and is a milk-giver ; and it should
be the finest (bull) in the herd.   And besides they
should adorn the best four young cows of the herd
and let them loose with this (verse), ' This young
(bull) I give you as your husband ; run about sporting with him, your lover.   Do not bring down a
curse upon us, by nature blessed ones.   May we
rejoice in increase of wealth and in comfort.'

7. When (the bull) stands in the midst of the
cows, he recites over it (the texts beginning with)
' Bringing refreshment,' down to the end of the
Anuvâka (Vâg. Sa*m*h. XVIII, 45–50).

8. With the milk of all (the cows) he should cook
milk-rice and give it to the Brâhma*n*as to eat.

---

5. Rig-veda VI, 54, 5 ; *S*ânkhâyana, § 5.

6. *S*ânkhâyana, §§ 6–14.   On the Rudra hymns, see above,
chap. 8, § 13.   Perhaps the words mâ na*h* *s*âpta are corrupt;
the correct reading may possibly be, mâ *s*vasthâta.

7. *S*ânkhâyana, § 15.   There is no Mantra in the Vâgasaneyi
Sa*m*hitâ beginning with the word mayobhû*h*, but this word occurs
in the middle of XVIII, 45 a ; the texts which he recites begin at
that word and extend down to the end of the Anuvâka.   It is clear
that mayobhû*h* was intended in the original text, from which both
*S*ânkhâyana and Pâraskara have taken this Sûtra, as the *R*i'k-
Pratika, Rig-veda X, 169, 1.

9. Some also sacrifice an animal.

10. The ritual thereof has been declared by the (ritual for the) spit-ox.

KANDIKÂ 10.

1. Now the water libations (which are performed for deceased persons).

2. When (a child) that has not reached the age of two years dies, his father and mother become impure.

3. The other (relations) remain pure.

4. (The impurity lasts) through one night or three nights.

5. They bury the body without burning it.

6. If (a child dies) during the impurity of his mother (caused by the child's birth), the impurity lasts till the (mother's) getting up (from child-bed), in the same way as the impurity caused by a child's birth.

7. In this case (of the child being younger than two years) no water libations (are performed).

8. If a child of more than two years dies, all his relations should follow (the corpse) to the cemetery—

9. Singing the Yama song and murmuring the Yama hymn, according to some (teachers).

10. If (the dead person) has received the initiation,

---

9. According to the commentators, a goat is sacrificed.

10. See chap. 8.

10, 2. Manu V, 68; Yâgñavalkya III, 1.

7. Manu V, 68; Yâgñavalkya III, 1.

9. The Yama song is stated to be the second verse of Taittirîya Âranyaka VI, 5, 3 ('He who day by day leads away cows, horses, men, and everything that moves, Vivasvat's son Yama is insatiable of the five human tribes'); the Yama hymn is Rig-veda X, 14. Comp. Yâgñavalkya III, 2.

10. The bhûmigoshana (election of the site for the Smasâna) is

(the rites) from the election of the site (for the *Smasâna*) down to their descending into water (in order to bathe themselves) are the same as those prescribed for persons who have set up the (sacred *Srauta*) fires.

11. They burn him with his (sacred) domestic fire, if he has kept that;

12. Silently, with a common fire, other persons.

13. They should ask one who is related (to the deceased person) by blood or by marriage, for (his permission to perform) the water-libation, in the words, 'We shall perform the libation.'

14. (He replies), 'Do so now and never again,' if the deceased person was not a hundred years old.

15. (He says) only, 'Do so,' if he was.

16. All relations (of the deceased), to the seventh or to the tenth degree, descend into water.

17. If dwelling in the same village, (all) as far as they can trace their relationship.

18. They wear (only) one garment, and have the sacred cord suspended over the right shoulder.

19. With the fourth finger of the left hand they spirt away (the water) with (the words), 'May he drive evil away from us with his splendour' (Vâg. Sa*m*h. XXXV, 6).

20. Facing the south, they plunge (into the water).

21. They pour out with joined hands one libation of water to the deceased person with (the words), 'N. N.! This water to thee!'

22. When they have come out (of the water) and

---

treated of in *Satapatha Brâhma*n*a* XIII, 8, 1, 6 seqq.; Kâtyâyana *Srauta*-sûtra XXI, 3, 15 seqq. On the bath taken after the ceremony, see *Satapatha* Brâhma*n*a XIII, 8, 4, 5; Kâtyâyana XXI, 4, 24.

16. Yâg*ñ*avalkya III, 3.

22. Yâg*ñ*avalkya III, 7: apavadeyus tân itihâsai*h* purâtanai*h*.

have sat down on a pure spot that is covered with grass, (those who are versed in ancient tales) should entertain them (by telling such tales).

23. They return to the village without looking back, in one row, the youngest walking in front.

24. In the doors of their houses they chew leaves of the Pikumanda (or Nimba) tree, sip water, touch water, fire, cowdung, white mustard seeds, and oil, tread upon a stone, and then they enter.

25. Through a period of three nights they should remain chaste, sleep on the ground, do no work and charge nobody (to do it for them).

26. Let them eat food which they have bought or received (from others); (they should eat it) only in the day-time, (and should eat) no meat.

27. Having offered to the deceased person the Pinda, naming his name at the washing, at the offering (of the Pinda), and at the second washing—

28. They should that night put milk and water in an earthen vessel into the open air with (the words), ' Deceased one, bathe here !'

29. The impurity caused by death lasts through three nights;

30. Through ten nights, according to some (teachers).

31. (During that period they) should not perform Svâdhyâya (or study the Vedic texts for themselves).

23. Yâgñavalkya III, 12.
24. Yâgñavalkya III, 12. 13.
25. 26. Yâgñavalkya III, 16; Manu V, 73; Vasishtha IV. 15.
27. See on the washing and on the offering of the Pinda, Kâtyâyana-Srauta-sûtra IV, 1, 10. 11. Comp. Weber, Indische Studien, X, 82.
28. Yâgñavalkya III, 17.
29. 30. Yâgñavalkya III, 18; Manu V, 59.

32. They should intermit the standing rites, except those performed with the three (*S*rauta) fires,

33. And (with the exception of those performed) with the (sacred) domestic fire, according to some (teachers).

34. Others should perform (those rites for them).

35. Those who have touched the dead body should not enter the village until the stars appear.

36. If (they have touched it) in the night-time, (they should not enter) till sunrise.

37. The entering and what follows after it is the same (for these persons) as for the others.

38. (Their) impurity lasts through one or two fortnights.

39. The same (rites should be performed) when the teacher (has died),

40. Or the maternal grandfather or grandmother,

41. Or unmarried females.

42. For those who were married, the others should do it,

43. And they for the (others).

44. If one dies while being absent on a journey, (his relations) shall sit (on the ground, as prescribed for impure persons) from the time when they have heard (of his death), performing the water libation

37. The position of this Sûtra after 35, 36 seems to me to indicate that it refers to those who have touched the dead body; comp. Yâg*ñ*avalkya III, 14 : prave*s*anâdika*m* karma pretasa*m*spar*s*inâm api. I believe that the same persons are concerned also in Sûtra 38.

42. I.e. the husband and his relatives. Comp. Vasish*th*a IV, 19.

43. A married female should perform the rites for her husband and his relatives. See Professor Bühler's note on Vasish*th*a IV, 19; S. B. E., XIV, 28.

44. Yâg*ñ*avalkya III, 21; Manu V, 75, 76. Comp. Gautama XIV, 37; Vasish*th*a IV, 14.

(at that time), until the period (of their impurity) has expired;

45. If (that period has already) elapsed, through one night or three nights.

46. Optional is the water libation for an officiating priest, a father-in-law, a friend, for (distant) relations, for a maternal uncle, and for a sister's son;

47. And for married females.

48. On the eleventh day he should give to an uneven number of Brâhmanas a meal at which meat is served.

49. Some also kill a cow in honour of the deceased person.

50. When the Pindas are prepared, the deceased person, if he has sons, shall be considered as the first of the (three) Fathers (to whom Pindas are offered).

51. The fourth one should be left out.

52. Some (make Pinda offerings to a deceased person) separately through one year (before admitting him to a share in the common Pitriyagña).

53. But there is a rule, 'There can be no fourth Pinda'—for this is stated in the Sruti.

54. Every day he shall give food to him (i.e. to the deceased person), and if he was a Brâhmana, a vessel with water.

55. Some offer also a Pinda.

---

47. See above, § 42.

51. See Sânkhâyana-Grihya IV, 2, 8.

52. Sânkhâyana-Grihya VIII, 2. Comp. the description of the Sapindikarana, ibid., chap. 3.

53. There would be four Pindas, if one were to be offered to the recently deceased person, and three others to those Fathers who had received Pinda offerings before his death. Therefore one of these three Fathers is omitted; see § 51.

54. Comp. Âpastamba I, 13, 1; Baudhâyana II, 11. 3.

KANDIKÂ 11.

1. If an animal (is to be sacrificed), let him wash it, if it is not a cow; let him walk round the fires and drive in front (of them) a Palâsa branch into the ground.

2. The winding (of a Kusa rope) round (that branch), the touching (of the animal with the grass-blade), the binding (of it to the branch), and the sprinkling (of the animal with water) should be performed in the way prescribed (in the Srauta-sûtra), and whatever else (is to be done).

3. After he has sacrificed the two oblations before and after the killing of the animal, (he) silently (sacrifices) five other (oblations, directed to Pragâpati).

4. And the omentum is taken out (of the killed animal). He should besprinkle it (with water) and name the deity (to whom the sacrifice is directed).

5. (He should name that deity also) at the touching (of the animal with the grass-blade), at (its) being bound (to the branch), at its being sprinkled (with water), and at (the preparation and oblation) of the mess of cooked food.

6. After he has sacrificed the omentum, he cuts off the Avadâna portions,

---

11, 1. The branch replaces the sacrificial post (yûpa) of the Srauta ritual. As to agrena, comp. Kâty.-Sraut. VI, 2, 11 and the commentary.

2. See Kâty.-Sraut.VI, 3, 15 on the parivyayana, ibid. §§ 19, 26 on the upâkarana, § 27 on the niyogana, § 33 on the prokshana.

3. Kâtyâyana VI, 5, 22 : He sacrifices (Âgya) with the words, 'Svâhâ to the gods.' § 24 : He sacrifices (Âgya) with the words, 'To the gods svâhâ.' In the commentary on § 25 these two oblations are called paripasavyâhutî.

4. See Kâtyâyana VI, 6, 13 ; Âsvalâyana-Grihya I, 11, 10.

5. See above, Sûtra 2.

7. All of them, or three, or five.

8. He sacrifices the Avadâna portions together with the mess of cooked food.

9. A limb of the animal is the sacrificial fee.

10. At (a sacrifice) directed to a special deity he should sacrifice (an animal) belonging to that deity, should make a portion for that (god), and should say to him (i.e. to the messenger who is to convey that offering to a place sacred to that deity) : ' Take care that this may reach that (god).'

11. If there is a river between (the sacrificer and that sacred place), he may have a boat made, or he may dispense with this.

KANDIKÂ 12.

1. Now (follows) the penance for a student who has broken the vow of chastity.

2. On a new-moon day he shall sacrifice an ass on a cross-road (to the goddess Nirriti).

3. (And) he shall offer a mess of cooked food to Nirriti.

4. The Avadâna portions are sacrificed into water (and not into fire).

---

7. The complete number of the Avadânas (i.e. the portions of the killed animal which have to be cut off, such as the heart, the tongue, &c.) is eleven; see Kâty.-Sraut. VI, 7, 6; Âsvalâyana-Grihya I, 11, 12.

8. Âsvalâyana-Grihya, loc. cit. § 13.

10,11. The way for interpreting these Sûtras is shown by Âsvalâyana-Grihya I, 12. I do not think that they have anything to do, as Gayarâma states, with reference to Sûtra 11, with the offering due to a relative who has died while being absent on a journey (chap. 10, 44).

12, 1. See the parallel passages quoted by Professor Bühler in his note on Âpastamba I, 26, 8 (S. B. E., II, 85), and besides, Kâtyâyana I, 1, 13 seqq.; Gautama XXIII, 17 seqq., &c.

4. This Sûtra is identical with Kâtyâyana I, 1, 16.

5. The Puro*d*âsa (or sacrificial cake), which belongs to the animal sacrifice, is cooked on the ground (and not in the Kapâlas).

6. (The guilty person) should put on the skin (of the ass),

7. With the tail turned upwards, according to some (teachers).

8. He should through one year go about for alms, proclaiming his deed.

9. After that time he sacrifices two Âg*y*a oblations with (the formulas), 'O Lust, I have broken my vow of chastity. I have broken my vow of chastity, O Lust. To Lust svâhâ!'—'O Lust, I have done evil. I have done evil, O Lust. To Lust svâhâ!'

10. He then approaches (the fire) with (the verse), 'May the Maruts besprinkle me, may Indra, may Br*i*haspati, may this Agni besprinkle me with offspring and with wealth.'

11. This is the penance.

KA*N*DIKÂ 13.

1. Now the entering of a court of justice.

2. He approaches the court with (the words), 'Court! Thou that belongest to the Angiras! Trouble art thou by name; vehemence art thou by name. Thus be adoration to thee!'

3. He then enters (the court) with (the words), '(May) the court and the assembly, the two unani-

---

5. This Sûtra is identical with Kâtyâyana I, 1, 15.

9. Baudhâyana II, 1, 34.   10. Baudhâyana II, 1, 35.

13, 2. The regular Sandhi would be sabha (for sabhe)ângirasi, instead of which the text has sabhângirasi.

3. In Sanskrit the words sabhâ (court) and samiti (assembly) are of feminine gender. I have translated upa mâ sa tish*th*et in the sense indicated by Pâ*n*ini I, 4, 87.

mous daughters of Pragâpati (protect me). May one who does not know me, be below me. May (all) people be considerate in what they say.'

4. When he has arrived at the assembly, he should murmur, 'Superior (to my adversaries) I have come hither, brilliant, not to be contradicted. The lord of this assembly is a man insuperable in his power.'

5. Should he think, 'This person is angry with me,' he addresses him with (the verses), 'The destroying power of wrath and anger that dwells here on thy forehead, that the chaste, wise gods may take away.

'Heaven am I and I am Earth; we both take away thy anger; the she-mule cannot bring forth offspring; N. N.!'

6. But if he should think, 'This person will do evil to me,' he addresses him with (the words), ' I take away the speech in thy mouth, I take away (the speech) in thy heart. Wheresoever thy speech dwells, thence I take it away. What I say, is true. Fall down, inferior to me.'

7. The same is the way to make (a person) subject (to one's self).

KANDIKÂ 14.

1. Now the mounting of a chariot (is declared).

2. After he has given the order, ' Put the horses to it,' and it has been announced, ' They are,' he goes to (the chariot, saying), ' This is the Virâg,' and touches the two wheels,

---

5. Perhaps we should read garbhenâsvataryâh saha : we take away thy anger together with the offspring of the she-mule (that cannot foal). Comp. Kullavagga VII, 2, 5; S. B. E., XX, 238.

6. It is impossible to give a sure restoration of this corrupt Mantra. Perhaps we should read something like this: â te vâkam âsya â te hridaya âdade. Comp. Hirany.-Grihya I, 4, 15, 6.

3. The right (wheel) with (the words), ' The Rathantara art thou '—

4. The left with (the words), ' The Br*i*hat art thou '—

5. The pole with (the words), ' The Vâmadevya art thou.'

6. He touches the interior of the chariot with his hand (saying), ' The two Aṅkas, the two Nyaṅkas which are on both sides of the chariot, which move forward with the rushing wind, the far-darting one with keen senses, the winged one, may these fires, the promoters, promote us.'

7. With (the words), ' Adoration to Mâ*ni*kara,' he drives on the beast on the right side.

8. (If going in his chariot) toward (images of) gods, let him descend (from the chariot) before he has reached them; if toward Brâhma*n*as, just before (reaching them); if toward cows, when amid them; if toward fathers, when he has reached them.

9. A woman or a Vedic student shall not be charioteers.

14, 6. The meaning of aṅkau and nyaṅkau cannot be determined, as far as I can see. The commentators explain the words as the two wheels and the two sides of the chariot, or as the two right wheels and the two left wheels of a four-wheeled chariot. Professor Zimmer (Altindisches Leben, pp. 251 seq.) compares aṅka with ἄντυξ, and says, 'Mit aṅkau (resp. aṅkû) wäre daher die obere Einfassung des Wagenkastens (ko*s*a, vandhura) bezeichnet, mit nyaṅkau (resp. nyaṅkû) ein zu grösserer Befestigung etwas weiter unten (ni) herumlaufender Stab.' To me it seems that aṅkau and nyaṅkau are to be understood both as designations of certain parts of the chariot and as names of different forms of Agni dwelling in the chariot.—Comp. Taittirîya Sa*m*hitâ I, 7, 7, 2; Pañka-vi*m*sa Brâhma*n*a I, 7, 5.

7. The name of the demon Mâ*ni*kara occurs, as far as I know, only here.

10. Having driven a moment beyond (the point to which he intends to go) he should murmur, ' Here is rest, rest here' (Vâg. Samh. VIII, 51).

11. Some add (the words), ' Here shall be no rest.'

12. If the chariot is weak, he should murmur, after he has mounted it, ' May this your chariot, O Asvins, suffer no damage on bad ways or by being over-thrown.'

13. If the horses run away with the chariot, he should touch the post (?) or the earth and should murmur, ' May this your chariot, O Asvins, suffer no damage on bad ways or by being overthrown.'

14. Thus he will suffer no harm and no damage.

15. When he has finished his way, and has un-yoked the horses, let him have grass and water given to them. ' For thus satisfaction is given to the beast that draws (the cart) '—says the Sruti.

KANDIKÂ 15.

1. Now how he should mount an elephant.

2. He goes to the elephant and touches it (saying), ' The elephants' glory art thou. The elephants' honour art thou.'

3. He then mounts it with (the words), ' With Indra's thunder-bolt I bestride thee. Make me arrive safely.'

4. Thereby it has also been declared how he should mount a horse.

---

11. If the reading of the text is correct, the meaning would seem to be : We will rest here for a while, but then we will go further.

13. I cannot say what 'the post' (stambha) here means; it may be a part of the chariot. Gayarâma has dhvagastambha, i.e. the staff of a flag, which we are to suppose was carried on the chariot. This may be the right explanation.

15. Satapatha Brâhmana I, 8, 2, 9.

5. When he is going to mount a camel, he addresses it : ' Thou art the son of Tvash*tri* ; Tvash*tri* is thy deity. Make me arrive safely.'

6. When he is going to mount a he-ass, he addresses it: 'A *Sûdra* art thou, a *Sûdra* by birth. To Agni thou belongest, with twofold sperm. Make me arrive safely.'

7. A path he addresses : 'Adoration to Rudra who dwells on the paths. Make me arrive safely.'

8. A cross-road he addresses : 'Adoration to Rudra who dwells at the cross-roads. Make me arrive safely.'

9. When he intends to swim across a river, he addresses it : 'Adoration to Rudra who dwells in the waters. Make me arrive safely.'

10. When going on board a ship, he addresses her : ' The good ship ' (Vâg. Sa*m*h. XXI, 7).

11. When going to cross (the river), he addresses (the ship) : ' The well-protecting ' (Vâg. Sa*m*h. XXI, 6).

12. A forest (through which he is wandering) he addresses : ' Adoration to Rudra who dwells in the forests. Make me arrive safely.'

13. A mountain (which he is going to cross) he addresses : ' Adoration to Rudra who dwells on the mountains. Make me arrive safely.'

14. A burial-ground he addresses : ' Adoration to Rudra who dwells among the Fathers. Make me arrive safely.'

15. A cow-stable he addresses : ' Adoration to Rudra who dwells among the dung-heaps. Make me arrive safely.'

---

6. The he-ass has twofold sperm, because he begets both asses and mules. Taittirîya Sa*m*hitâ VII, 1, 1, 2.

16. And wheresoever else it be, let him always say, 'Adoration to Rudra.' For the Sruti says, 'Rudra is this universe.'

17. If the skirt (of his garment) is blown upon him (by the wind), he addresses (that skirt): 'A skirt art thou. Thou art not a thunder-bolt. Adoration be to thee. Do no harm to me!'

18. The thunder he addresses: 'May the rains be friendly to us; may (Indra's) darts be friendly to us—may they be friendly to us which thou throwest, O killer of Vritra.'

19. A howling jackal he addresses: 'Friendly by name' (Vâg. Samh. III, 63).

20. A shrieking bird he addresses: 'Golden-winged bird who goest where the gods send thee! Messenger of Yama, adoration be to thee! What has the Kârkârina told thee?'

21. A tree that serves as a mark (of a boundary, &c.), he addresses: 'May neither the flash of lightning (destroy thee), nor axe nor wind nor punishment which the king sends. May thy shoots grow up; may rain fall on thee, in safety from the wind. May fire not destroy thy root. Blessing on thee, O lord of the forest! Blessing on me, O lord of the forest!'

22. If he receives something (given to him), he accepts it with (the formula), 'May Heaven give thee; may the Earth accept thee.' Thus (the thing given) does not decrease to him who gives it, and what he receives increases.

---

19. The play on words is untranslatable; 'jackal' is sivâ, 'friendly,' sivah.

20. I do not know the meaning of kârkârinah. Gayarâma takes it for a genitive standing instead of an accusative, and explains it by asmadbâdhakam.

23. If boiled rice is given to him, he accepts it with (the formula), 'May Heaven, &c.,' and he partakes thereof twice with (the formulas), 'May Brahman eat thee!'—'May Brahman partake of thee!'

24. If gruel is given to him, (as above) . . . . three times with (the formulas), 'May Brahman eat thee!'—'May Brahman partake of thee!'—'May Brahman drink thee!'

K*a*ndikâ 16.

1. Now each time after a lesson (of the Veda) is finished, in order to prevent his forgetting (the texts he has studied, the following prayer should be recited) :

'May my mouth be skilful ; my tongue be honey-sweet speech. With my ears I have heard much ; do not take away that which I have heard, which dwells in me.

'The Brahman's word art thou ; the Brahman's stand art thou ; the Brahman's store-house art thou. Fulfilment art thou ; peace art thou ; unforgetfulness art thou ; enter into my store-house of the Brahman. With the voice I cover thee! With the voice I cover thee! May I be able to form the vowels, to produce, to hold fast and to utter the guttural, pectoral, dental, and labial sounds. May my limbs grow strong, my voice, breath, eye, ear, honour, and power. What I have heard and studied, may that be fixed in my mind ; may that be fixed in my mind.'

End of the Third Kâ*nd*a.

End of Pâraskara's G*r*ihya-sûtra.

16, 1. As to anirâkara*n*a, comp. anirâkarish*n*u above, II, 4, 3. Possibly we should read, *g*ihvâ me madhumad va*k*a*h*.

KHÂDIRA-GRIHYA-SÛTRA.

B b

KHÂDIRA-GR/HYA-SÛTRA.

Among the Grantha MSS. collected by the late Dr.
Burnell and now belonging to the India Office Library,
there are some MSS. (numbers CLXXII and following
of the Catalogue) of a Gr/hya-sûtra hitherto unpublished,
which is ascribed to Khâdirâ*k*ârya. It belongs to the
Drâhyâya*n*a school of the Sâma-veda, which prevails in
the south of the Indian peninsula[1], and it is based on
the Gobhilîya-sûtra, from which it has taken the greater
number of its aphorisms, just as the Drâhyâya*n*a-*S*rauta-
sûtra, as far as we can judge at present, is nothing but a
slightly altered redaction of Lâ*t*yâyana[2]. Like the Gobhila-
Gr/hya it very seldom gives the Mantras in their full extent, but quotes them only with their Pratîkas, and it is
easy to identify these quotations in the Mantrabrâhma*n*a
(published at Calcutta, 1873), which contains the texts
prescribed by Gobhila for the Gr/hya ceremonies.

The Khâdira-Gr/hya has evidently been composed with
the intention of abridging Gobhila's very detailed and
somewhat lengthy treatise on the domestic rites. Digres-
sions, such as, for instance, that introduced by the words
tatraihad âhu*h*, Gobhila I, 2, 10–27, or such as Gobhila's
explication of the terms paur*n*amâsî and amâvâsyâ,
I, 5, 7 seqq., or most of the regulations concerning the
*S*akvaryas, III, 3, or the *S*lokas, IV, 7, are invariably left

---

[1] See Dr. Burnell's Catalogue, p. 56.

[2] Weber, Vorlesungen über indische Literaturgeschichte (2nd edition), p. 87:
'Almost the entire difference between this Sûtra and that of Lâ*t*yâyana lies in
the arrangement of the matter treated of, which is in itself very nearly the same
in both texts, and is expressed in the same words.' Comp. Ânanda*k*andra
Vedântavâgîsa's Introduction to his edition of Lâ*t*yâyana (in the Bibliotheca
Indica), pp. 2, 3, and his statements on Drâhyâya*n*a in the notes of that edition.

out, and in the descriptions of the single ceremonies
throughout the principal points only are given, with the
omission of all words and of all matter that it seemed
possible to dispense with. On the other hand, the arrangement of the Sûtras has undergone frequent changes, in
which the compiler clearly shows his intention of grouping
together, more carefully than was done in the original text,
the Sûtras which naturally belong to each other. Of the
Sûtras of the Khâdira-Gr*i*hya which cannot be identified in
Gobhila, several are to be traced back to Lâ*t*yâyana, or we
should perhaps rather say, to Drâhyâya*n*a. Thus Khâd.
I, 1, 14 mantrântam avyakta*m* parasyâdigraha-
*n*ena vidyât evidently corresponds to Lâ*t*yâyana I, 1, 3,
uttarâdi*h* pûrvântalakshana*n*am, and Khâd. I, 1, 24
avyâv*r*itti*m* yag*ñ*âṅgair avyavâya*m* *k*e*kk*et is
identical with Lâ*t*y. I, 2, 15, avyavâyo·vyâv*r*ittis *k*a
yag*ñ*âṅgai*h*.

Upon the whole, though certainly the Khâdira-Gr*i*hya
does not contain much matter which is not known to us
from other sources, it notwithstanding possesses a certain
interest, since it shows by a very clear example how a
Sûtrakâra of the later time would remodel the work of a
more ancient author, trying to surpass him by a more
correct arrangement, and especially by what became more
and more appreciated as the chief accomplishment of Sûtra
composition, the greatest possible succinctness and econo-
mising of words. To an interpreter of Gobhila the comparison of the Khâdira-Gr*i*hya no doubt will suggest in
many instances a more correct understanding of his text
than he would have been likely to arrive at without that
aid, and perhaps even readings of Gobhila which seemed
hitherto subject to no doubt, will have to give way to
readings supplied by the Grantha MSS. of the Khâdira-
Gr*i*hya. Thus, Gobhila III, 8, 16, I do not hesitate to
correct asa*m*svâdam, on the authority of Khâd. III, 3.
13, into asa*m*khâdam or asa*m*khâdan[1].

---

[1] Comp. Pâraskara II, 10, 15, and the quotations given by Böhtlingk-Roth
s. v. sa*m*-khâd. Forms derived from the two roots, khâd and svad, are frequently interchanged in the MSS.; see the two articles in the Dictionary.

As the text of the Khâdira-Gr*i*hya is very short and has not yet been published, it has been printed at the foot of the page, together with references to the parallel passages of Gobhila. For further explanations of the single Sûtras, I refer to my translation of Gobhila which will form part of the second volume of the Gr*i*hya-sûtras, where I shall also hope to give some extracts from Rudraskanda's commentary on the Khâdira-Gr*i*hya.

KHÂDIRA-GR*I*HYA-SÛTRA.

Patala I, Khanda 1.

1. Now henceforth the domestic sacrifices (will be explained).

2. During the northern course of the sun, at the time of the increasing moon, on auspicious days, before noon: this is the time at which the constellations are lucky, unless a special statement is given.

3. At the end (of the ceremonies) he should give to the Brâhma*n*as to eat according to his ability.

4. The sacrificial cord is made of a string or of Ku*s*a grass.

5. If he suspends it round his neck and raises the right arm (so as to wear the cord on his left shoulder), he becomes yag*n*opavîtin.

6. (If he raises) the left (arm and wears the cord on his right shoulder, he becomes) prâ*k*inâvîtin.

7. After having sipped water three times, let him wipe off the water twice.

I, 1, 1. athâto gr*i*hyâkarmâ*n*y. 2. udagayanapûrvapakshapu-*n*yâheshu prâg âvartanâd anubha*h* kâlo*s*nâde*s*e. 3. *s*pavarge ya-thotsâha*m* brâhma*n*ân â*s*ayed. 4. yag*n*opavîta*m* sautra*m* kau*s*a*m* vâ. 5. grîvâyâm pratimu*k*ya dakshi*n*a*m* bâhum uddh*r*itya yag*n*opavîtî bhavati. 6. savya*m* prâ*k*inâvîtî. 7. trir â*k*amyâpo dvi*h* parim*r*igîta.

I, 1, 1 = Gobhila I, 1, 1. 2 = I, 1, 3. 3 = I, 1, 6. 4–6 = I, 2, 1 seqq. 7–10 = I, 2, 5 seqq.

8. Having besprinkled his feet (with water), let him besprinkle his head.

9. Let him touch the organs of his senses (i.e. his eyes, his nose, and his ears) with water (i. e. with a wet hand).

10. When he has finally touched (water) again, he becomes pure.

11. (If) sitting, standing, or lying down (is prescribed), he should understand (that it is to be done) on northward-pointed Darbha grass, with the face turned to the east, to the west of the fire with which the sacrifice is performed.

12. If the word Snâna (or bathing) is used, (this refers to the whole body) with the head.

13. (The different ceremonies are) performed with the right hand, if no special rule is given.

14. If it is not clear where a Mantra ends, one should discern it by (adverting to) the beginning of the next Mantra.

15. The Mantras have the word svâhâ at their end, when offerings are made.

16. The term Pâkayag̃a is used of every sacrifice that is performed with one fire.

17. There the Brahman is (present as) officiating priest, with the exception of the morning and evening oblations.

8. pâdâv abhyukshya siro·bhyukshed. 9. indriyâny adbhih samsprísed. 10. antatah pratyupasprísya sukir bhavaty. 11. âsanasthânasamvesanâny udagagreshu darbheshu prânmukhasya pratiyât paskâd agner yatra homa syât. 12. sahasirasam snânasabde. 13. dakshinena pânina krityam anâdese. 14. mantrântam avyaktam parasyâdigrahanena vidyât. 15. svâhântâ mantrâ homeshu. 16. pâkayag̃a ityâkhya yah kas kaikâgnau. 17. tatra rítvig brahmâ sâyamprâtarhomavargam.

11-14 desunt. 15=I, 9, 25. 16 deest. 17, 18=I. 9, 8. 9.

18. The Hotri's place is filled by (the sacrificer) himself.

19. To the south of the fire the Brahman sits facing the north, silently, until the oblation has been performed, on eastward-pointed (Darbha grass).

20. But if he likes, he may speak of what refers to the sacrifice.

21. Or if he has spoken (words) which are unworthy of the sacrifice, let him murmur the Mahâvyâhritis,

22. Or (the verse), ʻ Thus has Vishnu ' (Sv. I, 222).

23. If he does himself the work both of the Brahman and of the Hotri, let him sit down on the Brahman's seat, and (leave that seat) placing a parasol on it, or an outer garment, or a water-pot, and then let him perform his other duties.

24. Let him take care not to turn his back to, or become separated (by any person or thing interposed) from what belongs to the sacrifice.

KHANDA 2.

1. In the eastern part of his dwelling he should besmear (the place on which the sacrifice will be

---

18. svayamhautram. 19. dakshinato-gner udanmukhas tûshnîm âste brahmâ homât prâgagreshu. 20. kâmam tv adhiyagñam vyâhared. 21. ayagñiyâm vâ vyâhritya mahâvyâhritîr gaped. 22. idam vishnur ita vâ. 23. hautrabrahmatve svayam kurvan brahmâsanam [sic] upavisya khattram uttarâsangam kamandalum vâ tatra kritvâthânyat kuryâd. 24. avyâvritim yagñângair avyavâyam kekhet.

2, 1. pûrve bhâge vesmano gomayenopalipya tasya madhyadese lakshanam kuryâd.

19=I, 6, 13 seqq. 20–22=I, 6, 17 seqq. 23=I, 6, 21. 24 deest.
2, 1 seqq.=Gobhila I, 1, 9 seqq.

performed) with cowdung, and should draw in the middle of it the lines.

2. To the south he should draw a line from west to east.

3. From the beginning of that line (he should draw a line) from south to north ; from the end (of the last-mentioned line) one from west to east; between (the first and the third line) three (lines) from west to east.

4. He besprinkles that (place) with water,

5. Establishes the fire (thereon),

6. Wipes along around (the fire) with the three verses, ' This praise ' (MB. II, 4, 2–4).

7. To the west of the fire he touches the earth with his two hands turned downwards, with (the verse), ' We partake of the earth's ' (MB. II, 4, 1).

8. In night-time (he pronounces that Mantra so that it ends with the word) ' goods' (vasu).

9. Having strewn Darbha grass to the west (of the fire), let him draw (some grass) from the south-end and from the north-end (of what he has strewn), in an eastern direction.

10. Or let him omit this drawing (of Darbha grass to the east),

11. And let him strew (the grass) beginning in the east, so as to keep his right side turned to the

---

2. dakshi*n*ata*h* prâ*k*i*m* rekhâm ullikhya. 3. tadârambhâd udi*k*i*m* tadavasânât prâ*k*i*m* tisro madhye prâ*k*îs. 4. tad abhyukshyâ. 5. ♦gnim upasamâdhâya. 6. ima*m* stomam iti parisamûhya t*r*i*k*ena. 7. pa*sk*âd agner bhûmau nya*ñk*au pâ*n*î k*r*itvedam bhûmer iti. 8. vasvanta*m* râtrau. 9. pa*sk*âd darbhân âstirya dakshi*n*ata*h* prâ*k*i*m* prakarshed uttarata*s k*â. 10. ♦prak*r*ishya vâ. 11. pûrvopakra-ma*m* pradakshi*n*am agni*m* st*r*i*n*uyân mûlâny agrai*s k*hâdayan tri-v*r*ita*m* pa*ñk*av*r*ita*m* vo.

6–8 = IV, 5, 3 seqq. 9–11 = I, 7, 9 seqq.

fire, covering the roots (of the Darbha blades) with the points, in three layers or in five layers.

12. Sitting down he cuts off two span-long Darbha points, not with his nail, with (the words), ' Purifiers are ye, sacred to Vish*n*u.'

13. He wipes them with water, with (the words), ' By Vish*n*u's mind are ye purified.'

14. Holding them with his two thumbs and fourth fingers so that their points are turned to the north, he three times purifies the Â*g*ya (with them), with (the words), ' May the god Savit*ri* purify thee with this uninjured purifier, with the rays of the good sun.'

15. Having sprinkled them (with water) he should throw them into the fire.

16. Having put the Â*g*ya on the fire he should take it (from the fire) towards the north.

17. Bending his right knee he should pour out to the south of the fire his joined hands full of water with (the words), 'Aditi! Give thy consent!'

18. To the west with (the words), 'Anumati! Give thy consent!'

19. To the north with (the words), ' Sarasvatî! Give thy consent!'

12. ⸱pavi*s*ya darbhâgre prâde*s*amâtre pra*kh*inatti na nakhena pavitre stho vaish*n*avyâv ity. 13. adbhir unm*ri*gya Vish*n*or manasâ pûte stha ity. 14. udagagre ⸱ngush*th*âbhyâm anâmikâbhyâ*m* *k*a sa*m*gr*ih*ya trir â*g*yam utpunâti devas tvâ Savitotpunâtv a*kh*idre*n*a pavitre*n*a vasos sûryasya ra*s*mibhir ity. 15. abhyu-kshyâgnâv anuprahared. 16. â*g*yam adhi*s*rityottarata*h* kuryâd. 17. daksh*in*agânvakto dakshi*n*enâgnim Adite ⸱numanyasvety udakâ*ñ*gali*m* prasi*ñk*ed. 18. Anumate ⸱numanyasveti pa*sk*ât. 19. Sarasvate [sic, comp. Hira*n*yakesi-Gr*ih*ya I, 1, 2, 9] ⸱numanya-svety uttarata*h*.

12–16=I, 7, 21–27. 17–21=I, 3, 1 seqq.

20. With (the words), 'God Savit*ri*! Give thy
impulse!' (MB. I, 1, 1) he should sprinkle (water)
round the fire so as to keep his right side turned
towards it, encompassing what he is going to offer
(with the water).

21. (This he does) once or thrice.

22. He puts a piece of wood on (the fire).

23. He should murmur the Prapada formula
(MB. II, 4, 5), hold his breath, fix his thoughts on
something good, and should emit his breath when
beginning the Virûpâksha formula (MB. II, 4, 6).

24. At ceremonies for the attainment of special
wishes (he should do so) for each of the objects
(which he wishes to attain). ●

25. He should do so always at sacrifices.

KHANDA 3.

1. A student after he has studied the Veda and
has offered a present to his teacher, should, with
permission (of his parents), take a wife.

2. And (he should take) the bath (which signifies
the end of studentship).

3. Of these two (acts the taking of) the bath
comes first.

20. deva Savita*h* prasuveti pradakshi*n*am agni*m* paryukshed
abhipariharan havya*m*. 21. sak*ri*t trir vâ. 22. samidham âdhâya.
23. prapada*m* *g*apitvopatâmya kalyâ*n*am dhyâyan vairûpâksham
ârabhyo*kkh*vaset. 24. pratikâma*m* kâmyeshu. 25. sarvatraitad
dhomeshu kuryât.

3, 1. brahma*k*ârî vedam adhîtyopanyâhr*it*ya gurave *nu*gñ*âto dârân
kurvitâ. 2. *plavana*n* *k*a. 3. tayor âplavana*m* pûrva*m*.

22=I, 8, 26. 23=IV, 5, 6 seqq. 24, 25 desunt. 3, 1=Gobhila III, 4, 1. 2=III, 4, 7. 3, 4 desunt.

4. As, however, in the (collection of) Mantras
marriage is treated of (first), it is explained (here)
before (the bath).

5. A Brâhmana with a water-pot, wrapped in his
robe, keeping silence, should step in front of the
fire and should station himself (to the south of it)
with his face to the north.

6. After (the bride) has taken a bath, (the bridegroom) should dress her in a garment that has not
yet been washed, with (the verse), 'They who spun'
(MB. I, 1, 5). While she is led up (to him), the
bridegroom should murmur (the verse), 'Soma gave
her' (l. l. 7).

♦ 7. To the south of the bridegroom he (who has
led her to him) should make her sit down.

8. While she touches him, (the bridegroom) should
make oblations of Âgya with the Sruva, picking
out (portions of it [comp. Pâraskara II, 14, 13]),
with the Mahâvyâhritis.

9. A fourth (oblation) with (the three Mahâvyâhritis) together.

10. The same at the ceremonies of the tonsure
(of the child's head), of the initiation (of the Brahmakârin), and of the cutting of the beard.

---

4. mantrâbhivâdât tu pânigrahanasya (correct, pânigrahanam?)
pûrvam vyâkhyâtam.   5. brâhmanas sahodakumbhah prâvrito
vâgyato · grenâgnim gatvodanmukhas tishthet.   6. snâtâm ahatenâkhâdya yâ akrintann ity ânîyamânâyâm pânigrâho gapet Somo · dadad
iti.   7. pânigrâhasya dakshinata upavesayed.   8. anvârabdhâyâm
sruvenopaghâtam mahâvyâhritibhir âgyam guhuyât.   9. samastâ-
bhis katurthîm.   10. evam kaulopanayanagodâneshv.

5=II, 1, 13.   6=II, 1, 17–19.   7 seqq.=II, 1, 23 seqq.; I, 9,
26 seqq.

11. And at the marriage (he makes oblations) with the six verses, 'May Agni go as the first' (MB. I, 1, 9 seqq.).

12. At Âgya oblations, unless a special rule is given, the two Âgya portions and the Svish/akr*it* oblation (are) not (offered).

13. After (the chief oblations he should) always (make oblations) with the Mahâvyâhr*i*tis,

14. And with the (verse) sacred to Pragâpati.

15. He should make an expiatory oblation.

16. After the sacrifice they both arise.

17. (The bridegroom) should pass behind (the bride's) back, station himself to the south, and seize the bride's hand.

18. Her mother who has, towards the east, put fried grain mixed with *S*amî leaves into a basket,

19. Should make the bride tread with the tip of her right foot on an upper mill-stone, to the west of the fire, with (the verse which the bridegroom repeats), 'On this stone' (MB. I, 2, 1).

20. Her brother, filling once his joined hands

11. Agnir etu prathama iti sha*d*bhi*s* *k*a pâ*n*igraha*n*e. 12. nâgya-bhâgau na svish/akr*i*d âgyâhutishv anâde*s*e. 13. sarvatropari*s*h/ân mahâvyâhr*i*ibhi*h* ¹. 14. prâgâpatyayâ *k*a. 15. prâya*s*kitta*m* gu-huyâd. 16. dhutvopottish/*h*ato. 17. *nupr*i*sh/*h*am gatvâ dakshi-*n*ato·vasthâya vadhva*n*gali*m* gr*i*h*n*îyât. 18. pûrvâ mâtâ samîpalâ-*s*ami*s*rân (var. lect. °mi*s*râl) lâg*â*n *kh*ûrpe kr*i*lvâ. 19. pa*s*kâd agner dr*i*shatputram âkramayed vadhû*m* dakshi*n*ena prapadenemam a*s*-mânam iti. 20. sakr*i*dgr*i*hîtam a*n*gali*m* lâgânâ*m* vadhva*n*galâv âvaped bhrâtâ.

14, 15 desunt. 16–31 = II, 2, 1 seqq.

¹ Possibly the Sûtras 12 and 13 should be divided thus: 12. nâgyabhâgau na svish/akr*i*d âgyâhutishv. 13. anâde*s*e sarvatr° &c. Comp. Gobhila I, 9, 26. 27; *S*ânkhâyana I, 12, 13; 9, 10.

with fried grain, should pour it into the bride's joined hands.

21. Or some friend (instead of the brother).

22. That she should sacrifice over the fire without opening her joined hands with (the verse which the bridegroom repeats), 'This woman' (MB. I, 2, 2).

23. (The verses), 'Aryaman' and 'Pûshan' (l. l. 3, 4) (are repeated) at the two following (oblations of fried grain).

24. After that sacrifice he should go back in the same way (see Sûtra 17), and should lead her round the fire, so that their right sides are turned towards it with (the formula), 'The maid from the fathers' (l. l. 5).

25. (These rites), beginning from his stationing himself (to the south, Sûtra 17), (are performed) thrice.

26. After (she) has poured the remnants (of the fried grain) into the fire, he should make her step forward in a north-eastern direction with (the formula), 'For sap with one step' (l. l. 6, 7).

27. The looking at the lookers-on, the mounting of the chariot, the reciting (of Mantras) at places difficult to pass (on the way of the bridegroom and the bride, is performed) with (verses) suited (to those different occasions).

---

21. suhrid vâ kaskit. 22. tam sâgnau guhuyâd avikhidyâṅgalim iyam nârîty. 23. Aryamanam Pûshanam ity uttarayor. 24. hute tenaiva gatvâ pradakshinam agnim parinayet kanyalâ pitribhya ity. 25. avasthânaprabhrity evam tris. 26. sûrpena sishtân agnâv opya prâgudîkîm utkramayed ekam isha itî. 27. ikshakâvekshanaratârohanadurgânumantranâny abhirûpâbhir.

(21 and a part of 27 desunt.)

28. Walking forward behind the fire, the water-carrier (see Sûtra 5) should besprinkle the bridegroom on his forehead.

29. So also the bride.

30. When he has thus been besprinkled, (he should repeat the verse), 'May (the Viṣve devâs) anoint (or, unite)' (MB. I, 2, 9).

31. He should seize her right hand, together with the thumb, with the six (verses), 'I seize thy hand' (MB. I, 2, 10 seqq.).

KHANDA 4.

1. He should carry her away in a north-eastern direction.

2. In a Brâhmaṇa's house he should establish the (nuptial) fire, should spread out to the west of the fire a red bull's hide with the hair outside and with the neck to the east, and should make her, who has to keep silence, sit down (thereon).

3. When (somebody) has said that a star has appeared, he should, while she touches him, make oblations (of Âgya) with the Sruva, picking out (portions of it), with the six (verses) commencing with (the verse), 'In the lines' (MB. I, 3, 1 seqq.). The remnants he should pour out over the bride's head.

---

28. apareṇâgnim auduko gatvâ pâṇigrâhaṃ mûrdhany avasiṅked.
29. vadhûm ka. 30. samaṅgantv ity avasikto. 31. dakshiṇaṃ pâṇiṃ sâṅgushṭham gṛhṇîyâd gṛbhṇâmi ta iti shaḍbhiḥ.
4, 1. prâgudikîm udvahed. 2. brâhmaṇakule ‹gnim upasamâdhâya paskâd agner lohitaṃ karmânaḍuham uttaraloma prâggrivam âstîrya vâgyatâm upaveṣayet. 3. prokte nakshatre‹nvârabdhâyâṃ sruveṇopaghâtam guhuyât shaḍbhir lekhâprabhṛtibhiḥ sampâtân avanayan mûrdhani vadhvâḥ.

4, 1-11 = Gobhila II, 3, 1 seqq.

4. Having circumambulated the fire so that their right sides are turned towards it, he shows her the polar star (literally, the firm one), with the verse, 'Firm is the sky' (l. l. 7).

5. She should break her silence by respectfully calling her Gurus by their Gotra names.

6. A cow constitutes the sacrificial fee.

7. Here the Arghya ceremony should be performed.

8. (Or rather it should be performed) when they have come (to their house), according to some (teachers) : [comp. *Sânkh.* I, 12, 10.]

9. Through a period of three nights they should avoid eating saline food and drinking milk, and should sleep together without having conjugal intercourse.

10. Having murmured over food which is fit for sacrifice, the (verses), 'With the tie of food' (MB. I, 3, 8–10), he should pronounce the wife's name, 'N. N.!'

11. After he has sacrificed (or, eaten ?) he should give the rest to the wife.

12. After the lapse of that period of three nights, he should make oblations of Âgya with the four

---

4. pradakshi*n*am agni*m* parikramya dhruva*m* dar*s*ayati dhruvâ dyaur ity. 5. abhivâdya gurûn (guru*m*, Gobhila) gotre*n*a vis*r*î*g*ed vâ*k*am. 6. gaur dakshi*n*â. 7. *s*trârghyam. 8. âgateshv ity eke. 9. trirâtra*m* kshâralava*n*e dugdham iti varga*y*antau (varga*y*ânau the MSS.) saha *s*ayîyâtâ*m* (*s*ayyâtâ*m*, sar*y*yatâ*m* the MSS.) brahma-*k*âri*n*au. 10. havishyam annam pari*g*apyânnapâ*s*enety asâv iti vadhvâ nâma brûyâd. 11. hutvo*kkh*ish*t*am (bhuktv°?) vadhvai dadyâd. 12. ûrdhva*m* trirâtrâ*k* *k*atasr*i*bhir âgya*m* *g*uhuyâd Agne prâya*s*kittir iti samasya pa*nk*amî*m* sampâtân avanayann udapâtre.

---

verses, 'Agni, thou art expiation' (MB. I, 4, 1 seqq.).
A fifth (oblation) combining (the names of the four
gods invoked in those verses). The remnants (of
Âgya) he should pour into a water-pot.

13. With that (Âgya) he should wash her, including her hair and nails.

14. Thenceforward he should behave as required
by circumstances.

15. At the time of her courses he should touch
with his right hand her secret parts with (the verse),
' May Vish*n*u make thy womb ready' (MB. I, 4, 6).

16. When (that verse) is finished, he should
cohabit with her, with (the verse), 'Give conception'
(l. l. 7).

Khanda 5.

1. The fire used at his wedding (is kept as) his
(sacred) domestic fire.

2. Or that on which he (as a student) puts the
last piece of wood.

3. Or (a fire) kindled by attrition: that is pure,
but it does not bring prosperity.

4. Or he may get it from a frying-pan.

5. Or from the house of one who offers many
sacrifices, with the exception of a Sûdra.

---

13. tenainâ*m* sake*s*anakhâm âplâvayet.   14. tato yathârtha*m*
syâd.   15. *r*itukâle dakshi*n*ena pâ*n*inopastham âlabhed Vish*n*ur
yoni*m* kalpayatv iti.   16. samâptâyâ*m* sambhaved garbhan
dhehiti.

5, 1. yasminn agnau pâ*n*i*m* g*r*ih*n*iyât sa g*r*ihyo.   2. yasmin
vântyâ*m* samidham âdadhyân.   3. nirmanthyo vâ pu*n*yas so ₊ nar-
dhuko.   4. ₊ mbarîshâd vânayed.   5. bahuyâ*g*ino vâgârâ*k k*hûdra-
var*g*a*m*.

---

6. The service (at that sacred domestic fire) begins with an evening oblation.

7. After (the fire) has been set in a blaze before sunset or sunrise—

8. The sacrifice (is performed) after sunset,

9. (And) after sunrise or before sunrise.

10. He should with his hand make oblations of food which is fit for sacrifice, having washed it, if it is raw.

11. If it consists in curds or milk, with a brazen bowl,

12. Or with the pot in which the oblations of cooked rice are prepared.

13. (In the evening the first oblation with the formula), 'To Agni Svâhâ!' in the middle (of the sacred fire);

14. The second (oblation) silently in the north-eastern part (of the fire).

15. In the morning the first (oblation with the formula), 'To Sûrya (Svâhâ)!'

16. The wiping round the fire and the similar acts, with the exception of the sprinkling (of water) round (the fire), are omitted here.

17. Some (teachers say) that his wife may offer these oblations, for the wife is (as it were) the house, and that fire is the domestic fire.

---

6. sâyamâhutyupakramam parikaranam. 7. prâg astamayodayâ-bhyâm prâdushkritya. 8. astam ite homa. 9. udite kânudite vâ. 10. havishyasyânnasyâkritam ket prakshâlya guhuyât pâninâ. 11. dadhi ket payo vâ kamsena. 12. karusthâlyâ vâ. 13. agnaye svâheti madhye. 14. tûshnîm prâgudikîm uttarâm. 15. Sûryâyeti prâtah pûrvâm. 16. nâtra parisamûhanâdini paryukshanavargam. 17. patnî guhuyâd ity eke grihâh patnî grihyo gnir esha iti.

10–19=I, 3, 6–18 (16 deest).

18. When (the meal) is ready, in the evening and in the morning, (the wife) should say, 'It is ready!' and (the husband) with loud voice, 'Om!'

19. Then in a low voice: 'May it not fail! Adoration to thee!'

20. Of food which is fit for sacrifice he should make oblations to Pragâpati and to (Agni) Svishṭakṛit.

21. Then he should make the Bali offerings.

22. He should put down (a Bali) at four places, inside or outside (the Agnyagâra);

23. (Another Bali) near the water-barrel;

24. (Another) at the middle door;

25. (Another) in the bed,

26. Or in the privy;

27. Another on the heap of sweepings.

28. He should sprinkle each (Bali with water) before and afterwards.

29. The remnants he should pour out together with water towards the south.

30. Of chaff, of water, and of the scum of boiled rice (he should offer a Bali) when a donation has been made.

---

18. siddhe sâyamprâtar bhûtam ity ukta om ity ukkair brûyât. 19. mâ kshâ namas ta ity upâṃsu. 20. havishyasyânnasya guhuyât prâgâpatyaṃ sauvishṭakṛitaṃ ka. 21. baliṃ nayed. 22. bahir antar vâ katur nidhâya. 23. maṇikadeṣe. 24. madhye dvâri. 25. ṣayyâm anu. 26. varkaṃ [sic] vâ. 27. ·tha ṣastûpam. 28. ekaikam ubhayataḥ parishiṅkek. 29. khesham adbhis sârdhaṃ dakshiṇâ ninayet. 30. phalikaraṇânâm apâm âkâmasveti (read, âkâmasyeti) viṣrâṇite.

20-37 = I, 4, 1 seqq.

31. The gods to whom the Bali offerings belong, are, the Earth, Vâyu, Pragâpati, the Visve devâs, the Waters, the Herbs and Trees, the Ether, Kâma or Manyu, the hosts of Rakshas, the Fathers, Rudra.

32. He should do so silently.

33. He should do so (i.e. offer Balis) of all food.

34. If for one meal the food gets ready at different times, he should do so only once.

35. If (food is prepared) at different places, (he should take) that which belongs to the householder.

36. Of all food he should offer (something) in the fire, and give the due portion to a Brâhmana; he should do so himself.

37. From the rice(-harvest) till the barley(-harvest), or from the barley(-harvest) till the rice(-harvest) he should offer (the Balis) himself. He should offer (the Balis) himself.

End of the First Patala.

---

31. Prithivî Vâyuh Pragâpatir Visve devâ Âpa Oshadhivanaspataya Âkâsah Kâmo Manyur vâ Rakshoganâh Pitaro Rudra iti balidaivatâni.   32. tûshnîm tu kuryât.   33. sarvasya tv annasyaitat kuryâd.   34. asakrik ked ekasmin kâle siddhe sakrid eva kuryâd.   35. bahudhâ ked yad grihapateh.   36. sarvasya tv annasyâgnau kritvâgram brâhmanâya dadyât; svayam kuryâd.   37. vrîhiprabhrity â yavebhyo yavebhyo vâ ʼvrîhibhya svayam haret svayam haret.   prathamapatalah.

1. Of the sacrifices of the new and full moon, the full-moon sacrifice should be performed first.

2. If (the term for the sacrifice) of the new moon comes first, he should first celebrate the full-moon sacrifice and then perform that.

3. Some say that he should not perform it, and wait till the day of the full moon.

4. In the afternoon, husband and wife, after having bathed, should eat fast-day food.

5. Mânadantavya has said: 'He who eats fast-day food, obtains offspring better than himself; he gains favour; hunger will not attack him.'

6. Therefore one should eat (fast-day food) which he likes.

7. He should do nothing unholy (such as cohabiting with his wife).

8. After he has sacrificed the morning oblation,

9. He should pour out the sacrificial food with (the formula), 'Agreeable to such and such (a deity) I pour thee out:' (this formula) referring to the

---

II, 1, 1. paur*n*amâsopakramau dar*s*apaur*n*amâsau.   2. dâr*s*a*m* *k*et pûrvam upapadyeta paur*n*amâsenesh*t*vâtha tat kuryâd.   3. akur-van paur*n*amâsîm âkânkshed ity eke.   4. *a*parâh*n*e snâtvaupava-sathika*m* dampatî bhu*ñ*gîyâtâm.   5. Mânadantavya uvâ*k*a: *s*reyasi*m* pra*g*â*m* vindate kâmyo bhavaty akshodhuko ya aupavasathika*m* bhunkte.   6. tasmâd yat kâmayeta tad bhu*ñ*gîta.   7. nâvratyam â*k*aret.   8. prâtarâhuti*m* hutvâ   9. havir nirvaped amushmai tvâ *g*ush*t*a*m* nirvapâmîti devatâsraya*m* sak*r*id *y*a*g*ur vâ dvis tûsh*n*î*m*.

---

deity, or a Ya*g*us, (is repeated) once; twice (it is done) silently.

10. He should wash (the food) thrice, (if it is destined) for gods;

11. Twice, if for men;

12. Once, if for the Fathers.

13. Stirring it up with the pot-ladle from the left to the right he should cook it.

14. When he has cooked it, he should sprinkle (Â*g*ya) on it, should take it from the fire towards the north, and should again sprinkle (Â*g*ya) on it.

15. Thus all kinds of Havis (are prepared).

16. Having put (the Havis) on the sacrificial grass,

17. He should sacrifice the two Â*g*ya portions (in the following way): Having taken four portions of Â*g*ya—five portions are taken by the Bh*r*igus (or at least?) by the *G*âmadagnyas [see Indische Studien, 10, 95]—(he should make two oblations), to the north with (the formula), 'To Agni Svâhâ!' to the south with (the formula), 'To Soma Svâhâ!'

18. Others (do it) conversely.

19. Having 'spread under' Â*g*ya, he should cut off with the pot-ladle (portions) of the Havis from the middle and from the eastern side;

---

10. trir devebhya*h* prakshâlayed.　　11. dvir manushyebhya*h*.
12. sak*ri*t pit*ri*bhyo.　13. meksha*n*ena pradakshi*n*am udâyuva*n* *s*rapayc*k*.　14. *kh*r*i*tam abhighâryodag udvâsya pratyabhighârayet.
15. sarvâ*ny* eva*m* havî*m*shi.　16. barhishy âsâdyâ.　17. *s*gyabhâgau *g*uhuyâ*k* *k*aturg*ri*hîtam â*g*ya*m* g*ri*hîtvâ pa*nk*âvatta*m* Bh*ri*gû*n*âm *G*âmadagnyânâm Agnaye svâhet*y* uttarata*h* Somâyeti dakshi*n*ato.
18. viparîtam itara.　19. â*g*yam upastirya havisho *v*advyen mekshana madhyât purastâd iti.

17–27 (18, 23 desunt)=I, 8, 3–29.

20. One who takes five cut-off portions (see Sûtra 17), also from the western side.

21. After he has sprinkled (Âg̃ya) on (the cut-off portions), he anoints the places from which he has cut them off, (with Âg̃ya).

22. (This anointing) is omitted at the Svish/akṛit oblation.

23. He should sacrifice with (the formula), 'To N. N. Svâhâ!'—according to the god to whom the oblation belongs.

24. At the Svish/akṛit oblation he 'spreads under' once—twice if he is a Bhṛigu—, (cuts off) once (a portion) of the Havis, sprinkles (Âg̃ya) on it twice, and sacrifices it in a north-eastern direction with (the formula), 'To Agni Svish/akṛit Svâhâ!'

25. Having put a piece of wood (on the fire),

26. He should dip Darbha-blades (of the sacrificial grass strewn round the fire) three times, the points, the middle, and the roots, into the Âg̃ya or into the Havis with (the words), 'May the birds come, licking what has been anointed.' Then, after having sprinkled (those Darbha-blades with water), he should throw them into the fire, with (the verse), 'Thou who art the lord of cattle, Rudra, who walkest with the lines (of cattle), the manly one: do no harm to our cattle; let this be offered to thee. Svâhâ!'

---

20. pas̃kâk ka paṅkâvatty.   21. abhighârya pratyanakty avadânasthânâni.   22. na svish/akṛito.   23. ·mushmai svâheti g̃uhuyâd yaddevatya͡m syât.   24. svish/akṛita͡h sakṛid upastîrya dvir Bhṛigûnâ͡m sakṛid dhavisho [sic] dvir abhighâryâgnaye svish/akṛite svâheti prâgudîkyâm g̃uhuyât.   25. samidham âdhâya.   26. darbhân âg̃ye havishi vâ trir avadhâyâgramadhyamûlâny akta͡m rihânâ viyantu vaya ity abhyukshyâgnâv anupraharcd ya͡h pasûnâm adhipatî Rudras tantikaro vṛishâ pasûn asmâka͡m mâ hi͡msîr etad astu hutan tava svâheti.

27. This (ceremony is called) Yag̃navâstu.

28. He should perform it at all (sacrifices).

29. The remnants of the Havis he should take away in a northern direction, and should give them to the Brahman.

30. A full vessel constitutes the fee for the sacrifice;

31. Or as much as he can afford.

KHANDA 2.

1. By one who has not set up the sacred fires, a mess of cooked food, sacred to Agni, is offered at the festivals of the full and new moon;

2. By one who has set them up, one sacred to Agni and Soma at the full moon;

3. One sacred to Indra, or to Mahendra, or to Indra and Agni, at the new moon;

4. Or as (the sacrifice is performed) by one who has not set up the sacred fires.

5. The time at which the morning oblation may be offered, is the whole day;

6. For the evening oblation the night;

7. For the sacrifice of the full moon the whole second fortnight (of the month);

---

27. tad yag̃navâstu.   28. sarvatra kuryâd.   29. dhavir ukkhish-
*t*am udag udvâsya brahmane dadyât.   30. pûrnapâtram dakshinâ.
31. yathotsâham vâ.

2, 1. Âgneya sthâlîpâko‑nâhitâgner darsapûrnamâsayor.   2. agnî-
shomîyah paurnamâsyâm âhitâgner.   3. aindro mâhendro vaindrâgno
vâmâvâsyâyâm.   4. yathâ vânâhitâgnes.   5. sarvam ahah prâtarâ-
hute sthânam.   6. râtris sâyamâhutes.   7. sarvo‑parapakshah
paurnamâsasya.

---

28 deest.   29–31 = I, 9, 1. 6. 11.
2, 1–4 = Gobhila I, 8, 22–25.   5–14 = I, 9, 14 seqq.

8. For the sacrifice of the new moon the first fortnight.

9. Some say that he should keep his vow (until the sacrifice is performed) by abstaining from food.

10. If (the proper) sacrificial food is wanting, let him offer fruits of sacrificially pure (plants or trees);

11. Or leaves (of such plants or trees);

12. Or water.

13. For (even if he offers water) the sacrifice has been performed.

14. A penance (is prescribed) for one who does not perform the sacrifice.

15. If no Havis is indicated, one should offer Âgya.

16. The deity (only should be named), if no Mantra is indicated.

17. In the third month of the first pregnancy (of the sacrificer's wife he should perform) the Pu*m*-savana (i. e. the ceremony to secure the birth of a son).

18. After she has bathed, her husband should put on her a (new) garment that has not yet been washed, and after having sacrificed he should stand behind her.

19. Grasping down over her right shoulder he

<hr/>

8. pûrvapaksho dârsasyâ. 9. ›bho*g*anena santanuyâd ity eke. 10. ›vidyamâne havye ya*gñ*iyânâ*m* phalâni *g*uhuyât. 11. palâsâni vâ. 12. ›po vâ. 13. huta*m* hi. 14. prâya*sk*ittam ahutasyâ. 15. ›gya*ñ g*uhuyâd dhavisho›nâde*s*e. 16. devatâ [corr. devatâ*m*?] mantrânâde*s*e. 17. prathamagarbhe tr*i*tîye mâsi pu*m*savana*m*. 18. snâtâm ahatenâ*khh*âdya hutvâ pati*h* pr*i*sh*th*atas tish*th*ed. 19. dakshi*n*am a*m*sam anvabhimr*i*syânantarhita*m* (*ᶜ*hitâ*m*, *ᶜ*hitân, the MSS.) nâbhide*s*am abhimr*i*set pumâ*m*sâv ity.

<hr/>

15, 16 desunt. 17–23 = II, 6.

should touch the uncovered place of her navel with (the verse), 'The two men' (MB. I, 4, 8).

20. Then another (ceremony). Having bought for three times seven barley corns or beans, a Nyagrodha-shoot which has fruits on both sides, which is not dry, and not touched by worms, he should set that up with (the formula), 'Ye herbs everywhere, being well-minded, bestow strength on this (shoot); for it will do its work.'

21. He then should take it and place it in the open air.

22. A girl, or a (wife) addicted (to her husband), or a student, or a Brâhmanî should pound (that Nyagrodha-shoot) without moving backward (the stone with which she pounds it).

23. (The husband) should make (the wife) who has bathed, lie down, and should insert (that pounded substance) into her right nostril with (the verse), 'A man is Agni' (MB. I, 4, 9).

24. Then in the fourth or sixth month (of her pregnancy) the Sîmantonnayana (or parting of the hair is performed) for her.

25. After she has bathed, her husband should put on her a garment that has not yet been washed,

---

20. athâparam nyagrodhasungâm ubhayatahphalâm asrâmâm akrimiparisriptâm trissaptair yavaih parikrîyotthâpayen mâshair vâ sarvatraushadhayas sumanaso bhûtvâ (hutvâ, hutvâm the MSS.) syâm vîryam samâdhatteyam karma karishyatîty.   21. âhritya vaihâyasîm kuryât.   22. kumârî vratavatî brahmakârî brâhmanî vâ peshayed apratyâharantî.   23. snâtâm samvesya dakshine nâsikâ-srotasy âsiñket pumân Agnir ity.   24. athâsyâs katurthe mâsi shashthe vâ sîmantonnayanam.   25. snâtâm ahatenâkhâdya hutvâ patih prishthatas tishthann anupûrvayâ phalavrikshasâkhayâ sakrit sîmantam unnayet trisvetayâ salalyâyam ûrgâvato vriksha iti.

24-27 = II, 7. 1 seqq.

and after having sacrificed, he should stand behind
her and should part her hair once with a well-pro-
portioned (?) branch of a tree, on which there are
fruits, (and) with a porcupine's quill that has three
white spots, with (the verse), 'Rich in sap is this
tree' (MB. I, 5, 1).

26. While she looks at a mess of boiled rice with
sesamum seeds, covered with ghee, he should ask
her, 'What dost thou see?'

27. He should make her reply, 'Offspring!'

28. When the child is appearing, the sacrifice for
the woman in labour (is to be performed)—

29. With the two verses, 'She who athwart'
(MB. I, 5, 6 seq.).

30. He should give a name to the child, 'N.N.!'

31. That (is his) secret (name).

32. Before the navel-string is cut off and the
breast is given (to the child, the father) should have
rice and barley grains pounded in the way prescribed
for the Nyagrodha-shoot (see Sûtra 22).

33. He should take thereof with his (right) thumb
and fourth finger and give it to the child to eat,
with (the formula), 'This order' (MB. I, 5, 8).

34. And butter with (the verse), 'May intelligence
to thee' (MB. I, 5, 9).

---

26. krisarasthâlîpâkam uttaraghr/tam aveksha[n]ûm pr/kk/et
kim pasyasîti. 27. pragâm iti vâkayet. 28. pratish/hite vastau
soshyantihomah. 29. yâ tiraskîti dvâbhyâm. 30. asâv iti nâma
dadhyât. 31. tad guhyam. 32. prâñ nâbhikr/ntanât stanadânâk
ka vrîhiyavau peshayek khuṅgâvr/tâ. 33. aṅgush/henânâmikayâ
kâdâya kumâram prâsayed iyam âgñeti. 34. sarpis ka medhân
ta iti.

28-34=II, 7. 13 seqq.

1. On the third (Tithi) of the third bright fortnight after his birth, the father should have the child
bathed in the morning, and after sunset he should,
holding up his joined hands, towards the auspicious
directions (of the horizon), worship the moon.

2. The mother, having dressed (the son) in a
clean (garment), should hand him, with his face
turned to the north, to the father.

3. She then should pass behind (her husband's)
back, and should station herself towards the north.

4. After he has performed worship (to the moon)
with the three (verses), 'Thy heart, O thou with
the well-parted hair' (MB. I, 5, 10 seqq.), and has
handed over the son, turning him towards the north,
to his mother, he should pour water out of his joined
hands with (the verse), 'What in the moon' (l. l. 13).

5. (He should do the same) twice silently.

6. After a period of ten nights, or of a hundred
nights, or of one year after (the child's birth) he
should give him a name.

7. He who is going to perform (that ceremony—
the father or a representative of the father), after he

3, 1. gananâg gyautsne triitiye triiîyâyâm prâta snâpya kumâram
astam ite sântâsu dikshu pitâ kandramasam upatishthet prâñgalih.
2. sukinâkhâdya mâtâ prayakhed udaksirasam.   3. anuprishtham
gatvottaratas tishthed.   4. yat te susîma iti tisrribhir upasthâ-
yodañkam mâtre pradâya yad ada ity apâm añgalim avasiñked.
5. dvis tûshnîm.   6. gananâd ûrdhvam dasarâtrâk khatarâtrât sam-
vatsarâd vâ nâma kuryât.   7. snâpya kumâram karishyata upa-
vishtasya sukinâkhâdya mâtâ prayakhed udaksirasam.

3, 1–5 = Gobhila II, 8, 1–7.   6–12 = II, 8, 8–17.

has had the boy bathed, should sit down, and the mother, having dressed him in a clean (garment), should hand him, with his face turned to the north, to the performer (of the ceremony).

8. She then should walk around behind (his) back and should sit down towards the north.

9. He should sacrifice and should touch the sense-organs at (the boy's) head with the (Mantra), 'Who art thou?' (MB. I, 5, 14, 15.)

10. 'N. N.!'—(at the place thus indicated in the Mantra) he should give him a name.

11. The same (he should pronounce) at the end of the Mantra.

12. He should tell it to the mother first.

13. (The father) when returning from a journey, should grasp (with his two hands) his son round the head, with (the verses), 'From limb by limb' (MB. I, 5, 16–18).

14. With (the formula), 'With the cattle's' (l. l. 19), he should kiss him.

15. Silently (he should do the same) with a daughter.

16. In the third year the tonsure (of the child's head is performed).

17. There the barber, warm water, a mirror, or a

---

8. anuprishtham gatvottarata upavised.   9. dhutvâ ko▸sîti tasya mukhyân prânân abhimrised.   10. asâv iti nâma kuryât.   11. tad eva mantrânte.   12. mâtre prathamam âkhyâya.   13. viproshyâṅgâd aṅgâd iti putrasya mûrdhânam parigrihnîyât.   14. pasûnâm tvety abhigighret.   15. tûshnîm striyas.   16. tritîye varshe kaulan.   17. tatra nâpita ushnodakam âdarsah kshuro vaudumbarah piṅgûlya iti dakshinata.

13-15=II, 8, 21–25.   16–33=II, 9.

razor of Udumbara-wood, and (Darbha)-blades (are placed) towards the south.

18. A bull's dung and a mess of boiled rice with sesamum seeds which may be more or less cooked, to the north;

19. And the mother with the son in her lap.

20. (The performer of the ceremony), after having sacrificed, should look, with (the Mantra), 'Hither has come' (MB. I, 6, 1), at the barber, fixing his thoughts on (the god) Savit*ri*.

21. With (the Mantra), 'With warm water' (l. l. 2), he should look at the warm water, fixing his thoughts on Vâyu.

22. With (the Mantra), 'May the waters ' (l. l. 3), he moistens (the boy's hair).

23. With (the Mantra), 'Vish*n*u's' (l. l. 4), he should look at the mirror or at the razor of Udumbara-wood.

24. With (the Mantra), ' Herb !' (l. l. 5) he puts seven Darbha-blades, with their points upwards (i. e. towards the boy's head ?), into (his hair).

25. With (the formula), 'Axe !' (l. l. 6) (he presses them down) with the mirror or with the razor of Udumbara-wood.

26. With (the Mantra), 'With which Pûshan' (l. l. 7), he should move forward (the razor) three

---

18. ân*d*uho gomaya*h* k*ri*sarasthâlîpâko v*ri*thâpakva ity uttarato. 19. mâtâ *k*a kumâram âdâya.   20. hutvâyam agâd iti nâpita*m* prekshet Savitâra*m* dhyâyann. 21. ush*n*enety ush*n*odaka*m* prekshed Vâyu*m* dhyâyann.   22. âpa ity untte (ante, u*m*de, u*n*tte, unte the MSS.).   23. Vish*n*or ity âda*rs*a*m* prekshetaudumbara*m* vau. 24. *ʼ*shadha iti darbhapi*ñg*ûlîs saptordhvâgrâ abhinidhâya.   25. sva-dhita ity âda*rs*ena kshure*n*audumbare*n*a vâ.   26. yena Pûsheti da-kshi*n*atas tri*h* prâ*ñk*a*m* prohet.

times towards the east on the right side (of the
boy's hair).

27. Cutting (the hair) once with a razor of metal
he should throw the hair on the bull's dung.

28. The same rites, beginning from the moistening (of the hair, are repeated) on the left side and
on the back side (of the child's head).

29. Grasping (with his two hands) the boy round
his head he should murmur (the verse), 'The threefold age' (l. l. 8).

30. Walking away (from the fire) in a northern
direction he should have the arrangement of (the
boy's) hair made according to the custom of his
Gotra and of his family.

31. Let them bury the hair in the forest.

32. Some throw them on a bunch (of grass or
the like).

33. A cow constitutes the sacrificial fee.

KHANDA 4.

1. Let him initiate a Brâhmana in his eighth year.

2. For him the time (for being initiated) has
not passed until his sixteenth (year).

3. In the eleventh a Kshatriya.

---

27. sakr*id* âyasena pra*khi*dyâna*du*he gomaye ke*s*ân kuryâd. 28.
undanaprabhr*ity* eva*m* pa*s*kâd uttarata*s ka*. 29. tryâyusham iti
putrasya mûrdhâna*m* parig*ri*hya *ga*ped. 30. udañ uts*ri*pya kusa-
likârayed yathâgotrakulakalpam. 31. ara*ny*e ke*s*ân nikhaneyu*h*.
32. stambe nidadhaty eke. 33. gaur dakshi*nâ*.

4, 1. ash*ta*me varshe brâhma*n*am upanayet. 2. tasyâ sho*da*sâd
anatîta*h* kâla. 3. ekâda*s*e kshatriya*m*.

4, 1 = Gobhila II, 10.

4. For him (the time has not passed) until the twenty-second.

5. In the twelfth a Vaisya.

6. For him (the time has not passed) until the twenty-fourth.

7. After (the student's) hair has been arranged, and he has been adorned, and dressed in a garment which has not yet been washed, (the teacher) should sacrifice with (the Mantras which the student recites), 'Agni! Lord of the vow!' (MB. I, 6, 9–13.)

8. He should cause (the student) to stand northwards of the fire, facing the west, and to join his hands.

9. And he should himself join his hands above (the student's hands).

10. A Brâhma*n*a versed in the Mantras who stands towards the south, should fill the teacher's joined hands with water.

11. While (the student?) looks at him, (the teacher) should murmur (the Mantra), 'With him who comes to us' (MB. I, 6, 14).

12. (The student) to whom (the teacher) has said, 'What is thy name?' should pronounce a name which he is to use at respectful salutations, derived from (the name of) a deity or a· Nakshatra, 'I am N. N.!' (l. l. 17.)

---

4. tasyâ dvâvim*s*âd.   5. dvâda*s*e vai*s*ya*m*.   6. tasyâ *k*aturvim*s*ât.
7. ku*s*alîkr*i*tam ala*m*kr*i*tam ahatenâ*kh*âdya hutvâgne vratapata ity.
8. uttarato·gne*h* pratyaṅmukham avasthâpyâṅgali*m* kârayet.   9.
svaya*m* *k*opari kuryâd.   10. dakshi*n*atas tish*th*an mantravân brâhma*n*a â*kk*âryâyodakâṅgalim pûrayed.   11. âgantreti *g*apet prekshamâ*n*e [sic].   12. ko nâmâsîty ukto devatâ*s*raya*m* nakshatrâ*s*raya*m*
vâbhivâdanîya*m* nâma brûyâd asâv asmîty.

13. Having let the water run (out of his joined hands over the student's hands) the teacher should seize with his two hands, holding the right uppermost, (the student's) joined hands, with (the formula), ' By the impulse of the god Savit*ri*' (l. l. 18).

14. With (the formula), 'Move in the sun's course' (l. l. 19) he should make him turn round from left to right.

15. Grasping down over his right shoulder he should touch his uncovered navel with (the formula), ' (Thou art the knot) of all breath ' (l. l. 20).

16. He then should give him in charge (to the gods) with the Antaka and the other formulas (l. l. 20 seqq.).

17. (He touches) his right shoulder with (the formula), 'To Pra*g*âpati (I give) thee (in charge)' (l.l. 23),

18. His left shoulder with his left (hand) with (the formula), ' To the god Savit*ri* (I give) thee (in charge) ' (l. l. 24).

19. Having directed him (to observe the duties of Brahma*k*arya, by the formula), 'A student art thou ' (l. l. 25, 26), (the teacher) sitting down should from left to right tie round the student, who bends his right knee and clasps his hands, the girdle made of Mu*ñg*a grass, and should cause him to repeat (the verse), ' Protecting us from evil word ' (l. l. 27).

---

13. uts*ri*g*y*âpo devasya ta iti dakshi*n*ottarâbhyâ*m* hastâbhyâm a*n*gali*m* g*ri*h*n*îyâd â*k*âryas. 14. Sûryasyeti pradakshi*n*am âvartayed. 15. dakshi*n*am a*m*sam anvavam*ri*syânantarhitâ*m* nâbhim âlabhet prâ*n*ânâm ity. 16. athaina*m* paridadyâd antakaprabh*ri*tibhir. 17. dakshi*n*am a*m*sa*m* Pra*g*âpataye tveti. 18. savyena savya*m* devâya tveti. 19. brahma*k*âry asîti sa*m*preshyopavisya (sa*m*preksh*y*°, sa*m*proksh*y*° the MSS.) dakshi*n*agânvaktam a*n*galik*ri*ta*m* pradakshi*n*a*m* mu*ñg*amekhalâm âbadhnan vâ*k*ayed iya*m* duruktâd ity.

20. With (the words), ' Recite, sir!' (the student) should respectfully sit down near (the teacher).

21. He then recites the Sâvitrî (l. l. 29) to him, Pâda by Pâda, hemistich by hemistich, (and finally) the whole—thus he should teach him the Sâvitrî,

22. And the Mahâvyâh*ri*tis, one by one,

23. And the word Om.

24. He hands over to him the staff, which should be made of (the wood of) a tree—

25. With (the formula which the student has to recite), 'O glorious one, make me glorious' (l. l. 31).

26. Let him put a piece of wood (on the fire) with (the verse), ' To Agni a piece of wood' (l. l. 32).

27. Let him go to beg food ;

28. First of his mother,

29. Then of other women friends.

30. He should announce the alms (received) to his teacher.

31. He should stand silently till sunset.

32. Through a period of three nights he should avoid eating saline food and drinking milk.

KHANDA 5.

1. At the Godâna (or cutting of the beard) the

---

20. adhîhi bho ity upasîdet.   21. tasmâ anvâha sâvitrî*m* pa*kkh*o *s*rdhar*k*a*s*as sarvâm iti sâvitrî*m* vâ*k*ayed.   22. mahâvyâh*ri*tis *k*ai-kaika*s*a.   23. o*m*kâra*ñ k*a.   24. praya*kh*aty asmai vârksha*m* da*nd*am.   25. su*s*ravas su*s*ravasa*m* meti.   26. samidham âdadhyâd Agnaye samidham iti.   27. bhaiksha*m k*aren.   28. mâtaram agre.   29. *s*thânyâs suh*ri*da.   30. â*k*âryâya bhaikshan nivedayet.   31. tish*th*ed âstamayât tûsh*n*îm.   32. trirâtra*m* kshâralava*n*e dugdham iti var*g*ayet.
5, 1. atha godâne *k*aulavat kalpa*h*.

---

rite is identical with the *K*aula (cutting of the hair ; see above, chap. 3, 16 seqq.).

2. He should have (his beard) and the hair of his body shaven.

3. The sacrificial fee consists of an ox and a cow, or of a pair of horses, or of sheep, for the (three) castes respectively,

4. Or of a cow for all (castes).

5. A goat (is given) to the person who catches up the hair.

6. The initiation (connected with the Godânakarman, &c.) has been declared.

7. (One should) not initiate one who does not intend to keep the vow through one year.

8. (The use of) a garment, however, which has not yet been washed (see chap. 4, 7), is not prescribed (here),

9. Nor the adornment (chap. 4, 7).

10. (The observances prescribed for the Godâna-vrata are the following :)

He should sleep on the ground.

11. He should avoid eating honey and flesh.

12. He should avoid sexual intercourse, shaving, (luxurious) bathing, combing his head, and cleansing his teeth and his feet (in a luxurious way).

13. nâsya kâme reta skandet.

14. Let him not mount a chariot yoked with cows,

2. saloma*m* vâpayed.   3. go·svâvimithunâni dakshi*nâh* *pri*thag var*nânâm*.   4. sarveshâ*m* vâ gaur.   5. *a*ga*h* ke*s*apratigrahâyo. 6. ·ktam upanayana*m*.   7. nâ*k*arishyanta*m* *sam*vatsaram.   8. aniyuktan tv ahatam.   9. athâla*m*kâro.   10. ·dhassa*m*ve*sy*.   11. amadhumâ*m*sâsî syân.   12. maithunakshurakr*i*tyasnânâvalekhanadantadhâvanapâdadhâvanâni vargayen.   13. nâsya kâme reta skanden. 14. na goyuktam ârohen.

D d 2

15. Nor (wear) shoes in the village.

16. Wearing the girdle, going the rounds for alms, (carrying) a staff, putting fuel (on the fire), touching water, reverentially saluting (the teacher) in the morning : (these are the) standing (duties).

17. The Godâna-vrata, the Vrâtika-vrata, the Âditya-vrata, the Upanishad-vrata, and the Gyesh-*th*asâma-vrata (last) one year (each).

18. The Âditya-vrata some (do) not (undergo).

19. They who undergo it, wear one garment.

20. They allow nothing to be between (themselves and) the sun.

21. And they do not descend into water.

22. For the *S*akvarî verses, twelve, nine, six, or three (years through which the Vrata is to be kept) make up the various possibilities.

23. He (who keeps the *S*âkvara-vrata) wears dark clothes.

24. He eats dark food.

25. He is entirely addicted to his teacher.

26. He should stand in day-time.

27. He should sit at night.

28. According to some (teachers, the Vrata may last only) one year, if the ancestors (of the student) have learnt (the *S*akvarî verses).

---

15. na grâma upânahau.   16. mekhalâdhâra*n*abhaikshâ*k*ara*n*a-da*n*dasamidâdhânopaspar*s*anaprâtarabhivâdâ nitya*m*.   17. godâna-vrâtikâdityavratopanisha*gg*yesh*th*asâmikâs sa*m*vatsarâ.   18. nâditya-vratam ekeshâ*m*.   19. ye *k*aranty ekavâsaso bhavanty.   20. âdit-ya*ñ k*a nântardadhate.   21. na *k*apo‹bhyupayanti.   22. *s*akvarî*n*âm dvâda*s*a nava sha*t* traya iti vikalpâ*h*.   23. k*ri*sh*n*avastra*h*.   24. k*ri*sh*n*abhaksha.   25. â*k*âryâdhînas.   26. tish*th*ed divâ.   27. ‹sîta nakta*m*.   28. sa*m*vatsaram ekeshâm pûrvai*s srutâs *k*ed.

22-34 = III, 2.

29. (The teacher) should sing (those verses) to (the student) who has fasted and veiled his eyes (thinking), 'May (the teacher) not burn me (with the *Sakvari* verses).'

30. In the morning they make (the student) look at such things as they expect will not burn him, viz. water, fire, a calf, the sun.

31. At water (he should look) with (the words), 'Water have I beheld!' At fire with (the words), 'Light have I beheld!' At the calf with (the words), 'Cattle have I beheld!' At the sun with (the words), 'The sky have I beheld!'—thus he should break his silence.

32. A cow is the fee (for the teacher),

33. A brazen vessel, a garment, and a golden ornament.

34. At the Anuprava*k*anîya ceremonies (see Âsvalâyana-Gri*hya I, 22, 12) he should sacrifice Âg*ya with (the two verses), 'To the *Rik*, to the Sâman we sacrifice' (Sâma-veda I, 369), and, 'The lord of the seat' (Sv. I, 171).

35. If he has touched a fire-altar or a sacrificial post, if he has humming in his ears, or if his eye

29. uposhitâya pari*n*addhâkshâyânugâpayed yathâ mâ na pradhakshyatîti.		30. ta*m* prâtar abhivîkshayanti yâny apradhakshyanti manyante ʻpo ʻgni*m* vatsam âdityam.		31. apo ʻbhivyakhyam ity apo *g*yotir abhivyakhyam ity agni*m* pa*s*ûn abhivyakhyam iti vatsa*m* sur [sic] abhivyakhyam ity âdjtya*m* vis*r*i*g*ed vâ*k*am.		32. gaur dakshi*n*â.		33. ka*m*so vâso rukma*s* *k*â.		34. ʻnuprava*k*anîyeshv *r*i*k*am sâma Sadasaspatim iti *k*âg*ya*m* *g*uhuyâ*k*.		35. *k*ityayû*p*opaspar*s*anakar*m*akro*s*âkshivepaneshu sûryâbhyuditas sûryâbhinimrukta indriyai*s* *k*a pâpaspar*s*ai*h* punar mâm ity etâbhyâm âhutîr (correct, âhutî?) *g*uhuyâd.

35-37=III, 3, 34-36.

palpitates, or if the sun rises or sets while he is sleeping, or if his organs of sense have been defiled by something bad, he should sacrifice two oblations of Âgya with the two (verses), 'May (my strength) return to me;'

36. Or two pieces of wood anointed with Âgya.

37. Or he may murmur (those verses) at light (offences). Or he may murmur (those verses) at light (offences).

End of the Second Pa/ala.

---

36. âgyalipte vâ samidhau.   37. gaped vâ laghushu, gaped vâ laghushu.   dvitîyapa/ala/.

PATALA III, KHANDA 1.

1. When (the student) is going to take the bath (at the end of his studentship), he seats himself in an enclosure to the east of his teacher's house.

2. The teacher (sits) facing the north,

3. On eastward-pointed (Darbha-grass).

4. Thus one (should act) who is desirous of holy lustre.

5. (The student should sit) in a cow-stable, if he is desirous of cattle,

6. In an assembly-hall, if desirous of renown.

7. Let him boil water with all kinds of herbs,

8. And with scents.

9. With that water, which must be lukewarm, the teacher should besprinkle (the student).

10. Or (the student should do so) himself, because that is signified by the Mantra.

11. Some say that both (should do so).

12. The teacher should say (in the Mantra), 'Therewith (I besprinkle) him,' (instead of, 'Therewith I besprinkle myself').

13. With (the verses), 'Which in the waters' (MB. I, 7, 1) (the student) should pour out his joined hands full of water;

III, 1, 1. âplavane purastâd âkâryakulasya parivrria âsta. 2. udanmukha âkâryah. 3. prâgagreshv. 4. evam brahmavarkasakâmo. 5. goshthe pasukâmas. 6. sabhâyâm yasaskâmah. 7. sarvaushadhenâpah phânayet. 8. surabhibhis ka. 9. tâbhis sitoshnâbhir âkâryo*bhishinket. 10. svayam vâ mantrâbhivâdâd. 11. ubhâv ity eke. 12. tenemam ity âkâryo brûyâd. 13. ye apsv ity apâm angalim avasinked.

III, 1, 1-32 = Gobhila III, 4, 7 seqq. (4–6, 11, 12, 15, 20 desunt).

14. And with (the formula), 'What (is dreadful) in the waters' (l. l. 2);

15. And silently.

16. With (the formula), 'The shining one' (l. l. 3), he should draw (some water) and should besprinkle himself (therewith);

17. And with (the verse), 'By which the wife' (l. l. 5);

18. And silently.

19. With (the formulas), 'Rising' (l. l. 6–8), he should worship the sun.

20. He may repeat (the sections of that Mantra) continuously.

21. If he repeats them separately, he should add at the end (of each section), 'The eye art thou' (l. l. 9).

22. With (the verse), 'Loosen the highest' (l. l. 10), he should take off the girdle.

23. After he has eaten something, he should have his hair, his beard, the hair of his body, and his nails cut, so as to leave the lock of hair (as required by the custom of his family).

24. Having adorned himself and put on clothes which have not yet been washed, he should put a garland (on his head) with (the formula), 'Luck' (l. l. 11).

25. The two shoes (he puts on) with (the formula), 'Leaders are you' (l. l. 12).

---

14. yad apâm iti *k*a.   15. tûsh*nî*n *k*a.   16. yo ro*k*ana iti *grî*hyâtmânam abhishi*nk*ed.   17. yena striyam iti *k*a.   18. tûsh-*nî*n *k*o.   19. *dyann ity âdityam upatish*th*et.   20. samasyed vâ. 21. viharann anusa*m*hare*k* *k*akshur asîty.   22. ud uttamam iti me-khalâm avamu*nk*et.   23. prâsya vâpaye*k* *kh*ikâva*rg*a*m* kesasma-*s*rulomanakhâny.   24. ala*m*k*r*ito*s*hatavâsasâ *s*rîr iti sra*g*a*m* prati-mu*nk*en.   25. netryau stha ity upânahau.

26. With (the formula), 'The Gandharva art thou'
(l. l. 13), he takes a bamboo staff.

27. He should approach the teacher and look at
the assembly (of pupils, &c.) with (the formula),
' Like an eye-ball' (l. l. 14).

28. Sitting down, he should touch the sense-
organs at his head with (the Mantra), 'Covered by
the lips' (l. l. 15).

29. Let him touch a chariot yoked with oxen,
with (the verse), 'O tree' (l. l. 16).

30. With (the words), ' He who stands on thee'
(l. l. 16), he should mount it.

31. Having driven (some distance) in an eastern
or northern direction, he should turn round from
left to right.

32. Some say that when he has come back, (his
teacher should offer to him) the Argha reception.

33. From that time he shall assume a dignified
demeanour.

34. nâgâtalomnyopahâsam ikkhet.

35. Nor (should he wish for sport) with a girl
who is the only child of her mother,

36. Nor with a woman during her courses,

37. Nor with (a woman) who descends from the
same Rishis.

38. Let him not eat food which has been brought

26. vainavam dandam âdadyâd Gandharvo·sity.　27. upetyâ-
kâryam parishadam prekshed yaksham ivety.　28. upavisyaushthâ-
pidhâneti mukhyân prânân abhimrised.　29. goyuktam ratham
âlabhed vanaspata ity.　30. âsthâtâ ta ity ârohet.　31. prâkîm
prayâyodikîm vâ gatvâ pradakshinam âvartayet.　32. pratyâgatâ-
yârghyam ity eke.　33. vriddhasilî syâd ata ûrdhvam.　34. nâgâtalomnyopahâsam ikkhen.　35. nâyugyâ (read, nâyugvâ).　36. na
ragasvalayâ.　37. na samânarshyâ.　38. ·parayâ dvârâ prapannah
(read, prapanna-) dvihpakvaparyushitâni nâsniyâd.

33-44=III, 5 (40 deest).

by another door (than the usual), or which has been cooked twice, or which has stood over-night—

39. Except such as is prepared of vegetables, flesh, barley, or flour—

40. Or of milk.

41. He shall avoid gathering fruits, looking into wells, running while it is raining, and taking his shoes in his hands.

42. He should not wear a scentless wreath,

43. If it is not a wreath of gold.

44. He should not use the word 'blessed' without a reason.

45. If he is desirous of thriving (in his cattle), he should with (the Mantra), 'May these' (MB. I, 8, 1) have his cows driven out.

46. When they have come back, (he should recite the Mantra), 'These which are rich in sweet' (l. l. 2).

47. If he is desirous of thriving (in his cattle), he should lick the forehead of the first-born calf, before it is licked by its mother, and should gulp with (the formula), ('Thou art the phlegm) of the cows' (l. l. 3).

48. When the cows have calved, he should at night sacrifice in the cow-stable churned curds with drops of ghee, with (the verse), 'Seizer' (l. l. 4).

---

39. anyatra *s*âkamâ*m*sayavapish*t*avikârebhya*h*. 40. pâyasâ*k* *k*a.
41. phalapra*k*ayanodapânâveksha*n*avarshatidhâvanopânatsvaya*m*hara*n*âni na kuryân.   42. nâgandhâ*m* srag*am* dhârayen.   43. na *k*ed dhira*n*yasrag.   44. bhadram iti na v*ri*thâ vyâharet.   45. push-*t*ikâmo gâ*h* prakâlayed imâ ma iti.   46. pratyâgatâ imâ madhu-matîr iti.   47. push*t*ikâma eva prathamagâtasya vatsasya prâṅ mâtu*h* pralehanâl lalâ*t*am ullihya nigired gavâm iti.   48. sampra-gâtâsu gosh*t*he ni*s*âyâ*m* vilayana*n* guhuyât sa*m*grahana*t*y.

45-52 = III, 6.

49. Now another (ceremony). He should make marks on the ears of a male and of a female calf with (the formula), ' The world art thou ' (l. l. 5, 6).

50. First on the male.

51. He should recite over them (the Mantra), ' With metal ' (l. l. 7).

52. When the rope (to which the calves are bound) is spread out, (let him recite over it the Mantra), ' This rope ' (l. l. 8).

KHANDA 2.

1. On the full-moon day of (the month) *Srâvaṇa*, let him carry forward fire from his house, and let him besmear (the place around it) to the extent of more than one prakrama (i. e. step) towards the different directions (of the horizon).

2. Having once taken a quantity of flour, and having put it into (the spoon called) Darvi, he should pour out water on the besmeared place to the east (of the fire), and should offer a Bali with (the formula), (' O king of serpents) dwelling towards the east ' (MB. II, 1, 1).

3. He should pour out the rest of the water.

4. Having touched water, he should do the same

---

49. athâparam vatsamithunayoḥ karṇe lakshaṇam kuryâd bhuvanam iti. 50. pumso·gre. 51. lohitenety anumantrayeta. 52. tantîm prasâritâm iyan tantîti.

2, 1. srâvaṇyâm paurṇamâsyâm gṛhâd agnim atipraṇîya pratidisam upalimped adhike prakrame. 2. sakṛidgṛhitân saktûn darvyâm kṛitvâ pûrvopalipte ninîyâpo yaḥ prâkyâm iti balim nirvapen. 3. ninayed apâm sesham. 4. apa upaspṛisyaivam pratidisam yathâliṅgam.

2. 1–7. 14. 15 = III, 7.

towards the other directions (of the horizon) according as they are mentioned in the Mantras.

5. Between (the besmeared surface) towards the south and that towards the east and the fire (there should be) a passage.

6. After he has thrown the remnants (of flour) out of the basket into the fire, he should go from (the fire) which has been carried forward, to that (fire) which has not (been carried forward), and should turn his hands downwards (so as to touch the earth with them) and should murmur (the Mantra), 'Adoration to the earth's ' (l. l. 3).

7. Thence rising he should place (to the north of the fire) a bunch of Darbha-grass with (the Mantra), ' The king Soma' (l. l. 4), and should fix his thoughts on the serpents that are in that bunch.

8. Taking a portion of fried grain, he should go out of the village in a northern or eastern direction, and should sacrifice it with his joined hands with the four (verses), ' Hearken, Râkâ!' (MB. II, 6, 2 seqq.).

9. Walking eastwards he should murmur, ' Be a giver of wealth ' (l. l. 6).

10. Thus three times to the different quarters and intermediate quarters (of the horizon).

---

5. dakshinapaskime antarenâgniñ ka samkarah. 6. sûrpena sish-tân agnâv opyâtipramîtâd anatipramîtasyârdham gatvâ nyañkau pânî kritvâ namah Prithivyâ iti gapet. 7. tata utthâya Somo râgeti darbhastambam upasthâya (correct, upasthâpya) stambasthân sarpân manasâ dhyâyann. 8. akshatân âdâya prân vodañ vâ grâmân nish-kramya guhuyâd añgalinâ haye Râka iti katasribhih. 9. prân utkramya gaped vasuvana edhiti. 10. tris trih pratidisam avân-taradeseshu ko.

8-13 = IV, 8, 1 seqq. (10 deest).

11. Looking upwards (he should offer a Bali) to the hosts of divine beings,

12. (Looking) towards the side, to the hosts of other beings;

13. Looking downwards, he should go back (to the fire) without looking back, and should eat the fried grain.

14. On the following day he should prepare flour of fried grain, should put it into a new vessel, and after sunset he should offer Balis.

15. (The same is repeated every day) till the Âgrahâya*n*î day.

16. On the full-moon day of Praush*th*apada (or) under (the Nakshatra) Hasta they should begin the Veda-study;

17. On the full-moon day of *S*râva*n*a, according to some (teachers).

18. Having sacrificed as at the Upanayana—

19. He should cause (the students) to recite the Sâvitrî,

20. (The verse), 'Soma, the king' (Sâma-veda I, 91), and the first verses of the Parvans.

21. Let them eat grain and curds with two appropriate (verses).

22. On the following day in the morning let them repeat (the Veda) to their pupils.

---

11. *r*dhva*m* prekshan devayaganebhyas (correct, deva*g*anebhyas).   12. tiryañ itara*g*anebhyo.   13. *r*vân prekshan *j*ratyetyânavekshann akshatân prâsnîyâ*k*.   14. *kh*vobhûte *j*kshatasaktûn k*r*itvâ nave pâtre nidhâyâstam ite balîn hared.   15. âgrahâya*n*yâ*h*.   16. praush*th*apadî*m* hastenâdhyâyân upâkuryu*h*.   17. *s*râva*n*îm ity eke.   18. hutvopanayanavat.   19. sâvitrîm anuvâ*k*ayet.   20. Soma*m* râgânam parvâdî*m*s *k*a.   21. dhânâ dadhi *k*a prâsniyur abhirûpâbhyâ*m*.   22. *s*vobhûte prâtar adhîyîra*ñ* *kh*ishyebhyo.

16–33 = III. 3 (22, 25, 29, 33 desunt).

23. (After each section of the text) they should repeat (as a sort of index ?) the beginnings of the *Rik*as and the Prastâvas (of the Sâmans).

24. Then the Rahasya texts are chanted,

25. Except when lightning is seen or thunder heard.

26. When they have studied four months and a half, they finish on the full-moon day of Pausha.

27. From that time studying is forbidden when clouds appear,

28. And when lightning is seen, or thunder heard, or when it is drizzling.

29. When these three things happen together, (studying is forbidden) till the twilight has thrice passed.

30. On an Ash*t*akâ, on a new-moon day, on the (three) festivals which come once in four months, and at (the beginning of) the northern course of the sun, (studying is forbidden) for one night with one day before and one day after it.

31. And if a fellow-pupil has died.

32. On the falling of a meteor, or after an earthquake, or an eclipse of the sun or of the moon, on these occasions one should know (that studying is forbidden) until the same time next day.

33. The Ka*th*as and Kauthumas, however, state

---

23. *nuvâkyâ*h* kuryur *r*igâdibhi*h* prastâvai*s* *k*â.   24. *nugâna*m* rahasyânâ*m*.   25. vidyutstanayitnuvar*g*am.   26. ardhapa*ñk*amân mâsân adhîtya paushîm utsargas.   27. tata ûrdhvam mantrânâ-dhyâyo (correct, abhrânâdhyâyo).   28. vidyutstanayitnuv*r*ish*t*iteshu (correct, °prushiteshu or °*p*r*ish*iteshu ; see Ludwig's note on Rig-veda VIII, 1, 12) *k*a.   29. trisannipâte trisandhyam.   30. ash*t*akâm amâvâsyâ*m* *k*âturmâsîr udagayane *k*a pakshi*n*i*m* râtrî*m*.   31. sa-brahma*k*âri*n*i *k*a preta.   32. ulkâpâte bhûmi*k*ale *g*yotisho*s* *k*opa-sarga eteshv âkâlika*m* vidyât.   33. kârshvan tu Ka*th*akauthumâ*h*.

that (when rain has fallen, studying is forbidden) as long as the water stands in the ditches.

KHANDA 3.

1. On the full-moon day of Âsvayuga milk-rice sacred to Rudra (is prepared).

2. He should offer it with (the Mantra), 'Not to our children.'

3. Let him pour Âgya into milk; this is called a Prishâtaka.

4. Therewith he should besprinkle the cows when they have come home, with (the Mantra), 'May Mitra and Varuna' (Sâma-veda I, 220).

5. That night he should let the calves join their mothers.

6. At the sacrifice of the first-fruits, milk-rice sacred to Indra and Agni (is prepared).

7. Let him sacrifice Âgya with the four (verses), 'To the bearer of the hundred weapons' (MB. II, 1, 9 seqq.),

8. And afterwards with (the verse), 'May Agni eat' (l. l. 15).

9. All of them who have received the initiation, should eat the remainder of that (sacrificial food).

10. Having 'spread under' water, he should cut off two portions of the new fruits.

3, 1. âsvayugîm Rudrâya pâyaso.   2. mâ nas toka iti guhuyât.
3. payasy avanayed âgyam tat prishâtakam.   4. tenâbhyâgatâ gâ
ukshed â no Mitrâvaruneti.   5. vatsâms ka mâtribhis saha vâsayet
tâm râtrîm.   6. navayagñe pâyasa aindrâgnah.   7. satâyudhâ-
yeti katasribhir âgyam guhuyâd.   8. uparishtâd Agnih prâsnâtv
iti ka.   9. tasya sesham prâsnîyur yâvanta upetâ.   10. upastîryâpo
dvir navasyâvadyet.

3, 1–15 = Gobhila III, 8 (3 deest).

11. Three (portions are cut off) by descendants of Bhrigu.

12. Over (these portions) water (is poured).

13. He should swallow (some part of that food) three times without chewing it, with (the Mantra), 'From the good' (l. l. 13);

14. Or at (the partaking of) barley with (the Mantra), 'This barley' (l. l. 16).

15. With (the Mantra), 'This art thou' (l. l. 14), let him touch the different sense-organs at his head.

16. The Âgrahâyana ceremony has been explained by the Srâvana (ceremony).

17. Let him (not?) murmur (the Mantra), 'Adoration to the Earth' (see chap. 2, 6).

18. In the evening let him make an oblation of milk-rice with (the verse), 'As the first' (MB. II, 2, 1).

19. Turning downwards his two hands (so as to touch the sacrificial grass) he should murmur (the Mantra), 'In worldly strength' (l. l. 2, 3).

20. Having spread out to the west of the fire a layer of northward-pointed grass, so that it is inclined towards the north, the householder sits down on that layer,

21. (And) the other persons in due order.

22. Then, without an interval, their wives,

---

11. trir Bhrigûnâm.　12. apâñ koparishtâd.　13. bhadrân na ity asamkhâdya pragiret tris trir.　14. etam u tyam iti vâ yavânâm. 15. amo‿síti mukhyân prânân abhimrised.　16. âgrahâyanam karma srâvanenaiva vyâkhyâtam.　17. namah Prithivyâ iti gapet (read. iti na gapet?).　18. pradoshe pâyasasya guhuyât prathameti. 19. nyañkau pânî krítvâ prati kshatra iti gapet.　20. paskâd agne svastaram udagagrais trinair udakpravanam âstîrya tasminn âstarane grihapatir âste.　21. ‿nupûrvam itare.　22. ‿nantarâ bhâryâh.

16-31 = III, 9 and 10, 1-17 (29 deest).

23. And their children.

24. The householder, turning his hands downwards (so as to touch the layer of grass), should murmur (the Mantra), ' Be soft ' (l. l. 4).

25. When he has finished that (verse), they should lie down on their right sides. They should turn round three times, turning themselves towards themselves (i. e. turning round forwards, not backwards, and thus returning to their former position ?).

26. Let them repeat the auspicious hymns.

27. Then let them do what they like.

28. The eighth days of the three dark fortnights after the Âgrahâyaṇî are called the Ashṭakâs.

29. On (each of) these a mess of cooked food (is sacrificed),

30. And eight cakes on the first.

31. These he should bake in a dish without turning them round.

32. On the last (Ashṭakâ) vegetables (are offered). (So also) at the Anvâhârya (Srâddha).

33. Let him sacrifice with (the formula), ' To the Ashṭakâ Svâhâ ! '

KHANDA 4.

1. On the middle (Ashṭakâ) a cow (is sacrificed).

23. putrâs ka. 24. nyaṅkau pâṇi kṛitvâ syoneti gṛihapatir gapet. 25. samâptâyâm dakshiṇaiḥ pârsvaiḥ saṃviseyus tris trir abhyâtmam âvṛitya. 26. svastyayanâni kuryus. 27. tato yathârtham syâd. 28. ûrdhvam âgrahâyaṇyâs tisras tâmisrâshṭamyo ◦shṭakâ ity âkakshate. 29. tâsu sthâlîpâkâ. 30. ashṭau kâpûpâḥ prathamâyâm. 31. tân aparivartayan kapâle srapayed. 32. uttamâyâm sâkam anvâhârye. 33. ◦shṭakâyai svâheti guhuyât. 4, 1. madhyamâyâm gaus.

32, 33 = IV, 4, 17. 21.
4, 1–13 = Gobhila III, 10, 18 seqq.

[29]   E e

2. He should place that (cow) to the east of the fire, facing the west, and should sacrifice (Âgya) with (the verse), 'What, O beasts' (MB. II, 2, 5).

3. After having made that oblation he should recite over (the cow the verse), 'May to thee' (l. l. 6).

4. Let him sprinkle it with water in which barley is, with (the formula), 'Agreeable to the Ash/akâ I sprinkle thee!'

5. Having sprinkled it and carried a fire-brand round it, he should give the Proksha*nî* water (to the cow) to drink.

6. Going in a northern direction (from the fire) he should kill (the cow), the head of which is turned to the west, the feet to the north.

7. After it has been killed, he should sacrifice (Âgya) with (the verse), 'If the beast' (l. l. 8).

8. His wife should wash the apertures of its body.

9. After (the cow's body) has been opened, so that two purifiers (i. e. grass-blades) have been put under (the knife), he should have the omentum drawn out.

10. Seizing it with one branch and with another forked branch of a sacrificially pure tree he should roast it.

11. When it has ceased to drop, he should hew (the cow) to pieces.

---

2. tâ*m* purastâd agne*h* pratyan̄mukhîm avasthâpya *g*uhuyâd yat pasava iti.   3. hutvâ *k*ânumantrayetânu tveti.   4. yavamatîbhir adbhi*h* prokshed ash/akâyai tvâ *g*ush/a*m* (correct, *g*ush/â*m*) prokshâmîti.   5. prokshyolmukena parih*ri*tya proksha*nî*h pâyayed.   6. udan̄n uts*ri*pya pratyak*s*irasam (°sim, °sim the MSS.) udakpadî*m* sa*m*g*ñ*apayet.   7. sa*m*g*ñ*aptâyâ*m* *g*uhuyâd yat pa*s*ur iti.   8. tasyâ*h* patnî srotâ*m*si prakshâlayet.   9. pavitre antardhâyotk*ri*tya vapâm uddhârayed.   10. ya*g*ñiyasya v*ri*kshasya visâkhâsâkhâbhyâ*m* parig*ri*hyâgnau *s*rapayet.   11. pras*ri*tâyâ*m* *vi*sased.

12. The 'spreading under' and sprinkling (of Âgya) on (the omentum) has been described. (It is done) as at the Svish/akr*t* oblation (see II, 1, 24).

13. He should sacrifice with (the formula), ' To the Ash/akâ Svâhâ!'

14. The Avadânas (or portions which have to be cut off) he should have taken from all its limbs.

15. Not from the left thigh and the lungs.

16. The left thigh he keeps (for the Anvash/akya).

17. He should cook the Avadânas and a mess of sacrificial food, (stirring up the ones and the other) with two different pot-ladles.

18. The juice he lets drop into a brazen vessel.

19. The Avadânas he puts on branches of the Plaksha tree.

20. From each (Avadâna) he should cut off (the prescribed portions, and should put them) into a brazen vessel ;

21. And from the mess of cooked food.

22. Let him take four portions or eight portions of Âgya (?) and let him sacrifice it with (the verses), ' Into Agni ' (MB. II, 2, 9 seqq.).

23. Let him make oblations out of the brazen vessel, each oblation with two of the following (verses).

---

12. uktam upastara*n*âbhighâra*n*a*m* yathâ svish/akr*i*to. 13. *sh/a-kâyai svâheti *g*uhuyât. 14. sarvâ*n*gebhyo*vadânây uddhârayen. 15. na savyât sakthno na klomna*h*. 16. savya*m* sakthi nidhâya. 17. pr*i*thañ meksha*n*âbhyâm avadânâni sthâlîpâka*ñ* *k*a *s*rapayitvâ. 18. ka*m*se rasa*m* prasrâvya. 19. plaksha*s*âkhâsv avadânâni kr*i*tvai. 20. *kaikasmât ka*m*se*vadyet. 21. sthâlîpâkâ*k* *k*a. 22. *k*aturgr*i*-hîtam ash/agr*i*hîta*m* vâtra (vâ*g*ya*m*? vâtra*m*, vâtra the MSS.) *g*uhu-yâd Agnâv iti. 23. ka*m*sât parâbhir dvâbhyâ*m* dvâbhyâm ekaikâm âhuti*m*.

14-24=IV, 1, 3-17.

24. The oblation to (Agni) Svish*takr*i*t with the eighth (verse).

25. At a sacrifice to the Fathers the omentum is sacrificed with (the verse), ' Carry the omentum ' (MB. II, 3, 16).

26. At one to the gods with (the verse), ' *G*âtavedas !' (l. l. 17.)

27. If (the deity is) unknown, (in the formula for) assigning (the oblation, instead of the name of a deity the name of) that (ceremony is put)—

28. As (for instance), ' To the Ash*t*akâ.'

29. An animal is the sacrificial fee at (the sacrifice of) an animal ;

30. A full vessel at (that of) a mess of cooked food.

KHA*N*DA 5.

1. On the ninth or tenth (of the dark fortnight) the Anvash*t*akya (ceremony is performed).

2. To the south-east (of the house) they partition off (a place with mats or the like), and to the northern part of that (place) he should carry a fire which has been kindled by attrition.

3. Let him take one portion of rice, let him remove the husks once, and let him cook it, stirring it up from right to left.

---

24. sauvish*t*ak*ri*tam ash*t*amyâ. 25. vaha vapâm iti pitrye vapâhomo. 26. *G*âtave*s*a iti daivatye. 27. tadâde*s*am anâg*ñ*âte. 28. yathâsh*t*akâyâ iti. 29. pa*s*ur eva pa*s*or dakshi*n*â. 30. sthâlipâkasya pûr*n*apâtram.

5, 1. navamî*m* da*s*amî*m* vânvash*t*akya*m*. 2. dakshi*n*apûrvabhâge parivârya tatrottarârdhe mathitvâgni*m* pra*n*ayet. 3. sak*ri*dgr*i*hîtân vrîhîn sak*ri*tphalîk*ri*tân prasavyam udâyuva*ñ* *s*rapayed.

25-28=IV, 4, 22-24 (29 deest). 30=I, 9, 6. 10.
5. 1-12=Gobhila IV, 2.

4. And some flesh of that thigh (see above, chap. 4, 16).

5. He should take it from the fire in a southern direction, and should omit the second sprinkling (of Âgya) on it.

6. To the west of the fire he should dig, in the southern part (of the place mentioned in Sûtra 2) three pits, four inches in depth and breadth.

7. He should carry the fire to the east of them.

8. He should strew (Darbha-grass round the fire),

9. And (into) the pits.

10. Having spread out to the west of the fire a layer of southward-pointed grass so that it is inclined towards the south, he should put (a mat) on it.

11. On that (grass) he should place the sacrificial implements, one by one.

12. Cutting off (the prescribed portions of the sacrificial food, and putting those portions) into the brazen vessel he should sacrifice, picking out (portions of the Havis) with the pot-ladle, with (the formulas), 'Svâhâ to Soma Pitrimat! Svâhâ to Agni Kavyavâhana!' (MB. II, 3, 1, 2.)

13. With his left hand he should lay down a fire-brand on the southern side of the pits (Sûtra 6), with

---

4. amushmâk ka sakthno mâmsam iti. 5. dakshinodvâsya na pratyabhighârayet. 6. paskâd agner dakshinâs tisrah karshûh khanyâk katurangulam adhas tiryak ka. 7. tâsâm purastâd agnim pranayet. 8. strinuyât. 9. karshûs ka. 10. paskâd agne svastaram dakshinâgrais trinair dakshinâpravanam âstirya brisîm upari nidadhyât. 11. tasminn ekaikam âharet. 12. kamse samavadâya mekshanenopaghâtam guhuyât svâhâ Somâya pitrimate svâhâgnaye kavyavâhanâyeti. 13. savyenolmukam dakshinatah karshûr nidadhyâd apahatâ iti.

13-31 = IV, 3 (23 deest).

(the formula), ' (The Asuras have been) driven away' (MB. II, 3, 3).

14. (He should perform the different rites) in the eastern pit for his father,

15. In the middle for his grandfather,

16. In the last for his great-grandfather.

17. Let him pour out vessels of water, from right to left, into the pits, pronouncing the name of each one (of his ancestors), with (the formula), ' N. N.! Wash thyself, and they who follow thee here, and they whom thou followest. To thee Svadhâ!'

18. In the same way he should put down the Pinḍas for them and should murmur, 'Here, O Fathers, enjoy yourselves; show your manly vigour each for his part' (MB. II, 3, 6).

19. After he has spoken thus, he should turn to the north, doubling his left arm, turning round from right to left.

20. Holding his breath and fixing his thoughts on something good he should, while turning back (in the same way), murmur: 'The Fathers have enjoyed themselves; they have shown their manly vigour each for his part' (MB. II, 3, 7).

21. He should sprinkle collyrium on three Darbha-

---

14. pûrvasyâm karshvâm pitur.   15. madhyamâyâm pitâmahasyo.   16. ̂ttamâyâm prapitâmahasyo.   17. ̂dapâtrâṇy apasalavi karshûshu ninayed ekaikasya nâmoktvâsâv avanenikshva ye kâtra tvânu yâms ka tvam anu tasmai te svâheti (correct, svadheti).   18. tathaiva pinḍân nidhâya gaped atra pitaro mâdayadhvam yathâbhâgam âvrishâyadhvam ity.   19. uktvodaṅṅ âvarteta savyam bâhum upasamhritya prasavyam âvrityo.   20. ̇patâmya kalyâṇam dhyâyann abhiparyâvartamâno gaped amîmadanta pitaro yathâbhâgam âvrishâyishateti.   21. tisro darbhapiṅgûlîr aṅganena nighrishya karshûshu nidadhyâd yathâpinḍam.

blades, and should put them down into the pits in the same way as the Pi*nd*as,

22. And sesamum oil and perfumes.

23. For the Pi*nd*as and the following offerings he should alter the formula (Sûtra 17) accordingly.

24. Now (follows) the deprecation.

25. On the eastern pit he lays his hands, turning the inside of the right hand upwards, with (the formula), 'Adoration to you, O Fathers, for the sake of life! Adoration to you, O Fathers, for the sake of vital breath !' (MB. II, 3, 8.)

26. On the middle, turning the inside of the left hand upwards, with (the formula), 'Adoration to you, O Fathers, for the sake of terror! Adoration to you, O Fathers, for the sake of sap !' (MB. I. I.)

27. On the western, turning the inside of the right hand upwards, with (the formula), 'Adoration to you, O Fathers, for the sake of comfort (svadhâ)! Adoration to you, O Fathers, for the sake of wrath !' (MB. II, 3, 9.)

28. Joining his hands—

29. (He should murmur the formula), 'Adoration to you' (MB. II, 3, 9).

30. He should lay down threads into the pits in the same way as the Pi*nd*as, with (the formula), 'This (garment) to you.'

---

22. taila*m* surabhi *k*a.   23. pi*nd*aprabhr*ĭ*ti yathârtham ûhed. 24. atha nihnavana*m*.   25. pûrvasyâ*m* karshvâ*m* dakshi*n*ottânau pâ*n*i kr*ĭ*tvâ namo va*h* pitaro *g*îvâya namo va*h* pitara*s* sûshâyeti. 26. savyottânau madhyamâyâ*m* namo va*h* pitaro ghorâya namo va*h* pitaro rasâyeti.   27. dakshi*n*ottânau pa*sk*imâyâm namo va*h* pitara svadhâyai namo va*h* pitaro manyava ity.   28. a*ṅg*ali*m* kr*ĭ*tvâ   29. namo va iti.   30. sûtratantûn karshûshu nidadhyâd yathâpi*nd*am etad va ity.

31. He should recite over the pits (the verse), ' Bringing strength ' (MB. II, 3, 13).

32. The middle Pi*nd*a he should give to his wife to eat, if she is desirous of a son, with (the verse), ' Give fruit.'

33. With (the verse), ' (*G*âtavedas) has been our messenger ' (MB. II, 3, 15), he should throw the firebrand into the fire.

34. They should take the sacrificial vessels back two by two.

35. The same is the rite of the Pi*nd*apit*ri*yag*ñ*a.

36. Let him cook the Havis in the (sacred) domestic fire.

37. From that fire (let him take the fire which) he carries forward (see above, Sûtra .2).

38. (Here is only) one pit.

39. No layer of grass (Sûtra 10).

40. Of the mess of cooked food sacred to Indrâ*ni* he should sacrifice with (the verse), ' The Ekâsh*t*akâ ' (MB. II, 3, 19). He should sacrifice with (the verse), ' The Ekâsh*t*akâ.'

End of the Third Pa*t*ala.

---

31. ûr*ga*m vahantîr iti karshûr anumantrayeta.   32. madhyama*m* pi*nd*am putrakâmâ*m* prâ*s*ayed âdhattety.   33. abhûn no dûta ity ulmukam agnau prakshiped.   34. dvandva*m* pâtrâ*ny* atihareyur. 35. esha eva pi*nd*apit*ri*yag*ñ*akalpo.   36. g*ri*hye*-*gnau havi*s* *s*rapayet.   37. tata evâtipra*n*ayed.   38. ekâ karshûr.   39. na svastara.   40. Indrâ*ny*â sthâlipâkasyaikâsh*t*aketi *g*uhuyâd ekâsh*t*aketi *g*uhuyât.   t*ri*tîyapa*t*ala*h*.

35–39=IV, 4, 1 seqq.   40=IV, 4, 32. 33.

1. When undertaking ceremonies for the obtainment of special wishes, let him omit six meals or three.

2. At such ceremonies as are repeated daily, (let him do so only) in the beginning;

3. After (the ceremony), if it is performed on account of a prodigy.

4. Thus also at the performances of the sacrificial day (i. e. of the first day of the fortnight).

5. One who keeps the vow (of fasting) through one fortnight, (may avail himself of the following indulgence) :

6. If he is not able (to subsist entirely without food, let him drink) rice-water once a day.

7. Let him murmur the Prapada formula (MB. II, 4, 5), sitting in the forest on eastward-pointed grass-blades.

8. Thus one who is desirous of holy lustre.

9. One who is desirous of cattle, as stated above (III, 1, 5?).

10. One who desires that his stock of cattle

IV, 1, 1. kâmyeshu sha*d* bhaktâni tri*n*i vâ nâ*s*nîyân. 2. nitya-prayuktânâm âdita. 3. uparish*t*ât sânnipâtika. 4. eva*m* ya*g*anî-yaprayogeshv. 5. ardhamâsavraty. 6. a*s*aktau peyam (read, peyâm) eka*m* kâlam. 7. ara*n*ye prapada*m* *g*aped âsina*h* prâg-agreshv. 8. eva*m* brahmavar*k*asakâmo. 9. yathokta*m* pa*s*u-kâma*h*. 10. sahasrabâhur iti pa*s*usvastyayanakâmo vrihiyavau *g*uhuyâd.

IV, 1, 1–18=Gobhila IV, 5, 1, 9, 10, 11, 13, 12, 27, 24, 25, 14, 15, 18, 19, 20, 27, 28, 22, 23, 30–34 (9 deest).

may increase, should sacrifice rice and barley, with
(the verse), 'He who has a thousand arms' (MB.
II, 4, 7).

11. To one with whom he wishes to become
associated, he should give fruits of a big tree,
over which he has murmured the Kautomata verse
(MB. II, 4, 8).

12. Having kept the vow (of fasting) through one
fortnight, he should in the full-moon night plunge up
to his navel into a pool which does not dry up, and
should sacrifice with his mouth fried grain into the
water, with the five (verses), 'Like a tree' (MB. II,
4, 9-13).

13. This ceremony procures (property on) the
earth.

14. One who is desirous of the enjoyment (of
riches), should worship the sun with the first (of those
five verses), while one who is rich in wealth should
look at him.

15. One who desires that his stock of horses and
elephants may increase, (should sacrifice) fried grain
with the second (of those verses), while the sun has
a halo.

16. One who desires that his flocks may increase,
(should sacrifice) sesamum seeds with the third (verse),
while the moon has a halo.

---

11. yenek/et sahakâra*m* kautomatenâsya mahâvr*i*kshaphalâni
parig*r*apya dadyâd. 12. ardhamâsavratî paur*n*amâsyâm râtrau
nâbhimâtra*m* pragâhyâvidâsini hrade ◦kshatata*nd*ulân âsyena *g*uhuyâd udake vr*i*ksha iveti pa*ñk*abhi*h*. 13. pârthiva*m* karma. 14.
prathamayâdityam upatish*th*ed bhogakâmo ◦rthapatau prekshamâ*n*e.
15. dvitîyayâkshatata*nd*ulân âditye parivishyamâ*n*e br*i*hatpattra-
svastyayanakâmas. 16. tr*i*tîyayâ *k*andramasi tilata*nd*ulân kshudra-
pa*s*usvastyayanakâma*s*.

17. Having worshipped the sun with the fourth (verse), let him try to gain great wealth.

18. Having worshipped the sun with the fifth, let him return home.

19. In order to avert involuntary death let him murmur every day (the formula), 'Bhûh!' (MB. II, 4, 14.)

20. On the sacrificial day (i. e. the first day of the fortnight) let him make oblations with the six verses, 'From the head' (MB. II, 5, 1 seqq.), with the Vâmadevya verses, with the Mahâvyâhritis, and with the verse sacred to Pragâpati (l. l. 8).

21. Thus he will drive away misfortune.

22. On an unsafe road let him murmur the verse, 'Go away' (Rig-veda X, 164, 1).

23. One who is desirous of glory should worship the sun in the forenoon, at noon, and in the afternoon, with (the formula), 'I am glory' (MB. II, 5, 9).

24. Let him change (the word), 'Of the forenoon,' according (to the different times of the day).

25. Worshipping (the sun) at twilight with the formula, 'O sun! the ship' (MB. II, 5, 14), procures happiness.

26. At the morning twilight (he says), 'When thou risest' (l. l. 15).

---

17. *k*aturthyâdityam upasthâya gurum artham abhyuttish*/h*et. 18. pa*ñk*amyâdityam upasthâya g*ri*hân eyâd. 19. anakâmamâra*m* nitya*m* *g*aped bhûr iti. 20. ya*g*anîye *g*uhuyân mûrdhno ‹ dhi ma iti sha*d*bhir vâmadevyargbhir mahâvyâh*ri*tibhi*h* prâ*g*âpatyayâ *k*â. 21. ‹lakshmînir*n*odo. 22. ‹ksheme pathy apehiti *g*aped. 23. ya*s*o ‹ham ity âditya upatish*/h*ed ya*s*askâma*h* pûrvâh*n*amadhyandinâparâh*n*eshu. 24. prâtarah*n*asyeti yathârtham ûhed. 25. âditya nâvam iti sandhyopasthâna*m* svastyayanam. 26. udyanta*m* tveti pûrvâ*m*.

19–27 = IV, 6, 1, 4, 5, 7, 8, 9, 3, 10–12 (22 deest).

27. At the evening twilight, ' When thou goest to rest ' (l. l. 16).

KHANDA 2.

1. Having kept the vow (of fasting) through one fortnight, he should, on the first day of the dark fortnight, feed the Brâhmanas with boiled milk-rice prepared of one Kamsa of rice.

2. The small grains of that (rice) he should sacrifice (day by day) at the evening twilight to the west of the village, on a place which he has besmeared (with cowdung), with the formula, ' To Phala' (MB. II, 5, 17).

3. And with (the formula), ' To Phalla!' The same on the first day of the next dark fortnight.

4. He shall observe chastity till the end (of the rite).

5. A hundred cart-loads (of gold) will be his.

6. A Brâhmana should elect the site for building his house on white ground, a Kshatriya on red, a Vaisya on black, which should be even, covered with grass, not salinous, not dry—

7. Where the water flows off to the north-west.

8. (Plants) with milky juice or with thorns or acrid plants should not be there.

---

27. pratitish/hantam tveti paskimâm.

2, 1. ardhamâsavratî tâmisrâdau brâhmanân âsayed vrîhikam-saudanam.   2. tasya kanân aparâsu sandhyâsu pratyag grâmât sthandilam upalipya Phalâyeti guhuyât.   3. Phallâyeti kaivam evâparasmims tâmisrâdau.   4. brahmakaryam â samâpter.   5. âkitasatam bhavati.   6. gaure bhûmibhâge brâhmano lohite kshatriyah krishne vaisyo·vasânam goshayet samam lomasam anîrinam asushkam.   7. yatrodakam pratyagudikim pravartate. 8. kshîrinah kantakinah [sic] katukâs kâtraushadhayo na syur.

2, 1–5=Gobhila IV, 6, 13–16.   6–23=IV, 7.

9. (Soil) on which Darbha-grass grows, brings holy lustre ;

10. Big sorts of grass, strength ;

11. Tender grass, cattle.

12. Or (the site of the house) should have the form of bricks (?) or of . . . . . . (?)

13. Or there should be natural holes (in the ground) in all directions.

14, 15. (A house) with its door to the east brings wealth and fame ; with its door to the north, children and cattle. By one with its door to the south all wishes (are obtained). The back-door should not face (?) the house-door.

16. Milk-rice should be offered,

17. And a black cow,

18. Or a white goat. Or only milk-rice.

19. In the middle of the house he should sacrifice the fat (of the animal) and the milk-rice, mixed with Âgya, taking eight portions (of that mixture), with (the verse), 'Vâstoshpati!' (MB. II, 6, 1.)

20. And with the seven last (texts) used at the driving away of misfortune (see above, chap. 1, 20, 21).

21. After he has sacrificed, he should distribute Balis in the different directions (of the horizon).

9. darbhasammita*m* brahmavar*k*asya*m*.   10. br*i*hattr*i*nair balyam.   11. mr*i*dutr*i*nai*h* pasavya*m*.   12. sâtâbhir (corr. *s*âdâbhir?) ma*nd*aladvipibhir vâ.   13. yatra vâ svaya*m*krîtâ*h* svabhrâ*h* sarvato-*bhimukhâ syu*h*.   14. prâgdvâra*m* dhanya*m* ya*s*asya*m* *k*odagdvâra*m* putrya*m* pasavya*m* *k*a dakshi*n*advâre sarve kâmâ. anudvâra*m* gehadvâram   15. asa*m*lokî (asa*m*loki?) syât.   16. pâyaso havi*h*.   17. kr*i*sh*n*â *k*a gaur.   18. a*g*o vâ *s*veta*h* pâyasa eva vâ.   19. madhye ve*s*mano vasâ*m* pâyasa*m* *kâg*yena misram ash*t*agrihîta*m* *g*uhuyâd Vâstoshpata iti.   20. yâ*s* *k*a parâs saptâlakshmînir*n*ode tâbhi*s* *k*a.   21. hutvâ disâ*m* bali*m* nayed.

22. And towards the intermediate points, and upwards and downwards.

23. This (he should repeat) every year, or at the
two sacrifices of the first-fruits (of rice and barley).

24. With the two (formulas), 'Obeying the will'
(MB. II, 6, 7, 8), he should sacrifice two oblations.

25. He should pronounce the name of the person
whom he wishes to subdue to his will, ' N. N. ;' then
that person will obey him.

KHANDA 3.

1. Keeping the observance (of fasting) through one
fortnight, let him sacrifice in a full-moon night one
hundred pegs with the Ekâksharyâ verse (MB. II, 6,
9), if he is desirous of having (a large) family.

2. (Those pegs should be) of Khâdira wood, if he
is desirous of long life.

3. Now another (ceremony performed with the
same verse). He should go out of the village in
an eastern or northern direction, should brush up an
elevated surface, or (should raise it) on a mountain
with the dung of beasts of the forest, should set it on

22. avântaradisâm kordhvâvâkibhyâm kai.   23. svam samvatsare
samvatsare navayagñayor vâ.   24. vasamgamâv ity etâbhyâm âhutî
guhuyâd.   25. yam ikhed vasam âyântam tasya nâma grihîtvâsâv
iti vasî hâsya bhavati.

3, 1. ardhamâsavratî paurnamâsyâm râtrau sankusatam guhuyâd
ekâksharyayâ sânvayakâmah.   2. khâdirân âyushkâmo.   3. sthâ-
param. prân vodan vâ grâmân nishkramya sthandilam samûhya
parvate vâranyair gomayai sthâpayitvâ (read, gomayais tâpayitvâ?)
sngârân apohyâsyena guhuyâd.

24=IV, 8, 7 (25 deest).
3, 1-5=Gobhila IV, 8, 10-16.   6=IV, 9, 15.

fire, should sweep the coals away (from that surface), and should make an oblation (of butter) with his mouth.

4. If (the butter) catches fire, twelve villages (will be his).

5. If smoke rises, at least three.

6. Let him sacrifice in the evening and in the morning the fallings-off of rice-grains. Thus his means of livelihood will not be exhausted.

7. Of articles of trade let him make an oblation with (the formula), ' Here (this Visvakarman),' (MB. II, 6, 10.)

8. On the sacrificial day (i. e. on the first day of the fortnight) let him sacrifice a full oblation (with the verse MB. II, 6, 11, 'A full oblation I sacrifice,' &c.).

9. One who is desirous of companions (should sacrifice) with (the formula), 'Indrâmavadât' (?), (MB. II, 6, 12.)

10. He should fast through a period of eight nights, and then should kindle a fire to the east or to the north of the village, at a place where four roads meet. The fuel should be Udumbara wood, and the Sruva and the cup (for water should be of the same wood). Let him sacrifice (Âgya) with (the formulas), ' Food indeed,' and ' Bliss indeed ' (MB. II, 6, 13, 14).

11. A third (oblation) in the village with (the formula), ' The food's ' (l. l. 15).

---

4. dvâdasa grâmâ gvalite.   5. tryavarâ dhûme.   6. kambûkân sâyamprâtar guhuyân nâsya vrittih kshîyata.   7. idam aham imam iti panyahomam guhuyât.   8. pûrnahomam yaganîye guhuyâd. 9. Indrâmavadâd iti sahâyakâmo.   10. .shtarâtroposhito.param prân vodan vâ grâmâk katushpathe samidhyâgnim audumbara idhma syât sruvakamasau ka guhuyâd annam vâ iti srîr vâ iti.   11. grâme tritîyâm annasyety.

7-9=IV, 8, 19 seqq.   10-16=IV, 9, 1 seqq.

12. Then he will become a ruler.

13. When (his cows) are sick, let him sacrifice milk-rice in the cow-stable.

14. On a dangerous road let him make knots in the skirts of the garments (of those who travel together). This will bring a prosperous journey to (himself) and his companions.

15. With the two (formulas), ' To Hunger Svâhâ!' (MB. II, 6, 16, 17), let him sacrifice a thousand oblations, if he desires to obtain a thousand cart-loads (of gold).

16. One who is desirous of cattle (should sacrifice one thousand oblations) of the excrements of a male and a female calf. Of a male and a female sheep, if he is desirous of flocks.

17. Let him make oblations of fresh cowdung in the evening and in the morning; then his means of livelihood will not be exhausted.

KHANDA 4.

1. One who has been bitten by a venomous animal, he should besprinkle with water, murmuring (the verse), ' Do not fear' (MB. II, 6, 18).

12. âdhipatyam prâpnoty.   13. upatâpinîshu goshthe pâyasam guhuyâd.   14. aksheme pathi vastradasânâm granthîn kuryât sahâyinâm (sahâyânâm?) ka svastyayanâni.   15. kshudhe svâhety etâbhyâm âhutisahasram guhuyâd âkitasahasrakâmo.   16. vatsamithunayoh purîshena pasukâmo=vimithunayoh kshudrapasukâmo.   17. haritagomayena sâyamprâtar guhuyân nâsya vrittih kshîyate.

4, 1. vishavatâ dashtam adbhir abhyukshan gapen mâ bhaishîr iti.

17=IV, 8, 18.
4, 1–4=Gobhila IV, 9, 16 seqq.

2. A Snâtaka should, when lying down to sleep, put his bamboo staff near (his bed) with (the formula), 'Strong one, protect' (l. l. 19). This will bring him luck.

3. A place where he has a worm he should be-sprinkle with water, murmuring (the verses), 'Thy worm is killed' (MB. II, 7, 1–4).

4. (If doing this) for his cattle, let him fetch in the afternoon an earth-clod taken out of a furrow, and let him in the morning strew the dust of it (on the place attacked by worms), murmuring (the same texts).

5. (A guest) who is going to accept the Madhu-parka should come forward murmuring, 'Here I tread on this' (MB. II, 8, 2).

6. They announce three times (to the guest) each (of the following things which are brought to him): a bed (of grass), water for washing the feet, the Argha water, water for sipping, and the Madhuparka;

7. And the cow.

8. Having spread out the bed (of grass, so that the points of the grass are) turned to the north, he should sit down thereon with (the verse), 'The herbs which' (MB. II, 8, 3).

9. With the feet (he treads on another bundle of

---

2. snâtakas samvisan vainavam dandam upanidadhyât tura gopâ-yeti svastyayanam. 3. hatas ta (hastata, ha/hsta, hasta, vitasta, the MSS.) iti krimimantam‘ desam adbhir abhyukshañ gapet. 4. pasûnâm ked aparâhne sitâlosh/am âhritya tasya prâta/h pâmsubhi/h pratishkirañ gapen. 5. madhuparkam pratigrahîshyann idam aham imâm iti pratitish/hañ gaped. 6. vish/arapâdyârghyâ/amaniyamadhuparkânâm ekaikam trir vedayante. 7. gâm ko. 8. dañkam vish/aram âstîrya yâ oshadhîr ity adhyâsîta. 9. pâdayor dvitîyayâ dvau ked.

5-23 = IV, 10.

grass), if there are two, with the second (verse) (l. l. 4).

10. Let him look at the water with (the formula), 'From which side I see the goddesses' (l. l. 5).

11. Let him wash his left foot with (the formula), 'The left' (l. l. 6), the right with, 'The right' (l. l. 7); both with the rest (8).

12. Let him accept the Arghya water with (the formula), 'Thou art the queen of food' (l. l 9).

13. The water which he is to sip, (he accepts) with (the formula), 'Glory art thou' (l. l. 10).

14. The Madhuparka with (the formula), 'The glory's glory art thou' (l. l. 11).

15. Let him drink three times with (the formulas), 'The glory's,' 'The might's,' 'The fortune's' (l. l. 12).

16. Having drunk more of it a fourth time silently he should give the remainder to a Brâhmana.

17. Over the cow, when it has been announced to him, he should recite (the formula), 'Let loose the cow.'

18. Instead of 'and of N. N.' (in that formula) he should put the name of the person who offers the Arghya reception.

19. Thus if it is no sacrifice (by which the Arghya ceremony has been occasioned).

20. 'Make it (ready),' if it is a sacrifice.

---

10. apah pasyed yato devîr iti.   11. savyam pâdam avasinked savyam iti dakshinam dakshinam ity ubhau seshenâ.   12. snnasya râshtrir asîty arghyam pratigrihniyâd.   13. yaso sîty âkamanîyam. 14. yasaso yaso sîti madhuparkam.   15. trih pibed yasaso mahasa sriyâ iti.   16. tûshnîm katurtham bhûyo bhipâya brâhmanâyokkhishtam dadyâd.   17. gâm veditâm anumantrayeta munka gâm ity.   18. amushya kety arhayitur nâma brûyâd.   19. evam ayagñe.   20. kuruteti yagña.

21. The six persons to whom the Arghya reception is due are, a teacher, an officiating priest, a Snâtaka, a king, the father-in-law, a friend.

22. He should honour them (with the Arghya reception) once a year;

23. But repeatedly in the case of a sacrifice and of a wedding. But repeatedly in the case of a sacrifice and of a wedding.

End of the Fourth Paṭala.

End of the Gṛihyakhaṇḍa.

21. âkârya ṛitvik snâtako râgâ vivâhyaḥ priya iti shaḍ arghyâḥ.
22. pratisaṃvatsarân arhayet.   23. punar yagñavivâhayos ḳa punar yagñavivâhayos ḳa.   ḳaturthapaṭalaḥ.
gṛihyakhaṇḍam samâptam.

OF THE SACRED BOOKS OF THE EAST.

CONSONANTS.	MISSIONARY ALPHABET.			Sanskrit.	Zend.	Pehlevi.	Persian.	Arabic.	Hebrew.	Chinese.
	I Class.	II Class.	III Class.							
Gutturales.										
1 Tenuis	k			क	୭	୭	୭	୭	⊓	k
2 „ aspirata	kh			ख	୪	๚			∩	kh
3 Media	g			ग	୯	ๅ			⊓	
4 „ aspirata	gh			घ	୯	ๅ			⊓	
5 Gutturo-labialis	q			व			૭	૭	⊓	
6 Nasalis	ṅ (ng)			ङ	{ ʒ (ng) }					h, hs
7 Spiritus asper	h			ह	⟨(h)⟩	ๅ	૭	๛	⧵	
8 „ lenis	’			स	℧(hv)		-	-	⅀	
9 „ asper faucalis	‘h						∪	∪	⅀	
10 „ lenis faucalis	’h						௳	௳	⅀	
11 „ asper fricatus		’h					∪	∪	⅀	
12 „ lenis fricatus		’h								
Gutturales modificatae (palatales, &c.)										
13 Tenuis		k		च	૭	૭	௳			k
14 „ aspirata		kh		छ						kh
15 Media		y		ज	૩	ౝ	૪	ౝ		
16 „ aspirata		gh		झ						
17 „ Nasalis		ñ		ञ						

CONSONANTS (continued)	Missionary Alphabet I Class	Missionary Alphabet II Class	Missionary Alphabet III Class	Sanskrit	Zend	Pehlevi	Persian	Arabic	Hebrew	Chinese
18 Semivocalis	y			य	𐬫 (init.)		ی	ی	י	y
19 Spiritus asper		(y)								
20 ,, lenis		(y)								
21 ,, asper assibilatus		s		श			ژ	ژ		
22 ,, lenis assibilatus		n								z
Dentales.										
23 Tenuis	t			त			ت	ت	ת	t
24 ,, aspirata	th		TH	थ			ث	ث	ט	th
25 ,, assibilata										
26 Media	d			द			د	د	ד	n
27 ,, aspirata	dh		DH	ध			ذ	ذ	ד	l
28 ,, assibilata										
29 Nasalis	n			न			ن	ن	נ ן	
30 Semivocalis	l	l	L	ल			ل	ل	ל	s
31 ,, mollis 1										
32 ,, mollis 2										
33 Spiritus asper 1	s		s (ς)	स			س	س	ס	z
34 ,, asper 2							ص	ص	ם	
35 ,, lenis	z						ز	ز	ז	ḍ, ḍh
36 ,, asperrimus 1			z (ʒ)				ض	ض		
37 ,, asperrimus 2			z (ʒ)				ظ	ظ		

Dontales modificatae (linguales, &c.)			
38 Tenuis			
39 „ aspirata			
40 Media			
41 „ aspirata			
42 Nasalis			
43 Semivocalis			
44 „ fricata		sh	
45 „ diacritica			
46 Spiritus asper			
47 „ lenis			
Labiales.			
48 Tenuis		p	
49 „ aspirata		ph	
50 Media		b	
51 „ aspirata		bh	
52 Tenuissima			
53 Nasalis		m	
54 Semivocalis		w	
55 „ aspirata		hw	
56 Spiritus asper		f	
57 „ lenis		v	
58 Anusvâra		m	
59 Visarga		h	

VOWELS.	MISSIONARY ALPHABET. I Class.	II Class.	III Class.	Sanskrit.	Zend.	Pehlevi.	Persian.	Arabic.	Hebrew.	Chinese.
1 Neutralis	0									ă
2 Laryngo-palatalis	ə					) fin.				
3 „ labialis	ŏ					ꝺ init.				
4 Gutturalis brevis	a	(a)		ऋ	ꝛ	ꝛ	ٲ	ٲ	־	a
5 „ longa	â			ॠ	ꝩ		ل	ل	־	ā
6 Palatalis brevis	i	(ĭ)		ॡ	ꝵ		ٮ	ٮ	־	i
7 „ longa	ī			ॣ	ꝳ		ؠ	ؠ	־	ī
8 Dentalis brevis	ĭ			ऌ						
9 „ longa	ī			ॢ						
10 Lingualis brevis	ṛi			ऋ						
11 „ longa	ṛī			ॠ						
12 Labialis brevis	u	(u)		उ	ꝯ		ٷ	ٷ	־	u
13 „ longa	û			ऊ						
14 Gutturo-palatalis brevis	e	(e)		ए	ᴇ(e) ꞁ(e)	ꝴ	ٸ	ٸ	־	e
15 „ longa	ê (ai)	(ai)		ऐ	ꝺ ꝺ				־	ê
16 Diphthongus gutturo-palatalis	äi									äi
17 „	ei (ĕi)									ei, ĕi
18 „	oi (ŏu)									
19 Gutturo-labialis brevis	o	(o)		ओ	ꝺ		ٷ	ٷ	־	o
20 „ longa	ô (au)	(au)		औ	ꝺꝴ (au)				־	
21 Diphthongus gutturo-labialis	âu									âu
22 „	eu (ĕu)									
23 „	ou (ŏu)									
24 Gutturalis fracta	ä									ü
25 Palatalis fracta	ï									
26 Labialis fracta	ŏ									
27 Gutturo-labialis fracta	ö									

January, 1888.

Clarendon Press, Oxford.

A SELECTION OF

BOOKS

PUBLISHED FOR THE UNIVERSITY BY

HENRY FROWDE,

AT THE OXFORD UNIVERSITY PRESS WAREHOUSE.

AMEN CORNER, LONDON.

ALSO TO BE HAD AT THE

CLARENDON PRESS DEPOSITORY, OXFORD.

[*Every book is bound in cloth, unless otherwise described.*]

LEXICONS, GRAMMARS, ORIENTAL WORKS, &c.

ANGLO-SAXON.—*An Anglo-Saxon Dictionary*, based on the MS. Collections of the late Joseph Bosworth, D.D., Professor of Anglo-Saxon, Oxford. Edited and enlarged by Prof. T. N. Toller, M.A. (To be completed in four parts.) Parts I-III. A—SAR. 4to. 15*s.* each.

ARABIC.—*A Practical Arabic Grammar.* Part I. Compiled by A. O. Green, Brigade Major. Royal Engineers, Author of ' Modern Arabic Stories ' Second Edition, Enlarged and Revised. Crown 8vo. 7*s.* 6*d.*

CHINESE.—*A Handbook of the Chinese Language.* By James Summers. 1863. 8vo. half bound, 1*l.* 8*s.*

—— *A Record of Buddhistic Kingdoms*, by the Chinese Monk FÂ-HIEN. Translated and annotated by James Legge, M.A., LL.D. Crown 4to. cloth back, 10*s.* 6*d.*

ENGLISH.—*A New English Dictionary, on Historical Principles:* founded mainly on the materials collected by the Philological Society. Edited by James A. H. Murray, LL.D., with the assistance of many Scholars and men of Science. Part I. A—ANT. Part II. ANT—BATTEN. Part III. BATTER—BOZ. Imperial 4to. 12*s.* 6*d.* each.

B

ENGLISH.—*An Etymological Dictionary of the English Language.* By W. W. Skeat, Litt.D. *Second Edition.* 1884. 4to. 2l. 4s.

——Supplement to the First Edition of the above. 4to. 2s. 6d.

—— *A Concise Etymological Dictionary of the English Language.* By W. W. Skeat, Litt.D. *Second Edition.* 1885. Crown 8vo. 5s. 6d.

GREEK.—*A Greek-English Lexicon,* by Henry George Liddell, D.D., and Robert Scott, D.D. Seventh Edition, Revised and Augmented throughout. 1883. 4to. 1l. 16s.

—— *A Greek-English Lexicon,* abridged from Liddell and Scott's 4to. edition. chiefly for the use of Schools. Twenty-first Edition. 1884. Square 12mo. 7s. 6d.

—— *A copious Greek-English Vocabulary,* compiled from the best authorities. 1850. 24mo. 3s.

—— *A Practical Introduction to Greek Accentuation,* by H. W. Chandler, M.A. Second Edition. 1881. 8vo. 10s. 6d.

HEBREW.—*The Book of Hebrew Roots,* by Abu 'l-Walid Marwân ibn Janâh, otherwise called Rabbî Yônâh. Now first edited, with an Appendix, by Ad. Neubauer. 1875. 4to. 2l. 7s. 6d.

—— *A Treatise on the use of the Tenses in Hebrew.* By S. R. Driver, D.D. Second Edition. 1881. Extra fcap. 8vo. 7s. 6d.

—— *Hebrew Accentuation of Psalms, Proverbs, and Job.* By William Wickes, D.D. 1881. Demy 8vo. 5s.

—— *A Treatise on the Accentuation of the twenty-one so-called Prose Books of the Old Testament.* By William Wickes, D.D. 1887. Demy 8vo. 10s. 6d.

ICELANDIC.—*An Icelandic-English Dictionary,* based on the MS. collections of the late Richard Cleasby. Enlarged and completed by G. Vigfússon. M.A. With an Introduction, and Life of Richard Cleasby, by G. Webbe Dasent, D.C.L. 1874. 4to. 3l. 7s.

—— *A List of English Words the Etymology of which is illustrated by comparison with Icelandic.* Prepared in the form of an APPENDIX to the above. By W. W. Skeat, Litt.D. 1876. stitched, 2s.

—— *An Icelandic Primer,* with Grammar, Notes, and Glossary. By Henry Sweet, M.A. Extra fcap. 8vo. 3s. 6d.

—— *An Icelandic Prose Reader,* with Notes, Grammar and Glossary, by Dr. Gudbrand Vigfússon and F. York Powell, M.A. 1879. Extra fcap. 8vo. 10s. 6d.

LATIN.—*A Latin Dictionary,* founded on Andrews' edition of Freund's Latin Dictionary, revised, enlarged, and in great part rewritten by Charlton T. Lewis, Ph.D., and Charles Short, LL.D. 1879. 4to. 1l. 5s.

MELANESIAN.—*The Melanesian Languages.* By R. H. Codrington, D.D., of the Melanesian Mission. 8vo. 18s.

SANSKRIT.—*A Practical Grammar of the Sanskrit Language*, arranged with reference to the Classical Languages of Europe. for the use of English Students, by Sir M. Monier-Williams, M.A. Fourth Edition, 8vo. 15s.

—— *A Sanskrit-English Dictionary*, Etymologically and Philologically arranged, with special reference to Greek, Latin, German, Anglo-Saxon, English, and other cognate Indo-European Languages. By Sir M. Monier-Williams. M.A. 1872. 4to. 4l. 14s. 6d.

—— *Nalopákhyánam.* Story of Nala, an Episode of the Mahá-Bhárata: the Sanskrit text, with a copious Vocabulary, and an improved version of Dean Milman's Translation, by Sir M. Monier-Williams, M.A. Second Edition, Revised and Improved. 1879. 8vo. 15s.

—— *Sakuntalá.* A Sanskrit Drama, in Seven Acts. Edited by Sir M. Monier-Williams, M.A. Second Edition, 1876. 8vo. 21s.

SYRIAC.—*Thesaurus Syriacus:* collegerunt Quatremère, Bernstein, Lorsbach, Arnoldi, Agrell, Field, Roediger: edidit R. Payne Smith. S.T.P. Fasc. I-VI. 1868-83. sm. fol. each, 1l. 1s. Fasc. VII. 1l. 11s. 6d.

Vol. I, containing Fasc. I-V, sm. fol. 5l. 5s.

—— *The Book of Kalilah and Dimnah.* Translated from Arabic into Syriac. Edited by W. Wright, LL.D. 1884. 8vo. 21s.

GREEK CLASSICS, &c.

Aristophanes: A Complete Concordance to the Comedies and Fragments. By Henry Dunbar, M.D. 4to. 1l. 1s.

Aristotle: The Politics, with Introductions. Notes. etc.. by W. L. Newman, M.A., Fellow of Balliol College, Oxford. Vols. I. and II. Medium 8vo. 28s. *Just Published.*

Aristotle: The Politics, translated into English, with Introduction, Marginal Analysis, Notes, and Indices, by B. Jowett, M.A. Medium 8vo. 2 vols. 21s.

Catalogus Codicum Graecorum Sinaiticorum. Scripsit V. Gardthausen Lipsiensis. With six pages of Facsimiles. 8vo. *linen*, 25s.

Heracliti Ephesii Reliquiae. Recensuit I. Bywater, M.A. Appendicis loco additae sunt Diogenis Laertii Vita Heracliti, Particulae Hippocratei De Diaeta Libri Primi, Epistolae Heracliteae. 1877. 8vo. 6s.

Herculanensium Voluminum Partes II. 1824. 8vo. 10s.

Fragmenta Herculanensia. A Descriptive Catalogue of the Oxford copies of the Herculanean Rolls, together with the texts of several papyri, accompanied by facsimiles. Edited by Walter Scott, M.A., Fellow of Merton College, Oxford. Royal 8vo. *cloth*, 21s.

Homer: A Complete Concordance to the Odyssey and Hymns of Homer; to which is added a Concordance to the Parallel Passages in the Iliad, Odyssey, and Hymns. By Henry Dunbar, M.D. 1880. 4to. 1l. 1s.

—— *Scholia Graeca in Iliadem.* Edited by Professor W. Dindorf, after a new collation of the Venetian MSS. by D. B. Monro, M.A., Provost of Oriel College. 4 vols. 8vo. 2l. 10s. Vols. V and VI. *In the Press.*

—— *Scholia Graeca in Odysseam.* Edidit Guil. Dindorfius. Tomi II. 1855. 8vo. 15s. 6d.

Plato: *Apology,* with a revised Text and English Notes, and a Digest of Platonic Idioms, by James Riddell, M.A. 1878. 8vo. 8s. 6d.

—— *Philebus,* with a revised Text and English Notes, by Edward Poste, M.A. 1860. 8vo. 7s. 6d

—— *Sophistes and Politicus,* with a revised Text and English Notes, by L. Campbell. M.A. 1867. 8vo. 18s.

—— *Theaetetus,* with a revised Text and English Notes. by L. Campbell, M.A. Second Edition. 8vo. 10s. 6d.

—— *The Dialogues,* translated into English, with Analyses and Introductions, by B. Jowett, M.A. A new Edition in 5 volumes, medium 8vo. 1875. 3l. 10s.

—— *The Republic,* translated into English, with an Analysis and Introduction, by B. Jowett, M.A. Medium 8vo. 12s. 6d.

Thucydides: Translated into English, with Introduction, Marginal Analysis, Notes, and Indices. By B. Jowett, M.A. 2 vols. 1881. Medium 8vo. 1l. 12s.

THE HOLY SCRIPTURES, &c.

STUDIA BIBLICA.—Essays in Biblical Archæology and Criticism, and kindred subjects. By Members of the University of Oxford. 8vo. 10s. 6d.

ENGLISH.—*The Holy Bible in the earliest English Versions,* made from the Latin Vulgate by John Wycliffe and his followers: edited by the Rev. J. Forshall and Sir F. Madden. 4 vols. 1850. Royal 4to. 3l. 3s.

[Also reprinted from the above, with Introduction and Glossary by W. W. Skeat, Litt. D.

—— *The Books of Job, Psalms, Proverbs. Ecclesiastes, and the Song of Solomon:* according to the Wycliffite Version made by Nicholas de Hereford, about A.D. 1381, and Revised by John Purvey, about A.D. 1388. Extra fcap. 8vo. 3s. 6d.

—— *The New Testament in English,* according to the Version by John Wycliffe, about A.D. 1380, and Revised by John Purvey, about A.D. 1388. Extra fcap. 8vo. 6s.]

ENGLISH.—*The Holy Bible:* an exact reprint, page for page, of the Authorised Version published in the year 1611. Demy 4to. half bound, 1l. 1s.

—— *The Psalter, or Psalms of David, and certain Canticles,* with a Translation and Exposition in English, by Richard Rolle of Hampole. Edited by H. R. Bramley, M.A., Fellow of S. M. Magdalen College, Oxford. With an Introduction and Glossary. Demy 8vo. 1l. 1s.

—— *Lectures on the Book of Job.* Delivered in Westminster Abbey by the Very Rev. George Granville Bradley, D.D., Dean of Westminster. Crown 8vo. 7s. 6d.

—— *Lectures on Ecclesiastes.* By the same Author. Crown 8vo. 4s. 6d.

GOTHIC.—*The Gospel of St. Mark in Gothic,* according to the translation made by Wulfila in the Fourth Century. Edited with a Grammatical Introduction and Glossarial Index by W. W. Skeat, Litt. D. Extra fcap. 8vo. 4s.

GREEK.—*Vetus Testamentum* ex Versione Septuaginta Interpretum secundum exemplar Vaticanum Romae editum. Accedit potior varietas Codicis Alexandrini. Tomi III. Editio Altera. 18mo. 18s.

—— *Origenis Hexaplorum* quae supersunt; sive, Veterum Interpretum Graecorum in totum Vetus Testamentum Fragmenta. Edidit Fridericus Field, A.M. 2 vols. 1875. 4to. 5l. 5s.

—— *The Book of Wisdom:* the Greek Text, the Latin Vulgate, and the Authorised English Version; with an Introduction, Critical Apparatus, and a Commentary. By William J. Deane, M.A. Small 4to. 12s. 6d.

—— *Novum Testamentum Graece.* Antiquissimorum Codicum Textus in ordine parallelo dispositi. Accedit collatio Codicis Sinaitici. Edidit E. H. Hansell, S.T.B. Tomi III. 1864. 8vo. 24s.

—— *Novum Testamentum Graece.* Accedunt parallela S. Scripturae loca, etc. Edidit Carolus Lloyd, S.T.P.R. 18mo. 3s.

On writing paper, with wide margin, 10s.

GREEK.—*Novum Testamentum Graece* juxta Exemplar Millia-num. 18mo. 2s. 6d. On writing paper, with wide margin, 9s.

—— *Evangelia Sacra Graece.* Fcap. 8vo. limp, 1s. 6d.

—— *The Greek Testament*, with the Readings adopted by the Revisers of the Authorised Version:—

(1) Pica type, with Marginal References. Demy 8vo. 10s. 6d.
(2) Long Primer type. Fcap. 8vo. 4s. 6d.
(3) The same, on writing paper, with wide margin, 15s.

—— *The Parallel New Testament*, Greek and English; being the Authorised Version, 1611; the Revised Version, 1881; and the Greek Text followed in the Revised Version. 8vo. 12s. 6d.

The Revised Version is the joint property of the Universities of Oxford and Cambridge.

—— *Canon Muratorianus:* the earliest Catalogue of the Books of the New Testament. Edited with Notes and a Facsimile of the MS. in the Ambrosian Library at Milan, by S. P. Tregelles, LL.D. 1867. 4to. 10s. 6d.

—— *Outlines of Textual Criticism applied to the New Testament.* By C. E. Hammond, M.A. Fourth Edition. Extra fcap. 8vo. 3s. 6d.

HEBREW, etc.—*Notes on the Hebrew Text of the Book of Genesis.* With Two Appendices. By G. J. Spurrell, M.A. Crown 8vo. 10s. 6d.

—— *The Psalms in Hebrew without points.* 1879. Crown 8vo. Price reduced to 2s., in stiff cover.

—— *A Commentary on the Book of Proverbs.* Attributed to Abraham Ibn Ezra. Edited from a MS. in the Bodleian Library by S. R. Driver, M.A. Crown 8vo. paper covers, 3s. 6d.

—— *The Book of Tobit.* A Chaldee Text, from a unique MS. in the Bodleian Library; with other Rabbinical Texts, English Transla-tions, and the Itala. Edited by Ad. Neubauer, M.A. 1878. Crown 8vo. 6s.

—— *Horae Hebraicae et Talmudicae*, a J. Lightfoot. A new Edition, by R. Gandell, M.A. 4 vols. 1859. 8vo. 1l. 1s.

LATIN.—*Libri Psalmorum* Versio antiqua Latina, cum Para-phrasi Anglo-Saxonica. Edidit B. Thorpe, F.A.S. 1835. 8vo. 10s. 6d.

—— *Old-Latin Biblical Texts: No. I.* The Gospel according to St. Matthew from the St. Germain MS. (g₁). Edited with Introduction and Appendices by John Wordsworth, D.D. Small 4to., stiff covers, 6s.

—— *Old-Latin Biblical Texts: No. II.* Portions of the Gospels according to St. Mark and St. Matthew, from the Bobbio MS. (k), &c. Edited by John Wordsworth, D.D., W. Sanday, M.A., D.D., and H. J. White, M.A. Small 4to., stiff covers, 21s.

LATIN.—*Old-Latin Biblical Texts: No. III.* The Four Gospels from the Munich MS. (q) of the Sixth Century. Edited by H. J. White, M.A., under the direction of the Bishop of Salisbury. *Nearly ready.*

OLD-FRENCH.—*Libri Psalmorum* Versio antiqua Gallica e Cod. MS. in Bibl. Bodleiana adservato, una cum Versione Metrica aliisque Monumentis pervetustis. Nunc primum descripsit et edidit Franciscus Michel, Phil. Doc. 1860. 8vo. 10s. 6d.

FATHERS OF THE CHURCH, &c.

St. Athanasius: Historical Writings, according to the Benedictine Text. With an Introduction by William Bright, D.D. 1881. Crown 8vo. 10s. 6d.

—— *Orations against the Arians.* With an Account of his Life by William Bright, D.D. 1873. Crown 8vo. 9s.

St. Augustine: Select Anti-Pelagian Treatises, and the Acts of the Second Council of Orange. With an Introduction by William Bright, D.D. Crown 8vo. 9s.

Canons of the First Four General Councils of Nicaea, Constantinople, Ephesus, and Chalcedon. 1877. Crown 8vo. 2s. 6d.

—— *Notes on the Canons of the First Four General Councils.* By William Bright, D.D. 1882. Crown 8vo. 5s. 6d.

Cyrilli Archiepiscopi Alexandrini in XII Prophetas. Edidit P. E. Pusey, A.M. Tomi II. 1868. 8vo. cloth, 2l. 2s.

—— *in D. Joannis Evangelium.* Accedunt Fragmenta varia necnon Tractatus ad Tiberium Diaconum duo. Edidit post Aubertum P. E. Pusey, A.M. Tomi III. 1872. 8vo. 2l. 5s.

—— *Commentarii in Lucae Evangelium* quae supersunt Syriace. E MSS. apud Mus. Britan. edidit R. Payne Smith, A.M. 1858. 4to. 1l. 2s.

—— Translated by R. Payne Smith, M.A. 2 vols. 1859. 8vo. 14s.

Ephraemi Syri, Rabulae Episcopi Edesseni, Balaei, aliorumque Opera Selecta. E Codd. Syriacis MSS. in Museo Britannico et Bibliotheca Bodleiana asservatis primus edidit J. J. Overbeck. 1865. 8vo. 1l. 1s.

Eusebius' Ecclesiastical History, according to the text of Burton, with an Introduction by William Bright, D.D. 1881. Crown 8vo. 8s. 6d.

Irenaeus: The Third Book of St. Irenaeus, Bishop of Lyons, against Heresies. With short Notes and a Glossary by H. Deane, B.D. 1874. Crown 8vo. 5*s.* 6*d.*

Patrum Apostolicorum, S. Clementis Romani, S. Ignatii, S. Polycarpi, quae supersunt. Edidit Guil. Jacobson, S.T.P.R. Tomi II. Fourth Edition, 1863. 8vo. 1*l.* 1*s.*

Socrates' Ecclesiastical History, according to the Text of Hussey, with an Introduction by William Bright, D.D. 1878. Crown 8vo. 7*s.* 6*d.*

ECCLESIASTICAL HISTORY, BIOGRAPHY, &c.

Ancient Liturgy of the Church of England, according to the uses of Sarum, York, Hereford, and Bangor, and the Roman Liturgy arranged in parallel columns, with preface and notes. By William Maskell, M.A. Third Edition. 1882. 8vo. 15*s.*

Baedae Historia Ecclesiastica. Edited, with English Notes, by G. H. Moberly, M.A. 1881. Crown 8vo. 10*s.* 6*d.*

Bright (W.).   Chapters of Early English Church History. 1878. 8vo. 12*s.*

Burnet's History of the Reformation of the Church of England. A new Edition. Carefully revised, and the Records collated with the originals, by N. Pocock, M.A.   7 vols. 1865. 8vo. *Price reduced to* 1*l.* 10*s.*

Councils and Ecclesiastical Documents relating to Great Britain and Ireland. Edited, after Spelman and Wilkins, by A. W. Haddan, B.D., and W. Stubbs, M.A. Vols. I. and III. 1869-71. Medium 8vo. each 1*l.* 1*s.*

> Vol. II. Part I. 1873. Medium 8vo. 10*s.* 6*d.*

> Vol. II. Part II. 1878. Church of Ireland; Memorials of St. Patrick. Stiff covers, 3*s.* 6*d.*

Hamilton (John, Archbishop of St. Andrews), The Catechism of. Edited, with Introduction and Glossary, by Thomas Graves Law. With a Preface by the Right Hon. W. E. Gladstone. 8vo. 12*s.* 6*d.*

Hammond (C. E.). Liturgies, Eastern and Western. Edited, with Introduction, Notes, and Liturgical Glossary. 1878. Crown 8vo. 10*s.* 6*d.*

> An Appendix to the above. 1879. Crown 8vo. paper covers, 1*s.* 6*d.*

John, Bishop of Ephesus. The Third Part of his Ecclesiastical History. [In Syriac.]   Now first edited by William Cureton, M.A. 1853. 4to. 1*l.* 12*s.*

—— Translated by R. Payne Smith, M.A. 1860. 8vo. 10*s.*

Leofric Missal, The, as used in the Cathedral of Exeter during the Episcopate of its first Bishop. A.D. 1050-1072; together with some Account of the Red Book of Derby, the Missal of Robert of Jumièges, and a few other early MS. Service Books of the English Church. Edited, with Introduction and Notes, by F. E. Warren, B.D. 4to. half morocco, 35s.

Monumenta Ritualia Ecclesiae Anglicanae. The occasional Offices of the Church of England according to the old use of Salisbury, the Prymer in English, and other prayers and forms, with dissertations and notes. By William Maskell, M.A. Second Edition. 1882. 3 vols. 8vo. 2l. 10s.

Records of the Reformation. The Divorce, 1527-1533. Mostly now for the first time printed from MSS. in the British Museum and other libraries. Collected and arranged by N. Pocock, M.A. 1870. 2 vols. 8vo. 1l. 16s.

Shirley (W. W.). Some Account of the Church in the Apostolic Age. Second Edition, 1874. Fcap. 8vo. 3s. 6d.

Stubbs (W.). Registrum Sacrum Anglicanum. An attempt to exhibit the course of Episcopal Succession in England. 1858. Small 4to. 8s. 6d.

Warren (F. E.). Liturgy and Ritual of the Celtic Church. 1881. 8vo. 14s.

ENGLISH THEOLOGY.

Bampton Lectures, 1886. The Christian Platonists of Alexandria. By Charles Bigg, D.D. 8vo. 10s. 6d.

Butler's Works, with an Index to the Analogy. 2 vols. 1874. 8vo. 11s.

Also separately,

Sermons, 5s. 6d.   *Analogy of Religion*, 5s. 6d.

Greswell's Harmonia Evangelica. Fifth Edition. 8vo. 1855. 9s. 6d.

Heurtley's Harmonia Symbolica: Creeds of the Western Church. 1858. 8vo. 6s. 6d.

Homilies appointed to be read in Churches. Edited by J. Griffiths, M.A. 1859. 8vo. 7s. 6d.

Hooker's Works, with his life by Walton, arranged by John Keble, M.A. Sixth Edition, 1874. 3 vols. 8vo. 1l. 11s. 6d.

Hooker's Works, the text as arranged by John Keble, M.A.
2 vols. 1875. 8vo. 11s.

Jewel's Works.   Edited by R. W. Jelf, D.D.   8 vols.   1848.
8vo. 1l. 10s.

Pearson's Exposition of the Creed.   Revised and corrected by
E. Burton, D.D.   Sixth Edition, 1877. 8vo. 10s. 6d.

Waterland's Review of the Doctrine of the Eucharist, with
a Preface by the late Bishop of London.   Crown 8vo. 6s. 6d.

—— *Works,* with Life, by Bp. Van Mildert.   A new Edition,
with copious Indexes.   6 vols.   1856.   8vo.   2l. 11s.

Wheatly's Illustration of the Book of Common Prayer.   A new
Edition, 1846. 8vo. 5s.

Wyclif.   A Catalogue of the Original Works of John Wyclif,
by W. W. Shirley, D.D.   1865. 8vo. 3s. 6d.

—— *Select English Works.*   By T. Arnold, M.A.   3 vols.
1869–1871. 8vo.   1l. 1s.

—— *Trialogus.*   With the Supplement now first edited.
By Gotthard Lechler. 1869. 8vo. 7s.

HISTORICAL AND DOCUMENTARY WORKS.

British Barrows, a Record of the Examination of Sepulchral
Mounds in various parts of England.   By William Greenwell, M.A., F.S.A.
Together with Description of Figures of Skulls, General Remarks on Pre-
historic Crania, and an Appendix by George Rolleston, M.D., F.R.S.   1877.
Medium 8vo. 25s.

Clarendon's History of the Rebellion and Civil Wars in
England. 7 vols. 1839. 18mo. 1l. 1s.

Clarendon's History of the Rebellion and Civil Wars in
England.   Also his Life, written by himself. in which is included a Con-
tinuation of his History of the Grand Rebellion. With copious Indexes.
In one volume, royal 8vo. 1842. 1l. 2s.

Clinton's Epitome of the Fasti Hellenici.   1851.   8vo.   6s. 6d.

—— *Epitome of the Fasti Romani.*   1854.   8vo.   7s.

Corpvs Poeticvm Boreale. The Poetry of the Old Northern Tongue, from the Earliest Times to the Thirteenth Century. Edited, classified, and translated, with Introduction, Excursus, and Notes, by Gudbrand Vigfússon, M.A., and F. York Powell, M.A. 2 vols. 1883. 8vo. 42s.

Freeman (E. A.). *History of the Norman Conquest of England;* its Causes and Results. In Six Volumes. 8vo. 5l. 9s. 6d.

—— *The Reign of William Rufus and the Accession of* Henry the First. 2 vols. 8vo. 1l. 16s.

Gascoigne's Theological Dictionary ("Liber Veritatum"): Selected Passages, illustrating the condition of Church and State, 1403–1458. With an Introduction by James E. Thorold Rogers, M.A. Small 4to. 10s. 6d.

Johnson (Samuel, LL.D.), Boswell's Life -of; including Boswell's Journal of a Tour to the Hebrides, and Johnson's Diary of a Journey into North Wales. Edited by G. Birkbeck Hill, D.C.L. In six volumes, medium 8vo. With Portraits and Facsimiles of Handwriting. Half bound, 3l. 3s.

Magna Carta, a careful Reprint. Edited by W. Stubbs, D.D. 1879. 4to. stitched, 1s.

Passio et Miracula Beati Olaui. Edited from a Twelfth-Century MS. in the Library of Corpus Christi College, Oxford, with an Introduction and Notes, by Frederick Metcalfe, M.A. Small 4to. stiff covers, 6s.

Protests of the Lords, including those which have been expunged, from 1624 to 1874; with Historical Introductions. Edited by James E. Thorold Rogers, M.A. 1875. 3 vols. 8vo. 2l. 2s.

Rogers (J. E. T.). *History of Agriculture and Prices in* England, A.D. 1259–1793.

    Vols. I and II (1259–1400). 1866. 8vo. 2l. 2s.

    Vols. III and IV (1401–1582). 1882. 8vo. 2l. 10s.

    Vols. V and VI (1583–1702). 8vo. 2l. 10s. *Just Published.*

—— *The First Nine Years of the Bank of England.* 8vo. 8s. 6d.

Saxon Chronicles (Two of the) parallel, with Supplementary Extracts from the Others. Edited, with Introduction, Notes, and a Glossarial Index, by J. Earle, M.A. 1865. 8vo. 16s.

Stubbs (W., D.D.). *Seventeen Lectures on the Study of* Medieval and Modern History, &c., delivered at Oxford 1867–1884. Crown 8vo. 8s. 6d.

Sturlunga Saga, including the Islendinga Saga of Lawman Sturla Thordsson and other works. Edited by Dr. Gudbrand Vigfússon. In 2 vols. 1878. 8vo. 2l. 2s.

York Plays. The Plays performed by the Crafts or Mysteries
of York on the day of Corpus Christi in the 14th, 15th, and 16th centuries.
Now first printed from the unique MS. in the Library of Lord Ashburnham.
Edited with Introduction and Glossary by Lucy Toulmin Smith. 8vo. 21s.

Manuscript Materials relating to the History of Oxford.
Arranged by F. Madan, M.A. 8vo. 7s. 6d.

Statutes made for the University of Oxford, and for the Colleges
and Halls therein, by the University of Oxford Commissioners. 1882. 8vo.
12s. 6d.

Statuta Universitatis Oxoniensis. 1887. 8vo. 5s.

The Examination Statutes for the Degrees of B.A., B. Mus.,
B.C.L., and B.M. Revised to Trinity Term, 1887. 8vo. sewed, 1s.

The Student's Handbook to the University and Colleges of
Oxford. Extra fcap. 8vo. 2s. 6d.

The Oxford University Calendar for the year 1887. Crown
8vo. 4s. 6d.

The present Edition includes all Class Lists and other University distinctions
for the seven years ending with 1886.

Also, supplementary to the above, price 5s. (pp. 606),

The Honours Register of the University of Oxford. A complete
Record of University Honours, Officers, Distinctions, and Class Lists; of the
Heads of Colleges, &c., &c., from the Thirteenth Century to 1883.

MATHEMATICS, PHYSICAL SCIENCE, &c.

Acland (H. W., M.D., F.R.S.). *Synopsis of the Pathological*
Series in the Oxford Museum. 1867. 8vo. 2s. 6d.

Burdon-Sanderson (J., M.D., F.R.SS. L. and E.). *Transla-*
tions of Foreign Biological Memoirs. I. Memoirs on the Physiology of Nerve,
of Muscle, and of the Electrical Organ. Medium 8vo. 21s.

De Bary (Dr. A.). *Comparative Anatomy of the Vegetative*
Organs of the Phanerogams and Ferns. Translated and Annotated by F. O.
Bower, M.A., F.L.S., and D. H. Scott, M.A., Ph.D., F.L.S. With 241
woodcuts and an Index. Royal 8vo., half morocco, 1l. 2s. 6d.

Goebel (Dr. K.). *Outlines of Classification and Special Mor-*
phology of Plants. A New Edition of Sachs' Text Book of Botany, Book II.
English Translation by H. E. F. Garnsey, M.A. Revised by I. Bayley Balfour,
M.A., M.D., F.R.S. With 407 Woodcuts. Royal 8vo. half morocco, 21s.

Sachs (Julius von). Lectures on the Physiology of Plants.
Translated by H. Marshall Ward, M.A. With 445 Woodcuts. Royal 8vo.
half morocco, 1l. 11s. 6d.

*De Bary (Dr. A). Comparative Morphology and Biology of
the Fungi, Mycetozoa and Bacteria.* Authorised English Translation by
Henry E. F. Garnsey, M.A. Revised by Isaac Bayley Balfour, M.A., M.D.,
F.R.S. With 198 Woodcuts. Royal 8vo., half morocco, 1l. 2s. 6d.

—— *Lectures on Bacteria.* Second improved edition. Authorised translation by H. E. F. Garnsey, M.A. Revised by Isaac Bayley
Balfour, M.A., M.D., F.R.S. With 20 Woodcuts. Crown 8vo. 6s.

Annals of Botany. Edited by Isaac Bayley Balfour, M.A.,
M.D., F.R.S., Sydney H. Vines, D.Sc., F.R.S., and William Gilson Farlow,
M.D., Professor of Cryptogamic Botany in Harvard University, Cambridge,
Mass., U.S.A., and other Botanists. Royal 8vo.
Vol. I. No. 1. Price 8s. 6d. Vol. I. No. 2. Price 7s. 6d.

*Müller (J.). On certain Variations in the Vocal Organs of
the Passeres that have hitherto escaped notice.* Translated by F. J. Bell, B.A.,
and edited, with an Appendix, by A. H. Garrod, M.A., F.R.S. With Plates.
1878. 4to. paper covers. 7s. 6d.

*Price (Bartholomew, M.A., F.R.S.). Treatise on Infinitesimal
Calculus.*

Vol. I. Differential Calculus. Second Edition. 8vo. 14s. 6d.

Vol. II. Integral Calculus, Calculus of Variations, and Differential Equations.
Second Edition, 1865. 8vo. 18s.

Vol. III. Statics, including Attractions; Dynamics of a Material Particle.
Second Edition. 1868. 8vo. 16s.

Vol. IV. Dynamics of Material Systems; together with a chapter on Theoretical Dynamics, by W. F. Donkin, M.A., F.R.S. 1862. 8vo. 16s.

Pritchard (C., D.D., F.R.S.). Uranometria Nova Oxoniensis.
A Photometric determination of the magnitudes of all Stars visible to the naked
eye, from the Pole to ten degrees south of the Equator. 1885. Royal 8vo.
8s. 6d.

—— *Astronomical Observations* made at the University
Observatory, Oxford, under the direction of C. Pritchard, D.D. No. 1.
1878. Royal 8vo. paper covers. 3s. 6d.

Rigaud's Correspondence of Scientific Men of the 17th Century,
with Table of Contents by A. de Morgan, and Index by the Rev. J. Rigaud,
M.A. 2 vols. 1841-1862. 8vo. 18s. 6d.

*Rolleston (George, M.D., F.R.S.). Scientific Papers and Ad-
dresses.* Arranged and Edited by William Turner, M.B., F.R.S. With a
Biographical Sketch by Edward Tylor, F.R.S. With Portrait, Plates, and
Woodcuts. 2 vols. 8vo. 1l. 4s.

Westwood (*J. O., M.A., F.R.S.*). Thesaurus *Entomologicus Hopeianus*, or a Description of the rarest Insects in the Collection given to the University by the Rev. William Hope. With 40 Plates. 1874. Small folio, half morocco, 7*l*. 10*s*.

The Sacred Books of the East.

TRANSLATED BY VARIOUS ORIENTAL SCHOLARS, AND EDITED BY
F. MAX MÜLLER.

[Demy 8vo. cloth.]

Vol. I. The Upanishads. Translated by F. Max Müller.
Part I. The *Kh*ândogya-upanishad, The Talavakâra-upanishad, The Aitareya-âra*n*yaka, The Kaushîtaki-brâhma*n*a-upanishad, and The Vâ*g*asaneyi-sa*m*hitâ-upanishad. 10*s*. 6*d*.

Vol. II. The Sacred Laws of the Âryas, as taught in the
Schools of Âpastamba, Gautama, Vâsish*th*a, and Baudhâyana. Translated by Prof. Georg Bühler. Part I. Âpastamba and Gautama. 10*s*. 6*d*.

Vol. III. The Sacred Books of China. The Texts of Con-
fucianism. Translated by James Legge. Part I. The Shû King, The Religious portions of the Shih King, and The Hsiâo King. 12*s*. 6*d*.

Vol. IV. The Zend-Avesta. Translated by James Darme-
steter. Part I. The Vendîdâd. 10*s*. 6*d*.

Vol. V. The. Pahlavi Texts. Translated by E. W. West.
Part I. The Bundahi*s*, Bahman Ya*s*t, and Shâyast lâ-shâyast. 12*s*. 6*d*.

Vols. VI and IX. The Qur'ân. Parts I and II. Translated
by E. H. Palmer. 21*s*.

Vol. VII. The Institutes of Vish*n*u. Translated by Julius
Jolly. 10*s*. 6*d*.

Vol. VIII. The Bhagavadgîtâ, with The Sanatsu*g*âtîya, and
The Anugîtâ. Translated by Kâshinâth Trimbak Telang. 10*s*. 6*d*.

Vol. X. The Dhammapada, translated from Pâli by F. Max
Müller; and The Sutta-Nipâta, translated from Pâli by V. Fausböll; being Canonical Books of the Buddhists. 10*s*. 6*d*.

Vol. XI. Buddhist Suttas. Translated from Pâli by T. W.
Rhys Davids. 1. The Mahâparinibbâna Suttanta; 2. The Dhamma-*k*akka-
ppavattana Sutta; 3. The Tevigga Suttanta; 4. The Akaṅkheyya Sutta;
5. The *K*etokhila Sutta; 6. The Mahâ-sudassana Suttanta; 7. The Sabbâsava
Sutta. 10s. 6d.

Vol. XII. The *S*atapatha-Brâhma*n*a, according to the Text
of the Mâdhyandina School. Translated by Julius Eggeling. Part I.
Books I and II. 12s. 6d.

Vol. XIII. Vinaya Texts. Translated from the Pâli by
T. W. Rhys Davids and Hermann Oldenberg. Part I. The Pâtimokkha.
The Mahâvagga, I-IV. 10s. 6d.

Vol. XIV. The Sacred Laws of the Âryas, as taught in the
Schools of Âpastamba, Gautama, Vâsish*th*a and Baudhâyana. Translated
by Georg Bühler. Part II. Vâsish*th*a and Baudhâyana. 10s. 6d.

Vol. XV. The Upanishads. Translated by F. Max Müller.
Part II. The Ka*th*a-upanishad, The Mu*nd*aka-upanishad, The Taittirîyaka-
upanishad, The B*ri*hadâra*n*yaka-upanishad, The *S*veta*s*vatara-upanishad, The
Pra*s*ña-upanishad, and The Maitrâya*n*a-Brâhma*n*a-upanishad. 10s. 6d.

Vol. XVI. The Sacred Books of China. The Texts of
Confucianism. Translated by James Legge. Part II. The Yî King.
10s. 6d.

Vol. XVII. Vinaya Texts. Translated from the Pâli by
T. W. Rhys Davids and Hermann Oldenberg. Part II. The Mahâvagga,
V-X. The *K*ullavagga, I-III. 10s. 6d.

Vol. XVIII. Pahlavi Texts. Translated by E. W. West.
Part II. The Dâ*d*istân-î Dînîk and The Epistles of Mânû*sk*îhar. 12s. 6d.

Vol. XIX. The Fo-sho-hing-tsan-king. A Life of Buddha
by A*s*vaghosha Bodhisattva, translated from Sanskrit into Chinese by
Dharmaraksha, A.D. 420, and from Chinese into English by Samuel Beal.
10s. 6d.

Vol. XX. Vinaya Texts. Translated from the Pâli by T. W.
Rhys Davids and Hermann Oldenberg. Part III. The *K*ullavagga, IV-XII.
10s. 6d.

Vol. XXI. The Saddharma-pu*nd*arîka; or, the Lotus of the
True Law. Translated by H. Kern. 12s. 6d.

Vol. XXII. *G*aina-Sûtras. Translated from Prâkrit by Hermann Jacobi. Part I. The Â*k*ârâṅga-Sûtra. The Kalpa-Sûtra. 10s. 6d.

Vol. XXIII. The Zend-Avesta. Translated by James Dar-
mesteter. Part II. The Sîrôzahs, Yasts, and Nyâyis. 10s. 6d.

Vol. XXIV. Pahlavi Texts. Translated by E. W. West.
Part III. Dînâ-î Maînôg-î Khirad, Sikand-gûmânîk, and Sad-Dar.
10s. 6d.

Second Series.

Vol. XXV. Manu. Translated by Georg Bühler. 21s.

Vol. XXVI. The Satapatha-Brâhmana. Translated by
Julius Eggeling. Part II. 12s. 6d.

Vols. XXVII and XXVIII. The Sacred Books of China.
The Texts of Confucianism. Translated by James Legge. Parts III and IV.
The Lî Kî, or Collection of Treatises on the Rules of Propriety, or Ceremonial
Usages. 25s.

Vols. XXIX and XXX. The Grihya-Sûtras, Rules of Vedic
Domestic Ceremonies. Translated by Hermann Oldenberg.

Part I (Vol. XXIX), 12s. 6d. *Just Published.*
Part II (Vol. XXX). *In the Press.*

Vol. XXXI. The Zend-Avesta. Part III. The Yasna,
Visparad, Âfrînagân, and Gâhs. Translated by L. H. Mills. 12s. 6d.

The following Volumes are in the Press:—

Vol. XXXII. Vedic Hymns. Translated by F. Max Müller.
Part I.

Vol. XXXIII. Nârada, and some Minor Law-books.
Translated by Julius Jolly. [*Preparing.*]

Vol. XXXIV. The Vedânta-Sûtras, with Sankara's Commentary. Translated by G. Thibaut. [*Preparing.*]

* *The Second Series will consist of Twenty-Four Volumes.*

𝕮𝖑𝖆𝖗𝖊𝖓𝖉𝖔𝖓 𝕻𝖗𝖊𝖘𝖘 𝕾𝖊𝖗𝖎𝖊𝖘

I. ENGLISH, &c.

A First Reading Book. By Marie Eichens of Berlin; and
edited by Anne J. Clough. Extra fcap. 8vo. stiff covers, 4*d.*

Oxford Reading Book, Part I. For Little Children. Extra
fcap. 8vo. stiff covers, 6*d.*

Oxford Reading Book, Part II. For Junior Classes. Extra
fcap. 8vo. stiff covers, 6*d.*

An Elementary English Grammar and Exercise Book. By
O. W. Tancock, M.A. Second Edition. Extra fcap. 8vo. 1*s.* 6*d.*

An English Grammar and Reading Book, for Lower Forms
in Classical Schools. By O W. Tancock, M.A. Fourth Edition. Extra
fcap. 8vo. 3*s.* 6*d.*

Typical Selections from the best English Writers, with Introductory Notices. Second Edition. In 2 vols. Extra fcap. 8vo. 3*s.* 6*d.* each.
Vol. I. Latimer to Berkeley.   Vol. II. Pope to Macaulay.

Shairp (*J. C., LL.D.*). *Aspects of Poetry;* being Lectures
delivered at Oxford. Crown 8vo. 10*s.* 6*d.*

A Book for the Beginner in Anglo-Saxon. By John Earle,
M.A. Third Edition. Extra fcap. 8vo. 2*s.* 6*d.*

An Anglo-Saxon Reader. In Prose and Verse. With Grammatical Introduction, Notes, and Glossary. By Henry Sweet. M.A. Fourth
Edition, Revised and Enlarged. Extra fcap. 8vo. 8*s.* 6*d.*

A Second Anglo-Saxon Reader. By the same Author. Extra
fcap. 8vo. 4*s.* 6*d.* *Just Published.*

An Anglo-Saxon Primer, with Grammar, Notes, and Glossary.
By the same Author. Second Edition. Extra fcap. 8vo. 2*s.* 6*d.*

Old English Reading Primers; edited by Henry Sweet. M.A.
I. Selected Homilies of Ælfric. Extra fcap. 8vo., stiff covers. 1*s.* 6*d.*
II. Extracts from Alfred's Orosius. Extra fcap. 8vo., stiff covers, 1*s.* 6*d.*

c

First Middle English Primer, with Grammar and Glossary.
By the same Author. Extra fcap. 8vo. 2s.

Second Middle English Primer. Extracts from Chaucer,
with Grammar and Glossary. By the same Author. Extra fcap. 8vo. 2s.

Principles of English Etymology. First Series. *The Native
Element.* By W. W. Skeat, Litt.D. Crown 8vo. 9s.

The Philology of the English Tongue. By J. Earle, M.A.
Fourth Edition. Extra fcap 8vo. 7s. 6d.

An Icelandic Primer, with Grammar, Notes, and Glossary.
By Henry Sweet, M.A. Extra fcap. 8vo. 3s 6d.

An Icelandic Prose Reader, with Notes, Grammar, and Glossary.
By G. Vigfússon, M.A., and F. York Powell, M.A. Ext. fcap. 8vo.
10s. 6d.

A Handbook of Phonetics, including a Popular Exposition of
the Principles of Spelling Reform. By H. Sweet, M.A. Extra fcap. 8vo.
4s. 6d.

Elementarbuch des Gesprochenen Englisch. Grammatik.
Texte und Glossar. Von Henry Sweet. Extra fcap. 8vo., stiff covers.
2s. 6d.

The Ormulum; with the Notes and Glossary of Dr. R. M.
White. Edited by R. Holt, M.A. 1878. 2 vols. Extra fcap. 8vo. 21s.

Specimens of Early English. A New and Revised Edition.
With Introduction, Notes, and Glossarial Index. By R. Morris, LL.D., and
W. W. Skeat, Litt.D.

   Part I. From Old English Homilies to King Horn (A.D. 1150 to A.D. 1300).
   Second Edition. Extra fcap. 8vo. 9s.

   Part II. From Robert of Gloucester to Gower (A.D. 1298 to A.D. 1393).
   Second Edition. Extra fcap. 8vo. 7s. 6d.

Specimens of English Literature, from the 'Ploughmans
Crede' to the 'Shepheardes Calender' (A.D. 1394 to A.D. 1579). With Introduction, Notes. and Glossarial Index. By W. W. Skeat, Litt.D. Extra fcap.
8vo. 7s. 6d.

The Vision of William concerning Piers the Plowman, in three
Parallel Texts; together with *Richard the Redeless.* By William Langland
(about 1362-1399 A.D.). Edited from numerous Manuscripts, with Preface,
Notes, and a Glossary, by W. W. Skeat, Litt.D. 2 vols. 8vo. 31s. 6d.

The Vision of William concerning Piers the Plowman, by
William Langland. Edited, with Notes, by W. W. Skeat, Litt.D. Fourth
Edition Extra fcap. 8vo. 4s. 6d.

Chaucer. I. *The Prologue to the Canterbury Tales;* the
Knightes Tale; The Nonne Prestes Tale. Edited by R. Morris, Editor of
Specimens of Early English, &c.. &c. Extra fcap. 8vo. 2s. 6d.

—— II. *The Prioresses Tale; Sir Thopas; The Monkes
Tale; The Clerkes Tale; The Squieres Tale,* &c. Edited by W. W. Skeat,
Litt.D. Third Edition. Extra fcap. 8vo. 4s. 6d.

—— III. *The Tale of the Man of Lawe;* The Pardoneres
Tale; The Second Nonnes Tale: The Chanouns Yemannes Tale. By the
same Editor. *New Edition, Revised.* Extra fcap. 8vo. 4s. 6d.

Gamelyn, The Tale of. Edited with Notes, Glossary, &c., by
W. W. Skeat. Litt.D. Extra fcap. 8vo. Stiff covers, 1s. 6d.

Minot (Laurence). Poems. Edited, with Introduction and
Notes, by Joseph Hall, M.A., Head Master of the Hulme Grammar School,
Manchester. Extra fcap. 8vo. 4s. 6d.

Spenser's Faery Queene. Books I and II. Designed chiefly
for the use of Schools. With Introduction, Notes, and Glossary. By G. W.
Kitchin, D.D. Extra fcap. 8vo. 2s. 6d. each.

Hooker. Ecclesiastical Polity, Book I. Edited by R. W.
Church. M.A. Second Edition. Extra fcap. 8vo. 2s.

OLD ENGLISH DRAMA.

The Pilgrimage to Parnassus with *The Two Parts of the
Return from Parnassus.* Three Comedies performed in St. John's College,
Cambridge, A.D. MDXCVII–MDCI. Edited from MSS. by the Rev. W. D.
Macray, M.A., F.S.A. Medium 8vo. Bevelled Boards, Gilt top, 8s. 6d.

*Marlowe and Greene. Marlowe's Tragical History of Dr.
Faustus,* and *Greene's Honourable History of Friar Bacon and Friar Bungay.*
Edited by A. W. Ward, M.A. *New and Enlarged Edition.* Extra fcap.
8vo. 6s. 6d.

Marlowe. Edward II. With Introduction, Notes, &c. By
O. W. Tancock, M.A. Extra fcap. 8vo. Paper covers, 2s. Cloth 3s.

SHAKESPEARE.

Shakespeare. Select Plays. Edited by W. G. Clark, M.A.,
and W. Aldis Wright, M.A. Extra fcap. 8vo. stiff covers.

The Merchant of Venice. 1s.	Macbeth. 1s. 6d.
Richard the Second. 1s. 6d.	Hamlet. 2s.

C 2

Shakespeare. Select Plays. Edited by W. Aldis Wright, M.A.

The Tempest. 1s. 6d.	Midsummer Night's Dream. 1s. 6d.
As You Like It. 1s. 6d.	Coriolanus. 2s. 6d.
Julius Cæsar. 2s.	Henry the Fifth. 2s.
Richard the Third. 2s. 6d.	Twelfth Night. 1s. 6d.
King Lear. 1s. 6d.	King John. 1s. 6d.

Shakespeare as a Dramatic Artist; a popular Illustration of the Principles of Scientific Criticism. By R. G. Moulton, M.A. Crown 8vo. 5s.

Bacon. I. *Advancement of Learning.* Edited by W. Aldis Wright, M.A. Second Edition. Extra fcap. 8vo. 4s. 6d.

—— II. *The Essays.* With Introduction and Notes. By S. II. Reynolds, M.A., late Fellow of Brasenose College. *In Preparation.*

Milton. I. *Areopagitica.* With Introduction and Notes. By John W. Hales, M.A. Third Edition. Extra fcap. 8vo. 3s.

—— II. *Poems.* Edited by R. C. Browne, M.A. 2 vols. Fifth Edition. Extra fcap. 8vo. 6s. 6d. Sold separately, Vol. I. 4s.; Vol. II. 3s.

In paper covers:—
Lycidas, 3d.   L'Allegro, 3d.   Il Penseroso, 4d.   Comus, 6d.
Samson Agonistes, 6d.

—— III. *Paradise Lost.* Book I. Edited by H. C. Beeching. Extra fcap. 8vo. *Nearly ready.*

—— IV. *Samson Agonistes.* Edited with Introduction and Notes by John Churton Collins. Extra fcap. 8vo. stiff covers, 1s.

Bunyan. I. *The Pilgrim's Progress, Grace Abounding, Relation of the Imprisonment of Mr. John Bunyan.* Edited, with Biographical Introduction and Notes, by E. Venables, M.A. 1879. Extra fcap. 8vo. 5s. In ornamental Parchment, 6s.

—— II. *Holy War, &c.* Edited by E. Venables, M.A. In the Press.

Clarendon. *History of the Rebellion.* *Book VI.* Edited by T. Arnold, M.A. Extra fcap. 8vo. 4s. 6d.

Dryden. *Select Poems.* Stanzas on the Death of Oliver Cromwell; Astræa Redux; Annus Mirabilis; Absalom and Achitophel; Religio Laici; The Hind and the Panther. Edited by W. D. Christie, M.A. Second Edition. Extra fcap. 8vo. 3s. 6d.

Locke's Conduct of the Understanding. Edited, with Introduction, Notes, &c., by T. Fowler, D.D. Second Edition. Extra fcap. 8vo. 2s.

Addison. Selections from Papers in the Spectator. With Notes.
By T. Arnold, M.A. Extra fcap. 8vo. 4s. 6d. In ornamental Parchment, 6s.

Steele. Selections from the Tatler, Spectator. and Guardian.
Edited by Austin Dobson. Extra fcap. 8vo. 4s. 6d. In white Parchment, 7s. 6d.

Pope. With Introduction and Notes. By Mark Pattison, B.D.

—— I. *Essay on Man.* Extra fcap. 8vo. 1s. 6d.

—— II. *Satires and Epistles.* Extra fcap. 8vo. 2s.

Parnell. The Hermit. Paper covers, 2d.

Gray. Selected Poems. Edited by Edmund Gosse. Extra
fcap. 8vo. Stiff covers, 1s. 6d. In white Parchment, 3s.

—— *Elegy and Ode on Eton College.* Paper covers, 2d.

Goldsmith. Selected Poems. Edited, with Introduction and
Notes, by Austin Dobson. Extra fcap. 8vo. 3s. 6d. In white Parchment,
4s. 6d.

—— *The Deserted Village.* Paper covers, 2d.

Johnson. I. *Rasselas; Lives of Dryden and Pope.* Edited
by Alfred Milnes, M.A. (London). Extra fcap. 8vo. 4s 6d., or *Lives of
Dryden and Pope* only, stiff covers, 2s. 6d.

—— II. *Rasselas.* Edited, with Introduction and Notes. by
G. Birkbeck Hill. D.C.L. Extra fcap. 8vo. Bevelled boards, 3s. 6d. In white
Parchment, 4s. 6d.

—— III. *Vanity of Human Wishes.* With Notes, by E. J.
Payne, M.A. Paper covers, 4d.

*Boswell's Life of Johnson. With the Journal of a Tour to
the Hebrides.* Edited, with copious Notes, Appendices, and Index, by G.
Birkbeck Hill, D.C.L., Pembroke College. With Portraits and Facsimiles.
6 vols. Medium 8vo. *Half bound,* 3l. 3s.

Cowper. Edited, with Life, Introductions, and Notes, by
H. T. Griffith, B.A.

—— I. *The Didactic Poems of* 1782, with Selections from the
Minor Pieces, A.D. 1779-1783. Extra fcap. 8vo. 3s.

—— II. *The Task, with Tirocinium.* and Selections from the
Minor Poems A.D. 1784-1799. Second Edition. Extra fcap. 8vo. 3s.

Burke. Select Works. Edited, with Introduction and Notes,
by E. J. Payne, M.A.

—— I. *Thoughts on the Present Discontents; the two Speeches
on America.* Second Edition. Extra fcap. 8vo. 4s. 6d.

Burke. II. *Reflections on the French Revolution.* Second Edition.
Extra fcap. 8vo. 5s.

—— III. *Four Letters on the Proposals for Peace with the*
Regicide Directory of France. Second Edition. Extra fcap. 8vo. 5s.

Keats. Hyperion, Book I. With Notes by W. T. Arnold, B.A.
Paper covers. 4d.

Byron. Childe Harold. Edited, with Introduction and Notes,
by H. F. Tozer, M.A. Extra fcap. 8vo. 3s. 6d. In white Parchment, 5s.

Scott. Lay of the Last Minstrel. Edited with Preface and
Notes by W. Minto. M.A. With Map. Extra fcap. 8vo. Stiff covers, 2s.
Ornamental Parchment, 3s. 6d.

—— *Lay of the Last Minstrel.* Introduction and Canto I,
with Preface and Notes, by the same Editor. 6d.

II. LATIN.

Rudimenta Latina. Comprising Accidence, and Exercises of
a very Elementary Character, for the use of Beginners. By John Barrow
Allen, M.A. Extra fcap. 8vo. 2s.

An Elementary Latin Grammar. By the same Author.
Fifty-Seventh Thousand. Extra fcap. 8vo. 2s. 6d.

A First Latin Exercise Book. By the same Author. Fourth
Edition. Extra fcap. 8vo. 2s. 6d.

A Second Latin Exercise Book. By the same Author. Extra
fcap. 8vo. 3s. 6d.

Reddenda Minora, or Easy Passages, Latin and Greek, for
Unseen Translation. For the use of Lower Forms. Composed and selected
by C. S. Jerram, M.A. Extra fcap. 8vo. 1s. 6d.

Anglice Reddenda, or Extracts. Latin and Greek, for
Unseen Translation. By C. S. Jerram, M.A. Third Edition, Revised and
Enlarged Extra fcap. 8vo. 2s. 6d.

Anglice Reddenda. Second Series. By the same Author.
Extra fcap. 8vo. 3s.

Passages for Translation into Latin. For the use of Passmen
and others. Selected by J. Y. Sargent, M.A. Seventh Edition. Extra fcap.
8vo. 2s. 6d.

Exercises in Latin Prose Composition; with Introduction,
Notes, and Passages of Graduated Difficulty for Translation into Latin. By
G. G. Ramsay, M.A., LL.D. Second Edition. Extra fcap. 8vo. 4s. 6d.

Hints and Helps for Latin Elegiacs. By H. Lee-Warner, M.A.
Extra fcap. 8vo. 3s. 6d.

First Latin Reader. By T. J. Nunns, M.A. Third Edition.
Extra fcap. 8vo. 2s.

Caesar. The Commentaries (for Schools). With Notes and
Maps. By Charles E. Moberly, M.A.

Part I. *The Gallic War.* Second Edition. Extra fcap. 8vo. 4s. 6d.
Part II. *The Civil War.* Extra fcap. 8vo. 3s. 6d.
The Civil War. Book I. Second Edition. Extra fcap. 8vo. 2s.

Cicero. Speeches against Catilina. By E. A. Upcott, M.A.,
Assistant Master in Wellington College. In one or two Parts. Extra fcap.
8vo. 2s. 6d.

Cicero. Selection of interesting and descriptive passages. With
Notes. By Henry Walford, M.A. In three Parts. Extra fcap. 8vo. 4s. 6d.
Each Part separately, limp, 1s. 6d.

Part I. Anecdotes from Grecian and Roman History. Third Edition.
Part II. Omens and Dreams: Beauties of Nature. Third Edition.
Part III. Rome's Rule of her Provinces. Third Edition.

Cicero. De Senectute. Edited, with Introduction and Notes,
by L. Huxley, M.A. In one or two Parts. Extra fcap. 8vo. 2s.

Cicero. Selected Letters (for Schools). With Notes. By the
late C. E. Prichard, M.A., and E. R. Bernard, M.A. Second Edition.
Extra fcap. 8vo. 3s.

Cicero. Select Orations (for Schools). In Verrem I. De
Imperio Gn. Pompeii. Pro Archia. Philippica IX. With Introduction and
Notes by J. R. King, M.A. Second Edition. Extra fcap. 8vo. 2s. 6d.

Cicero. In Q. Caecilium Divinatio, and *In C. Verrem Actio
Prima.* With Introduction and Notes, by J. R. King, M.A. Extra fcap. 8vo.
limp, 1s. 6d.

Cicero. Speeches against Catilina. With Introduction and
Notes, by E. A. Upcott, M.A. In one or two Parts. Extra fcap. 8vo.
2s. 6d.

Cornelius Nepos. With Notes. By Oscar Browning, M.A.
Second Edition. Extra fcap. 8vo. 2s. 6d.

Horace. Selected Odes. With Notes for the use of a Fifth
Form. By E. C. Wickham, M.A. In one or two Parts. Extra fcap. 8vo.
cloth, 2s.

Livy. Selections (for Schools). With Notes and Maps. By
H. Lee-Warner, M.A. Extra fcap. 8vo. In Parts, limp, each 1s. 6d.

Part I. The Caudine Disaster. Part II. Hannibal's Campaign
in Italy. Part III. The Macedonian War.

Livy. Books V–VII. With Introduction and Notes. By
A. R. Cluer, B.A. Second Edition. Revised by P. E. Matheson, M.A.
(In one or two vols.) Extra fcap. 8vo. 5s.

Livy. Books XXI, XXII, and XXIII. With Introduction and Notes. By M. T. Tatham, M.A. Extra fcap. 8vo. 4s. 6d.

Ovid. Selections for the use of Schools. With Introductions and Notes, and an Appendix on the Roman Calendar. By W. Ramsay. M.A. Edited by G. G. Ramsay, M.A. Third Edition. Extra fcap. 8vo. 5s. 6d.

Ovid. Tristia. Book I. The Text revised, with an Introduction and Notes. By S. G. Owen, B.A. Extra fcap. 8vo 3s. 6d.

Plautus. Captivi. Edited by W. M. Lindsay, M.A. Extra fcap. 8vo. (In one or two Parts.) 2s. 6d.

Plautus. The Trinummus. With Notes and Introductions. (Intended for the Higher Forms of Public Schools.) By C. E. Freeman, M.A., and A. Sloman. M.A. Extra fcap. 8vo. 3s.

Pliny. Selected Letters (for Schools). With Notes. By the late C. E. Prichard, M.A., and E. R. Bernard, M.A. Extra fcap. 8vo. 3s.

Sallust. With Introduction and Notes. By W. W. Capes, M.A. Extra fcap. 8vo. 4s. 6d.

Tacitus. The Annals. Books I–IV. Edited, with Introduction and Notes (for the use of Schools and Junior Students), by H. Furneaux, M.A. Extra fcap. 8vo. 5s.

Tacitus. The Annals. Book I. With Introduction and Notes, by the same Editor. Extra fcap. 8vo. limp, 2s.

Terence. Andria. With Notes and Introductions. By C. E. Freeman, M.A., and A. Sloman, M.A. Extra fcap. 8vo. 3s.

—— *Adelphi.* With Notes and Introductions. (Intended for the Higher Forms of Public Schools.) By A. Sloman, M.A. Extra fcap. 8vo. 3s.

—— *Phormio.* With Notes and Introductions. By A. Sloman, M.A. Extra fcap. 8vo. 3s.

Tibullus and Propertius. Selections. Edited by G. G. Ramsay, M.A. Extra fcap. 8vo. (In one or two vols.) 6s.

Virgil. With Introduction and Notes By T. L. Papillon. M.A. Two vols. Crown 8vo. 10s. 6d. The Text separately, 4s. 6d.

Virgil. Bucolics. Edited by C. S. Jerram. M.A. In one or two Parts. Extra fcap. 8vo. 2s. 6d.

Virgil. Aeneid I. With Introduction and Notes, by C. S. Jerram, M.A. Extra fcap. 8vo. limp, 1s. 6d.

Virgil. Aeneid IX. Edited, with Introduction and Notes. by A. E. Haigh, M.A., late Fellow of Hertford College, Oxford. Extra fcap. 8vo. limp, 1s. 6d. In two Parts, 2s.

Avianus, The Fables of. Edited, with Prolegomena, Critical Apparatus, Commentary, etc. By Robinson Ellis, M.A., LL.D. Demy 8vo 8s. 6d.

Catulli Veronensis Liber. Iterum recognovit, apparatum criticum prolegomena appendices addidit, Robinson Ellis A.M. 1878 Demy 8vo. 16s.

—— *A Commentary on Catullus.* By Robinson Ellis, M.A. 1876. Demy 8vo. 16s.

Catulli Veronensis Carmina Selecta, secundum recognitionem Robinson Ellis, A.M. Extra fcap. 8vo 3s 6d.

Cicero de Oratore. With Introduction and Notes. By A. S. Wilkins, M.A.
Book I. 1879. 8vo. 6s.   Book II. 1881. 8vo. 5s.

—— *Philippic Orations.* With Notes By J. R. King, M.A. Second Edition. 1879. 8vo. 10s. 6d.

Cicero. Select Letters. With English Introductions, Notes, and Appendices. By Albert Watson, M.A. Third Edition. Demy 8vo. 18s.

—— *Select Letters.* Text. By the same Editor. Second Edition. Extra fcap. 8vo. 4s.

—— *pro Cluentio.* With Introduction and Notes. By W. Ramsay, M.A. Edited by G. G Ramsay, M.A. 2nd Ed. Ext. fcap. 8vo. 3s. 6d.

Horace. With a Commentary. Volume I. The Odes, Carmen Seculare, and Epodes. By Edward C. Wickham, M.A. Second Edition. 1877. Demy 8vo. 12s.

—— A reprint of the above, in a size suitable for the use of Schools. In one or two Parts. Extra fcap. 8vo. 6s.

Livy, Book I. With Introduction, Historical Examination, and Notes. By J. R. Seeley. M.A. Second Edition. 1881. 8vo. 6s.

Ovid. P. Ovidii Nasonis Ibis. Ex Novis Codicibus edidit, Scholia Vetera Commentarium cum Prolegomenis Appendice Indice addidit, R. Ellis, A.M. 8vo. 10s. 6d.

Persius. The Satires. With a Translation and Commentary. By John Conington, M.A. Edited by Henry Nettleship. M.A. Second Edition. 1874. 8vo. 7s. 6d.

Juvenal. XIII Satires. Edited, with Introduction and Notes, by C. H. Pearson, M.A., and Herbert A. Strong. M.A., LL.D., Professor of Latin in Liverpool University College, Victoria University. In two Parts. Crown 8vo. Complete, 6s.
Also separately, Part I. Introduction, Text, etc., 3s.   Part II. Notes, 3s. 6d.

Tacitus. The Annals. Books I-VI. Edited, with Introduction and Notes, by H. Furneaux, M.A. 8vo. 18s.

Nettleship (H., M.A.)   Lectures and Essays on Subjects connected with Latin Scholarship and Literature. Crown 8vo. 7s. 6d.

—— *The Roman Satura:* its original form in connection with its literary development. 8vo. sewed, 1s.

—— *Ancient Lives of Vergil.* With an Essay on the Poems of Vergil, in connection with his Life and Times. 8vo. sewed. 2s.

Papillon (T. L., M.A.).   A Manual of Comparative Philology. Third Edition, Revised and Corrected. 1882. Crown 8vo. 6s.

Pinder (North, M.A.).   Selections from the less known Latin Poets. 1869. 8vo. 15s.

Sellar (W. Y., M.A.).   Roman Poets of the Augustan Age. VIRGIL. New Edition. 1883. Crown 8vo. 9s.

—— *Roman Poets of the Republic.* New Edition, Revised and Enlarged. 1881. 8vo. 14s.

Wordsworth (J., M.A.).   Fragments and Specimens of Early Latin. With Introductions and Notes. 1874. 8vo. 18s.

III. GREEK.

A Greek Primer, for the use of beginners in that Language. By the Right Rev. Charles Wordsworth, D.C.L. Seventh Edition. Extra fcap. 8vo. 1s. 6d.

Easy Greek Reader. By Evelyn Abbott, M.A. In one or two Parts. Extra fcap. 8vo. 3s.

Graecae Grammaticae Rudimenta in usum Scholarum. Auctore Carolo Wordsworth, D.C.L. Nineteenth Edition, 1882. 12mo. 4s.

A Greek-English Lexicon, abridged from Liddell and Scott's 4to. edition, chiefly for the use of Schools. Twenty-first Edition. 1886. Square 12mo. 7s. 6d.

Greek Verbs, Irregular and Defective; their forms, meaning, and quantity; embracing all the Tenses used by Greek writers, with references to the passages in which they are found. By W. Veitch. Fourth Edition. Crown 8vo. 10s. 6d.

The Elements of Greek Accentuation (for Schools): abridged from his larger work by H. W. Chandler, M.A. Extra fcap. 8vo. 2s. 6d.

A SERIES OF GRADUATED GREEK READERS:—

First Greek Reader. By W. G. Rushbrooke, M.L. Second Edition. Extra fcap. 8vo. 2s. 6d.

Second Greek Reader. By A. M. Bell, M.A. Extra fcap. 8vo. 3s. 6d.

Fourth Greek Reader; being Specimens of Greek Dialects. With Introductions, etc. By W. W. Merry, D.D. Extra fcap. 8vo. 4s. 6d.

Fifth Greek Reader. Selections from Greek Epic and Dramatic Poetry, with Introductions and Notes. By Evelyn Abbott, M.A. Extra fcap. 8vo. 4s. 6d.

The Golden Treasury of Ancient Greek Poetry: being a Collection of the finest passages in the Greek Classic Poets, with Introductory Notices and Notes. By R. S. Wright, M.A. Extra fcap. 8vo. 8s. 6d.

A Golden Treasury of Greek Prose, being a Collection of the finest passages in the principal Greek Prose Writers, with Introductory Notices and Notes. By R. S. Wright, M.A., and J. E. L. Shadwell, M.A. Extra fcap. 8vo. 4s. 6d.

Aeschylus. Prometheus Bound (for Schools). With Introduction and Notes, by A. O. Prickard, M.A. Second Edition. Extra fcap. 8vo. 2s.

—— *Agamemnon.* With Introduction and Notes, by Arthur Sidgwick, M.A. Third Edition. In one or two parts. Extra fcap. 8vo. 3s.

—— *Choephoroi.* With Introduction and Notes by the same Editor. Extra fcap. 8vo. 3s.

—— *Eumenides.* With Introduction and Notes, by the same Editor. In one or two Parts. Extra fcap. 8vo. 3s.

Aristophanes. In Single Plays. Edited, with English Notes. Introductions, &c., by W. W. Merry, D.D. Extra fcap. 8vo.

I. The Clouds, Second Edition, 2s.
II. The Acharnians, Third Edition.. In one or two parts, 3s.
III. The Frogs, Second Edition. In one or two parts, 3s.
IV. The Knights. In one or two parts, 3s.

Cebes. Tabula. With Introduction and Notes. By C. S. Jerram, M.A. Extra fcap. 8vo. 2s. 6d.

Demosthenes. Orations against Philip. With Introduction and Notes, by Evelyn Abbott, M.A., and P. E. Matheson, M.A. Vol. I. Philippic I. Olynthiacs I–III. In one or two Parts. Extra fcap. 8vo. 3s.

Euripides. Alcestis (for Schools). By C. S. Jerram, M.A. Extra fcap. 8vo. 2s. 6d.

—— *Helena.* Edited, with Introduction, Notes, etc., for Upper and Middle Forms. By C. S. Jerram, M.A. Extra fcap. 8vo. 3s.

—— *Iphigenia in Tauris.* Edited, with Introduction, Notes, etc., for Upper and Middle Forms. By C. S. Jerram, M.A. Extra fcap. 8vo. cloth, 3s.

—— *Medea.* By C. B. Heberden, M.A. In one or two Parts. Extra fcap. 8vo. 2s.

Herodotus, Book IX. Edited, with Notes, by Evelyn Abbott, M.A. In one or two Parts. Extra fcap. 8vo. 3s.

Herodotus, Selections from. Edited, with Introduction, Notes. and a Map, by W. W. Merry. D.D. Extra fcap. 8vo. 2s. 6d.

Homer. Odyssey, Books I–XII (for Schools). By W. W. Merry, D.D. Fortieth Thousand. In one or two Parts. Extra fcap. 8vo. 5s.

Books I, and II, *separately*. each 1s. 6d.

—— *Odyssey,* Books XIII–XXIV (for Schools). By the same Editor. Second Edition Extra fcap. 8vo. 5s.

—— *Iliad,* Book I (for Schools). By D. B. Monro, M.A. Second Edition. Extra fcap. 8vo. 2s.

—— *Iliad,* Books I–XII (for Schools). With an Introduction, a brief Homeric Grammar, and Notes. By D. B. Monro, M.A. Second Edition. Extra fcap. 8vo. 6s.

—— *Iliad,* Books VI and XXI. With Introduction and Notes. By Herbert Hailstone, M.A. Extra fcap. 8vo. 1s. 6d. each.

Lucian. Vera Historia (for Schools). By C. S. Jerram, M.A. Second Edition. Extra fcap. 8vo. 1s. 6d.

Lysias. Epitaphios. Edited, with Introduction and Notes, by F. J. Snell, B.A. (In one or two Parts.) Extra fcap. 8vo. 2s.

Plato. Meno. With Introduction and Notes. By St. George Stock, M.A., Pembroke College. (In one or two Parts.) Extra fcap. 8vo. 2s. 6d.

Plato. The Apology. With Introduction and Notes. By St. George Stock, M.A. (In one or two Parts. Extra fcap. 8vo. 2s. 6d.

Sophocles. For the use of Schools. Edited with Introductions and English Notes By Lewis Campbell, M.A., and Evelyn Abbott, M.A. *New and Revised Edition.* 2 Vols. Extra fcap. 8vo. 10s. 6d.

Sold separately, Vol. I, Text, 4s. 6d.; Vol. II, Explanatory Notes, 6s.

Sophocles. In Single Plays, with English Notes, &c. By Lewis Campbell. M.A., and Evelyn Abbott. M.A. Extra fcap. 8vo. limp

Oedipus Tyrannus, Philoctetes. New and Revised Edition, 2s. each.

Oedipus Coloneus, Antigone, 1s. 9d. each.

Ajax, Electra, Trachiniae, 2s. each.

—— *Oedipus Rex:* Dindorf's Text, with Notes by the present Bishop of St. David's. Extra fcap. 8vo. limp, 1s. 6d.

Theocritus (for Schools). With Notes. By H. Kynaston, D.D. (late Snow). Third Edition. Extra fcap. 8vo. 4s. 6d.

Xenophon. Easy Selections (for Junior Classes). With a Vocabulary, Notes, and Map. By J. S. Phillpotts, B.C.L., and C. S. Jerram, M.A. Third Edition. Extra fcap. 8vo. 3s. 6d.

Xenophon. Selections (for Schools). With Notes and Maps. By J. S. Phillpotts. B.C.L. Fourth Edition. Extra fcap. 8vo. 3s. 6d.

—— *Anabasis*, Book I. Edited for the use of Junior Classes and Private Students. With Introduction, Notes, etc. By J. Marshall. M.A., Rector of the Royal High School, Edinburgh. Extra fcap. 8vo. 2s. 6d.

—— *Anabasis*, Book II. With Notes and Map. By C. S. Jerram, M.A. Extra fcap. 8vo. 2s.

—— *Cyropaedia*, Books IV and V. With Introduction and Notes by C. Bigg, D.D. Extra fcap. 8vo. 2s. 6d.

———————

Aristotle's Politics. By W. L. Newman, M.A. [*In the Press.*]

Aristotelian Studies. I. On the Structure of the Seventh Book of the Nicomachean Ethics. By J. C. Wilson, M.A. 8vo. stiff, 5s.

Aristotelis Ethica Nicomachea, ex recensione Immanuelis Bekkeri. Crown 8vo. 5s.

Demosthenes and Aeschines. The Orations of Demosthenes and Aeschines on the Crown. With Introductory Essays and Notes. By G. A. Simcox, M.A., and W. H. Simcox, M.A. 1872. 8vo. 12s.

Head (Barclay V.). Historia Numorum: A Manual of Greek Numismatics. Royal 8vo. half-bound. 2l. 2s.

Hicks (E. L., M.A.). A Manual of Greek Historical Inscriptions. Demy 8vo. 10s. 6d.

Homer. Odyssey, Books I–XII. Edited with English Notes, Appendices, etc. By W. W. Merry, D.D., and the late James Riddell. M.A. 1886 Second Edition. Demy 8vo. 16s.

Homer. A Grammar of the Homeric Dialect. By D. B. Monro, M.A. Demy 8vo. 10s. 6d.

Sophocles. The Plays and Fragments. With English Notes and Introductions, by Lewis Campbell. M.A. 2 vols.

    Vol. I. Oedipus Tyrannus. Oedipus Coloneus. Antigone. 8vo. 16s.

    Vol. II. Ajax. Electra. Trachiniae. Philoctetes. Fragments. 8vo. 16s.

IV. FRENCH AND ITALIAN.

Brachet's Etymological Dictionary of the French Language, with a Preface on the Principles of French Etymology. Translated into English by G. W. Kitchin, D.D. Third Edition. Crown 8vo. 7s. 6d.

—— *Historical Grammar of the French Language.* Translated into English by G. W. Kitchin. D.D. Fourth Edition. Extra fcap. 8vo. 3s. 6d.

Works by GEORGE SAINTSBURY, M.A.

Primer of French Literature. Extra fcap. 8vo. 2s.

Short History of French Literature. Crown 8vo. 10s. 6d.

Specimens of French Literature. from Villon to Hugo. Crown 8vo. 9s

MASTERPIECES OF THE FRENCH DRAMA.

Corneille's Horace. Edited. with Introduction and Notes, by George Saintsbury, M.A. Extra fcap. 8vo. 2s. 6d.

Molière's Les Précieuses Ridicules. Edited, with Introduction and Notes, by Andrew Lang, M.A Extra fcap. 8vo. 1s. 6d.

Racine's Esther. Edited, with Introduction and Notes, by George Saintsbury, M.A. Extra fcap. 8vo. 2s.

Beaumarchais' Le Barbier de Séville. Edited, with Introduction and Notes. by Austin Dobson. Extra fcap. 8vo. 2s. 6d.

Voltaire's Mérope. Edited, with Introduction and Notes, by George Saintsbury. Extra fcap. 8vo. cloth, 2s.

Musset's On ne badine pas avec l'Amour, and *Fantasio.* Edited, with Prolegomena, Notes, etc., by Walter Herries Pollock. Extra fcap. 8vo. 2s.

The above six Plays may be had in ornamental case, and bound in Imitation Parchment, price 12s. 6d.

Sainte-Beuve. Selections from the Causeries du Lundi. Edited by George Saintsbury, M.A. Extra fcap. 8vo. 2s.

Quinet's Lettres à sa Mère. Selected and edited by George Saintsbury, M.A. Extra fcap. 8vo. 2s.

Gautier, Théophile. Scenes of Travel. Selected and Edited by George Saintsbury, M.A. Extra fcap. 8vo. 2s.

L'Éloquence de la Chaire et de la Tribune Françaises. Edited by Paul Blouët, B.A. (Univ. Gallic.). Vol. I. French Sacred Oratory. Extra fcap. 8vo. 2s. 6d.

Edited by **GUSTAVE MASSON, B.A.**

Corneille's Cinna. With Notes, Glossary, etc. Extra fcap. 8vo.
cloth, 2s. Stiff covers, 1s. 6d.

Louis XIV and his Contemporaries ; as described in Extracts
from the best Memoirs of the Seventeenth Century. With English Notes,
Genealogical Tables, &c. Extra fcap. 8vo. 2s. 6d.

Maistre, Xavier de. *Voyage autour de ma Chambre.* Ourika,
by *Madame de Duras;* Le Vieux Tailleur, by *MM. Erckmann–Chatrian ;*
La Veillée de Vincennes, by *Alfred de Vigny ;* Les Jumeaux de l'Hôtel
Corneille, by *Edmond About :* Mésaventures d'un Écolier, by *Rodolphe Töpffer.*
Third Edition, Revised and Corrected. Extra fcap. 8vo. 2s. 6d.

◄ ——- *Voyage autour de ma Chambre.* Separately, limp,
1s. 6d

Molière's Les Fourberies de Scapin, and *Racine's Athalie.*
With Voltaire's Life of Molière. Extra fcap. 8vo. 2s. 6d.

Molière's Les Fourberies de Scapin. With Voltaire's Life of
Molière. Extra fcap. 8vo. stiff covers, 1s. 6d.

Molière's Les Femmes Savantes. With Notes, Glossary, etc.
Extra fcap. 8vo. *cloth,* 2s. Stiff covers, 1s. 6d.

Racine's Andromaque, and *Corneille's Le Menteur.* With
Louis Racine's Life of his Father. Extra fcap. 8vo. 2s. 6d.

Regnard's Le Joueur, and *Brueys and Palaprat's Le Grondeur.*
Extra fcap. 8vo. 2s. 6d.

*Sévigné, Madame de, and her chief Contemporaries. Selections
from the Correspondence of.* Intended more especially for Girls' Schools.
Extra fcap. 8vo. 3s.

— —

Dante. Selections from the Inferno. With Introduction and
Notes. By H. B. Cotterill, B.A. Extra fcap. 8vo. 4s. 6d.

Tasso. *La Gerusalemme Liberata.* Cantos i, ii. With Introduction and Notes. By the same Editor. Extra fcap. 8vo. 2s. 6d.

V GERMAN.

Scherer (W.). *A History of German Literature.* Translated
from the Third German Edition by Mrs. F. Conybeare. Edited by F. Max
Müller. 2 vols. 8vo. 21s.

Max Müller. The German Classics, from the Fourth to the
Nineteenth Century. With Biographical Notices, Translations into Modern
German, and Notes. By F. Max Müller, M.A. A New Edition, Revised,
Enlarged, and Adapted to Wilhelm Scherer's 'History of German Literature,'
by F. Lichtenstein. 2 vols. crown 8vo. 21s.

The Germans at Home; a Practical Introduction to German Conversation, with an Appendix containing the Essentials of German Grammar. Third Edition. 8vo. 2s. 6d.

The German Manual; a German Grammar, Reading Book. and a Handbook of German Conversation. 8vo. 7s. 6d.

Grammar of the German Language. 8vo. 3s. 6d.

German Composition; A Theoretical and Practical Guide to the Art of Translating English Prose into German. Second Edition. 8vo. 4s. 6d.

German Spelling; A Synopsis of the Changes which it has undergone through the Government Regulations of 1880. Paper covers, 6d. •

Lessing's Laokoon. With Introduction, English Notes, etc. By A Hamann. Phil. Doc., M.A. Extra fcap. 8vo. 4s. 6d.

Schiller's Wilhelm Tell. Translated into English Verse by E. Massie, M.A. Extra fcap. 8vo. 5s.

Also, Edited by C. A. BUCHHEIM, Phil. Doc.

Becker's Friedrich der Grosse. Extra fcap. 8vo. *In the Press.*

Goethe's Egmont. With a Life of Goethe, &c. Third Edition. Extra fcap. 8vo. 3s.

—— *Iphigenie auf Tauris.* A Drama. With a Critical Introduction and Notes. Second Edition. Extra fcap. 8vo. 3s.

Heine's Prosa, being Selections from his Prose Works. With English Notes, etc. Extra fcap. 8vo. 4s. 6d.

Heine's Harzreise. With Life of Heine, Descriptive Sketch of the Harz, and Index. Extra fcap. 8vo. paper covers, 1s. 6d.; cloth, 2s. 6d.

Lessing's Minna von Barnhelm. A Comedy. With a Life of Lessing, Critical Analysis, etc. Extra fcap. 8vo. 3s. 6d.

—— *Nathan der Weise.* With Introduction, Notes. etc. Extra fcap. 8vo. 4s. 6d.

Schiller's Historische Skizzen; Egmont's Leben und Tod, and *Belagerung von Antwerpen.* With a Map. Extra fcap. 8vo. 2s. 6d.

—— *Wilhelm Tell.* With a Life of Schiller; an historical and critical Introduction, Arguments. and a complete Commentary and Map. Sixth Edition. Extra fcap. 8vo. 3s. 6d.

---- *Wilhelm Tell.* School Edition. With Map. 2s.

—— *Die Jungfrau von Orleans. In preparation.*

Modern German Reader. A Graduated Collection of Extracts in Prose and Poetry from Modern German writers :—

Part I. With English Notes, a Grammatical Appendix, and a complete Vocabulary. Fourth Edition. Extra fcap. 8vo. 2s. 6d.

Part II. With English Notes and an Index. Extra fcap. 8vo. 2s. 6d.

Niebuhr's Griechische Heroen-Geschichten. Tales of Greek Heroes. Edited with English Notes and a Vocabulary, by Emma S. Buchheim. School Edition. Extra fcap. 8vo., *cloth*, 2s. *Stiff covers*, 1s. 6d.

VI. MATHEMATICS, PHYSICAL SCIENCE, &c.

By LEWIS HENSLEY, M.A.

Figures made Easy : a first Arithmetic Book. Crown 8vo. 6d.

Answers to the Examples in Figures made Easy, together with two thousand additional Examples, with Answers. Crown 8vo. 1s.

The Scholar's Arithmetic. Crown 8vo. 2s. 6d.

Answers to the Examples in the Scholar's Arithmetic. Crown 8vo. 1s. 6d.

The Scholar's Algebra. Crown 8vo. 2s. 6d.

Aldis (W. S., M.A.). *A Text-Book of Algebra: with Answers to the Examples.* Crown 8vo. 7s. 6d.

Baynes (R. E., M.A.). *Lessons on Thermodynamics.* 1878. Crown 8vo. 7s. 6d.

Chambers (G. F., F.R.A.S.). *A Handbook of Descriptive Astronomy.* Third Edition. 1877. Demy 8vo. 28s.

Clarke (Col. A. R., C.B., R.E.). *Geodesy.* 1880. 8vo. 12s. 6d.

Cremona (Luigi). *Elements of Projective Geometry.* Translated by C. Leudesdorf, M.A. 8vo. 12s. 6d.

Donkin. *Acoustics.* Second Edition. Crown 8vo. 7s. 6d.

Euclid Revised. Containing the Essentials of the Elements of Plane Geometry as given by Euclid in his first Six Books. Edited by R. C. J. Nixon, M.A. Crown 8vo. 7s. 6d.

Sold separately as follows,

Book I. 1s.	Books I, II. 1s. 6d.
Books I-IV. 3s. 6d.	Books V, VI. 3s.

Galton (Douglas, C.B., F.R.S.). The Construction of Healthy Dwellings. Demy 8vo. 10s. 6d.

Hamilton (Sir R. G. C.), and J. Ball. Book-keeping. New and enlarged Edition. Extra fcap. 8vo. limp cloth, 2s.

Ruled Exercise books adapted to the above may be had, price 2s.

Harcourt (A. G. Vernon, M.A.), and *H. G. Madan, M.A. Exercises in Practical Chemistry.* Vol. I. Elementary Exercises. Fourth Edition. Crown 8vo. 10s. 6d.

Maclaren (Archibald). A System of Physical Education : Theoretical and Practical. Extra fcap. 8vo. 7s. 6d.

Madan (H. G., M.A.). Tables of Qualitative Analysis. Large 4to. paper, 4s. 6d.

Maxwell (J. Clerk, M.A., F.R.S.). A Treatise on Electricity and Magnetism. Second Edition. 2 vols. Demy 8vo. 1l. 11s. 6d.

—— *An Elementary Treatise on Electricity.* Edited by William Garnett, M.A. Demy 8vo. 7s. 6d.

Minchin (G. M., M.A.). A Treatise on Statics with Applications to Physics. Third Edition, Corrected and Enlarged. Vol. I. *Equilibrium of Coplanar Forces.* 8vo. 9s. Vol. II. *Statics.* 8vo. 16s.

—— *Uniplanar Kinematics of Solids and Fluids.* Crown 8vo. 7s. 6d.

Phillips (John, M.A., F.R.S.). Geology of Oxford and the Valley of the Thames. 1871. 8vo. 21s.

—— *Vesuvius.* 1869. Crown 8vo. 10s. 6d.

Prestwich (Joseph, M.A., F.R.S.). Geology, Chemical, Physical, and Stratigraphical. Vol. I. Chemical and Physical. Royal 8vo. 25s.

Rolleston's Forms of Animal Life. Illustrated by Descriptions and Drawings of Dissections. New Edition. (*Nearly ready.*)

Smyth. A Cycle of Celestial Objects. Observed, Reduced, and Discussed by Admiral W. H. Smyth. R.N. Revised, condensed, and greatly enlarged by G. F. Chambers, F.R.A.S. 1881. 8vo. *Price reduced to* 12s.

Stewart (Balfour, LL.D., F.R.S.). A Treatise on Heat, with numerous Woodcuts and Diagrams. Fourth Edition. Extra fcap. 8vo. 7s. 6d.

Vernon-Harcourt (L. F., M.A.). A Treatise on Rivers and Canals, relating to the Control and Improvement of Rivers, and the Design, Construction, and Development of Canals. 2 vols. (Vol. I, Text. Vol. II, Plates.) 8vo. 21s.

—— *Harbours and Docks;* their Physical Features, History, Construction, Equipment, and Maintenance; with Statistics as to their Commercial Development. 2 vols. 8vo. 25s.

Walker (James, M.A.) The Theory of a Physical Balance. 8vo. stiff cover, 3s. 6d.

Watson (H. W., M.A.). A Treatise on the Kinetic Theory of Gases. 1876. 8vo. 3s. 6d.

Watson (H. W., D. Sc., F.R.S.), and S. H. Burbury, M.A.
I. *A Treatise on the Application of Generalised Coordinates to the Kinetics of a Material System.* 1879. 8vo. 6s.
II. *The Mathematical Theory of Electricity and Magnetism.* Vol. I. Electrostatics. 8vo. 10s. 6d.

Williamson (A. W., Phil. Doc., F.R.S.). Chemistry for Students. A new Edition, with Solutions. 1873. Extra fcap. 8vo. 8s. 6d.

VII. HISTORY.

Bluntschli (J. K.). The Theory of the State. By J. K. Bluntschli, late Professor of Political Sciences in the University of Heidelberg. Authorised English Translation from the Sixth German Edition. Demy 8vo. half bound, 12s. 6d.

Finlay (George, LL.D.). A History of Greece from its Conquest by the Romans to the present time, B.C. 146 to A.D. 1864. A new Edition, revised throughout, and in part re-written, with considerable additions, by the Author, and edited by H. F. Tozer, M.A. 7 vols. 8vo. 3l. 10s.

Fortescue (Sir John, Kt.). The Governance of England: otherwise called The Difference between an Absolute and a Limited Monarchy. A Revised Text. Edited, with Introduction, Notes, and Appendices, by Charles Plummer, M.A. 8vo. half bound, 12s. 6d.

Freeman (E.A., D.C.L.). A Short History of the Norman Conquest of England. Second Edition. Extra fcap. 8vo. 2s. 6d.

George (H. B., M.A.). Genealogical Tables illustrative of Modern History. Third Edition, Revised and Enlarged. Small 4to. 12s.

Hodgkin (T.). Italy and her Invaders. Illustrated with Plates and Maps. Vols. I—IV., A.D. 376-553. 8vo. 3l. 8s.

Hughes (Alfred). Geography for Schools. With Diagrams.
Part I. Practical Geography. Crown 8vo. 2s. 6d. *Just Published.*
Part II. General Geography. *In preparation.*

Kitchin (G. W., D.D.). A History of France. With numerous
Maps, Plans, and Tables. In Three Volumes. *Second Edition.* Crown 8vo.
each 10s. 6d.
Vol. I. Down to the Year 1453.
Vol. II. From 1453-1624.   Vol. III. From 1624-1793.

*Lucas (C. P.). Introduction to a Historical Geography of the
British Colonies.* With Eight Maps. Crown 8vo. 4s. 6d.

*Payne (E. J., M.A.). A History of the United States of
America.* In the Press.

Ranke (L. von). A History of England, principally in the
Seventeenth Century. Translated by Resident Members of the University of
Oxford, under the superintendence of G. W. Kitchin, D.D., and C. W. Boase,
M.A. 1875. 6 vols. 8vo. 3l. 3s.

Rawlinson (George, M.A.). A Manual of Ancient History.
Second Edition. Demy 8vo. 14s.

Ricardo. Letters of David Ricardo to Thomas Robert Malthus
(1810-1823). Edited by James Bonar, M.A. Demy 8vo. 10s. 6d.

*Rogers (J. E. Thorold, M.A.). The First Nine Years of the
Bank of England.* 8vo. 8s. 6d.

*Select Charters and other Illustrations of English Constitutional
History,* from the Earliest Times to the Reign of Edward I. Arranged and
edited by W. Stubbs, D.D. Fifth Edition. 1883. Crown 8vo. 8s. 6d.

Stubbs (W., D.D.). The Constitutional History of England,
in its Origin and Development. Library Edition. 3 vols. demy 8vo. 2l. 8s.
Also in 3 vols. crown 8vo. price 12s. each.

—— *Seventeen Lectures on the Study of Medieval and
Modern History,* &c., delivered at Oxford 1867-1884. Crown 8vo. 8s. 6d.

Wellesley. A Selection from the Despatches, Treaties, and
other Papers of the Marquess Wellesley, K.G., during his Government
of India. Edited by S. J. Owen, M.A. 1877. 8vo. 1l. 4s.

Wellington. A Selection from the Despatches, Treaties, and
other Papers relating to India of Field-Marshal the Duke of Wellington, K.G.
Edited by S. J. Owen, M.A. 1880. 8vo. 24s.

A History of British India. By S. J. Owen, M.A., Reader
in Indian History in the University of Oxford. In preparation.

VIII. LAW.

Alberici Gentilis, I.C.D., I.C., De Iure Belli Libri Tres.
Edidit T. E. Holland, I.C.D. 1877. Small 4to, half morocco, 21*s.*

Anson (Sir William R., Bart., D.C.L.). Principles of the
English Law of Contract, and of Agency in its Relation to Contract. Fourth
Edition. Demy 8vo. 10*s. 6d.*

—— *Law and Custom of the Constitution.* Part I. Parlia-
ment. Demy 8vo. 10*s. 6d.*

Bentham (Jeremy). An Introduction to the Principles of
Morals and Legislation. Crown 8vo. 6*s. 6d.*

Digby (Kenelm E., M.A.). An Introduction to the History of
the Law of Real Property. Third Edition. Demy 8vo. 10*s. 6d.*

Gaii Institutionum Juris Civilis Commentarii Quattuor ; or,
Elements of Roman Law by Gaius. With a Translation and Commentary
by Edward Poste, M.A. Second Edition. 1875. 8vo. 18*s.*

Hall (W. E., M.A.). International Law. Second Ed. 8vo. 21*s.*

Holland (T. E., D.C.L.). The Elements of Jurisprudence.
Third Edition. Demy 8vo. 10*s. 6d.*

—— *The European Concert in the Eastern Question,* a Collection of Treaties and other Public Acts. Edited, with Introductions and
Notes, by Thomas Erskine Holland, D.C.L. 8vo. 12*s. 6d.*

Imperatoris Iustiniani Institutionum Libri Quattuor ; with
Introductions, Commentary, Excursus and Translation. By J. B. Moyle, B.C.L.,
M.A. 2 vols. Demy 8vo. 21*s.*

Justinian, The Institutes of, edited as a recension of the
Institutes of Gaius, by Thomas. Erskine Holland, D.C.L. Second Edition,
1881. Extra fcap. 8vo. 5*s.*

Justinian, Select Titles from the Digest of. By T. E. Holland,
D.C.L., and C. L. Shadwell, B.C.L. 8vo. 14*s.*

Also sold in Parts, in paper covers, as follows :—
Part I. Introductory Titles. 2*s. 6d.* Part II. Family Law. 1*s.*
Part III. Property Law. 2*s. 6d.* Part IV. Law of Obligations (No. 1). 3*s. 6d.*
Part IV. Law of Obligations (No. 2). 4*s. 6d.*

Lex Aquilia. The Roman Law of Damage to Property :
being a Commentary on the Title of the Digest ' Ad Legem Aquiliam ' (ix. 2).
With an Introduction to the Study of the Corpus Iuris Civilis. By Erwin
Grueber, Dr Jur., M.A. Demy 8vo. 10*s. 6d.*

Markby (*W., D.C.L.*). *Elements of Law* considered with reference to Principles of General Jurisprudence. Third Edition. Demy 8vo. 12s.6d.

Stokes (*Whitley, D.C.L.*). The Anglo-Indian Codes.
Vol. I. *Substantive Law.* 8vo. 30s. *Just Published.*
Vol. II. *Adjective Law.* In the Press.

Twiss (*Sir Travers, D.C.L.*). The Law of Nations considered as Independent Political Communities.
Part I. On the Rights and Duties of Nations in time of Peace. A new Edition, Revised and Enlarged. 1884. Demy 8vo. 15s.
Part II. On the Rights and Duties of Nations in Time of War. Second Edition, Revised. 1875. Demy 8vo. 21s.

IX. MENTAL AND MORAL PHILOSOPHY, &c.

Bacon's Novum Organum. Edited, with English Notes, by G. W. Kitchin, D.D. 1855. 8vo. 9s. 6d.

—— Translated by G. W. Kitchin, D.D. 1855. 8vo. 9s. 6d.

Berkeley. The Works of George Berkeley, D.D., formerly Bishop of Cloyne: including many of his writings hitherto unpublished. With Prefaces, Annotations, and an Account of his Life and Philosophy, by Alexander Campbell Fraser, M.A. 4 vols. 1871. 8vo. 2l. 18s.
The Life, Letters, &c. 1 vol. 16s.

Berkeley. Selections from. With an Introduction and Notes. For the use of Students in the Universities. By Alexander Campbell Fraser, LL.D. Second Edition. Crown 8vo. 7s. 6d.

Fowler (*T., D.D.*). *The Elements of Deductive Logic*, designed mainly for the use of Junior Students in the Universities. Eighth Edition, with a Collection of Examples. Extra fcap. 8vo. 3s. 6d.

—— *The Elements of Inductive Logic*, designed mainly for the use of Students in the Universities. Fourth Edition. Extra fcap. 8vo. 6s.

—— *and Wilson* (*J. M., B.D.*). *The Principles of Morals* (Introductory Chapters). 8vo. *boards*, 3s. 6d.

—— *The Principles of Morals.* Part II. (Being the Body of the Work.) 8vo. 10s. 6d.

Edited by T. FOWLER, D.D.

Bacon. Novum Organum. With Introduction, Notes, &c. 1878. 8vo. 14s.

Locke's Conduct of the Understanding. Second Edition. Extra fcap. 8vo. 2s.

Danson (J. T.). The Wealth of Households. Crown 8vo. 5s.

Green (T. H., M.A.). Prolegomena to Ethics. Edited by
A. C. Bradley, M.A. Demy 8vo. 12s. 6d.

Hegel. The Logic of Hegel; translated from the Encyclo-
paedia of the Philosophical Sciences. With Prolegomena by William
Wallace, M.A. 1874. 8vo. 14s.

Lotze's Logic, in Three Books; of Thought, of Investigation,
and of Knowledge. English Translation; Edited by B. Bosanquet, M.A.,
Fellow of University College, Oxford. Second Edition. 2 vols. Crown 8vo.
cloth, 12s.

—— *Metaphysic,* in Three Books; Ontology, Cosmology,
and Psychology. English Translation; Edited by B. Bosanquet, M.A.
Second Edition. 2 vols. Crown 8vo. 12s.

Martineau (James, D.D.). Types of Ethical Theory. Second
Edition. 2 vols. Crown 8vo. 15s.

—— *A Study of Religion : its Sources and Contents.* 2 vols.
8vo. 24s. *Just Published.*

Rogers (J. E. Thorold, M.A.). A Manual of Political Economy,
for the use of Schools. Third Edition. Extra fcap. 8vo. 4s. 6d.

Smith's Wealth of Nations. A new Edition, with Notes, by
J. E. Thorold Rogers. M.A. 2 vols. 8vo. 1880. 21s.

X. FINE ART.

*Butler (A. J., M.A., F.S.A.) The Ancient Coptic Churches of
Egypt.* 2 vols. 8vo. 30s.

*Head (Barclay V.). Historia Numorum. A Manual of Greek
Numismatics.* Royal 8vo. *half morocco,* 42s.

Hullah (John). The Cultivation of the Speaking Voice.
Second Edition. Extra fcap. 8vo. 2s. 6d.

Jackson (T. G., M.A.). Dalmatia, the Quarnero and Istria ;
with Cettigne in Montenegro and the Island of Grado. By T. G. Jackson,
M.A., Author of 'Modern Gothic Architecture.' In 3 vols. 8vo. With many
Plates and Illustrations. *Half bound,* 42s.

Ouseley (Sir F. A. Gore, Bart.). A Treatise on Harmony.
Third Edition. 4to. 10s.

—— *A Treatise on Counterpoint, Canon, and Fugue,* based
upon that of Cherubini. Second Edition. 4to. 16s.

—— *A Treatise on Musical Form and General Composition.*
Second Edition. 4to. 10s.

Robinson (J. C., F.S.A.). A Critical Account of the Drawings
by Michel Angelo and Raffaello in the University Galleries, Oxford. 1870.
Crown 8vo. 4s.

Troutbeck (J., M.A.) and R. F. Dale, M.A. A Music Primer
(for Schools). Second Edition. Crown 8vo. 1s. 6d.

Tyrwhitt (R. St. J., M.A.). A Handbook of Pictorial Art.
With coloured Illustrations, Photographs, and a chapter on Perspective by
A. Macdonald. Second Edition. 1875. 8vo. half morocco, 18s.

Upcott (L. E., M.A.). An Introduction to Greek Sculpture.
Crown 8vo. 4s. 6d.

Vaux (W. S. W., M.A.). Catalogue of the Castellani Collec-
tion of Antiquities in the University Galleries, Oxford. Crown 8vo. 1s.

The Oxford Bible for Teachers, containing Supplementary
HELPS TO THE STUDY OF THE BIBLE, including Summaries of the several
Books, with copious Explanatory Notes and Tables illustrative of Scripture
History and the characteristics of Bible Lands: with a complete Index of
Subjects, a Concordance, a Dictionary of Proper Names, and a series of Maps.
Prices in various sizes and bindings from 3s. to 2l. 5s.

Helps to the Study of the Bible, taken from the OXFORD
BIBLE FOR TEACHERS, comprising Summaries of the several Books, with
copious Explanatory Notes and Tables illustrative of Scripture History and
the Characteristics of Bible Lands ; with a complete Index of Subjects, a Concordance, a Dictionary of Proper Names, and a series of Maps. Crown 8vo.
cloth, 3s. 6d. ; 16mo. cloth, 1s.

LONDON: HENRY FROWDE,
OXFORD UNIVERSITY PRESS WAREHOUSE, AMEN CORNER,

OXFORD: CLARENDON PRESS DEPOSITORY,
116 HIGH STREET.

☞ *The* DELEGATES OF THE PRESS *invite suggestions and advice from all persons*
interested in education; and will be thankful for hints, &c. addressed to the
SECRETARY TO THE DELEGATES, *Clarendon Press, Oxford.*